England:
The Autobiography

England:
The Autobiography

*2,000 Years of English History
By Those Who Saw It Happen*

JOHN LEWIS-STEMPEL

VIKING
an imprint of
PENGUIN BOOKS

VIKING

Published by the Penguin Group

Penguin Books Ltd, 80 Strand, London WC2R ORL, England

Penguin Group (USA) Inc., 375 Hudson Street, New York, New York 10014, USA

Penguin Group (Canada), 90 Eglinton Avenue East, Suite 700, Toronto, Ontario, Canada M4P 2Y3

(a division of Pearson Penguin Canada Inc.)

Penguin Ireland, 25 St Stephen's Green, Dublin 2, Ireland

(a division of Penguin Books Ltd)

Penguin Group (Australia), 250 Camberwell Road,

Camberwell, Victoria 3124, Australia (a division of Pearson Australia Group Pty Ltd)

Penguin Books India Pvt Ltd, 11 Community Centre,

Panchsheel Park, New Delhi – 110 017, India

Penguin Group (NZ), cnr Airborne and Rosedale Roads, Albany,

Auckland 1310, New Zealand (a division of Pearson New Zealand Ltd)

Penguin Books (South Africa) (Pty) Ltd, 24 Sturdee Avenue,

Rosebank 2196, Johannesburg, South Africa

Penguin Books Ltd, Registered Offices: 80 Strand, London WC2R ORL, England

www.penguin.com

First published 2005

1

Set in 11.25/13.75pt Monotype Bembo
Typeset by Rowland Phototypesetting Ltd, Bury St Edmunds, Suffolk
Printed in Great Britain by Clays Ltd, St Ives plc

A CIP catalogue record for this book is available from the British Library

ISBN 0-670-91553-6

For an English oak and an English rose, Tristram and Freda

Contents

Contents

Editor's note

Spellings in the quoted extracts are reproduced as in the original texts.

Foreword

This is a history of England by her subjects. Her autobiography.

There is something about England. The verdant southern part of a small island off the coast of Europe, England was – with apologies to the essentially colonized Wales, Scotland and Ireland – the birthplace of parliamentary democracy, the engine of the Industrial Revolution, the hub of the greatest empire the world has seen, and the last-ditch stand against an expansionist Germany in two world wars. England, to put it plainly, was the making of the modern world.

The Victorian adventurer and statesman Cecil Rhodes once informed an audience of schoolboys, 'Remember that you are Englishmen, and have therefore won first prize in the lottery of life.' Hyperbole, yes – but also a truism: to have been born and lived in England, not just in times modern but in times medieval and even times Dark, has invariably been a better lot – freer, more stable, more plentiful – than to have been the subject of another realm.

Certainly, a more colourful lot: Henry VIII's six wives (and their fates), Oates at the South Pole, the Dambusters, the Armada, the Peasants' Revolt, the Battle of Agincourt, the Great Fire of London, the Gunpowder Plot, the Sex Pistols . . .

Of course, as that quintessentially English (awkward but loyal) writer George Orwell once pointed out, autobiography is not to be trusted unless it reveals something shameful. So this life of England does not forget the *holocaustum* of the Jews in York in 1190, the stomach-heaving slums of Manchester in 1844, the massacre of the reformers at Peterloo.

All these, and nearly 150 more events from England's past, are described in the following pages by those 'who were there'. Eyewitness reports may not have the in-depth analysis offered by historians but they are invariably more vivid, more pleasurable, and they allow a quality of understanding of bygone ages that is much underrated: an intuitive one.

Here the past speaks for itself. I have only added context and connections that allow the life story of England to be clear and flowing in the telling. It is not a complete life: to include every event of the last 2,000 years would not be possible. So this is the history of England in magic-lantern moments. I do mean England: the history of the rest of the isles is only included where it shares a common destiny with England herself.

This is England in her own words.

John Lewis-Stempel, Herefordshire, May 2005

Caesar Invades, 55 BC

JULIUS CAESAR

Julius Caesar gave a virtuous reason (the prevention of arms traffic from Britain to occupied Gaul) for his invasion of Britannia, but personal ambition squatted in the foreground. The conquest would bring the prestige Caesar needed if he was to escape his triumvirate partners and rule Rome alone.

By Caesar's usual, meticulous military standards the invasion of Britain was ill-prepared, and his 14,000 legionaries, like all Romans, were reluctant sailors. By the time the barges crossed the Channel to the south coast, their human cargo was sea-sick and dispirited. Caesar's account of the invasion is the first direct written record of events in England – the beginning of English history, indeed.

I reached Britain with the leading vessels at about 9 a.m., and saw the enemy forces standing under arms all along the heights. At this point of the coast precipitous cliffs tower over the water, making it possible to fire from above directly on to the beaches. It was clearly no place to attempt a landing, so we rode at anchor until about 3.30 p.m. awaiting the rest of the fleet. During this interval I summoned my staff and company commanders, passed on to them the information obtained by Volusenus, and explained my plans. They were warned that, as tactical demands, particularly at sea, are always uncertain and subject to rapid change, they must be ready to act at a moment's notice on the briefest order from myself. The meeting then broke up: both wind and tide were favourable, the signal was given to weigh anchor, and after moving about eight miles up channel the ships were grounded on an open and evenly shelving beach.

The natives, however, realized our intention: their cavalry and war chariots (a favourite arm of theirs) were sent ahead, while the main body followed close behind and stood ready to prevent our landing. In the circumstances, disembarkation was an extraordinarily difficult business. On account of their large draught the ships could not be beached except in deep water; and the troops, besides being ignorant of the locality, had their hands full: weighted with a mass of heavy armour, they had to jump from the ships, stand firm in the surf, and fight at the same time. But the enemy knew their ground: being quite unencumbered, they could hurl their weapons boldly from dry land or shallow water, and gallop their horses which were trained to this kind of work. Our men were terrified: they were inexperienced in this kind of fighting, and lacked that dash and drive which always characterized their land battles.

The warships, however, were of a shape unfamiliar to the natives; they were swift, too, and easier to handle than the transports. Therefore, as soon as I grasped the situation I ordered them to go slightly astern, clear of the transports, then full speed ahead, bringing up on the Britons' right flank. From that position they were to open fire and force the enemy back with slings, arrows, and artillery. The manœuvre was of considerable help to the troops. The Britons were scared by the strange forms of the warships, by the motion of the oars, and by the artillery which they had never seen before: they halted, then fell back a little; but our men still hesitated, mainly because of the deep water.

At this critical moment the standard-bearer of the Tenth Legion, after calling on the gods to bless the legion through his act, shouted: 'Come on, men! Jump, unless you want to betray your standard to the enemy! I, at any rate, shall do my duty to my country and my commander.' He threw himself into the sea and started forward with the eagle. The rest were not going to disgrace themselves; cheering wildly they leaped down, and when the men in the next ships saw them they too quickly followed their example.

The action was bitterly contested on both sides. But our fellows were unable to keep their ranks and stand firm; nor could they follow their appointed standards, because men from different ships were falling in under the first one they reached, and a good deal of confusion resulted. The Britons, of course, knew all the shallows: standing on dry land, they watched the men disembark in small parties, galloped down, attacked them as they struggled through the surf, and surrounded them with superior numbers while others opened fire on the exposed flank of isolated units. I therefore had the warships' boats and scouting vessels filled with troops, so that help could be sent to any point where the men seemed to be in difficulties. When every one was ashore and formed up, the legions charged: the enemy was hurled back, but pursuit for any distance was impossible as the cavalry transports had been unable to hold their course and make the island. That was the only thing that deprived us of a decisive victory.

The natives eventually recovered from their panic and sent a delegation to ask for peace, promising to surrender hostages and carry out my instructions. These envoys brought with them Commius, who, it will be remembered, had preceded us to Britain. When he had landed and was actually delivering my message in the character of an ambassador he had been arrested and thrown into prison. Now, after their defeat, the natives sent him back: in asking for peace they laid the blame for this outrage upon the common people and asked me to overlook the incident on the grounds of their ignorance. I protested against this unprovoked attack which they had launched after sending a mission to the Continent to negotiate a friendly settlement, but agreed to pardon their ignorance and demanded hostages. Some of these were handed over at once, others, they said, would have to be fetched from a distance and would be delivered in a few days. Meanwhile they were ordered to return to their occupations on the land, and chieftains began to arrive from the surrounding districts, commending themselves and their tribes to my protection. Peace was thus concluded.

The pax *proved temporary and the Britons resumed fighting. Their dismaying habit of refusing set-piece battle in favour of a guerrilla war from the woods was not the campaign that the Romans were either militarily or psychologically prepared for. The Britons were also disconcertingly good charioteers. ('They can run along the chariot pole, stand on the yoke, and get back into the chariot as quick as lightning.') And anyway, gales had blown most of Caesar's cavalry back to Gaul. He followed them shortly.*
A year later, 54 BC, Caesar mounted another invasion of Britain.

England: A Roman View, 54 BC

JULIUS CAESAR

Caesar's second invasion of Britain crossed the Thames (at Brentford) but otherwise was a dismal repetition of the first excursion. A closer acquaintance with the land at least enabled Caesar to pen its portrait.

The interior of Britain is inhabited by people who claim, on the strength of an oral tradition, to be aboriginal; the coast, by Belgic immigrants who came to plunder and make war – nearly all of them retaining the names of the tribes from which they originated – and later settled down to till the soil. The population is exceedingly large, the ground thickly studded with homesteads, closely resembling those of the Gauls, and the cattle very numerous. For money they use either bronze, or gold coins, or iron ingots of fixed weights. Tin is found inland, and small quantities of iron near the coast; the copper that they use is imported. There is timber of every kind, as in Gaul, except beech and fir. Hares, fowl, and geese they think it unlawful to eat, but rear them for pleasure and amusement. The climate is more temperate than in Gaul, the cold being less severe . . .

By far the most civilized inhabitants are those living in Kent (a purely maritime district), whose way of life differs little from that of the Gauls. Most of the tribes in the interior do not grow corn but live on milk and meat, and wear skins. All the Britons dye their bodies with woad, which produces a blue colour, and shave the whole of their bodies except the head and the upper lip. Wives are shared between groups of ten or twelve men, especially between brothers and between fathers and sons; but the offspring of these unions are counted as the children of the man with whom a particular woman cohabited first.

After extracting a face-saving promise by the British (who had the Iron Age equivalent of crossed fingers behind their backs) to pay tribute, Caesar, citing troubles in Gaul, withdrew. Definitively.

Caesar had come, seen, and failed to conquer. He had, however, put Britannia on the Roman map. Once there, it was inevitable that it would eventually be seized. Britannia's independence was an irritant. Moreover, Caesar had painted the place so positively that it tantalized unbearably. And so it was that in AD *43 Claudius invaded Britain.*

There was just one hiccup. Claudius' shining-armoured troops, as hydrophobic as their Julian predecessors, initially refused to get in their boats at Boulogne. Once across the Channel, the Romans made easy work of the British. Those his 40,000-strong invasion army did not beat, Claudius – no fool, despite his drooling stammer – contemptuously bought off.

By AD *47 the Claudian armies had occupied Britain as far as the Trent and Severn. A decade later nearly all of England and Wales was conquered. By then Claudius was dead, and Nero resplendent in the imperial purple.*

Under Nero Roman rule in Britain became more grasping.

Boudicca Revolts, AD 61

TACITUS

Boudicca (or Boadicea as the Victorians renamed her) was Queen of the Iceni, a tribe from the east of England hitherto given to collaboration with the Romans. Although the Roman writer and jurist Tacitus was not an eye-witness to the revolt, his source is unimpeachable: it is his father-in-law Agricola, the Roman commander who became Roman Britain's most capable governor. As Tacitus noted of the Britons, they could 'bear to be ruled by others but not be their slaves'.

Prasutagus, king of the Iceni, after a life of long and renowned prosperity, had made the emperor co-heir with his own two daughters. Prasutagus hoped by this submissiveness to preserve his kingdom and household from attack. But it turned out otherwise. Kingdom and household alike were plundered like prizes of war, the one by Roman officers, the other by Roman slaves. As a beginning, his widow Boudicca was flogged and their daughters raped. The Icenian chiefs were deprived of their hereditary estates as if the Romans had been given the whole country. The king's own relatives were treated like slaves.

And the humiliated Iceni feared still worse, now that they had been reduced to provincial status. So they rebelled. With them rose the Trinobantes and others. Servitude had not broken them, and they had secretly plotted together to become free again. They particularly hated the Roman ex-soldiers who had recently established a settlement at Camulodunum. The settlers drove the Trinobantes from their homes and land, and called them prisoners and slaves. The troops encouraged the settlers' outrages, since their own way of behaving was the same – and they looked forward to similar licence for themselves. Moreover, the temple erected to the divine Claudius was a blatant stronghold of alien rule, and its observances were a pretext to make the natives appointed as its priests drain the whole country dry.

It seemed easy to destroy the settlement; for it had no walls. That was a matter which Roman commanders, thinking of amenities rather than needs, had neglected. At this juncture, for no visible reason, the statue of Victory at Camulodunum fell down – with its back turned as though it were fleeing the enemy. Delirious women chanted of destruction at hand. They cried that in the local senate-house outlandish yells had been heard; the theatre had echoed with shrieks; at the mouth of the Thames a phantom settlement had been seen in ruins. A blood-red colour in the sea, too, and shapes like human corpses left by the ebb tide, were interpreted hopefully by the Britons – and with terror by the settlers.

Suetonius, however, was far away. So they appealed for help to the imperial agent Catus Decianus. He sent them barely two hundred men, incompletely armed. There was also a small garrison on the spot. Reliance was placed on the temple's protection. Misled by secret pro-rebels, who hampered their plans, they dispensed with rampart or trench. They omitted also to evacuate old people and women and thus leave only fighting men behind. Their precautions were appropriate to a time of unbroken peace.

Then a native horde surrounded them. When all else had been ravaged or burnt, the garrison concentrated itself in the temple. After two days' siege, it fell by storm. The ninth Roman division, commanded by Quintus Petilius Cerialis Caesius Rufus, attempted to relieve the town, but was stopped by the victorious Britons and routed. Its entire infantry force was massacred, while the commander escaped to his camp with his cavalry and sheltered behind its defences. The imperial agent Catus Decianus, horrified by the catastrophe and by his unpopularity, withdrew to Gaul. It was his rapacity which had driven the province to war.

But Suetonius, undismayed, marched through disaffected territory to Londinium. This town did not rank as a Roman settlement, but was an important centre for business-men and merchandise. At first, he hesitated whether to stand and fight there. Eventually, his numerical inferiority – and the price only too clearly paid by the divisional commander's rashness – decided him to sacrifice the single city of Londinium to save the province as a whole. Unmoved by lamentations and appeals, Suetonius gave the signal for departure. The inhabitants were allowed to accompany him. But those who stayed because they were women, or old, or attached to the place, were slaughtered by the enemy. Verulamium suffered the same fate.

The natives enjoyed plundering and thought of nothing else. By-passing forts and garrisons, they made for where loot was richest and protection weakest. Roman and provincial deaths at the places mentioned are estimated at seventy thousand. For the British did not take or sell prisoners, or practise other war-time exchanges. They could not wait to cut throats, hang, burn, and crucify – as though avenging, in advance, the retribution that was on its way.

Suetonius collected the fourteenth brigade and detachments of the twentieth, together with the nearest available auxiliaries – amounting to nearly ten thousand armed men – and decided to attack without further delay. He chose a position in a defile with a wood behind him. There could be no enemy, he knew, except at his front, where there was open country without cover for ambushes. Suetonius drew up his regular troops in close order, with the light-armed auxiliaries at their flanks, and the cavalry massed on the wings. On the British side, cavalry and infantry bands seethed over a wide area in unprecedented numbers. Their confidence was such that they brought their wives with them to see the victory, installing them in carts stationed at the edge of the battlefield.

Boudicca drove round all the tribes in a chariot with her daughters in front of her. 'We British are used to woman commanders in war,' she cried. 'I am descended from mighty men! But now I am not fighting for my kingdom and wealth. I am fighting as an ordinary person for my lost freedom, my bruised body, and my outraged daughters. Nowadays Roman rapacity docs not even spare our bodies. Old people are killed, virgins raped. But the gods will grant us the vengeance we deserve! The Roman division which dared to fight is annihilated. The others cower in their camps, or watch for a chance to escape. They will never face even the din and roar of all our thousands, much less the shock of our onslaught. Consider how many of you are fighting – and why. Then you will win this battle, or perish. That is what I, a woman, plan to do! – let the men live in slavery if they will.'

Suetonius trusted his men's bravery. Yet he too, at this critical moment, offered encouragements and appeals. 'Disregard the clamours and empty threats of the natives!' he said. 'In their ranks, there are more women than fighting men. Unwarlike, unarmed, when they see the arms and courage of the conquerors who have routed them so often, they will break immediately. Even when a force contains many divisions, few among them win the battles – what special glory for your small numbers to win the renown of a whole army! Just keep in close order. Throw your javelins, and then carry on: use shield-bosses to fell them, swords to kill them. Do not think of plunder. When you have won, you will have everything.'

The general's words were enthusiastically received: the old battle-experienced soldiers longed to hurl their javelins. So Suetonius confidently gave the signal for battle. At first the regular troops stood their ground. Keeping to the defile as a natural defence, they launched their javelins accurately at the approaching enemy. Then, in wedge formation, they burst forward. So did the auxiliary infantry. The cavalry, too, with lances extended, demolished all serious resistance. The remaining Britons fled with difficulty since their ring of wagons blocked the outlets. The Romans did not spare even the women. Baggage animals too, transfixed with weapons, added to the heaps of dead.

It was a glorious victory, comparable with bygone triumphs. According to one report almost eighty thousand Britons fell. Our own casualties were about four hundred dead and a slightly larger number of wounded. Boudicca poisoned herself.

In the aftermath of the uprising the Roman conquest proceeded ineluctably, until it dwindled out in the moorlands between the Humber and the Tyne, beyond which lay the drizzling land of the Picts. There were sporadic and optimistic attempts to conquer Caledonia, but always the Romans gave it up as a bad job, retreated behind Hadrian's Wall (AD 122–8) and hoped that the troublesome Picts would stay the other side of it. Or pay a toll to come through its gates.

'Roman Britain' was no such creature; Scotland was excluded, Wales was under military occupation – only what would become modern England was Romanized.

For three and a half centuries, England remained a far-flung outpost of the Roman Way. Pax Romana brought 10,000 miles of straight roads and the trappings of the Roman good life. But not many. Only Bath reached any level of degenerate luxury; only Lincoln had sewers.

Graffiti, *c.* AD 100–400

VARIOUS

Roman civilization in England may have been a poor cousin, but it was indisputably civilization (from the Latin civitas, *city-living). There was a boom in town-planning, and five settlements – St Albans, Colchester, Lincoln, Gloucester and York – eventually achieved municipal status. London was founded as a supply centre. There was a money economy and eventually there was Christianity. Probably, though, the import the locals adopted most keenly was the 'villa', a farm-cum-country estate, which became* de rigueur *for any landed Celt who could stretch to it (the 'gentleman farmer' is one of England's oldest social stereotypes). Other popular introductions were peas, parsnips, plums, apples, and domestic cats. (The islanders were already famous for their dogs.)*

The spread of literacy allowed the Romano-British to carve their thoughts, hopes, fears, prejudices and advertisements in, among other media, inscriptions and graffiti:

Gaius Valerius Amandus' Drops for dim sight
[Proprietary stamp]

The Club of his fellow-slaves set this up to a well-deserving comrade
[A gravestone for Hardalio]

Austalis has been going off on his own every day this fortnight
[Inscribed on a roof tile]

To the God Nodens. Silvianus has lost a ring, and dedicated half [its value] to Nodens.
Among those who are called Senicianus, permit no health until he brings it to the temple of Nodens.
[Curse found at Lydney temple in Gloucestershire]

Clementius made this box-tile.
[A posterity-minded potter]

Roman England began to decline around AD 350, as legion after legion was withdrawn to protect the heartland of the Roman Empire from the barbarian hordes. In AD 410, the last two legions sailed away and Britannia ceased to be a Roman colony. Over her remains there developed a three-cornered fight between Romano-Britons, Picts, and Germanic warriors who rowed across the North Sea to England in their open 'wave horses'. As the British monk Gildas asserts in his De Excidio Britanniae *of c. 540, these first Angles, Saxons, Jutes and Frisians were seemingly invited to England as mercenaries to fight the Picts. It was one of English history's bigger blunders:*

Then all the councillors, together with that proud tyrant Gurthrigern (Vortigern), the British king, were so blinded, that, as a protection to their country, they sealed its doom by inviting in among them (like wolves into the sheep-fold), the fierce and impious Saxons, a race hateful both to God and men, to repel the invasions of the northern nations. Nothing was ever so pernicious to our country, nothing was ever so unlucky. . . . They first landed on the eastern side of the island, by the invitation of the unlucky king, and there fixed their sharp talons, apparently to fight in favour of the island, but alas! more truly against it. Their mother-land, finding her first brood thus successful, sends forth a larger company of her wolfish offspring, which sailing over, join themselves to their bastard-born comrades.

Despite the Britons' victory at Mons Badonicus – which legend, at least, ascribes to King Arthur in c. 516 – they were unable to prevent the Anglo-Saxon takeover. By the end of the seventh century, the Anglo-Saxon kingdoms of Kent, Sussex (South Saxons), Essex (East Saxons), Wessex (West Saxons), East Anglia, Mercia and Northumbria covered most of England.

And the Romano-British? Some were pushed into the far south-west (Cornwall held out until 838) and Wales, taking their Christianity with them to found hundreds of little monasteries in the hills. Some were enslaved, and many were killed by war and its faithful followers, famine and disease. As a piece of ethnic cleansing the Anglo-Saxon invasion would never be surpassed in the isles. Perhaps 200,000 Angles, Saxons and their kin came to the land they would call Angelcynn, *then* Englaland, *in the 100 years from c. AD 430; they displaced 90 per cent of the resident males. And it was not just the Romano-British who disappeared. So did their 'civilization'. A determinedly non-urban people, the Anglo-Saxons turned up their noses at the Romans' towns, which fell into desolation and ruin.*

Their aversion to city life aside, the Anglo-Saxons had other defining characteristics. They were, notably, a warrior race. It was war, with its code of blood loyalty and its reward of plunder, that stuck Anglo-Saxon society together. 'Let he who can win glory before death' enjoined the epic Saxon poem Beowulf. *To the glorious dead, like the East Anglian warrior-king who came to be buried at Sutton Hoo, went rich funereal treasures and a conspicuous burial mound.*

So, these then were the English: a race of seafarers, who inclined towards farming (particularly if they could press some locals into servitude), fighting and pomp.

And, to the consternation of the Christian Church, an utter adherence to paganism.

King Edwin of Northumbria Is Converted to Christianity, c. 627

BEDE

The conversion of the English to Christianity was initiated by Pope Gregory the Great who, legendarily, saw some English slaves in Rome and declared them 'not Angles but angels'. In 597 Gregory's missionary, Augustine, duly if reluctantly landed amongst the heathen.

As Augustine had guessed, the English were stony soil for the Christian missionaries; it took thirty years for a Gregorian representative, Paulinus, even to reach the court of King Edwin of Northumbria.

The Venerable Bede, a monk at Jarrow, was the author of the Historia Ecclesiastica Gentis Anglorum (Ecclesiastical History of the English People), *731.*

King Edwin ... answered that he was both willing and bound to accept the faith which Paulinus taught. He said, however, that he would confer about this with his loyal chief men and his counsellors so that, if they agreed with him, they might all be consecrated together in the waters of life. Paulinus agreed and the king did as he had said. A meeting of his council was held and each one was asked in turn what he thought of this doctrine hitherto unknown to them and this new worship of God which was being proclaimed.

Coifi, the chief of the priests, answered at once, 'Notice carefully, King, this doctrine which is now being expounded to us. I frankly admit that, for my part, I have found that the religion which we have hitherto held has no virtue nor profit in it. None of your followers has devoted himself more earnestly than I have to the worship of our gods, but nevertheless there are many who receive greater benefits and greater honour from you than I do and are more successful in all their undertakings. If the gods had any power they would have helped me more readily, seeing that I have always served them with greater zeal. So it follows that if, on examination, these new doctrines which have now been explained to us are found to be better and more effectual, let us accept them at once without any delay.'

Another of the king's chief men agreed with this advice and with these wise words and then added, 'This is how the present life of man on earth, King, appears to me in comparison with that time which is unknown to us. You are sitting feasting with your ealdormen and thegns in winter time; the fire is burning on the hearth in the middle of the hall and all inside is warm, while outside the wintry storms of rain and snow are raging; and a sparrow flies swiftly through the hall. It enters in at one door and quickly flies out through the other. For the few moments it is inside, the storm and wintry tempest cannot touch it, but after the briefest moment of calm, it flits from your sight, out of the wintry storm and into it again. So this life of man appears but for a moment; what follows or indeed what went before, we know not at all. If this new doctrine brings us more certain information, it seems right that we should accept it.' Other elders and counsellors of the king continued in the same manner, being divinely prompted to do so.

Coifi added that he would like to listen still more carefully to what Paulinus himself had to say about God. The king ordered Paulinus to speak, and when he had said his say, Coifi exclaimed, 'For a long time now I have realized that our religion is worthless; for the more diligently I sought the truth in our cult, the less I found it. Now I confess openly that the truth shines out clearly in this teaching which can bestow on us the gift of life, salvation, and eternal happiness. Therefore I advise your Majesty that we should promptly abandon and commit to the flames the temples and the altars which we have held sacred without reaping any benefit.' Why need I say more? The king publicly accepted the gospel which Paulinus preached, renounced idolatry, and confessed his faith in Christ. When he asked the high priest of their religion which of them should be the first to profane the altars and the shrines of the idols, together with their precincts, Coifi answered, 'I will; for through the wisdom the true God has given me no one can more suitably destroy those things which I once foolishly worshipped, and so set an example to all.' And at once, casting aside his vain superstitions, he asked the king to provide him with arms and a stallion; and mounting it he set out to destroy the idols. Now a high priest of their religion was not allowed to carry arms or to ride except on a mare. So, girded with a sword, he took a spear in his hand and mounting the king's stallion he set off to where the idols were. The common people who saw him thought he was mad. But as soon as he approached the shrine, without any hesitation he profaned it by casting the spear which he held into it; and greatly rejoicing in the knowledge of the worship of the true God, he ordered his companions to destroy and set fire to the shrine and all the enclosures. The place where the idols once stood is still shown, not far from York, to the east, over the river Derwent. Today it is called

Goodmanham, the place where the high priest, through the inspiration of the true God, profaned and destroyed the altars which he himself had consecrated.

Edwin, like a good number of other Anglo-Saxon kings, was not slow in seeing the benefit of 'Christian kingship' – it enabled him to dress himself up as God's appointed local deputy on Earth, and to use the clergy (who were literate) as his civil service. The regent's subjects were less convinced by the Church's good news. On Edwin's death the Northumbrians apostatized – just as the East Angles of Raedwald had done on his demise. Meanwhile, the South Saxons and the Jutes on the Isle of Wight remained pagan and proud of it. It took an evangelical pincer-movement by the Roman mission and wandering monks sent over by the Irish Church to commit the English to Christianity entirely and irrevocably in c. 800.

Despite their commitment to converting the English, the Celtic and Roman missions were theological rivals, notably over the dating of Easter, which was eventually settled in the favour of Rome by King Oswiu of Northumbria at the Synod of Whitby in 664.

The decision to align with Rome was no trivial matter. In doing so England attached to Christian mainstream Europe. For Bede, at least, the English now began their walk with God as His other chosen people.

Over the course of three centuries, the Anglo-Saxons created in England a recognizably English language, culture, Church and landscape. In the grand council that was the Witan, they even had the notion of government by consent rather than kingly diktat. More than this, the Anglo-Saxons, uniquely in the Western world, melded a national identity unity that transcended kith and kin – after all, how else could Bede title his 731 masterpiece The Ecclesiastical History of the English People? *People, not peoples.*

Alas for the English, the work of national construction was about to be rudely interrupted.

The Vikings Raid England, 787–93

THE ANGLO-SAXON CHRONICLE

In 787 the English had never had it so good. In Offa of Mercia they had an overlord of the Anglo-Saxon kingdoms who brought stability (not least by constructing his 150-mile-long Dyke, from Basingwerk to Chepstow, to keep out the stock-rustling Welsh), which in turn brought trade.

In likelihood it was the very wealth of mercantile Anglo-Saxon England that attracted the Vikings there. Hailing and sailing from Denmark and Norway, the pagan Vikings peddled amber, fur and walrus ivory. However, their stock-in-trade was extortion: they raped and pillaged until paid to go away.

'Viking' is Anglo-Saxon for pirate.

AD 787. In this year Beorhtric took to wife Eadburh, daughter of king Offa. And in his days came first three ships of Norwegians from Hörthaland around Hardanger Fjord; and then the reeve rode thither and tried to compel them to go to the royal manor, for he did not know what they were: and then they slew him. These were the first ships of the danes to come to England.

AD 793. In this year terrible portents appeared over Northumbria, and miserably frightened the inhabitants: these were exceptional flashes of lightning, and fiery dragons were seen flying in the air. A great famine soon followed these signs; and a little after that in the same year on 8 January the harrying of the heathen miserably destroyed God's church in Lindisfarne by rapine and slaughter. In this year . . . Northumbria was ravaged by the heathen, and Ecgfrith's monastery at *Donemup* [Jarrow] looted; and there one of their leaders was slain, and some of their ships besides were shattered by storms: and many of them were drowned there, and some came ashore alive and were at once slain at the river mouth.

Viking hit-and-row raids continued sporadically until 851, when the Chronicle *records 'the heathen stayed in Thanet over the winter'. This was the Vikings' first, but abortive, attempt at settlement. Fifteen years later, they came for good. Essentially, the 'wolf-coats' had done what all other visitors to England had done: raided a bit, liked what they saw, and decided to conquer.*

But who could save England for the English?

The Viking Invasion: Alfred Saves Angelcynn from the Danes, 871–8

ASSER

Alfred, King of Wessex (871–99), is unique in English history in having the honorific title 'Great' attached to his name. By any standards he deserved it, foremost because he led the Saxon resistance to the 'heathen host'. Asser was Alfred's tutor and chaplain, and later Bishop of Sherborne.

The same year (871), the aforesaid Alfred, who had been up to that time only of secondary rank, whilst his brothers were alive, now, by God's permission, undertook the government of the whole kingdom, amid the acclamations of all the people; and if he had chosen, he might have done so before, whilst his brother above-named was still alive; for in wisdom and other qualities he surpassed all his brothers, and, moreover, was warlike and victorious in all his wars. And when he had reigned one month, almost against his will, for he did not think he could alone sustain the multitude and ferocity of the pagans, though even during his brothers' lives, he had borne the woes of many – he fought a battle with a few men, and on very unequal terms, against all the army of the pagans, at a hill called Wilton, on the south bank of the river Wily, from which river the whole of that district is named, and after a long and fierce engagement, the pagans, seeing the danger they were in, and no longer able to bear the attack of their enemies, turned their backs and fled. But, oh, shame to say, they deceived their too audacious pursuers, and again rallying, gained the victory. Let no one be surprised that the Christians had but a small number of men, for the Saxons had been worn out by eight battles in one year, against the pagans, of whom they had slain one king, nine dukes, and innumerable troops of soldiers, besides endless skirmishes, both by night and by day, in which the oft-named Alfred, and all his chieftains, with their men, and several of his ministers, were engaged without rest or cessation against the pagans. How many thousand pagans fell in these numberless skirmishes God alone knows, over and above those who were slain in the eight battles above-mentioned. In the same year the Saxons made peace with the pagans, on condition that they should take their departure, and they did so . . .

In the year 877, the pagans, on the approach of autumn, partly settled in Exeter, and partly marched for plunder into Mercia. The number of that disorderly crew increased every day, so that, if thirty thousand of them were slain in one battle, others took their places to double the number. Then King Alfred commanded boats and galleys, i.e. long ships, to be built throughout the kingdom, in order to offer battle by sea to the enemy as they were coming. On board of these he placed seamen, and appointed them to watch the seas. Meanwhile he went himself to Exeter, where the pagans were wintering, and having shut them up within the walls, laid siege to the town. He also gave orders to his sailors to prevent them from obtaining any supplies by sea; and his sailors were encountered by a fleet of a hundred and twenty ships full of armed soldiers, who were come to help their countrymen. As soon as the king's men knew that they were fitted with pagan soldiers, they leaped to their arms, and bravely attacked those barbaric tribes; but the pagans who had now for almost a month been tossed and almost wrecked among the waves of the sea, fought vainly against them; their bands were discomfited in a moment, and all were sunk and drowned in the sea, at a place called Suanewic . . .

In the year of our Lord's incarnation 878, which was the thirtieth of king Alfred's life, the army above-mentioned left Exeter, and went to Chippenham, a royal villa, situated in the west of Wiltshire, and on the eastern bank of the river, which is called in British, the Avon. There they wintered, and drove many of the inhabitants of that country beyond the sea by the force of their arms, and by want of the necessaries of life. They reduced almost entirely to subjection all the people of that country . . .

The same year, after Easter, king Alfred, with a few followers, made for himself a stronghold in a place called Athelney, and from thence sallied with his vassals and the nobles of Somersetshire, to make frequent assaults upon the pagans. Also, in the seventh week after Easter, he rode to the stone of Egbert, which is in the eastern part of the wood which is called Selwood. . . . Here he was met by all the neighbouring folk of Somersetshire, and Wiltshire, and Hampshire, who had not, for fear of the pagans, fled beyond the sea; and when they saw the king alive after such great tribulation, they received him, as he deserved, with joy and acclamations, and encamped there for one night. When the following day dawned, the king struck his camp, and went to Okely, where he encamped for one night. The next morning he removed to Edington, and there fought, bravely and perseveringly against all the army of the pagans, whom, with the divine help he defeated with great slaughter, and pursued them flying to their fortification. Immediately he slew all the men, and carried off all the booty that he could find without the fortress, which he immediately laid siege to with all his army; and when he had been there fourteen days, the pagans, driven by famine, cold, fear, and last of all by despair, asked for peace, on the condition that they should give the king as many hostages as he pleased, but should receive none of him in return, in which form they had never before made a treaty with any one. The king, hearing that, took pity upon them, and received such hostages as he chose; after which the pagans swore, moreover, that they would immediately leave the kingdom; and their king, Gothrun, promised to embrace Christianity, and receive baptism at king Alfred's hands. All of which articles he and his men fulfilled as they had promised.

For their baptism Gothrun (Gothrum) and his former axe-men wore white dresses.

By the subsequent Peace of Wedmore between Alfred and Gothrun a frontier was established between Alfred's Saxon England and the Danish territories in north, central and east England where Danelaw prevailed. In his share, Alfred built fortified towns (burhs) and supervised a flowering of law and of learning; the Anglo-Saxon Chronicle *itself, the age's semi-official record, was almost certainly begun in Alfred's court. Naturally, Alfred had it penned in Anglo-Saxon, not Latin. He was the saviour of English, not just of England. But Alfred did more than aloofly oversee the Anglo-Saxon arts; he was the only English king before Henry VIII to write books.*

In 899 King Alfred, 'Engele hirde, engele dirling' (England's shepherd, England's darling), died. But his bloodline carried on. Over the next fifty years the house of Wessex, the de facto *royal house of England, reconquered almost all of Danelaw. The claim by Alfred's grandson Athelstan (reigned 924–39) to be the first true King of England was no idle boast; he sought, and he got, his coinage to 'run throughout the land'. By the time of Edgar (959–75), Alfred's great-grandson, the duty of the monarch was less going off to the wars, more the maintenance of the national peace. (It was Edgar who founded the penny coinage, who divided England into 'shires', who devised the coronation ritual, including the acclamatory cry of 'Long live the king, may the king live forever' used to this day). Soon, the Anglo-Saxons would look upon Edgar's reign as their Golden Age. They had need of nostalgia, because the Vikings were on the seas again.*

A Saxon Warrior at the Battle of Maldon, 991

ANONYMOUS

Unlike the freebooting Viking raids of yore, those of the 980s were deliberate Danish policy: their aim was the subjugation of England. Occupying the English throne was the hapless Aethelred whose name (meaning 'counsel') was punned by his disillusioned subjects into 'Unraed' ('no counsel'). Later generations would mistranslate Unraed as 'Unready'. He was that too.

In 991 an English fyrd *(militia) under Ealdorman Brihtnoth met the Danes at Maldon in Essex. Overcome by bravado or a proto-English sense of fair play, Brihtnoth allowed the Vikings off Northey island, where they were trapped, and on to the battlefield proper.*

Then Brihtnoth began to array his men; he rode and gave counsel and taught his warriors how they should stand and keep their ground, bade them hold their shields aright, firm with their hands and fear not at all. When he had meetly arrayed his host, he alighted among the people where it pleased him best, where he knew his bodyguard to be most loyal.

Then the messenger of the vikings stood on the bank, he called sternly, uttered words, boastfully speaking the seafarers' message to the earl, as he stood on the shore. 'Bold seamen have sent me to you, and bade me say, that it is for you to send treasure quickly in return for peace, and it will be better for you all that you buy off an attack with tribute, rather than that men so fierce as we should give you battle. There is no need that we destroy each other, if you are rich enough for this. In return for the gold we are ready to make a truce with you. If you who are richest determine to redeem your people, and to give to the seamen on their own terms wealth to win their friendship and make peace with us, we will betake us to our ships with the treasure, put to sea and keep faith with you.'

Brihtnoth lifted up his voice, grasped his shield and shook his supple spear, gave forth words, angry and resolute, and made him answer: 'Hear you, sea-rover, what this folk says? For tribute they will give you spears, poisoned point and ancient sword, such war gear as will profit you little in the battle. Messenger of the seamen, take back a message, say to your people a far less pleasing tale, how that there stands here with his troop an earl of unstained renown, who is ready to guard this realm, the home of Ethelred my lord, people and land; it is the heathen that shall fall in the battle. It seems to me too poor a thing that you should go with our treasure unfought to your ships, now that you have made your way thus far into our land. Not so easily shall you win tribute; peace must be made with point and edge, with grim battle-play, before we give tribute.'

Then he bade the warriors advance, bearing their shields, until they all stood on the river bank. Because of the water neither host might come to the other. There came the tide, flowing in after the ebb; the currents met and joined. All too long it seemed before they might clash their spears together. Thus in noble array they stood about Pante's stream, the flower of the East Saxons and the shipmen's host. None of them might harm another, unless a man should meet his death through a javelin's flight.

The tide went out, the seamen stood ready, many a viking eager for war. Then the bulwark of heroes appointed a warrior, hardy in war, to hold the bridge, Wulfstan was his name, accounted valiant among his kin. It was he, Ceola's son, who with his javelin shot down the first man that was so hardy as to set foot upon the bridge. There with Wulfstan stood warriors unafraid, Ælfhere and Maccus, a dauntless pair; they had no thought of flight at the ford, but warded themselves stoutly against the foe, as long as they might wield their weapons. When the vikings knew and saw full well that they had to deal with grim defenders of the bridge, the hateful strangers betook themselves to guile, craved leave to land, to pass over the ford and lead their men across. Then the earl, in his pride, began to give ground all too much to the hateful folk; Brihthelm's son called over the cold water (the warriors gave ear): 'Now is the way open before you; come quickly, men, to meet us in battle. God alone knows to whom it shall fall to hold the field.'

The wolves of slaughter pressed forward, they recked not for the water, that viking host; west over Pante, over the gleaming water they came with their bucklers, the seamen came to land with their linden shields.

There, ready to meet the foe, stood Brihtnoth and his men. He bade them form the war-hedge with their shields, and hold their ranks stoutly against the foe. The battle was now at hand, and the glory that comes in strife. Now was the time when those who were doomed should fall. Clamour arose; ravens went circling, the eagle greedy for carrion. There was a cry upon earth.

They let the spears, hard as files, fly from their hands, well-ground javelins. Bows were busy, point pierced shield; fierce was the rush of battle, warriors fell on either hand, men lay dead. Wulfmær was wounded, he took his place among the slain; Brihtnoth's kinsman, his sister's son, was cruelly cut down with swords. Then was payment given to the vikings; I heard that Edward smote one fiercely with his blade, and spared not his stroke, so that the doomed warrior fell at his feet. For this his lord gave his chamberlain thanks when time allowed.

Thus the stout-hearted warriors held their ground in the fray. Eagerly they strove, those men at arms, who might be the first to take with his spear the life of some doomed man. The slain fell to the earth.

The men stood firm; Brihtnoth exhorted them, bade each warrior, who would win glory in fight against the Danes, to give his mind to war.

Then came one, strong in battle; he raised his weapon, his shield to defend him, and bore down upon the man; the earl, no less resolute, advanced against the 'churl'. Each had an evil intent toward the other. Then the pirate sent a southern spear, so that the lord of warriors was stricken. He pushed with his shield so that the shaft was splintered, and shivered the spear so that it sprang back again. The warrior was enraged; he pierced with his lance the proud viking who had given him the wound. The warrior was deft; he drove his spear through the young man's neck; his hand guided it so that it took the life of his deadly foe. Quickly he shot down another, so that his corselet burst asunder; he was wounded through his mail in the breast, a poisoned point pierced his heart. The earl was the more content; then the proud man laughed, and gave thanks to his Creator for the day's work that the Lord had granted him.

Then one of the warriors let a dart fly from his hand, so that it pierced all too deeply Ethelred's noble thegn. By his side stood a warrior not yet full grown, a boy in war. Right boldly he drew from the warrior the bloody spear, Wulfstan's son, Wulfmær the young, and let the weapon, wondrous strong, speed back again; the point drove in so that he who had so cruelly pierced his lord lay dead on the ground. Then a man, all armed, approached the earl, with intent to bear off the warrior's treasure, his raiment and his rings and his well-decked sword. Then Brihtnoth drew his blade, broad and of burnished edge, and smote upon his mail. All too quickly one of the seamen checked his hand, crippling the arm of the earl. Then his golden-hilted sword fell to the earth; he could not use his hard blade nor wield a weapon. Yet still the white-haired warrior spoke as before, emboldened his men and bade the heroes press on. He could no longer now stand firm on his feet. The earl looked up to heaven and cried aloud: 'I thank thee, Ruler of Nations, for all the joys that I have met with in this world. Now I have most need, gracious Creator, that thou grant my spirit grace, that my soul may fare to thee, into thy keeping, Lord of Angels, and pass in peace. It is my prayer to thee that fiends of hell may not entreat it shamefully.'

Then the heathen wretches cut him down, and both the warriors who stood near by, Ælfnoth and Wulfmær, lay overthrown; they yielded their lives at their lord's side.

Then those who had no wish to be there turned from the battle. Odda's sons were first in the flight; Godric for one turned his back on war, forsook the hero who had given him many a steed. He leapt upon the horse that had been his lord's, on the trappings to which he had no right. With him his brothers both galloped away, Godwine and Godwig, they had no taste for war, but turned from the battle and made for the wood, fled to the fastness and saved their lives, and more men than was fitting at all, if they had but remembered all the favours that he had done them for their good. It was as Offa had told them on that day, at the meeting place when he held a council, that many were speaking proudly there, who later would not stand firm in time of need.

Now was fallen the people's chief, Ethelred's earl. All the retainers saw how their lord lay dead. Then the proud thegns pressed on, hastened eagerly, those undaunted men. All desired one of two things, to lose their lives or to avenge the one they loved.

Maldon was not the end of Anglo-Saxon England, but it was the beginning of the end; in 1013 England finally fell to the Viking offensive of King Sweyn I – who promptly died, leaving the kingdom to his son, Cnut. (Or Canute, as the Victorians would have him.) The quick turnover of Danish rulers encouraged the exiled English King Aethelred and his son, Edmund Ironside, to launch a rebid for the country. It came close, but not close enough. At Ashingdon in 1016 Cnut decisively defeated the House of Wessex.

Cnut and the Waves, c. 1030

HENRY OF HUNTINGDON

*The Dane Cnut began his overlordship of England by marrying the matronly
Emma, Aethelred's widow, and slaughtering as many Saxon claimants to the
throne of England as he could lay his youthful hands on. Otherwise he left
England to tick along as before; it was, after all, the most ordered (and thus most
easily taxable) country in Europe.*

*Far from Cnut changing England, England changed Cnut – into a model
Christian king. The famous story of Cnut and the waves – seemingly a long
oral tradition put down on paper by Henry of Huntingdon around 1130 – was
not about his arrogance but about his piety.*

Canute reigned for twenty years. He died at Scaftesbirh (Shaftesbury)
and was buried at Winchester in the old monastery. A few facts about
his reign should be briefly told, for never before him was there a king
in England of such greatness. For he was lord of all Denmark, all England,
all Norway and at the same time of Scotland. Over and above the
number of the wars in which he was so glorious, he did three handsome
and magnificent acts. Firstly, he married his daughter (Gunhild) to the
Roman emperor (Henry III) with indescribable riches. Secondly, on his
path to Rome (1031) he paid money and reduced by as much as a half
all those evil exactions called tolls and pontages on the road which leads
to Rome through France. Thirdly, at the very summit of his power, he
ordered his throne to be set on the seaside when the tide was rising. He
addressed the mounting waters 'You are under my sway as is the land
on which is my throne and there has never been anyone who has resisted
my rule without being punished. I therefore command you not to rise
on to my land and you are not to dare to wet the clothes or limbs of
your master.' The sea rose in the usual way and wetted the feet and legs
of the monarch without showing any respect. The king accordingly
leapt up and said: 'Know all inhabitants of earth, that vain and trivial is
the power of kings nor is anyone worthy of the name of king save Him
whose nod heaven and earth, and sea obey under laws eternal.' King
Canute therefore, never again set the golden crown upon his neck but
set it for ever above an image of the Lord which is nailed to a cross, in
honour of God the great king. By His mercy may the soul of King
Canute rest in peace.

Within five years of Cnut's death in 1035, the royal Danish line in England ended, when Cnut's second son, Harthacnut, demised 'from excess of drinking'. With no obvious Danish contenders on the spot, the Witan restored the Anglo-Saxon line, and elected Aethelred's son Edward as king.

Edward 'the Confessor' was king in name, but the de facto *ruler of England was the upstart Earl Godwine, who obliged Edward to take his (Godwine's) daughter in marriage. Edward's sly revenge was to refuse carnal relations with Edith Godwine and so deprive the Godwines of a rightful heir to the throne.*

Edward's drastic chastity had profound implications for English history. With no blood heir to follow him, he willed his throne to William the Bastard, Duke of Normandy.

The king's sexual abstinence at least helped his reputation for saintliness. 'The Confessor' was the originator of the curing 'royal touch', his piety the cause of the construction of the greatest church in England, Westminster Abbey, consecrated in 1065.

The Battle of Hastings, 14 October 1066

WILLIAM OF POITIERS

With the death of the childless Edward the Confessor on 5 January 1066, the Witan elected Harold Godwineson to the throne of England, largely perforce of his being the mightiest Saxon earl in the place. The new king hastily issued coinage with 'PAX' writ large on the face. Peace, though, was not the sentiment on the minds of Duke William of Normandy or Hardrada of Norway, both of whom claimed the English throne. After a lightning march north which covered 190 miles in five days Harold met and bested Hardrada (aided by Harold's own, alienated brother, Tostig) at Stamford Bridge, Yorkshire, on 25 September. The victory party was short-lived. On 29 September Duke William landed at Pevensey on the south coast, and back down England Harold rushed.

There are no direct eye-witness accounts of the Norman invasion but William of Poitiers was in an unrivalled position as chronicler. He was Duke William's chaplain, and compiled his account of the battle of Hastings in Sussex from post-battle interviews with Norman combatants.

. . . the English . . . took up their position on higher ground, on a hill abutting the forest through which they had just come. There, at once dismounting from their horses, they drew themselves up on foot and in very close order. The duke and his men in no way dismayed by the difficulty of the ground came slowly up the hill, and the terrible sound of trumpets on both sides signalled the beginning of the battle. The eager boldness of the Normans gave them the advantage of attack, even as in a trial for theft it is the prosecuting counsel who speaks first. In such wise the Norman foot drawing nearer provoked the English by raining death and wounds upon them with their missiles. But the English resisted valiantly, each man according to his strength, and they hurled back spears and javelins and weapons of all kinds together with axes and stones fastened to pieces of wood. You would have thought to see our men overwhelmed by this death-dealing weight of projectiles. The knights came after the chief, being in the rearmost rank, and all disdaining to fight at long range were eager to use their swords. The shouts both of the Normans and of the barbarians were drowned in the clash of arms and by the cries of the dying, and for a long time the battle raged with the utmost fury. The English, however, had the advantage of the ground and profited by remaining within their position in close order. They gained further superiority from their numbers, from the impregnable front which they preserved, and most of all from the manner in which their weapons found easy passage through the shields and armour of their enemies. Thus they bravely withstood and successfully repulsed those who were engaging them at close quarters, and inflicted losses upon the men who were shooting missiles at them from a distance. Then the foot-soldiers and the Breton knights, panic-stricken by the violence of the assault, broke in flight before the English and also the auxiliary troops on the left wing, and the whole army of the duke was in danger of retreat. This may be said without disparagement to the unconquerable Norman race. The army of the Roman emperor, con-taining the soldiers of kings accustomed to victory on sea and land, sometimes fled on the report, true or false, that their leader was dead. And in this case the Normans believed that their duke and lord was killed. Their flight was thus not so much shameful as sad, for their leader was their greatest solace.

Seeing a large part of the hostile host pursuing his own troops, the prince thrust himself in front of those in flight, shouting at them and threatening them with his spear. Staying their retreat, he took off his helmet, and standing before them bareheaded he cried: 'Look at me well. I am still alive and by the grace of God I shall yet prove victor. What is this madness which makes you fly, and what way is open for your retreat? You are allowing yourselves to be pursued and killed by men whom you could slaughter like cattle. You are throwing away victory and lasting glory, rushing into ruin and incurring abiding disgrace. And all for naught since by flight none of you can escape destruction.' With these words he restored their courage, and, leaping to the front and wielding his death-dealing sword, he defied the enemy who merited death for their disloyalty to him their prince. Inflamed by his ardour the Normans then surrounded several thousands of their pursuers and rapidly cut them down so that not one escaped. Heartened by this success, they then furiously carried their attack on to the main body of the English host, which even after their losses scarcely seemed diminished in number. The English fought confidently with all their strength, striving in particular to prevent the attackers from penetrating within their ranks, which indeed were so closely massed together that even the dead had not space in which to fall. The swords of the bravest warriors hewed a gap in some places, and there they were followed by the men of Maine, by the French, by the Bretons and the men of Aquitaine, and by the Normans who showed the greatest valour . . .

Realising that they could not without severe loss overcome an army massed so strongly in close formation, the Normans and their allies feigned flight and simulated a retreat, for they recalled that only a short while ago their flight had given them an advantage. The barbarians thinking victory within their grasp shouted with triumph, and heaping insults upon our men, threatened utterly to destroy them. Several thousand of them, as before, gave rapid pursuit to those whom they thought to be in flight; but the Normans suddenly wheeling their horses surrounded them and cut down their pursuers so that not one was left alive. Twice was this ruse employed with the utmost success, and then they attacked those that remained with redoubled fury. This army was still formidable and very difficult to overwhelm. Indeed this was a battle of a new type: one side vigorously attacking; the other resisting as if rooted to the ground. At last the English began to weary, and as if confessing their crime in their defeat they submitted to their punishment. The Normans threw and struck and pierced. The movements of those who were cut down to death appeared greater than that of the living; and those who were lightly wounded could not escape because of the density of their formation but were crushed in the throng. Thus fortune crowned the triumph of William.

There were present in this battle: Eustace, count of Boulogne; William, son of Richard, count of Evreux; Geoffrey, son of Rotrou, count of Mortagne; William fitz Osbern; Haimo, *vicomte* of Thouars; Walter Giffard; Hughe of Montfort-sur-Risle; Rodulf of Tosny; Hugh of Grantmesnil; William of Warenne; and many other most renowned warriors whose names are worthy to be commemorated in histories among the bravest soldiers of all time. But Duke William excelled them all both in bravery and soldier-craft, so that one might esteem him as at least the equal of the most praised generals of ancient Greece and Rome. He dominated this battle, checking his own men in flight, strengthening their spirit, and sharing their dangers. He bade them come with him, more often than he ordered them to go in front of him. Thus it may be understood how he led them by his valour and gave them courage. At the mere sight of this wonderful and redoubtable knight, many of his enemies lost heart even before they received a scratch. Thrice his horse fell under him; thrice he leapt upon the ground; and thrice he quickly avenged the death of his steed. It was here that one could see his prowess, and mark at once the strength of his arm and the height of his spirit. His sharp sword pierced shields, helmets and armour, and not a few felt the weight of his shield. His knights seeing him thus fight on foot were filled with wonder, and although many were wounded they took new heart. Some weakened by loss of blood went on resisting, supported by their shields, and others unable themselves to carry on the struggle, urged on their comrades by voice and gesture to follow the duke. 'Surely,' they cried, 'you will not let victory slip from your hands.' William himself came to the rescue of many . . .

Evening was now falling, and the English saw that they could not hold out much longer against the Normans. They knew they had lost a great part of their army, and they knew also that their king with two of his brothers and many of their greatest men had fallen. Those who remained were almost exhausted, and they realised that they could expect no more help. They saw the Normans, whose numbers had not been much diminished, attack them with even greater fury than at the beginning of the battle, as if the day's fighting had actually increased their vigour. Dismayed at the implacable bearing of the duke who spared none who came against him and whose prowess could not rest until victory was won, they began to fly as swiftly as they could, some on horseback, some on foot, some along the roads, but most over the trackless country. Many lay on the ground bathed in blood, others who struggled to their feet found themselves too weak to escape, while a few, although disabled, were given strength to move by fear. Many left their corpses in the depths of the forest, and others were found by their pursuers lying by the roadside. Although ignorant of the countryside the Normans eagerly carried on the pursuit, and striking the rebels in the back brought a happy end to this famous victory. Many fallen to the ground were trampled to death under the hooves of runaway horses.

But some of those who retreated took courage to renew the struggle on more favourable ground. This was a steep valley intersected with ditches. These people, descended from the ancient Saxons (the fiercest of men), are always by nature eager for battle, and they could only be brought down by the greatest valour. Had they not recently defeated with ease the king of Norway at the head of a fine army?

The duke who was following the victorious standards did not turn from his course when he saw these enemy troops rallying. Although he thought that reinforcements had joined his foes he stood firm. Armed only with a broken lance he was more formidable than others who brandished long javelins. With a harsh voice he called to Eustace of Boulogne, who with fifty knights was turning in flight, and was about to give the signal for retreat. This man came up to the duke and said in his ear that he ought to retire since he would court death if he went forward. But at the very moment when he uttered the words Eustace was struck between the shoulders with such force that blood gushed out from his mouth and nose, and half dead he only made his escape with the aid of his followers. The duke, however, who was superior to all fear and dishonour, attacked and beat back his enemies. In this dangerous phase of the battle many Norman nobles were killed since the nature of the ground did not permit them to display their prowess to full advantage.

Having thus regained his superiority, the duke returned to the main battlefield, and he could not gaze without pity on the carnage, although the slain were evil men, and although it is good and glorious in a just war to kill a tyrant. The bloodstained battle-ground was covered with the flower of the youth and nobility of England. The two brothers of the king were found near him, and Harold himself stripped of all badges of honour could not be identified by his face, but only by certain marks on his body. His corpse was brought into the duke's camp, and William gave it for burial to William, surnamed Malet, and not to Harold's mother, who offered for the body of her beloved son its weight in gold. For the duke thought it unseemly to receive money for such merchandise, and equally he considered it wrong that Harold should be buried as his mother wished, since so many men lay unburied because of his avarice. They said in jest that he who had guarded the coast with such insensate zeal should be buried by the seashore . . .

*From Hastings William sent his army on a fire-and-sword circuit of London,
where the last English resistance had gathered. London got William's scorched-
earth message.*

The Coronation of William the Conqueror,
Christmas Day 1066

ORDERIC VITALIS

*William's coronation took place in Westminster Abbey, London. Orderic Vitalis,
befitting his half-Norman, half-English blood, was the most balanced of the
contemporary chroniclers.*

So at last on Christmas Day in the year of Our Lord 1067, the fifth
Indiction, the English assembled at London for the king's coronation,
and a strong guard of Norman men-at-arms and knights was posted
round the minster to prevent any treachery or disorder. And, in the
presence of the bishops, abbots, and nobles of the whole realm of Albion,
Archbishop Ealdred consecrated William duke of Normandy as king of
the English and placed the royal crown on his head. This was done in
the abbey church of St Peter the chief of the apostles, called Westminster,
where the body of King Edward lies honourably buried.

But at the prompting of the devil, who hates everything good, a
sudden disaster and portent of future catastrophes occurred. For when
Archbishop Ealdred asked the English, and Geoffrey bishop of Coutances
asked the Normans, if they would accept William as their king, all of
them gladly shouted out with one voice if not in one language that they
would. The armed guard outside, hearing the tumult of the joyful crowd
in the church and the harsh accents of a foreign tongue, imagined that
some treachery was afoot, and rashly set fire to some of the buildings.
The fire spread rapidly from house to house; the crowd who had been
rejoicing in the church took fright and throngs of men and women of
every rank and condition rushed out of the church in frantic haste. Only
the bishops and a few clergy and monks remained, terrified, in the
sanctuary, and with difficulty completed the consecration of the king
who was trembling from head to foot. Almost all the rest made for the
scene of conflagration, some to fight the flames and many others hoping
to find loot for themselves in the general confusion. The English, after
hearing of the perpetration of such misdeeds, never again trusted the

Normans who seemed to have betrayed them, but nursed their anger and bided their time to take revenge.

It was not often that William the Bastard was seen trembling 'from head to foot'.

William had the crown of England on his head, but not quite the kingdom in his hand. For the first five years of his reign he faced almost annual rebellions by the English and almost annual landings by the Danes.

The Harrying of the North, 1069–70

ORDERIC VITALIS

In 1069 York opened its gates to the Danes of Sweyn II as their liberators from Norman rule. To quell the insurrection William used his favourite weapons: the fire and the sword.

So at last they [William's army] approached York only to learn that the Danes had fled. The king assigned officers and castellans with armed retainers to repair the castles in the city, and left others on the bank of the Humber to ward off the Danes. He himself continued to comb forests and remote mountainous places, stopping at nothing to hunt out the enemy hidden there. His camps were spread out over an area of a hundred miles. He cut down many in his vengeance; destroyed the lairs of others; harried the land, and burned homes to ashes. Nowhere else had William shown such cruelty. Shamefully he succumbed to this vice, for he made no effort to restrain his fury and punished the innocent with the guilty. In his anger he commanded that all crops and herds, chattels and food of every kind should be brought together and burned to ashes with consuming fire, so that the whole region north of Humber might be stripped of all means of sustenance. In consequence so serious a scarcity was felt in England, and so terrible a famine fell upon the humble and defenceless populace, that more than 100,000 Christian folk of both sexes, young and old alike, perished of hunger. My narrative has frequently had occasion to praise William, but for this act which condemned the innocent and guilty alike to die by slow starvation I cannot commend him. For when I think of helpless children, young men in the prime of life, and hoary greybeards perishing alike of hunger I am so moved to pity that I would rather lament the griefs and sufferings of the wretched people than make a vain attempt to flatter the perpetrator of such infamy . . .

In the midst of the fighting William sent to the city of Winchester for his crown and other royal insignia and plate, left his army in camp, and came to York to celebrate Christmas there. He learned that another enemy band was lying hidden in a narrow neck of land sheltered on all sides by sea or marshes. It could be reached only by one narrow causeway, no more than twenty feet wide. They had laid in ample supplies and believed themselves safe, regarding their position as impregnable. In spite of this, on learning that a royal force was approaching, they instantly fled away by night. The king, raging, pursued his bitter enemies to the river Tees, forcing his way through trackless wastes, over ground so rough that he was frequently compelled to go on foot. He spent fifteen days encamped on the bank of the Tees. There Waltheof and Gospatric submitted to him and took oaths of fealty, Waltheof in person and Gospatric by proxies. Their recent allies the Danes were now in grave peril as wandering pirates, at the mercy of winds and waves. They suffered as much from hunger as from storms. Some perished through shipwreck. The remainder sustained life with vile pottage; princes, earls, and bishops being no better off than the common soldiers. Their supplies of meat – even of the rancid and putrid flesh they had long been eating – were completely exhausted. They dared not venture out to seek plunder, or even come to shore for fear of the inhabitants. Finally, the meagre remnants of the great fleet returned to Denmark and told King Swein the woeful story of all the hazards they had endured, the terrible savagery of the enemy, and the loss of their comrades.

Everywhere across the land the 10,000 accomplices of William built thick-walled stone castles and sat it out against the truculent 1.75 million English. The Normans persisted – despite the statistical odds – because they wanted their reward for victory: the entire green and pleasant land of England itself. To give it to them William confiscated – with scarcely an exception – the holdings of the 4,000 Saxon thegns. In one fell stroke the old English aristocracy was destroyed.

By 1085 William had secured England from his enemies within and without. There remained only for him to investigate its financial worth.

The Domesday Inquisition, 1085–6

THE ANGLO-SAXON CHRONICLE

So complete was William's inquisition of England that the subjugated English were put in mind of the Day of Judgement, hence their nickname for the register: 'The Domesdei [Doom's Day] Book'.

For Christmas, the King was at Gloucester with his nobles and held his court there for five days; afterwards the Archbishop and Clergy held a synod for three days. Present were Maurice, Bishop-elect of London, William of Norfolk, and Robert of Chester; all these were the King's clerks. Afterwards the King held his Great Council, and had deep speech with his nobles about this land, as to how and by what manner of men it was inhabited. He sent, therefore, into every County throughout the whole of England ministers of his with orders to investigate how many hundred hides there were in each County, and how much land and cattle the King himself had in that County; and how much in annual revenue he ought to enjoy from that County. He ordered also to be entered the quantity of land held by his Archbishops, Diocesan Bishops, Abbots, and Earls; and, to be brief, what and how much each person, who had lands in the English nation, possessed, whether in lands or in cattle, and how much it was worth in money. So diligently did he have the land surveyed, that not a single hide or virgate of land, and not even (though it is a shame to say what he thought it no shame to do) a single ox or cow or pig was omitted and not returned in the reckoning, and all these writings were afterwards brought to him.

The Domesday Assessment of Cumnor, 1086

ANONYMOUS

The Domesday Inquisition was arranged by holders of land, rather than by area, and allowed King William to tax his subjects directly. Here is the Abbey of Abbendone's (Abingdon's) holding at Cominore (Cumnor), a village in Berkshire.

The Abbey of Abbendone holds Cominore. It has belonged to the Abbey T.R.E.,* and always it was assessed at fifty hides,† now at thirty hides. There is land for fifty ploughs. On the demesne are nine ploughs; and there are sixty villeins‡ and sixty-nine bordars with twenty-six ploughs. There are four serfs¶ and two mills worth fifty shillings; and from the fisheries is yielded forty shillings; and there are two hundred acres of meadow. There is a church. T.R.E. it was worth thirty pounds; and afterwards, as now, fifty pounds.

Of these fifty hides Anschil holds five. Norman held them T.R.E. as one manor. It is called Seuacoorde, and he could not go to what lord he wished. It paid geld for five hides with the others above mentioned. There is land for seven ploughs. On the demesne are two ploughs; and twelve villeins and fifteen bordars with five ploughs. T.R.E. it was worth a hundred shillings; and afterwards seventy shillings; now eight pounds.

For anyone who cared to peruse Domesday Book's *two volumes a statistical picture of England was revealed. The cold proof of the demise of the Saxon aristocracy was found in the number of surviving Saxon* thegns *of any standing. Two. Of the rest of the population, 90 per cent were peasants who were bound to their Norman overlord to provide labour in peace and foot-soldiering in war. This 'feudal' socio-economic system had been extant in England for centuries, but whereas* thegn *and* ceorl *had been tied by communality and law, the Norman and his Saxon peasant were tied by obligation in law alone. There was nothing intimate in the Norman class system.*

As for William himself, he barely lived long enough to profit from his Domesday Inquisition.

---

* T.R.E: tempore regis Edwardi (in the time of King Edward).
† The hide: four virgates, or 120 acres.
‡ Villeins: unfree farmers.
¶ Serfs: the least free of the free farmers.

An Estimate of William the Conqueror at His Death, 1087

THE ANGLO-SAXON CHRONICLE

Aged sixty-one and gone to fat, William fell against the pommel of his saddle during the sack of Mantes (France) and ruptured an internal organ. His servants stripped his body and it was left abandoned until a pitying local knight took it for burial. When forced into the sarcophagus, William's cadaver split, filling the church with a foul smell.

On William's demise, the chroniclers penned an estimation of the man and his reign:

What can I say? That bitter death that spares neither high nor low seized him. He died in Normandy on the day following the Nativity of St Mary (9 September), and was buried at Caen in the abbey of St Stephen, which he had formerly built and afterwards endowed in various ways.

Alas! how deceitful and transitory is the prosperity of this world. He who was once a mighty king, and lord of many a land, was left of all the land with nothing save seven feet of ground: and he who was once decked with gold and jewels, lay then covered over with earth.

He left behind him three sons. The eldest was called Robert, who became duke of Normandy after him. The second was called William, who wore the royal crown in England after him. The third was called Henry, to whom his father bequeathed treasures innumerable.

If anyone desires to know what kind of man he was or in what honour he was held or how many lands he was lord over, then shall we write of him as we have known him, who have ourselves seen him and at one time dwelt in his court. King William, of whom we speak, was a man of great wisdom and power, and surpassed in honour and in strength all those who had gone before him. Though stern beyond measure to those who opposed his will, he was kind to those good men who loved God. On the very spot where God granted him the conquest of England he caused a great abbey to be built; and settled monks in it and richly endowed it. During his reign was built the great cathedral at Canterbury, and many another throughout all England. This land too was filled with monks living their lives after the rule of St Benedict. Such was the state of religion in his time that every man who wished to, whatever considerations there might be with regard to his rank, could follow the profession of a monk.

Moreover he kept a great state. He wore his royal crown three times a year as often as he was in England: at Easter at Winchester, at Whitsuntide at Westminster, at Christmas at Gloucester. On these occasions all the great men of England were assembled about him: archbishops, bishops, abbots, earls, thanes, and knights. He was so stern and relentless a man that no one dared do aught against his will. Earls who resisted his will he held in bondage. Bishops he deprived of their sees and abbots of their abbacies, while rebellious thanes he cast into prison, and finally his own brother he did not spare. His name was Odo. He was a powerful bishop in Normandy, and Bayeux was his episcopal see; he was the foremost man after the king. He had an earldom in England, and was master of the land when the king was in Normandy. William put him in prison. Among other things we must not forget the good order he kept in the land, so that a man of any substance could travel unmolested throughout the country with his bosom full of gold. No man dared to slay another, no matter what evil the other might have done him. If a man lay with a woman against her will, he was forthwith condemned to forfeit those members with which he had disported himself.

He ruled over England, and by his foresight it was surveyed so carefully that there was not a 'hide' of land in England of which he did not know who held it and how much it was worth; and these particulars he set down in his survey. Wales was in his domain, in which country he built castles and so kept its people in subjection. Scotland also he reduced to subjection by his great strength. Normandy was his by right of birth, while he also ruled over the county called Maine. If he had lived only two years more he would have conquered Ireland by his astuteness and without any display of force. Assuredly in his time men suffered grievous oppression and manifold injuries.

> He caused castles to be built
> Which were a sore burden to the poor.
> A hard man was the king
> And took from his subjects many marks
> In gold and many more hundreds of pounds in silver.
> These sums he took by weight from his people,
> Most unjustly and for little need.
> He was sunk in greed

And utterly given up to avarice.
He set apart a vast deer preserve and imposed laws concerning it.
Whoever slew a hart or a hind
Was to be blinded.
He forbade the killing of boars
Even as the killing of harts.
For he loved the stags as dearly
As though he had been their father.
Hares, also, he decreed should go unmolested.
The rich complained and the poor lamented,
But he was too relentless to care though all might hate him,
And they were compelled, if they wanted
To keep their lives and their lands
And their goods and the favour of the king.
To submit themselves wholly to his will.
Alas! that any man should bear himself so proudly
And deem himself exalted above all other men!
May Almighty God shew mercy to his soul
And pardon him his sins.

We have set down these things about him, both the good and the evil, so that men may cherish the good and utterly eschew the evil, and follow the path that leads us to the Kingdom of Heaven.

King William was succeeded on the throne of England by his son William II (invariably known as William Rufus on account of his florid complexion), who ruled the kingdom with brutal and avaricious efficiency for thirteen years. His end was premature – he was killed in a hunting accident in the New Forest, the great and unpopular game preserve created by his father. William of Malmesbury caught the popular reckoning of William Rufus in his Chronicles of the Kings of England: *'He was a man much to be pitied by the clergy for throwing away a soul which they could not save. He earned the love of hired soldiers for he was lavish in his gifts to them. But by the common people he was not mourned because he allowed them to be plundered.'*

With scarcely a moist fraternal eye, Rufus' younger brother Henry galloped off to have the Bishop of London crown him King of England (instead of elder brother Robert Curthose, Duke of Normandy) in a short-notice coronation. Having shamelessly seized power, Henry I was no less brazen about buying the support he needed to maintain his elevated station: he deftly issued a charter of liberties (in which 'the Lion of Justice' limited his own power over his subjects) and married Edith, of the House of Wessex, so that his offspring would have both Norman and English blood. When the Normans choked on the miscegenation, Henry changed Edith's name to the francophone Matilda.

Henry I thus had his father's political genius for ruling and his dynastic vision, too. In 1106 he defeated Robert Curthose at Tinchebrai to gain control of Normandy and reunite his father's Anglo-Norman empire. He sired scores of bastards but only one legitimate son.

In 1120 Henry's carefully planned dynasty was sunk in the English Channel.

The Loss of the White Ship, 25 November 1120

ORDERIC VITALIS

The White Ship *disaster was the* Titanic *of the Middle Ages. Lost with the* White Ship *was Henry I's heir William, 'educated and destined to the succession'. Orderic Vitalis was wrong in stating that the tragedy occurred under a full moon; it was a new one.*

On 25 November, when a great fleet had been fitted out in the port of Barfleur, and a body of noble knights of the king's company had assembled while a south wind blew, the king and earls embarked in the first watch of the night, hoisted their sails to catch the wind, and put to sea. In the morning those whom God allowed to do so landed in England.

A terrible disaster occurred during that voyage, which was the cause of deep mourning and countless tears. Thomas, son of Stephen, went to the king and offered him a mark of gold, saying, 'Stephen son of Airard was my father, and he served your father at sea during his lifetime, for he carried him in his ship to England when he set out for England to fight against Harold. He earned your father's favour by performing this service for him to the end of his days, and received many gifts from him which raised him to high honour among his companions. I ask you, my lord king, to grant me this fief: I have a vessel which is aptly called the *White Ship*, excellently fitted out and ready for the royal service.' To this the king replied, 'Your request meets with my approval. I have indeed chosen a fine ship for myself and will not change it; but I entrust to you my sons William and Richard, whom I love as my own life, and many nobles of my realm.' On hearing this the sailors were delighted, and fawned on the king's son, asking him for wine to drink. He ordered three muids of wine to be given to them. They received these, drank, and gave to their companions to drink their fill; too much drinking made them tipsy. At the king's command a great many barons embarked in the ship with his sons; I believe there were about three hundred in the ill-fated vessel. However, two monks of Tiron and Count Stephen with two knights, also William of Roumare, Rabel the chamberlain, Edward of Salisbury, and a number of others disembarked, because they realized that there was too great a crowd of wild and headstrong young men on board. There were fifty experienced rowers there, and high-spirited marine guards who had already found seats in the boat were showing off and, too drunk to know what they were doing, were paying respect to almost no one. Alas, how many of them had in their hearts no filial reverence for God, who tempers the raging fury of sea and wind. So when the priests came there with other ministers carrying holy water to bless them, they laughed and drove them away with abuse and guffaws. All too soon they were punished for their disrespect. Apart from the king's treasure and the casks of wine Thomas's boat carried only passengers, and they commanded him to try to overtake the king's fleet, which was already sailing in the open sea. As his judgement was impaired by drink, he trusted in his skill and that of his crew, and recklessly vowed to leave behind all those who had started first. At length he gave the signal to put to sea. Then the rowers made haste to take up their oars and, in high spirits because they knew nothing of what lay ahead, put the rest of the equipment ready and made the ship leap forward and race through the sea. As the drunken oarsmen were rowing with all their might, and the luckless helmsman paid scant attention to steering the ship through the sea, the port side of the *White Ship* struck violently against a huge rock, which was uncovered each day as the tide ebbed and covered once more at high tide. Two planks were shattered and, terrible to relate, the ship capsized without warning. Everyone cried out at once in their great peril, but the water pouring into the boat soon drowned their cries and all alike perished. Only two men grabbed hold of a spar from which the sail hung and, clinging to it for the greater part of the night, waited for help to come from any quarter. One was a butcher of Rouen named Berold, and the other a noble lad called Geoffrey, the son of Gilbert of Laigle.

At that time the moon was in the nineteenth day of the sign of the Bull, and its rays lit up the world for about nine hours, showing up everything in the sea to the mariners. Thomas, the skipper, gathered his strength after sinking for the first time and, remembering his duty, lifted his head as he came to the surface; seeing the heads of the men who were clinging somehow to the spar, he asked, 'The king's son – what has become of him?' When the shipwrecked men replied that he had perished with all his companions, he said, 'It is vain for me to go on living.' With these words, in utter despair, he chose rather to sink on the spot than to die beneath the wrath of a king enraged by the loss of his sons, or suffer long years of punishment in fetters. The men clinging to the spar called on God in the waters, trying to keep up each other's spirits, and waited trembling for the fate that God had in store for them.

The night was frosty, so that the young man, after enduring the bitter cold for a long time, finally lost his grip and, commending his companion to God, fell back to perish in the sea and was never seen again. But Berold, who was the poorest of all and was dressed in a pelisse made of rams' skins, was the only one of the great company to see the day. In the morning he was taken aboard a light vessel by three fishermen and reached dry land alone. Later, when he was somewhat revived, he told the whole sad tale to those who wished to learn, and subsequently lived for about twenty years in good health.

Roger, bishop of Coutances, had accompanied his son William (whom the king had already made one of his four chief chaplains), his brother, and three distinguished nephews to the ship condemned by God to destruction, and had given them and their fellows a bishop's blessing though they made light of it. He and many others who were still standing together on the shore, as well as the king and his companions who were already far out to sea, heard the terrible cries of the doomed men, but, not knowing the cause until the next day, marvelled at it and asked one another what it could mean.

The sad news spread swiftly from mouth to mouth through the crowds along the sea coast, and came to the ears of Count Theobald and other nobles of the court; but that day no one dared announce it to the anxious king, who earnestly asked for news. The magnates wept bitterly in private and mourned inconsolably for their loved kinsfolk and friends, but in the king's presence they struggled to restrain their tears to avoid betraying the cause of their distress. However, on the following day, by a wise plan of Count Theobald's, a boy threw himself, weeping, at the king's feet, and the king learned from him that the cause of his grief was the wreck of the *White Ship*. Immediately Henry fell to the ground overcome with anguish, and after being helped to his feet by friends and led into a private room, gave way to bitter laments.

The loss of the White Ship left Henry's daughter, Matilda, as his only direct legitimate heir. At the royal council of Christmas 1126 Henry made the bishops, abbots and barons accept Matilda as heir to the Anglo-Norman throne.

To little avail.

The Anarchy, 1137–54

THE ANGLO-SAXON CHRONICLE

On Henry I's death in December 1135 (after eating a meal of lampreys, against doctor's orders), his daughter and successor Matilda was out of the kingdom. On to the temptingly vacant throne leapt Henry's nephew, Stephen of Blois. Most of the baronage supported him; Matilda was widely loathed (she haughtily insisted on being called 'Empress'), as was her Plantagenet second husband, Geoffrey d'Anjou.

Matilda had no intention of relinquishing her inheritance, and civil war was joined. With the monarchy fighting itself, England's barons sniffed the opportunity to aggrandize power. The Anglo-Saxon Chronicle gloomily recorded:

1137. This year King Stephen went over sea to Normandy, and he was received there because it was expected that he would be altogether like his uncle, and because he had gotten possession of his treasure, but this he distributed and scattered foolishly. King Henry had gathered together much gold and silver, yet did he no good for his soul's sake with the same. When king Stephen came to England, he held an assembly at Oxford; and there he seized Roger bishop of Salisbury, and Alexander bishop of Lincoln, and Roger the chancellor, his nephew, and he kept them all in prison till they gave up their castles. When the traitors perceived that he was a mild man, and a soft, and a good, and that he did not enforce justice, they did all wonder. They had done homage to him, and sworn oaths, but they no faith kept; all became forsworn, and broke their allegiance, for every rich man built his castles, and defended them against him, and they filled the land full of castles. They greatly oppressed the wretched people by making them work at these castles, and when the castles were finished they filled them with devils and evil men. Then they took those whom they suspected to have any goods, by night and by day, seizing both men and women, and they put them in prison for their gold and silver, and tortured them with pains unspeakable, for never were any martyrs tormented as these were. . . . Many thousands they exhausted with hunger. I cannot and I may not tell of all the wounds, and all the tortures that they inflicted upon the wretched men of this land; and this state of things lasted the nineteen years that Stephen was king, and ever grew worse and worse. They were continually levying an exaction from the towns, which they called Tenserie, and when the miserable inhabitants had no more to give, then plundered they, and burnt all the towns, so that well mightest thou walk a whole day's journey nor ever shouldest thou find a man seated in a town, or its lands tilled.

Then was corn dear, and flesh and cheese, and butter, for there was none in the land – wretched men starved with hunger – some lived on alms who had been erewhile rich: some fled the country – never was there more misery, and never acted heathens worse than these. At length they spared neither church nor churchyard, but they took all that was valuable therein, and then burned the church and all together. Neither did they spare the lands of bishops, nor of abbats, nor of priests; but they robbed the monks and the clergy, and every man plundered his neighbour as much as he could. If two or three men came riding to a town, all the township fled before them, and thought that they were robbers. The bishops and clergy were ever cursing them, but this to them was nothing, for they were all accursed and forsworn, and reprobate. The earth bare no corn, you might as well have tilled the sea, for the land was all ruined by such deeds, and it was said openly that Christ and his saints slept. These things, and more than we can say, did we suffer during nineteen years because of our sins . . .

After a decade of reverses Matilda's regal hopes passed from herself to her teenage son, Henry Plantagenet. In 1152 the eighteen-year-old Henry was astutely married off to Eleanor of Aquitaine, recently on the international marriage market after her divorce from Louis VII of France. Eleanor was thirty, second-hand and childless (although she blamed Louis VII for that: 'more monk than king', she said). She was also black-eyed, beautiful and rich enough to pay for Henry to invade England.

Within a year of his marriage Henry crossed the Channel, armed to the teeth with money and levies; his own from Normandy and Anjou, Eleanor's from Aquitaine.

King Stephen had little heart for more fighting. He had recently lost his son, and his health was gone. A treaty was achieved with Henry at Westminster: Stephen would stay on the throne until his death, on condition that he named

Henry his rightful heir. A bare year later, on 19 December 1154, in the first un-disputed succession to the throne for over a century, Henry II was crowned King of England, Eleanor by his side.

The Virtues and Vices of Henry II, 1154–89

WALTER MAP

Map was one of Henry II's counsellors.

I witnessed the beginnings of his reign and the following years in which his life was praiseworthy in many things. He was a little over medium height, a man blest with sound limbs and a handsome countenance, one upon whom men gazed closely a thousand times, yet took occasion to return. In physical capacity he was second to none, capable of any activity which another could perform, lacking no courtesy, well read to a degree both seemly and profitable, having a knowledge of all tongues spoken from the coasts of France to the river Jordan, but making use only of Latin and French. In making laws and in ordering the affairs of government he showed discrimination, and was clever in devising new and undiscovered legal procedures; he was easy of approach, modest and humble; the discomforts of dust and mire he suffered patiently; though vexed by the importunity of suitors and litigants and provoked by injustice, he bore all in silence. Nevertheless he was ever on his travels, moving by intolerable stages like a courier, and in this respect he showed little mercy to his household which accompanied him. He had great experience of dogs and birds and was a very keen follower of hounds; in night-watches and labours he was unremitting. As often as the vain images of pleasure disturbed his slumbers, he used to revile his body, because neither labour nor abstinence availed to break or weaken it. I, however, used to ascribe his distresses not to his infidelities but to his fear of growing too plump . . .

. . . Moreover the said King Henry II was distinguished for many virtues and infamous for some vices. One fault he derived from his mother's teaching, as I have said before, is this. He was dilatory in settling the affairs of his subjects, whence it befell that many died before they could bring their suits to a conclusion, or withdrew from court sorrowful and empty-handed, impelled by hunger. Another fault was that when he was taking his ease, which was seldom, he did not permit himself to be seen as good men desired, but, shutting himself up within doors, he was accessible only to those who seemed unworthy of such approach. A third fault was that, impatient of repose, he did not scruple to disturb almost half Christendom. In these three respects he erred; yet in others he was exceedingly good and lovable. No man surpassed him in gentleness and friendliness. As often as he went abroad he was seized by the crowd, carried about by force from place to place whither he would not, and what is remarkable, he gave ear patiently to each man singly, and though assailed at one time by the shouts of the mob, and at another violently dragged and pushed about, yet for this he brought no charge against any man nor used it as an excuse for anger. When he was too hard pressed he fled in silence to havens of peace. He did naught insolently or pompously, but was temperate, moderate and virtuous, faithful and wise, liberal and victorious, bringing honour on good men.

I lately crossed the Channel with him in a fleet of twenty-five vessels, reserved for his crossing without charge. But a storm scattered them all and drove them upon rocks and shores inhospitable to ships, with the exception of his own ship which, by God's grace, was brought safely to port. In the morning therefore the king sent and recompensed each sailor according to the estimate of his loss, although he was not bound to do this, and the total sum was large. Perchance another king would not have paid this just debt.

The energetic first Angevin King of England immediately razed the crop of baronial fortresses which had mushroomed over the country in the dark days of the Anarchy, before reforming the legal system (trial by twelve-man jury, begun in Aethelred's reign, became standard in Henry's) and cowing Scotland into paying him homage. Ireland was invaded and sufficiently occupied for Henry to apportion it to his youngest son.

Henry Plantagenet turned England into a model medieval monarchy. But it is not for his regal powers and legal glories that he is remembered.

It is for inciting the murder of a Churchman.

The Murder of Thomas-à-Becket, Canterbury, 29 December 1170

EDWARD GRIM

Thomas-à-Becket was born into a London family on the make. Like the sons of other arrivistes, he was sent off for a career in the Church, the best fast track upwards in medieval society. In 1155, at the age of thirty-seven, he became Henry II's Chancellor, the first Englishman to hold high office since the Conquest. He also became Henry's closest friend. In 1162 Henry created Becket Archbishop of Canterbury. To Henry's chagrin, Becket in his new office became a zealous ecclesiast, and opposed Henry's attempt under the 'Constitutions of Clarendon' to enable lay courts to try clergy. The issue of 'criminous clerks' hid a bigger question: was the Church separate to the state or part of it?

Eventually Becket's intransigence caused Henry II to roar out the legendary invitation: 'Will no one rid me of this turbulent priest?' (More accurately, the king bellowed: 'What miserable drones and traitors have I nourished and brought up in my household who allow their lord to be treated with such shameful contempt by a low-born cleric!') Four knights – Hugh de Morville, Reginald fitzUrse, Richard le Breton and William de Tracy – took Henry's outburst as their cue to murder the fifty-two-year-old Becket in his cathedral.

Grim was Becket's attendant.

When the holy archbishop entered the church, the monks stopped vespers which they had begun and ran to him, glorifying God that they saw their father, whom they had heard was dead, alive and safe. They hastened, by bolting the doors of the church, to protect their shepherd from the slaughter. But the champion, turning to them, ordered the church doors to be thrown open, saying, 'It is not meet to make a fortress of the house of prayer, the church of Christ: though it be not shut up it is able to protect its own; and we shall triumph over the enemy rather in suffering than in fighting, for we came to suffer, not to resist.' And straightway they entered the house of prayer and reconciliation with swords sacrilegiously drawn, causing horror to the beholders by their very looks and the clanging of their arms.

All who were present were in tumult and fright, for those who had been singing vespers now ran hither to the dreadful sight.

Inspired by fury the knights called out, 'Where is Thomas Becket, traitor to the king and realm?' As he answered not, they cried out the more furiously, 'Where is the archbishop?' At this, intrepid and fearless, as it is written, 'The just, like a bold lion, shall be without fear,' he descended from the stair where he had been dragged by the monks in fear of the knights, and in a clear voice answered 'I am here, no traitor to the king, but a priest. Why do ye seek me?' And whereas he had already said that he feared them not, he added, 'So I am ready to suffer in His name, Who redeemed me by His Blood: be it far from me to flee from your swords, or to depart from justice.' Having thus said, he turned to the right, under a pillar, having on one side the altar of the blessed Mother of God and ever Virgin Mary, on the other that of S. Benedict the Confessor: by whose example and prayers, having crucified the world with its lusts, he bore all that the murderers could do with such constancy of soul as if he had been no longer in the flesh. The murderers followed him; 'Absolve,' they cried, 'and restore to communion those whom you have excommunicated, and restore their powers to those whom you have suspended.' He answered: 'There has been no satisfaction, and I will not absolve them.' 'Then you shall die,' they cried, 'and receive what you deserve.' 'I am ready,' he replied, 'to die for my Lord, that in my blood the Church may obtain liberty and peace. But in the name of Almighty God, I forbid you to hurt my people whether clerk or lay.' Thus piously and thoughtfully, did the noble martyr provide that no one near him should be hurt or the innocent be brought to death, whereby his glory should be dimmed as he hastened to Christ. Thus did it become the martyr-knight to follow in the footsteps of his Captain and Saviour Who when the wicked sought Him said: 'If ye seek Me, let these go their way.' Then they laid sacrilegious hands on him, pulling and dragging him that they might kill him outside the Church, or carry him away a prisoner, as they afterwards confessed. But when he could not be forced away from the pillar, one of them pressed on him and clung to him more closely. Him he pushed off calling him 'pander', and saying, 'Touch me not, Reginald; you owe me fealty and subjection; you and your accomplices act like madmen.' The knight, fired with terrible rage at this severe repulse, waved his sword over the sacred head. 'No faith', he cried, 'nor subjection do I owe you against my fealty to my lord the king.' Then the unconquered martyr seeing the hour at hand which should put an end to this miserable life and give him straightway the crown of immortality promised by the Lord, inclined his neck as one who prays and joining his hands he lifted them up, and commended his cause and that of the Church of God, to S. Mary, and to the blessed martyr Denys. Scarce had he said the words than the wicked knight fearing lest he should be rescued by the people and escape alive, leapt upon him suddenly and wounded this lamb, who was sacrificed to God, on the head, cutting off the top of the crown which the sacred unction of chrism had dedicated to God; and by the same blow he wounded the arm of him who tells this. For he, when the others, both monks and clerks, fled, stuck close to the sainted archbishop and held him in his arms till the one he interposed was almost severed . . .

Then he received a second blow on the head but still stood firm. At the third blow he fell on his knees and elbows, offering himself a living victim, and saying in a low voice, 'For the Name of Jesus and the protection of the Church I am ready to embrace death.' Then the third knight inflicted a terrible wound as he lay, by which the sword was broken against the pavement, and the crown which was large was separated from the head; so that the blood white with the brain and the brain red with blood, dyed the surface of the virgin mother Church with the life and death of the confessor and martyr in the colours of the lily and the rose. The fourth knight prevented any from interfering so that the others might freely perpetrate the murder. As to the fifth, no knight but that clerk who had entered with the knights, that a fifth blow might not be wanting to the martyr who was in other things like to Christ, he put his foot on the neck of the holy priest and precious martyr, and, horrible to say, scattered his brains and blood over the pavement, calling out to the others, 'Let us away, knights; he will rise no more.'

Under his outer garments the dead Becket was found to be wearing hairshirt and sackcloth. 'At this sight', recorded Benedict of Peterborough, 'the monks gazed at one another, astounded at this proof of piety greater than would have been credited the archbishop.'

Christendom was outraged by the murder and Becket was canonized within three years. In 1174 Henry did penance at St Thomas of Canterbury's shrine, where he was scourged by all the monks of Canterbury. The shrine of St Thomas was already a place of popular pilgrimage for the English – who saw Becket as their exclusive saint – and would remain one for centuries. It is the destination for Chaucer's pilgrims in The Canterbury Tales.

Henry II died on 6 July 1189, cursing his sons as 'real bastards' for their heart-breaking rebellion against him. Disloyal or no, the eldest son, Richard, succeeded his father; the Plantagenets were a family affair. Dynasty beat sentiment.

Holocaustum, 1190

ROGER OF WENDOVER

Unlike Christians, the Jews of medieval Europe were allowed to lend money with interest. Hostility to this 'usury', plus wild stories of Jews eating babies for breakfast, plus the anti-semitism whipped up by the Crusades, set off a wave of pogroms against England's Jews in 1189–90. The holocaustum, as the monk-historian Roger of Wendover termed it, culminated in the suicide and the slaughter of York's Jews.

In the same year, during Lent, that is, that on the 15th of March, the Jews of the city of York, to the number of five hundred, besides women and children, through fear of an attack on the part of the Christians, by permission of the sheriff and the governor of the castle, shut themselves up in that fortress, and when the garrison required them to give up possession of it, they refused to do so. On this refusal, repeated attacks were made both by day and night, and at length the Jews after reflecting, offered a large sum of money for their lives, but this was refused by the people. Then one of them skilled in the law, rose and addressed his companions thus, 'Oh, men of Israel, hear my counsel. It is better, as our law instructs us, to die for our law than to fall into the hands of our enemies.' This being agreed to by all, each head of a family came with a sharp razor, and cut the throats first of his wife, sons, and daughters, and afterwards of all his family, and threw the dead bodies, which they considered as sacrificed to devils, on the Christians outside the castle; they then shut themselves up in the king's house, and setting fire to it, both living dead were burned together with the buildings. After this the citizens and soldiers burned the Jews' houses, with the papers of their debtors, but retained the money for their own use.

Richard I Massacres His Muslim Prisoners After Seizing Acre, 2–20 August 1191

BEHA-ED-DIN

Whereas Henry II had been a statesman, Richard I was an absentee knight-errant who could not, in all probability, speak the King's English. Only weeks after his coronation, Richard departed England for the Third Christian Crusade to the Holy Land. His lack of interest in England notwithstanding, the 'Lionheart's' military exploits earned him an enduring, Arthurian-like place in national myth. More prosaically, his victory over Saladin at Acre secured the Crusader states for another century. The victory, however, was darkened by Richard's less than chivalric murder of his Turkish prisoners. A Saracen view of the massacre follows.

Acre is modern-day Akka in Israel.

The same day Hossam ad-Din Ibn Barîc, an interpreter working with the English, issued from Acre accompanied by two officers of the King of England. He brought news that the King of France had set out for Tyre, and that they had come to talk over the matter of a possible exchange of prisoners and to see the true cross of the Crucifixion if it were still in the Mussulman camp, or to ascertain if it really had been sent to Baghdad. The True Cross was shown to them, and on beholding it they showed the profoundest reverence, throwing themselves on the ground till they were covered with dust, and humbling themselves in token of devotion. These envoys told us that the European princes had accepted the Sultan's (Saladin's) proposition, viz., to deliver all that was specified in the treaty by three instalments at intervals of a month. The Sultan then sent an envoy to Tyre with rich presents, quantities of perfumes, and fine raiment – all of which were for the King of the French.

In the morning of the tenth day of Rajab (3 August), Ibn Barîc and his comrades returned to the King of England while the Sultan went off with his bodyguard and his closest friends to the hill that abuts on Shefa'Amr . . . Envoys did not cease to pass from one side to the other in the hope of laying the foundation of a firm peace. These negotiations continued till our men had procured the money and the number of prisoners that they were to deliver to the Christians at the end of the first period in accordance with the treaty. The first instalment was to consist of the Holy Cross, 100,000 dinars and 1,600 prisoners.

Trustworthy men sent by the Christians to conduct the examination found it all complete saving only the prisoners who had been demanded by name, all of whom had not yet been gathered together. And thus the negotiations continued to drag on till the end of the first term. On this day, the 18th of Rajab (11 August), the enemy sent demanding what was due.

The Sultan replied as follows: 'Choose one of two things. Either send us back our comrades and receive the payment fixed for this term, in which case we will give hostages to ensure the full execution of all that is left. Or accept what we are going to send you today, and in your turn give us hostages to keep until those of our comrades whom you hold prisoners are restored.' To this the envoys made answer: 'Not so. Send us what is due for this term and in return we will give our solemn oath that your people shall be restored you.'

This proposition the Sultan rejected, knowing full well that if he were to deliver the money, the Cross, and the prisoners, while our men were still kept captive by the Christians, he would have no security against treachery on the part of the enemy, and this would be a great disaster to Islam.

Then the King of England, seeing all the delays interposed by the Sultan to the execution of the treaty, acted perfidiously as regards his Mussulman prisoners. On their yielding the town of Acre he had engaged to grant them life, adding that if the Sultan carried out the bargain he would give them freedom and suffer them to carry off their children and wives; if the Sultan did not fulfil his engagements they were to be made slaves. Now the King broke his promises to them and made open display of what he had till now kept hidden in his heart, by carrying out what he had intended to do after he had received the money and the Christian prisoners. It is thus that people in his nation ultimately admitted.

In the afternoon of Tuesday, 27 Rajab (20 August), about four o'clock, he came out on horseback with all the Christian army, knights, foot-men, Turcopoles and advanced to the pits at the foot of the hill of Al 'Ayâdîyeh, to which place he had already sent on his tents. The Christians, on reaching the middle of the plain that stretches between this hill and that of Keisân, close to which place the Sultan's advanced guard had drawn back, ordered all the Mussulman prisoners, whose martyrdom God had decreed for this day, to be brought before him. They numbered more than three thousand and were all bound with ropes. The Christians then flung themselves upon them all at once and massacred them with sword and lance in cold blood. Our advanced guard had already told the Sultan of the enemy's movements and he sent it some reinforcements, but only after the massacre. The Mussulmans, seeing what was being done to the prisoners, rushed against the Christians and in the combat, which lasted till nightfall, several were slain and wounded on either side. On the morrow morning our people gathered at the spot and found the Mussulmans stretched out upon the ground as martyrs for the faith. They even recognized some of the dead, and the sight was a great affliction to them. The enemy had only spared the prisoners of note and such as were strong enough to work.

The motives of this massacre are differently told; according to some, the captives were slain by way of reprisal for the death of those Christians whom the Mussulmans had slain. Others again say that the King of England, on deciding to attempt the conquest of Ascalon, thought it unwise to leave so many prisoners in the town after his departure. God alone knows what the real reason was.

Richard probably ordered the slaughter in impetuous anger at Saladin's tardy ransom. A year later, in an ironic turn of fortune's whirligig, it was Richard's turn to be held to ransom when he was captured on his homeward journey by the Duke of Austria. Unlike the Mussulmans, Richard was too valuable to be killed. His release cost England 34 tons of gold.

Magna Carta, 1215

KING JOHN ET AL.

Richard I died in 1199 – inevitably, abroad, fighting a war. The Lionheart's successor to the throne of England, his younger brother John, lacked the Plantagenet military genius but not the family's bent to homicide; he was widely rumoured to have drunkenly slain his twelve-year-old-nephew Prince Arthur 'with his own hand and, tying a heavy stone to the body, cast it into the Seine'. Unloved and unesteemed, King John found it impossible to rally supporters to defend the Angevin Continental territories, which were largely lost to the French. John crept into England to find that the locals had dubbed him 'softsword'.

Whereas before the entire Angevin empire had paid for the upkeep of the Plantagenet monarch, the cost was now borne by England alone. Taxes and fines were ratcheted up. (The era's rapacity at least made a dramatic setting for that most enduring English legend: Robin Hood and his Merry Men). When John

failed in his 1214 bid to recover his Angevin inheritance at the battle of Bouvines,
the patience of the English with his ruinous and oppressive regime snapped.

   The barons, however, had a rare problem. There was no obvious successor to
John. So their rebellion took an entirely novel cast: constitutional reform. Deserted
by 'almost everyone, and having . . . only seven Lords about his person', King
John eventually bowed to the inevitable and agreed to a 'great assembly of the
King and barons . . . in a place betwixt Windsor and Stains, called Runingmede'.

   The Great Charter (Magna Carta) was negotiated over five days and, although
the baronial class sought mostly to secure itself from feudal financial abuse by the
king, they also codified notions of law and government which became essentials
of Englishness: notably, that the power of the king (i.e. government) is subject to
the law of the land and the voice of his subjects. In Clause 39, no freeman is to
be punished except by lawful judgement of his equals and the law of the land –
thus guaranteeing trial by jury; a subject is free to enter and leave the country
(except in times of war) under Clause 42; the beginnings of Parliament can be
seen in Clause 14, which provided for a meeting of those who held land off the
crown to consent (or not) to levies of 'aid' requested by the monarch.

   Here are the most significant provisions of Magna Carta:

John, by the grace of God King of England, Lord of Ireland, Duke of
Normandy and Aquitaine, and Count of Anjou, to his archbishops,
bishops, abbots, earls, barons, justices, foresters, sheriffs, stewards, servants, and to all his officials and loyal subjects, Greeting.

   Know that before God, for the health of our soul and those of our
ancestors and heirs, to the honour of God, the exaltation of the holy
Church, and the better ordering of our kingdom, at the advice of
our reverend fathers Stephen, archbishop of Canterbury, primate of all
England, and cardinal of the holy Roman Church, Henry archbishop of
Dublin, William bishop of London, Peter bishop of Winchester, Jocelin
bishop of Bath and Glastonbury, Hugh bishop of Lincoln, Walter bishop
of Coventry, Benedict bishop of Rochester, Master Pandulf subdeacon
and member of the papal household, Brother Aymeric master of the
knighthood of the Temple in England, William Marshal earl of Pem-
broke, William earl of Salisbury, William earl of Warren, William earl
of Arundel, Alan de Galloway constable of Scotland, Warin Fitz Gerald,
Peter Fitz Herbert, Hubert de Burgh seneschal of Poitou, Hugh de
Neville, Matthew Fitz Herbert, Thomas Basset, Alan Basset, Philip
Daubeny, Robert de Roppeley, John Marshal, John Fitz Hugh and
other loyal subjects:

   (1) First, that we have granted to God, and by this present charter

have confirmed for us and our heirs in perpetuity, that the English Church shall be free, and shall have its rights undiminished, and its liberties unimpaired. That we wish this so to be observed, appears from the fact that of our own free will, before the outbreak of the present dispute between us and our barons, we granted and confirmed by charter the freedom of the Church's elections – a right reckoned to be of the greatest necessity and importance to it – and caused this to be confirmed by Pope Innocent III. This freedom we shall observe ourselves, and desire to be observed in good faith by our heirs in perpetuity.

To all free men of our kingdom we have also granted, for us and our heirs for ever, all the liberties written out below, to have and to keep for them and their heirs, of us and our heirs:

. . .

(9) Neither we nor our officials will seize any land or rent in payment of a debt, so long as the debtor has movable goods sufficient to discharge the debt. A debtor's sureties shall not be distrained upon so long as the debtor himself can discharge his debt. If, for lack of means, the debtor is unable to discharge his debt, his sureties shall be answerable for it. If they so desire, they may have the debtor's lands and rents until they have received satisfaction for the debt that they paid for him, unless the debtor can show that he has settled his obligations to them.

. . .

(12) No 'scutage'* or 'aid' may be levied in our kingdom without its general consent, unless it is for the ransom of our person, to make our eldest son a knight, and (once) to marry our eldest daughter. For these purposes only a reasonable 'aid' may be levied. 'Aids' from the city of London are to be treated similarly.

(13) The city of London shall enjoy all its ancient liberties and free customs, both by land and by water. We also will and grant that all other cities, boroughs, towns, and ports shall enjoy all their liberties and free customs.

(14) To obtain the general consent of the realm for the assessment of an 'aid' – except in the three cases specified above – or a 'scutage', we will cause the archbishops, bishops, abbots, earls, and greater barons to be summoned individually by letter. To those who hold lands directly of us we will cause a general summons to be issued, through the sheriffs and other officials, to come together on a fixed day (of which at least

---

* 'Scutage' or 'shield-money' was paid in lieu of physical participation in the king's wars.

forty days notice shall be given) and at a fixed place. In all letters of summons, the cause of the summons will be stated. When a summons has been issued, the business appointed for the day shall go forward in accordance with the resolution of those present, even if not all those who were summoned have appeared.

. . .

(20) For a trivial offence, a free man shall be fined only in proportion to the degree of his offence, and for a serious offence correspondingly, but not so heavily as to deprive him of his livelihood. In the same way, a merchant shall be spared his merchandise, and a husbandman the implements of his husbandry, if they fall upon the mercy of a royal court. None of these fines shall be imposed except by the assessment on oath of reputable men of the neighbourhood.

. . .

(28) No constable or other royal official shall take corn or other movable goods from any man without immediate payment, unless the seller voluntarily offers postponement of this.

. . .

(35) There shall be standard measures of wine, ale, and corn (the London quarter), throughout the kingdom. There shall also be a standard width of dyed cloth, russett, and haberject, namely two ells within the selvedges. Weights are to be standardized similarly.

. . .

(39) No free man shall be seized or imprisoned, or stripped of his rights or possessions, or outlawed or exiled, or deprived of his standing in any other way, nor will we proceed with force against him, or send others to do so, except by the lawful judgement of his equals or by the law of the land.

(40) To no one will we sell, to no one deny or delay right or justice.

. . .

(42) In future it shall be lawful for any man to leave and return to our kingdom unharmed and without fear, by land or water, preserving his allegiance to us, except in time of war, for some short period for the common benefit of the realm. People that have been imprisoned or outlawed in accordance with the law of the land, people from a country that is at war with us, and merchants – who shall be dealt with as stated above – are excepted from this provision.

. . .

(60) All these customs and liberties that we have granted shall be observed in our kingdom in so far as concerns our own relations with

our subjects. Let all men of our kingdom, whether clergy or laymen, observe them similarly in their relations with their own men.

(61) Since we have granted all these things for God, for the better ordering of our kingdom, and to allay the discord that has arisen between us and our barons, and since we desire that they shall be enjoyed in their entirety, with lasting strength, for ever, we give and grant to the barons the following security:

The barons shall elect twenty-five of their number to keep, and cause to be observed with all their might, the peace and liberties granted and confirmed to them by this charter.

If we, our chief justice, our officials, or any of our servants offend in any respect against any man, or transgress any of the articles of the peace or of this security, and the offence is made known to four of the said twenty-five barons, they shall come to us – or in our absence from the kingdom to the chief justice – to declare it and claim immediate redress. If we, or in our absence abroad the chief justice, make no redress within forty days, reckoning from the day on which the offence was declared to us or to him, the four barons shall refer the matter to the rest of the twenty-five barons, who may distrain upon and assail us in every way possible, with the support of the whole community of the land, by seizing our castles, lands, possessions, or anything else saving only our own person and those of the queen and our children, until they have secured such redress as they have determined upon. Having secured the redress, they may then resume their normal obedience to us.

Any man who so desires may take an oath to obey the commands of the twenty-five barons for the achievement of these ends, and to join with them in assailing us to the utmost of his power. We give public and free permission to take this oath to any man who so desires, and at no time will we prohibit any man from taking it. Indeed, we will compel any of our subjects who are unwilling to take it to swear it at our command.

If one of the twenty-five barons dies or leave the country, or is prevented in any other way from discharging his duties, the rest of them shall choose another baron in his place, at their discretion, who shall be duly sworn in as they were.

In the event of disagreement among the twenty-five barons on any matter referred to them for decision, the verdict of the majority present shall have the same validity as a unanimous verdict of the whole twenty-five, whether these were all present or some of those summoned were unwilling or unable to appear.

The twenty-five barons shall swear to obey all the above articles faithfully, and shall cause them to be obeyed by others to the best of their power.

We will not seek to procure from anyone, either by our own efforts or those of a third party, anything by which any part of these concessions or liberties might be revoked or diminished. Should such a thing be procured, it shall be null and void and we will at no time make use of it, either ourselves or through a third party.

Both we and the barons have sworn that all this shall be observed in good faith and without deceit. Witness the above-mentioned people and many others.

Given by our hand in the meadow that is called Runnymede, between Windsor and Staines, on the fifteenth day of June in the seventeenth year of our reign.

Magna Carta, with justification, entered the English psyche as the 'Palladium of Liberty' for good reason; however, as a short-term political fix to maintain peace between barons and monarch it failed miserably. As soon as King John signed it he regretted doing so, and the provoked barons offered the English crown to Louis of France. The 'Barons' War' ensued, which was only halted with John's death from dysentery in 1217 and the accession of his nine-year-old son, Henry III.

The intermission from civil strife was brief. Henry III's penchant when adult for absolutism and Frenchified favourites – in a century when English identity was on the rise – discontented the baronage all over again. Matters came to a fatal close in the mid-1250s when Henry pressed for money for a fanciful war to put his son Edmund on the throne of Sicily, and the catastrophic weather of 1257 caused the harvest to fail.

The Weather, 1257

MATTHEW PARIS

Paris, a monk at St Albans, was arguably the greatest English chronicler of the Middle Ages.

. . . On the Innocents' day* in this year such a quantity of rain fell that it covered the surface of the ground, and the times of Deucalion seemed to be renewed. The furrows looked like caves or rivers, and the rivers covered the meadows and all the neighbouring country, so that it presented the appearance of a sea. That from one case other similar ones may be understood, I may mention, that one river alone in the northern parts of England carried away seven large bridges of wood and stone; the mills too, and the neighbouring houses, were carried away by the violence of the torrent-swollen streams and destroyed. On the aforesaid day, too, a fierce whirlwind, accompanied by a violent hailstorm, disturbed the atmosphere and obscured the sky with darkness like that of night. The clouds collected together, and from them the lightning darted forth with fearful vividness, followed by claps of thunder. This thunder was clearly a bad omen, for it was mid-winter, and the cold was equal to that generally felt in February. This weather was followed by sickly unseasonable weather, which lasted about three months. . . . About this time, that is to say at the commencement of the autumn, the abbot and brethren of St Albans, considering that the crops of hay and corn were in imminent danger of being spoiled by the excessive falls of rain, came to a determination in their chapter, as was the usual custom in cases of such danger, that a fast should be proclaimed through their archdeacon, to be observed by the public as well as the convent; and also that the bier of St Alban should be carried in solemn procession to the church of St Mary-in-the-Fields, the conventual brethren and the people following with bare feet and uttering devout prayers. This was accordingly done, and on the same day, through the merits of the martyr, the destructive rain ceased. . . . This year throughout was barren and meagre; for whatever had been sown in winter, had budded in spring, and grown ripe in summer, was stifled and destroyed by the autumnal inundations. The scarcity of money, brought on by the spoliation practised by the king

* i.e. 28 December 1256.

and the pope in England, brought on unusual poverty. The land lay uncultivated, and great numbers of people died from starvation. About Christmas, the price of a measure of wheat rose to ten shillings. Apples were scarce, pears more so; figs, beech-nuts, cherries, plums – in short all fruits which are preserved in jars were completely spoiled. This pestiferous year, moreover, gave rise to mortal fevers, which raged to such an extent that, not to mention other cases, at [Bury] St Edmunds alone more than two thousand dead bodies were placed in the large cemetery during the summer, the largest portion of them during the dog-days. There were old men, who had formerly seen a measure of wheat sold for a mark, and even twenty shillings, without the people being starved to death. To add to the misery, Richard, king of Germany, had stripped the kingdom of England of many thousand marks, which he had ordered to be raised from his lands in England. The Holy Land languished in desolation and in fear of the Tartars; for the king of the latter had four million of fighting men in his train; and, as we have heard from learned and credible persons, they had already reduced half the world to subjection to them by their ferocity. Any one making a careful search and inquiry at St Albans may find there an account of their most filthy mode of life. This year, too, generated chronic complaints, which scarcely allowed free power of breathing to any one labouring under them. Not a single frosty or fine day occurred, nor was the surface of the lakes at all hardened by the frost, as was usual; neither did icicles hang from the ledges of houses; but uninterrupted heavy falls of rain and mist obscured the sky until the Purification of the blessed Virgin.*

Such was the backcloth of distress and disaster against which the baronial reformers, led by Simon de Montfort, made their move on Henry III.

De Montfort's French birth was only one of the contradictions he presented as an English revolutionary. He was simultaneously a hairshirt Christian and an aristocrat (the king's brother-in-law, the Earl of Leicester indeed), a scholar and a soldier. It was the mesmeric de Montfort who drew up the constitutional Provisions of Oxford of 1258 obliging the king to share sovereignty with a standing council of barons, and it was de Montfort who led the barons to military victory at Lewes in May 1264 after the king repudiated the self-same Provisions. For a year post-Lewes de Montfort was 'Steward of England'. But he was not its dictator: he not only convened 'Parliaments', he summoned to them, as well as the great and the good, knights from the shires and burgesses from the boroughs.

* i.e. until 2 February 1258.

For the first time in England's history, the political order opened up to the middle ranks.

Some of de Montfort's baronial backers, however, had no intention of power-sharing with jumped-up 'mesne gentes'. Still others were alienated by the de Montfort family's habit of preying on England's assets.

Only a reduced baronial army accompanied de Montfort at the battle of Evesham in the high summer of 1265, where a royalist army under Henry III's eldest son, Prince Edward, was arraigned against him. Looking over at the superior force, de Montfort sighed, 'Let us, therefore commend our souls to God, for our bodies are theirs.' He scarcely exaggerated; after the brief battle, his head, hands, feet and testicles were severed from his corpse.

De Montfort might have lost the battle and his life, but the greater victory was his. England's first political hero had killed Plantagenet autocracy stone-dead. When Edward succeeded his father on the throne (as Edward I), he adopted much of de Montfort's reform programme.

Edward I Conquers Wales, 1281–2

THOMAS WYKES

Whereas his Angevin and Plantagenet forebears had looked France-wards for territorial conquest, Edward I decided that empire-building began at home. Wales offered an early opportunity when Llewelyn ap Gruffudd failed to pay Edward homage. The response of Edward – sometime crusader, victor of Evesham – was predictable to all but the reality-divorced 'Prince of Wales'. Edward invaded Wales in 1277 and reduced Llewelyn to ruler of a toy state in Gwynedd. Still unable to grasp the nature of the medieval balance of local power, Llewelyn then rebelled against English tutelage.

In the year 1281, about the feast of the Annunciation [March 25], Llewelyn, the disturber of the peace made between himself and the king of England, instigated by his brother David, began to attack Flint and Rhuddlan Castles, and to waste the surrounding country. And when this came to the king's ears, who was at that time at Devizes, holding Easter, he sent some few troops to those parts to drive back the wretched Welsh raiders, and defend the castles till the king could take proper measures. At length he summoned the nobles of the realm together and held a Parliament at Worcester on the feast of the Nativity of St John the Baptist [June 24], and it was there arranged that all the magnates of the realm should meet the king with horses and arms on the feast of St Peter in Chains, on the Welsh border. Meanwhile David and his accomplices mortally wounded and took prisoner lord Roger Clifford, after cruelly slaying many of his people.

The king, gathering an army, took vengeance on Llewelyn, Prince of Wales, by most cruelly laying waste his lands. One day, too, some of the king's men left the main body, and by way of taking vengeance on Llewelyn were intently plundering at an unwise distance, when the Welsh burst out from an ambush in the woods and from the marshes and began to attack the English, who were but few in comparison with themselves; and in this fight were slain the son of lord William of Valence, the king's uncle, and lord Richard d'Argentein; many were barbarously killed, and the others with difficulty escaped by flight. The king stayed in the neighbourhood of Rhuddlan till the feast of All Saints [November 1], and the archbishop of Canterbury was sent to Llewelyn in Snowdon to warn him and persuade him to keep the peace with the king, under which he chafed, and which he absolutely refused to keep; but he could not be induced to come to terms. Meanwhile, while the archbishop was spending three days in Snowdon, the royal leaders imperceptibly but gradually entered Snowdon, thinking that they could seize it in force by treachery; but the Welsh were forewarned and came to meet them, and at the first attack compelled them to flee; and the fugitives, thinking to save themselves by crossing some river, not knowing the ford, were drowned in large numbers – the more famous being Lucas de Tany, William of Dodingeseles, and William la Zuche, while the others escaped only with the greatest difficulty. When the archbishop withdrew and came back to the king he excommunicated Llewelyn, the perjured disturber of the peace, his brother David, and all their accomplices and abettors. All this took place about St Leonard's Day [November 6]. About the feast of St Thomas the Apostle [December 21], as Llewelyn was coming down from Snowdon with a small following, on some unknown business, he was met unexpectedly by Edmund Mortimer with a small escort, and slain with his accomplices, who were unable to take to flight. The prince's head, which he recognized among the slain, Edmund cut off and brought to the king. The king triumphantly had the head taken to London and fixed on a spear above the Tower of London as a token of his splendid victory. The king of England for this Welsh war took a scutage of forty shillings from his whole realm.

Encouraged by his success, the king of England had a suitable road laid open for him, and entered Snowdon in triumph, and kept Easter there in a Cistercian monastery called Aberconway, disposing of the whole of the principality of Wales at his pleasure, with the exception of the castle which in their language is called Bere, and which is surrounded by an impassable marsh, having difficult and very narrow entries and exits by a single road most ingeniously made. Into it, after his brother's death, David had thrown a garrison, while he himself was lying hid in the woods and practically inaccessible places. But the king besieged the castle, and so closely beset the garrison that, under the compulsion of necessity, they were compelled to surrender the castle to him; and on obtaining possession of it he made a bargain with some Welshmen that they should take David from his hiding-place and surrender him to the king as a prisoner; and the king sent him, with his wife and son, to Rhuddlan, and there imprisoned him and loaded him with fetters. And when Rhys Vychan [the little] heard what had happened, he surrendered himself and his followers to lord Humphrey de Bohun, earl of Hereford; and he forthwith sent them to the king, and the king to London, with orders that he should be put in the Tower and most strictly guarded . . .

About the feast of St Michael [September 29] the king summoned to Shrewsbury the chief men of his realm and the best counsellors, both from among the burgesses and the magnates, and had David brought thither – who had been kept in captivity at Rhuddlan – to submit to the punishment demanded by his crime, and it was there decided that he should die a fivefold death: firstly, to be torn asunder by horses; secondly, to be hanged; thirdly, to be executed; fourthly, to have his heart and entrails burned; and fifthly, to have his body quartered and hung up in four separate places in England. His head was carried off to London by the Londoners then at Shrewsbury, to be set as a conspicuous mark on the Tower of London, next to the head of his brother Llewelyn.

In 1284 Wales was formally annexed to the English crown. To ensure that this state of affairs endured, Edward ringed the principality with giant castles, architected by the Savoyard genius Master James of St George: Flint, Rhuddlan, Aberystwyth, Builth, Conwy, Caernarfon, Criccieth, Harlech and Beaumaris. They were the high-point of castle-building in Britain. To add insult to conquered Welsh pride, the title 'Prince of Wales' was granted to Edward's own eldest son.

Wales was never again independent.

Sex in the Country, 15 June 1300

ANONYMOUS COURT RECORDER

The proceedings of a rural dean's court at Salwarp, Worcestershire. The place in brackets refers to the defendant's village of residence.

(King's Norton) William le yrmongarre fornicated for the third time with Agnes Elyot. Purgation seven-handed is decreed for the man. The woman is suspended for contumacy. The man fails in the purgation and renounces his sin and is whipped in the usual way twice through the market place. The woman confesses and is whipped in the usual way once through the market place. The man withdrew.

Henry de Lee fornicated with Agnes of Alvechurch. Purgation six-handed is decreed for the man. The woman is suspended for contumacy. The woman withdrew. The man is cited.

William Miller fornicated with Alice de la Schave. Each appears and confesses and is whipped in the usual way. Each withdrew.

Edith Ythefrithe, pregnant, says on oath by Richard de Boscho whom she renounces and is whipped in the usual way. The man confesses and is whipped in the usual way. The woman did [penance]. The man withdrew.

(Bromsgrove) William de Coleweyk fornicated with Julia, a weaver. Each appears and confesses and is whipped in the usual way. Each did [penance].

Roger Miller fornicated with Isabella Clerk and with Alice Clerk, sister of the said Isabella. The man confesses with regard to each and is whipped in the usual way once through the market place. Isabella confesses and is whipped in the usual way. Each withdrew.

Thomas de Brandel fornicated with Agnes daughter of Gilbert the smith. The man confesses and is whipped in the usual way. The woman is suspended for contumacy. The woman is excommunicated. The man is doing [penance]. The woman is reconciled and confesses and is whipped in the usual way. Withdrew.

Geoffrey of Langley fornicated for the fifth time with Agnes daughter of Aldich. Purgation six-handed is decreed for each. They each make their purgation.

Walter of Morton fornicated with Alice le Carter. The man is cited.

The woman appears and confesses and is whipped in the usual way. The woman withdrew. The man is not found.

Thomas Noppe fornicated with Isabella of Holywalle. Each confesses and is whipped in the usual way. Each *recessit.*

Henry de Frankel fornicated with Matilda Honderwode. The woman confesses and renounces her sin and is whipped in the usual way once through the market place. The man is suspended for contumacy. The woman did [penance]. The man is excommunicated *cum communi.*

The Age of Chivalry: A Mass Knighting, May 1306

ANONYMOUS MONK

Edward I was widely considered 'the best lance in the world' (despite his lisp and droopy eyelid), and his court was the English headquarters for the chivalric cult of perfect manners and battlefield prowess by which the elite of the era defined itself. On the eve of Edward's resumed campaign to crush the Scots the most fabulous chivalric ceremony of medieval England took place at Westminster. The scene was recorded by a monk of Westminster in the Flowers of History.

To increase the numbers that were to set out for Scotland, the king issued a public proclamation that as many as were knights by inheritance, and who had the wherewithal for campaigning, should appear at Westminster on 12 May, where each individual would be equipped, from the royal wardrobe, with every knightly accoutrement except a horse.

So it was that to the three hundred young men who assembled, sons of earls, barons and knights, were distributed purple satin, fine linen and robes sewn with the finest gold.

The royal palace of Westminster, though big, was too small for the great crowd that had gathered, so the apple trees at the New Temple were cut down and walls demolished, and pavilions and tents erected where the young men might adorn themselves with their golden robes.

That night in the Temple church, these esquires, or as many of them as the place would hold, kept vigil. But on the instructions of his father, Edward, prince of Wales, together with certain very noble aspirants to knighthood, kept his vigil in the abbey church at Westminster. So loud were the voices of those shouting for joy, and so great the clamour of trumpets and horns, that the rejoicing of the congregation could not be heard from one side of the choir to the other.

In the palace the next day, King Edward I girded his son with the sword belt of a knight and granted him the dukedom of Aquitaine. And thus Prince Edward was made a knight in the abbey church of Westminster, that he might make his companions resplendent likewise with knightly glory.

There was such a crush of people before the high altar that two knights died, several fainted and at least three had to be taken away and attended to.

Then two swans were brought before King Edward I in pomp and splendour, adorned with golden nets and gilded reeds, the most astounding sight to the onlookers. Having seen them, the king swore by the God of Heaven and by the swans that he wished to set out for Scotland and, whether he lived or died, to avenge the wrong done to the Holy Church, the death of John Comyn and the breach of faith by the Scots.

The oath was pledged by all the other magnates, who asserted with the king that they were ready to journey to Scotland both during his lifetime and after, under his son the prince, to fulfil his vow.

On 30 May, when all had been roused to courage, the young men saluted the king and left Westminster, men who were to appear before the king in Scotland on 8 July.

For the knighting of the king's son, the clergy and people ceded a thirtieth part of their goods to the king, and the merchants a twentieth.

Edward I died in 1307 aged sixty-eight. 'The Hammer of the Scots' (as his Westminster tomb was inscribed) tasked his son, Prince Edward, with carrying on the work of English domination north of the border.

The Battle of Bannockburn, 24 June 1314

THE CHRONICLE OF LANERCOST

The pursuits of Edward II were unkingly (ditch-digging, thatching), his bed-companions preferably male (notoriously Piers Gaveston, elevated to Earl of Cornwall), his interest in effective government slight, his ability as war-leader of the English nation thinner still.

At Bannockburn on the Forth plain, Edward II faced a Scottish army (led by Robert the Bruce) a third the size of his Plantagenet force.

The Chronicle of Lanercost was compiled by clergy in Cumberland.

In early May, the king of England approached the Scottish March with a fine and mighty army.

Yet whereas his father, Edward I, when going to war with the Scots, had been accustomed to visit the shrines of English saints and to make splendid offerings to them, Edward II rode along in great pomp with elaborate trappings, took goods from the monasteries and, so it is reported, said and did much that was harmful to the shrines.

In June, King Edward II gathered his forces together and approached Stirling Castle in great might, in order to break up the siege, and to do battle with the Scots, who had assembled there with their entire strength. On 23 June, after midday, the English forces reached Tor Wood. The Scots, who were in the wood, fell upon the leading column of Robert Clifford's force, killing a number of men and forcing the rest to flee. After this incident, the English grew fearful, while the Scots became bolder.

When the two armies had drawn much closer to each other, all the Scots fell to their knees, saying the Lord's Prayer, commending themselves to God's protection and seeking divine assistance. This done, they marched boldly against the English. The Scottish army was drawn up with the first two lines each a little ahead of the one next to it, so that no line was in front of another. Robert Bruce was in the third and final line.

When the two armies joined battle, the great English horses rushed on to the Scottish pikes, which bristled like a dense forest. An appalling din arose from the splintering pikes and the warhorses, mortally wounded. This brought matters to a standstill for a while. The English could not pass the Scots' front line in order to reach the enemy; indeed they could do nothing to improve their situation, and their only recourse was to flight.

I heard the tale of these events from a trustworthy eyewitness.

In the fighting in the front line, the dead included Gilbert of Clare, earl of Gloucester, Robert Clifford, and many other nobles, besides a great number of footsoldiers.

Yet another misfortune befell the English, who had a little earlier crossed a deep ditch, a tidal inlet, called the Bannock Burn: now, as they struggled to retreat in confusion, many noblemen and others fell into this ditch in the crush, with their horses. Some managed to scramble out, but many were completely unable to extricate themselves. 'Bannockburn' was a name on all English lips for many years to come.

The king, with Hugh Despenser, who had become the apple of the king's eye after Piers Gaveston, and numerous English cavalry and infantry, were guided away by a Scottish knight who knew an escape route. Thus, to their eternal shame, they fled wretchedly to the castle at Dunbar. Some stragglers were killed by the Scots, who were in hot pursuit. From Dunbar, the king and a few of his closest companions took a boat to Berwick upon Tweed, leaving the rest to their fate.

The Murder of Edward II, 22 September 1327

GEOFFREY LE BAKER

Humiliated once too often by Edward II's homosexual infatuations, his wife Isabella exiled herself to her native France, taking as her lover the English Marcher lord, Roger de Mortimer. In September 1326 Isabella and Mortimer invaded England, Edward's supposedly loyal subjects flocked to their standard, and within four months a great council at Westminster had deposed Edward II in favour of his son, Edward III.

There remained only the problem of what to do with the ex-king. In April 1327 Edward II was placed in the custody of Thomas, Lord of Berkeley. Geoffrey le Baker was almost alone among fourteenth-century chroniclers in showing sympathy for Edward II.

These things were told me by William Bishop, in the time after the great plague. He had seen them with his own eyes for he had been among those who took Edward to Berkeley.

Finally they arrived at Berkeley Castle, where, ever patient in the face of his misfortunes, the noble Edward was shut up like a hermit. He was robbed of his earthly kingdom and stripped bare like the blessed Job, not by his rivals but by his own wife, his servants and serving women.

Despoiled of his command, his honours, his goods, Edward II looked forward to the kingdom of Heaven. However, his wife, Isabella, was angered that his life which had become most hateful to her should be so prolonged. She asked advice of the bishop of Hereford, pretending that she had had a dreadful dream from which she feared, if it was true, that her husband would at some time be restored to his former dignity and would condemn her, as a traitress, to be burned or to perpetual slavery. The bishop of Hereford feared greatly for himself, just as Isabella did, if this should come to pass, conscious as he was that he was guilty of treason.

And so, letters were written to Edward's keepers, setting forth in vivid detail the false accusation that they had been too lenient with him and fed him on delicacies. Moreover, it was hinted that the death of Edward would cause these nobles no great displeasure, whether it were natural or violent. Concerning this point, the bishop of Hereford penned a message of double meaning: *Edwardum occidere nolite timere bonum est.*

This saying may be resolved into two parts: the first consists of the first three words of the bishop's puzzle: *'Edwardum occidere nolite'* – 'Do not kill Edward!' – followed by the second three: *'timere bonum est'* – 'fear is a good thing.' Read thus, the message would not be construed as treason.

But those who received the message were aware of the true import of the bishop's communication. They construed the message thus: *'Edwardum occidere nolite timere'* – 'Do not fear to kill Edward!' – followed by *'bonum est'* – 'it is good!' Those who were guilty of evil, read the message as evil. Thus did that skilful trickster have recourse to a puzzle, for he knew that without his authority, Edward's keepers would not dare to carry out their cruel instructions and kill him, lest they should later be brought to trial for this crime.

The bishop of Hereford himself made careful provision that the authority which he gave might appear to mean the opposite of what he intended, but to have been misread by the thick-witted keepers who then took the life of an innocent man as a consequence of their own mistake. Taken in the contrary sense, his message made him safe from any accusation of treason. And indeed, events were to prove the bishop correct.

In the end, Edward's murderers, who had believed that the favour of Isabella and the slippery and deceitful bishop made them secure, found instead that these two were eager to take vengeance for the murder of their hostage, Edward.

The keepers were dumbfounded and did not know what to do. They showed the letters with the seals of Isabella, the bishop of Hereford and the other conspirators to prove that the latter had indeed given their consent.

The bishop did not deny the letter, agreeing that he and his accomplices had sent it, but he explained it as being perfectly innocent and loyal in its meaning. It was the keepers, he claimed, who had misinterpreted it and used it as authority for their own wicked deed. He so terrified them with his threats that they fled. So much for the letter of double meaning.

Edward II was welcomed kindly at the castle and treated well by

Thomas Berkeley, lord of the estate. After receipt of the letter, however, Edward's torturers took control of the castle.

They gave orders that Thomas Berkeley was to have no contact with Edward. This caused him not only sadness but also shame for he was unable to do as he wished and as before had been his right. Sighing, he bade Edward farewell and removed to another of his estates.

Then began the most extreme part of Edward's persecution which was to continue until his death.

Firstly, he was shut up in a secure chamber, where he was tortured for many days until he was almost suffocated by the stench of corpses buried in a cellar hollowed out beneath. Carpenters, who one day were working near the window of his chamber, heard him, God's servant, as he lamented that this was the most extreme suffering that had ever befallen him.

But when his tyrannous warders perceived that the stench alone was not sufficient to kill him, they seized him on the night of 22 September as he lay sleeping in his room.

There, with cushions heavier than fifteen strong men could carry, they held him down, suffocating him.

Then they thrust a plumber's soldering iron, heated red hot, guided by a tube inserted into his bowels, and thus they burnt his innards and his vital organs. They feared lest, if he were to receive a wound in those parts of the body where men generally are wounded, it might be discovered by some man who honoured justice, and his torturers might be found guilty of manifest treason and made to suffer the consequent penalty.

As this brave knight was overcome, he shouted aloud so that many heard his cry both within and without the castle and knew it for the cry of a man who suffered violent death. Many in both the town and castle of Berkeley were moved to pity for Edward, and to watch and pray for his spirit as it departed this world.

The Hundred Years War: Sea Fight at Sluys, 24 June 1340

GEOFFREY LE BAKER

Even more so than his grandfather, Edward III, founder of the Order of the Garter, was the epitome of the chivalric king; even more so than his grandfather, Edward III defined Englishness through war. He banned village sports other than archery as too distracting, and he reorganized the navy to such a degree that an admiring Parliament dubbed him 'King of the Sea'.

In 1337 Edward led his nation into what would become a Hundred Years War against France. Aside from Edward's own longing for martial honours, geo-politics necessitated that England protect her remaining possessions in France and her outlets for the wool trade (England's major money-earner) in the Low Countries. Three years later, Edward raised the stakes by claiming the French throne after the extinction of the male Capetian line and adding the fleur-de-lis to his heraldic arms.

The English could not but love him, especially after the 'King of the Sea' captained the first of England's historic naval victories over her Channel neighbours, at Sluys, off the Flanders coast.

King Edward [III] kept his Whitsuntide at Ipswich, because he intended from thence to make his passage into Flanders; but, being informed that the French King had sent a great navy of Spanish ships and also the whole fleet of France to stop his passage, he caused his ships of the Cinque Ports and others to be assembled, so that he had in his fleet, great and small, 260 ships.

Wherefore, on the Thursday before the Nativity of Saint John the Baptist, having a favourable wind, he began to sail; and the next day, in the even of the said feast, they descried the French fleet lying in Swinehaven. Wherefore the King caused all his fleet to come to anchor.

The next day, being the Feast of Saint John the Baptist, early in the morning the French fleet divided themselves into three parts, withdrew about a mile, and then approached the King's fleet. When the King saw this, about nine o'clock, having the wind and sun on his back, he set forward and met his enemies as he would have wished; at which the whole fleet gave a terrible shout, and a shower of arrows out of long wooden bows so poured down on the Frenchmen that thousands were slain in that meeting. At length they closed and came to hand blows with pikes, poleaxes, and swords, and some threw stones from the tops of ships, wherewith many were brained. The size and height of the Spanish ships caused many Englishmen to strike many a blow in vain. But, to be short, the first part of the French ships being overcome and all the men spent, the Englishmen entered and took them. The French ships were chained together in such a way that they could not be separated from each other, so that a few Englishmen kept that part of the fleet. They then set upon the second part and with great difficulty made the attack; but when this had been done, the second part was sooner overcome than the first because many of the Frenchmen abandoned their ships and leapt overboard. The Englishmen, having thus overcome the first and second parts of the fleet, and now finding night drawing on, partly for want of light and partly because they were weary, determined to take some rest till the next morning. On this account, during the night thirty ships of the third part fled away, but a large ship called the 'James' of Dieppe, thinking to have carried away a certain ship of Sandwich belonging to the prior of Canterbury, was stopped, for the sailors so stoutly defended themselves by the help of the Earl of Huntingdon that they saved themselves and their ship from the Frenchmen.

The fight continued all night, and in the morning, the Normans being overcome and taken, there were found in the ship 400 men slain. Moreover, the King understanding that the ships were fled, sent forty well-equipped ships to follow them. . . . In the first group of ships that were taken they found these conquered ships: the 'Denis', the 'George', the 'Christopher' and the 'Blacke Cocke', all of which had been captured by Frenchmen at Sluys and carried into Normandy. The number of ships of war that were taken was about 230 barges; the number of enemies that were slain and drowned was about 25,000, and of Englishmen about 4,000, among whom were four knights . . .

The Hundred Years War: The Battle of Crécy, 26 August 1346

SIR JOHN FROISSART

The battle of Crécy ensued when Edward III's invasion army was trapped by a superior French force under King Philip in Picardy. Among Edward's soldiers was his sixteen-year-old son, the Prince of Wales, known as the Black Prince.

The English . . . were drawn up in three divisions, and seated on the ground, on seeing their enemies advance, rose up undauntedly and fell into their ranks. The Prince's battalion, whose archers were formed in the manner of a portcullis, and the men-at-arms in the rear, was the first to do so. The Earls of Northampton and Arundel, who commanded the second division, posted themselves in good order on the Prince's wing to assist him if necessary.

You must know that the French troops did not advance in any regular order, and that as soon as their King came in sight of the English his blood began to boil, and he cried out to his marshals, 'Order the Genoese forward and begin the battle in the name of God and St Denis.' There were about 15,000 Genoese crossbow men; but they were quite fatigued, having marched on foot that day six leagues, completely armed and carrying their crossbows, and accordingly they told the Constable they were not in a condition to do any great thing in battle. The Earl of Alençon hearing this, said, 'This is what one gets by employing such scoundrels, who fall off when there is any need for them.' During this time a heavy rain fell, accompanied by thunder and a very terrible eclipse of the sun; and, before this rain, a great flight of crows hovered in the air over all the battalions, making a loud noise; shortly afterwards it cleared up, and the sun shone very bright; but the French had it in their faces; and the English on their backs. When the Genoese were somewhat in order they approached the English and set up a loud shout, in order to frighten them; but the English remained quite quiet and did not seem to attend to it. They then set up a second shout, and advanced a little forward; the English never moved. Still they hooted a third time, advancing with their crossbows presented, and began to shoot. The English archers then advanced one step forward, and shot their arrows with such force and quickness, that it seemed as if it snowed. When the Genoese felt these arrows, which pierced through their armour, some of them cut the strings of their crossbows, others flung them to the ground, and all turned about and retreated quite discomfited.

The French had a large body of men-at-arms on horseback to support the Genoese, and the King, seeing them thus fall back, cried out, 'Kill me those scoundrels, for they stop up our road without any reason.' The English continued shooting, and some of their arrows falling among the horsemen, drove them upon the Genoese, so that they were in such confusion, they could never rally again.

In the English army there were some Cornish and Welsh men on foot, who had armed themselves with large knives, these advancing through the ranks of the men-at-arms and archers, who made way for them, came upon the French when they were in this danger, and falling upon earls, barons, knights, and squires, slew many, at which the King of England was exasperated. The valiant King of Bohemia was slain there; he was called Charles of Luxembourg, for he was the son of the gallant king and emperor, Henry of Luxembourg, and, having heard the order for the battle, he inquired where his son the Lord Charles was; his attendants answered that they did not know, but believed he was fighting. Upon this, he said to them, 'Gentlemen, you are all my people, my friends, and brethren at arms this day; therefore, as I am blind, I request of you to lead me so far into the engagement that I may strike one stroke with my sword.' The knights consented, and in order that they might not lose him in the crowd, fastened all the reins of their horses together, placing the King at their head that he might gratify his wish, and in this manner advanced towards the enemy. The Lord Charles of Bohemia, who already signed his name as King of Germany, and bore the arms, had come in good order to the engagement; but when he perceived that it was likely to turn out against the French he departed. The King, his father, rode in among the enemy, and he and his companions fought most valiantly; however, they advanced so far that they were all slain, and on the morrow they were found on the ground with all their horses tied together.

The Earl of Alençon advanced in regular order upon the English, to fight with them, as did the Earl of Flanders in another part. These two lords with their detachments, coasting, as it were, the archers, came to the Prince's battalion, where they fought valiantly for a length of time. The King of France was eager to march to the place where he saw their banners displayed, but there was a hedge of archers before him: he had that day made a present of a handsome black horse to Sir John of Hainault, who had mounted on it a knight of his, called Sir John de

Fusselles, who bore his banner; the horse ran off with the knight and forced his way through the English army, and when about to return, stumbled and fell into a ditch and severely wounded him; he did not, however, experience any other inconvenience than from his horse, for the English did not quit their ranks that day to make prisoners: his page alighted and raised him up, but the French knight did not return the way he came, as he would have found it difficult from the crowd. This battle, which was fought on Saturday, between La Broyes and Crécy, was murderous and cruel; and many gallant deeds of arms were performed that were never known: towards evening, many knights and squires of the French had lost their masters, and wandering up and down the plain, attacked the English in small parties; but they were soon destroyed, for the English had determined that day to give no quarter, nor hear of ransom from anyone.

Early in the day some French, Germans, and Savoyards had broken through the archers of the Prince's battalion, and had engaged with the men-at-arms; upon this the second battalion came to his aid, and it was time they did so, for otherwise he would have been hard pressed. The first division, seeing the danger they were in, sent a knight off in great haste to the King of England, who was posted upon an eminence near a windmill. On the knight's arrival he said, 'Sir, the Earl of Warwick, the Lord Stafford, the Lord Reginald Cobham, and the others who are about your son, are vigorously attacked by the French, and they entreat that you will come to their assistance with your battalion, for if numbers should increase against him, they fear he will have too much to do.' The King replied, 'Is my son dead, unhorsed, or so badly wounded that he cannot support himself?' 'Nothing of the sort, thank God,' rejoined the knight, 'but he is in so hot an engagement that he has great need of your help.' The King answered, 'Now, Sir Thomas, return to those that sent you, and tell them from me not to send again for me this day, nor expect that I shall come, let what will happen, as long as my son has life; and say that I command them to let the boy win his spurs, for I am determined, if it please God, that all the glory of this day shall be given to him, and to those into whose care I have entrusted him.' The knights returned to his lords and related the King's answer, which mightily encouraged them, and made them repent they had ever sent such a message.

It is a certain fact, that Sir Godfrey de Harcourt, who was in the prince's battalion, having been told by some of the English that they had seen the banner of his brother engaged in the battle against him, was exceedingly anxious to save him; but he was too late, for he was left dead on the field, and so was the Earl of Aumarle, his nephew. On the other hand, the Earls of Alençon and Flanders were fighting lustily under their banners with their own people; but they could not resist the force of the English, and were there slain, as well as many other knights and squires, who were attending on, or accompanying them.

The Earl of Blois, nephew to the King of France, and the Duke of Lorraine, his brother-in-law, with their troops, made a gallant defence; but they were surrounded by a troop of English and Welsh, and slain in spite of their prowess. The Earl of St Pol, and the Earl of Auxerre, were also killed, as well as many others. Late after vespers, the King of France had not more about him than sixty men, every one included. Sir John of Hainault, who was of the number, had once remounted the King, for his horse had been killed under him by an arrow: and seeing the state he was in, he said, 'Sir, retreat whilst you have an opportunity, and do not expose yourself so simply; if you have lost this battle, another time you will be the conqueror.' After he had said this he took the bridle of the King's horse and led him off by force, for he had before entreated him to retire. The king rode on until he came to the castle of La Broyes, where he found the gates shut, for it was very dark: he ordered the Governor of it to be summoned, who, after some delay, came upon the battlements, and asked who it was that called at such an hour. The King answered, 'Open, open, Governor, it is the fortune of France.' The Governor hearing the King's voice immediately descended, opened the gate, and let down the bridge; the King and his company entered the castle, but he had with him only five barons: Sir John of Hainault, the Lord Charles of Montmorency, the Lord of Beaujeu, the Lord of Aubigny, and the Lord of Montfort. It was not his intention, however, to bury himself in such a place as this, but having taken some refreshments, he set out again with his attendants about midnight, and rode on under the direction of guides, who were well acquainted with the country, until about daybreak he came to Amiens, where he halted. This Saturday the English never quitted their ranks in pursuit of anyone, but remained on the field guarding their position and defending themselves against all who attacked them. The battle ended at the hour of vespers, when the King of England embraced his son and said to him, 'Sweet son, God give you perseverance: you are my son; for most loyally have you acquitted yourself; you are worthy to be a sovereign.' The Prince bowed very low, giving all honour to the King, his father. The English during the night made frequent thanks-givings to the Lord for the happy issue of the day; and with them there was no rioting, for the King had expressly forbidden all riot or noise.

On the following day, which was Sunday, there were a few encounters with the French troops; however, they could not withstand the English, and soon either retreated or were put to the sword. When Edward was assured that there was no appearance of the French collecting another army, he sent to have the number and rank of the dead examined. This business was entrusted to Lord Reginald Cobham and Lord Stafford, assisted by three heralds to examine the arms, and two secretaries to write down the names. They passed the whole day upon the field of battle, and made a very circumstantial account of all they saw: according to their report it appeared that 80 banners, the bodies of 11 princes, 1,200 knights, and about 30,000 common men were found dead on the field.

The English won at Crécy because of their longbowmen (who could fire ten arrows per minute, compared to the French / Genoese crossbowmen's five), their superior tactics and their patriotism, which bound them together above class. So socially polarized were the French at Crécy that their lords rode roughshod – literally – over their peasant foot soldiers. Who needed sophisticated English arms when the French were happy to kill one another?

After Crécy, Edward III seized Calais (which would remain an English possession until 1558). But a deadlier enemy than the French lay in wait for Edward's England. King Death.

The Black Death, 1348–9

HENRY KNIGHTON

The population of England stood at around 4 million in 1348, up threefold since the Norman Conquest, courtesy of two centuries of economic prosperity. Perhaps 2 million of these English were lost to the Black Death, a form of bubonic plague carried by the fleas of the black rat. The first symptoms were buboes (swellings) in the lymph system; death came within two to five days.

Henry Knighton was a canon of St Mary's Abbey, Leicester. The plague arrived in England via the port of Melcombe Regis in Dorset, not Southampton as Knighton says.

The dreadful pestilence penetrated the sea coast by Southampton and came to Bristol, and there almost the whole population of the town perished, as if it had been seized by sudden death; for few kept their beds more than two or three days, or even half a day. Then this cruel death spread everywhere around, following the course of the sun. And there died at Leicester in the small parish of St Leonard more than 380 persons, in the parish of Holy Cross, 400; in the parish of St Margaret's, Leicester, 700; and so in every parish, a great multitude. Then the Bishop of London sent word throughout his whole diocese giving general power to each and every priest, regular as well as secular, to hear confessions and to give absolution to all persons with full episcopal authority, except only in case of debt. In this case, the debtor was to pay the debt, if he was able, while he lived, or others were to fulfil his obligations from his property after his death. Likewise the Pope granted full remission of all sins to anyone receiving absolution when in danger of death, and granted that this power should last until Easter next following, and that everyone might choose whatever confessor he pleased.

In the same year there was a great murrain of sheep everywhere in the kingdom, so that in one place in a single pasture more than 5,000 sheep died; and they putrefied so that neither bird nor beast would touch them. Everything was low in price because of the fear of death, for very few people took any care of riches or property of any kind. A man could have a horse that had been worth 40s for half a mark [6s 8d], a fat ox for 4s, a cow for 12d, a heifer for 6d, a fat wether for 4d, a sheep for 3d, a lamb for 2d, a large pig for 5d; a stone of wool [24 lbs] was worth 9d. Sheep and cattle ran at large through the fields and among the crops, and there was none to drive them off or herd them; for lack of care they perished in ditches and hedges in incalculable numbers throughout all districts, and none knew what to do. For there was no memory of death so stern and cruel since the time of Vortigern, King of the Britons, in whose day, as Bede testifies, the living did not suffice to bury the dead.

In the following autumn a reaper was not to be had for a lower wage than 8d, with his meals; a mower for not less than 10d, with meals. Wherefore many crops wasted in the fields for lack of harvesters. But in the year of the pestilence, as has been said above, there was so great an abundance of every kind of grain that almost no one cared for it.

The Scots, hearing of the dreadful plague among the English, suspected that it had come about through the vengeance of God, and, according to the common report, they were accustomed to swear 'be the foul deth of Engelond'. Believing that the wrath of God had befallen the English, they assembled in Selkirk forest with the intention of invading the kingdom, when the fierce mortality overtook them, and in a short time about 5,000 perished. As the rest, the strong and the feeble, were preparing to return to their own country, they were followed and attacked by the English, who slew countless numbers of them.

Master Thomas of Bradwardine was consecrated by the Pope Archbishop of Canterbury, and when he returned to England he came to London, but within two days was dead . . .

Meanwhile the King sent proclamation into all the counties that reapers and other labourers should not take more than they had been accustomed to take, under the penalty appointed by statute. But the labourers were so lifted up and obstinate that they would not listen to the King's command, but if anyone wished to have them he had to give them what they wanted, and either lose his fruit and crops, or satisfy the lofty and covetous wishes of the workmen. And when it was known to the King that they had not observed his command, and had given greater wages to the labourers, he levied heavy fines upon abbots, priors, knights, greater and lesser, and other great folk and small folk of the realm, of some 100s, of some 40s, of some 20s, from each according to what he could give. And afterwards the King had many labourers arrested, and sent them to prison; many withdrew themselves and went into the forests and woods; and those who were taken were heavily fined. Their ringleaders were made to swear that they would not take daily wages beyond the ancient custom, and then were freed from prison. And in like manner was done with the other craftsmen in the boroughs and villages . . . After the aforesaid pestilence, many buildings, great and small, fell into ruins in every city, borough, and village for lack of inhabitants, likewise many villages and hamlets became desolate, not a house being left in them, all having died who dwelt there; and it was probable that many such villages would never be inhabited.

Many thought the plague a judgement by God for society's sins, especially Lust. The Benedictine preacher Thomas Brinton complained: 'We are not constant in faith . . . It is undoubtedly for that reason that there exists in the kingdom of England so marked a diminution of fruitfulness; so cruel a pestilence, so much injustice, so many illegitimate children – for on every side there is so much lechery and adultery that few men are contented with their wives but each man lusts after the wife of his neighbour or keeps a stinking concubine.'

Having tried everything else – flight, bleedings, enemas, lavender or columbine potions – to save themselves from the buboes, the English sought God's intercession.

Flagellants Come to London, Michaelmas 1349

ROBERT OF AVESBURY

Usually members of the Dominican and Franciscan orders, flagellants voluntarily whipped themselves in public to atone for society's sins.

About Michaelmas 1349 over six hundred men came to London from Flanders, mostly of Zeeland and Holland origin. Sometimes at St Paul's and sometimes at other points in the city they made two daily public appearances wearing cloths from the thighs to the ankles, but otherwise stripped bare. Each wore a cap marked with a red cross in front and behind. Each had in his right hand a scourge with three tails. Each tail had a knot and through the middle of it there were sometimes sharp nails fixed. They marched naked in a file one behind the other and whipped themselves with these scourges on their naked and bleeding bodies. Four of them would cant in their native tongue and, another four would chant in response like a litany. Thrice they would all cast themselves on the ground in this sort of procession, stretching out their hands like the arms of a cross. The singing would go on and, the one who was in the rear of those thus prostrate acting first, each of them in turn would step over the others and give one stroke with his scourge to the man lying under him. This went on from the first to the last until each of them had observed the ritual to the full tale of those on the ground. Then each put on his customary garments and always wearing their caps and carrying their whips in their hands they retired to their lodgings. It is said that every night they performed the same penance.

The Peasant's Life, c. 1362

WILLIAM LANGLAND

Langland set his epic alliterative poem The Vision of Piers Plowman *in the plague-stricken England of the declining years of Edward III. A Mass-priest, Langland dressed as a beggar to experience the lot of the lower orders, and* Piers Plowman *has been called the first 'authentic cry of the poor' in British history. Here Hunger is interrogating Piers:*

'Can you serve,' he said, 'or sing in churches,
Or cock hay in my harvest, or handle a hay-fork,
Mow or mound it or make sheaves or bindings,
Reap, or be an head reaper, and rise early,
Or have an horn and be an hayward, and be out till morning,
And keep my corn in my croft from pickers and stealers?
Or make shoes, or sew cloth, or tend sheep or cattle,
Or make hedges, or harrow, or drive geese, or be swineherd?
Or can you work at any craft which the commune calls for,
To be means of livelihood to the bed-ridden?'

'I have no penny,' said Piers, 'to buy pullets,
Nor geese nor pigs, but two green cheeses,
A few curds of cream, a cake of oatmeal,
Two loaves of beans and bran, baked for my children;
And, by my soul, I swear I have no salt bacon,
Nor cook to make collops, I take Christ to witness!
But I have parsley and pot herbs and a plenty of cabbages,
And a cow and a calf, and a cart mare
To draw my dung afield till the drought is over.
This is the little we must live on till the Lammas season.
And then I hope to have my harvest in the garner.
And then I may spread your supper to my soul's content.'

So all the poor people fetched peascods,
And brought him beans and baked apples by the lapful,
Ripe cherries, chervils and many small onions,
And offered Piers the present to please Hunger.

The needy are our neighbours, if we note rightly;
As prisoners in cells, or poor folk in hovels,
Charged with children and overcharged by landlords.
What they may spare in spinning they spend on rental,
On milk, or on meal to make porridge
To still the sobbing of the children at meal time.
Also they themselves suffer much hunger.
They have woe in winter time, and wake at midnight
To rise and to rock the cradle at the bedside,
To card and to comb, to darn clouts and to wash them,
To rub and to reel and to put rushes on the paving.

The woe of these women who dwell in hovels
Is too sad to speak of or to say in rhyme.
And many other men have much to suffer
From hunger and from thirst; they turn the fair side outward,
For they are abashed to beg, lest it should be acknowledged
At their neighbours what they need at noon and even.

I know all this well; for the world has taught me
What befalls another who has many children,
With no claim but his craft to clothe and feed them,
When the mouths are many and the money scarce.
They have bread and penny ale in place of a pittance,
And cold flesh and cold fish for venison from the butcher.
On Fridays and fast days a farthing worth of mussels
Would be a feast for such folk, with a few cockles.
It were an alms to help all with such burdens,
And to comfort such cottagers and crooked men and blind folk.

Langland was angry about the peasants' plight. Although not, as it would turn out, as angry as the peasants themselves.

The Peasants' Revolt, May–June 1381

THE ANONIMALLE CHRONICLE

Something like foreboding settled upon late-fourteenth-century England. The plague came back in 1374 and 1379; the harvest failed in 1369.

At the top all was awry. The last days of Edward III were marked alternately by his senility and his seduction by his mistress Alice Perrers. When he died in 1377 his heir was a minor, his ten-year-old grandson, Richard II; the de facto ruler was Richard's uncle John of Gaunt, who persisted in the Hundred Years War with France – now on a losing streak for the English – and ham-fisted attempts to curtail an increasingly assertive Parliament (which in 1376 had elected its first Speaker).

At the bottom all was bitterness. The Statute of Labourers pegged wages at pre-Black Death levels, whereas the shortage of labour caused by the plague drove the peasants (who made up 90 per cent of the population) to demand more pay and the ending of demeaning serf services.

The spark to the tinderbox was the 1380 poll tax, to raise revenue for the French war, set at the flat rate of 3 groats per household.

In the year 1380, because the subsidies were lightly granted at the parliament of Northampton and because various lords and commons were advised that the subsidies were not duly or loyally levied, but commonly exacted from the poor and not from the rich, to the great profit and advantage of the collectors, and the deception of the king and the commons, the King's council ordained certain commissions to make inquiry in each township how they were levied. One of these commissions was sent to Essex to a certain Thomas Bampton [i.e. John Bampton] steward of a lord, who was regarded as a king or great magnate in that area because of the great estate that he kept. And one day before Whitsuntide he held a court at Brentwood in Essex to make inquisition, and showed the commission directed to him to raise the money which was in default, and to inquire how the collectors had levied the subsidy. He had summoned before him a hundred of the neighbouring townships and wished to have from them a new subsidy, commanding the people of those townships to inquire diligently and to give their replies and to pay their dues. Amongst these townships all the people of Fobbing gave answer that they would not pay a penny more because they already had a receipt from him for the said subsidy. On this Thomas menaced them strongly, and he had with him two sergeants-at-arms of our lord the king; and for fear of his wrath the people of Fobbing took counsel with the people of Corringham, and the folks of these two townships made levies and assemblies, and sent messages to the men of Stanford-le-Hope to urge them to rise too, for their common profit. And then the men of the three townships came together to the number of a hundred or more and with one assent went to Thomas Bampton and roundly gave him answer that they would have nothing to do with him nor give him one penny. On this Thomas ordered the sergeants at arms to arrest these folks and put them into prison; and the commons rose against him and would not be arrested, but tried to kill Thomas and the two sergeants. On this Thomas fled towards London to the king's council and the commons fled to the woods for fear of his malice and lay there a long time, till they were almost famished; and afterwards they went from place to place to stir up other people to rise against the lords and good folk of the countryside. And because of these doings of Thomas Sir Robert Belknap, Chief Justice of the Common Pleas of our lord the king, was sent to the shire with a commission of trailbaston, and indictments against various persons were laid before him, so that the people of the countryside were in such fear that they proposed to abandon their homes. Therefore the commons rose against him and came before him and told him that he was a traitor to the king and the realm, and that it was of pure wickedness and malice that he wished to put them in default by means of the false inquests made before him. And because of this evil they caused him to swear on the Bible that he would never again hold such a session nor act as a justice in such inquiries. And they made him tell them the names of all the jurors, and they took all that they could catch and cut off their heads and cast their houses to the ground, and Sir Robert took his way home with all possible speed. And afterwards the commons assembled together before Whitsunday to the number of 50,000 and went to the manors and townships of those who did not wish to rise with them and rased their houses to the ground or set fire to them. At this time they caught three clerks of Thomas Bampton and cut off their heads, which they carried about with them for several days as an example to others; for it was their purpose to slay all lawyers and all jurors and all the servants of the king whom they could find. Meanwhile all the great lords of the countryside and other people of substance fled towards London and to other shires where they might be safe.

At the same time the high master of the hospital of St John of Clerkenwell in London had a very beautiful and delectable manor-house in Essex, where he had ordered victuals and other necessities to hold his chapter general, and it was well furnished with wines and was suitably appointed, as befits such a lord and his brethren. And at this time the commons came to the manor and ate the victuals and drank three tuns of good wine and rased the manor-house to the ground and set it alight, to the great damage and loss of the master. And then the commons sent various letters into Kent and Suffolk and Norfolk to urge them to rise with them; and when they had assembled they went about in many bands doing great mischief in all the countryside. After this on the Monday next after the feast of Whitsuntide [3 June] a knight of the household of our lord the king, Sir Simon Burley by name, had in his company two sergeants at arms of the king, and came on the Monday abovesaid to Gravesend and there challenged a man as being his serf. And the good folks of the town came to make a bargain for the man in civil fashion, because of their respect for the king; but Sir Simon would not take less than £300, a sum which would have been the man's undoing. The good folks prayed him to lessen the sum, but they could not come to terms nor induce him to take a lesser sum, though they told Sir Simon that the man was a Christian and of good character and that therefore he ought not to be ruined for ever. But Sir Simon was very angry and irritable, and greatly despised these good folk, and for haughtiness of heart he bade his sergeants bind the said man and take him to Rochester Castle, to be kept in custody there; from which there came later great evil and mischief. And after his departure the commons began to rise, gathering to them the men of many townships of Kent.

And at this juncture a justice was assigned by the king and council to go into Kent with a commission of trailbaston, as had been done before in Essex, and with him went a sergeant-at-arms of our lord the king, Master John Legge by name, carrying with him a great number of indictments against various folks of that area to make the king rich. And they would have held a session at Canterbury, but they were driven away by the commons. And after this the commons of Kent gathered together in great numbers day by day, without head and without chieftain, and on Friday before [a mistake for 'after'] Whitsuntide came to Dartford; and they took counsel there and ordained that no one who dwelt near the sea in any place for the space of 12 leagues should come with them, but keep the coasts of the sea from the enemies, saying amongst themselves that there were more kings than one and that they would not suffer or have any king except King Richard.

At the same time the commons of Kent came to Maidstone and cut off the head of one of the best men of the town, and rased to the ground various places and tenements of people who would not rise with them, as had been done before in Essex. And on the Friday following they came to Rochester and there met a great number of the commons from Essex. And because of the man of Gravesend, they laid siege to Rochester Castle, to deliver their friend from Gravesend, whom the aforesaid Sir Simon had imprisoned. They laid siege with energy to the Castle, and the constable defended himself vigorously for half a day, but at last, for fear that he had of such a multitude of men deaf to reason from Essex and Kent, he delivered up the castle to them. And the commons entered and took their companion and all the other prisoners out of prison: and those who had come from Gravesend repaired home with their fellow with great joy, without doing any more, but the men of Maidstone took their way with the other commons through the countryside. And there they made their chief a certain Wat Tyghler of Maidstone to maintain them and be their counsellor. And on the next Monday after the feast of the Holy Trinity they came to Canterbury before the hour of noon, and 4,000 of them entered into the minster church of St Thomas and, kneeling down, they cried with one voice on the monks to elect a monk to be archbishop of Canterbury, 'for he who is now archbishop is a traitor, and will be beheaded for his iniquity'. And so he was five days afterwards! And when they had done this, they went into the town to their fellows, and by one assent they summoned the mayor, bailiffs and commons of the said town and examined them whether there were any traitors amongst them; and the townsfolk said that there were three and named them. These three the commons dragged out of their houses and cut off their heads. And afterwards they took 500 men of the town with them to London, and left the others to guard the town.

At this time the commons had as their counsellor a chaplain of evil character, Sir John Ball by name, who advised them to get rid of all the lords and archbishops, bishops, abbots, priors, and most of the monks and canons, saying that there should be no bishop in England except one archbishop, and that he should be that archbishop, and that there should be no monks or canons in any religious houses save two, and that their possessions should be shared out amongst the laity. For these sayings he was esteemed amongst the commons as a prophet, and laboured with them day by day to strengthen them in their malice; and a fitting reward he had afterwards, for he was drawn, hanged, disembowelled, and beheaded as a traitor.

After this the commons went to various towns and raised the people, whether they wished to do so or not, until they had gathered together fully 60,000. And as they journeyed towards London they encountered various lawyers and twelve knights of the king and the countryside, and they took them and made them swear to support them, or otherwise they would be beheaded. And they wrought much damage in Kent and especially to Thomas Haselden, a servant of the Duke of Lancaster, because of their hatred for the duke. They rased his manors to the ground and all his houses, and sold his beasts – his horses, oxen, cows, sheep, and pigs – and all his stores of corn, at cheap rates. And every day they wanted to have his head and that of Sir Thomas Orgrave, clerk of the receipt and sub-treasurer of England. And when the king heard of their doings he sent his messengers to them on the Tuesday next after Trinity Sunday, to ask them why they were behaving in this fashion and why they were raising a rebellion in his land. And they returned answer by the messengers that they were rising to deliver him and to destroy the traitors to him and to his kingdom. The king sent again to them to bid them cease their doings, in reverence for him, until he could speak with them, and he would make reasonable amends, according to their will, of all that was amiss; and the commons begged him, by the said messengers, that he would be pleased to come and talk with them at

Blackheath. And the king sent again the third time to say that he would willingly come next day at the hour of prime to hear their purpose; and then the king, who was at Windsor, removed with all speed to London. At this time the mayor and good folk of London came to meet him and conduct him safely to the Tower of London; there all the council and all the lords of the countryside round about assembled, that is, the Archbishop of Canterbury, chancellor of England, the Bishop of London, the Master of the Hospital of St John of Clerkenwell, then treasurer of England, and the Earls of Buckingham, Kent, Arundel, Warwick, Suffolk, Oxford, Salisbury and other persons to the number of 600.

And on the vigil of Corpus Christi Day [12 June] the commons of Kent came to Blackheath, three leagues from London, to the number of 50,000, to await the king's arrival, and they displayed two banners of St George and forty pennons and the commons of Essex came to the other side of the water to the number of 60,000 to help them and hear the king's response. And on the Wednesday the king who was at the Tower of London, thinking to settle the affair, caused his barges to be assembled and took with him in his barge the archbishop and the treasurer and others of his council and four other barges for his retinue, and went to Greenwich, three leagues from London; and there the chancellor and treasurer warned the king that it would be too great a folly to go to them, for they were men without reason, and had not the sense to behave properly. But as the king, by the advice of the chancellor and treasurer, would not come to the commons of Kent, they sent a petition to him requiring him to grant them the heads of the Duke of Lancaster and fifteen other lords, of whom fourteen [?three] were bishops present with him in the Tower of London; and these were their names – Sir Simon Sudbury, Archbishop of Canterbury and Chancellor of England, Sir Robert Hales, Prior of the Hospital, treasurer of England, the Bishop of London, Sir John Fordham, clerk of the privy seal and Bishop-elect of Durham, Sir Robert Belknap, chief justice of the common pleas, Sir Ralph Ferrers, Sir Robert Plessington, chief baron of the exchequer, John Legge, sergeant-at-arms of the king, and Thomas Bampton aforesaid and others. And to this the king would not agree, wherefore they sent again to him a yeoman, praying that he would come and speak with them; and he said that he would gladly do so, but the chancellor and treasurer gave him contrary advice, telling them that if they wished to come to Windsor the following Monday, they should have there a suitable answer.

And the commons had among themselves a watch word in English, 'With whom hold you?' and the response was, 'With king Richard and with the true commons', and those who could not or would not so answer were beheaded and put to death. And at this time there came a knight with all the haste that he could, crying to the king to wait; and the king was startled at this and awaited his arrival to hear what he had to say. And the knight came to the king to tell him that he had it from a servant who had been in the hands of the rebels that day, that if the king should come to them, all the land would be lost, for they would never let him loose for any consideration, but would take him round with them through all England, and that they would make him grant all their demands, and that their purpose was to slay all the lords and ladies of great renown, and all the archbishops, bishops, abbots, priors, monks, and canons, parsons, and vicars, by the advice and counsel of the aforesaid Sir John Ball. Therefore the king returned to London as fast as he could and arrived at the Tower at the hour of terce.

And at this time the yeoman already mentioned above hastened to Blackheath crying to his fellows that the king had gone, and that it would be well for them to press on to London to pursue their purpose. On the same day of Wednesday before the hour of vespers the commons of Kent came, as many as 60,000 of them, to Southwark, where the Marshalsea was, and they broke and threw down to the ground all the buildings of the Marshalsea, and took out of prison all the prisoners who were held captive there for debt or felony. And they levelled to the ground a fine house belonging to John Imworth, then marshal of the marshalsea of the king's bench, and keeper of the prisoners of the said place, and all the houses of the jurors and questmongers belonging to the marshalsea, throughout that night.

At the same time the commons of Essex reached Lambeth, near to London, a manor of the Archbishop of Canterbury, and entered the buildings there, and destroyed many goods of the archbishop, and burnt all the books of register and rolls of remembrance of the chancery which they found there. And the next day, Thursday, which was the feast of Corpus Christi, the 13th day of June, with the dominical letter F, the commons of Essex went in the morning to Highbury, two leagues north of London, a very fine manor-house of the Master of the Hospital of St John of Clerkenwell, and they set it on fire, to the great damage and loss of the Hospitallers of St John. Some of them then returned to London, while the others stayed in the open fields all night. And this same day of Corpus Christi, in the morning, the commons of Kent pulled down a house of ill fame near London Bridge, which was in the hands of Flemish women and they had the house to rent from the mayor of London. And then they surged on to the bridge to pass into the city, but the mayor was just before them and had the chain drawn up and the drawbridge lifted to stop their passage. And the commons of Southwark rose with them and cried to the keepers of the bridge to lower the drawbridge and let them in, or otherwise they would be undone. And for fear of their lives the keepers let them enter, though it was against their will. At this time all the religious and the parsons and the vicars of London were going devoutly in procession to pray God for peace. And at the same time the commons took their way through London and did no harm or molestation until they came to Fleet Street. (And at the same time, as was said, the commons of London set fire to the beautiful manor-house of the Savoy before the arrival of the commons from the country.) And in Fleet Street the said commons of Kent broke open the Fleet prison and released all the prisoners and let them go whither they would. Then they stopped and threw to the ground, and set fire to, the shop of a certain chandler and another shop of a certain blacksmith, in the middle of the said street. There there shall never again be houses, it is said, to deface the beauty of the street. And after that they went to the Temple to destroy the tenants of the Temple, and they cast down the house to the ground and tore off all the tiles, so that the buildings were in a bad state, without any roofing.

And they went into the Temple Church and took all the books and rolls and remembrances which were in the cupboards of the apprentices at law in the Temple, and carried them into the highway and burnt them. And then they went towards the Savoy, destroying all the buildings belonging to the Master of the Hospital of St John. And then they went to the house of the Bishop of Chester, near the church of St Mary-le-Strand, where was dwelling Sir John Fordham, the elect of Durham, and clerk of the privy seal, and they rolled barrels of wine out of his cellar, and drank their fill, and departed without doing further damage. And then they went towards the Savoy and set fire to various houses of various folks and questmongers on the western side, and at last they came to the Savoy. They broke open the gates and entered the place and came to the wardrobe, and they took all the torches they could find and set fire to all the sheets and coverlets and beds and head boards of great worth, for their whole value amounted, it was said, to 1,000 marks. And all the napery and other things which they could find they carried into the hall and set it on fire with their torches. And they burnt the hall and chambers and all the buildings within the gates belonging to the said palace or manor, which the commons of London had left unburnt. And, as was said, they found three barrels of gunpowder which they took to be gold or silver, and they threw them on the fire, and this powder blew up high and set the hall in a greater blaze than before, to the great loss and damage of the Duke of Lancaster. The commons of Kent got the blame, but some said that the Londoners were really responsible, because of their hatred for the said duke. Then one party of them went towards Westminster and set on fire a house belonging to John Butterwick, under-sheriff of Middlesex, and other houses of various people, and broke open the prison at Westminster and brought out all the prisoners condemned by the law, and afterwards they returned to London by way of Holborn, and in front of St Sepulchre's Church they set fire to the houses of Simon Hosteler and several other houses, and broke open Newgate prison and let loose all the prisoners, for whatever cause they had been imprisoned.

The same Thursday the commons went to St Martin-le-Grand and tore away from the high altar a certain Roger Legett, a great 'assizer' and took him to Cheapside and beheaded him there; on the same day eighteen others were beheaded in various parts of the town. At the same time a great body of commons went to the Tower to speak to the king, and could not gain speech with him, wherefore they laid siege to the Tower from the side of St Katherine's, towards the south. And another part of the commons who were in the city went to the hospital of St John of Clerkenwell and on the way burnt the house and buildings of Roger Legett the questmonger who had been beheaded in Cheapside and all the rented houses and tenements of the hospital of St John that they could; and afterwards they came to the beautiful priory of the said hospital and set on fire several fine and desirable buildings in the same priory, a great and horrible piece of damage for all time to come; and then they returned to London to rest or to do more mischief.

At this time the king was in a turret of the great Tower of London, from which he could see the manor of the Savoy and the hospital of Clerkenwell, and the buildings of Simon Hosteler near Newgate, and John Butterwick's house, all on fire at once. And he called all his lords about him to his chamber and asked their advice as to what he should do in such an emergency; and none of them could or would give him any counsel. Wherefore the young king said that he would send to the mayor of the city to bid him order the sheriffs and aldermen to have it cried round their wards that all men between the ages of 15 and 60, on pain of life and members, should go on the morrow, Friday, to Mile End and meet him at seven in the morning. He did this so that all the commons who were surrounding the Tower would raise the siege and go to Mile End to see and hear him, and all those who were in the Tower could go away safely whither they would and save themselves; but it was of no avail, for the besieged did not have the good fortune to get away.

After this on the same Thursday, the feast of Corpus Christi, the king being in the Tower pensive and sorrowful, climbed up into a little turret towards St Katherine's, where were lying a great number of the commons, and caused a proclamation to be made to them that they should all go home in a peaceful manner and that he would pardon them all manner of trespasses. But all cried with one voice that they would not leave before they had taken the traitors who were in the Tower and had been given charters to be free of all manner of serfdom and had been granted all the items which they wished to ask. And the king graciously granted all and caused a clerk to write a bill in their presence in this style: 'Richard, king of England and of France, greatly thanks his good commons because they have such a great desire to see and hear their king, and pardons them for all manner of trespasses and misprisions and felonies committed until now, and wills and commands that now everyone should hasten to his own home and wishes and commands that each one should put his grievances into writing, and cause them to be sent to him, and he will provide, with the aid of his loyal lords and of his good counsel such remedy as shall be profitable for him and them and for the realm.' And to this document he set his signet seal in their presence, and sent out the said bill with two of his knights to them before St Katherine's and caused it to be read to them. And the knight who read it stood up on an old chair before the others so that all could hear. All this time the king was in the Tower in great distress of mind. And when the commons had heard the bill, they said that this was nothing but trifles and mockery; wherefore they returned to London and caused it to be cried throughout the city that all lawyers and all the officials of the chancery and exchequer and all those who could write a writ or a letter should be beheaded, wherever they could be found; and at this time they burnt several more houses in the city. And the king climbed to a high garret of the Tower and watched the fires, and then came down again and sent for the lords to have their counsel; but they did not know how to advise him and all were wondrously abashed.

Next day, the Friday, the commons of the countryside and the commons of London assembled in fearful strength to the number of 100,000 or more, besides some four score or more who stayed on Tower Hill to watch those who were in the Tower. And some went to Mile End towards Brentwood to await the coming of the king, because of the proclamation he had made, and the others came to Tower Hill. And when the king knew that they were there, he sent them orders by a messenger to join their friends at Mile End and he himself would join them soon. And at this time of the morning he advised the Archbishop of Canterbury and the others who were in the Tower to go down to the Little Water Gate and take a boat and save themselves. And the archbishop did so, but a wicked woman raised a cry against him and he had to return to the Tower, to his destruction. And by seven o'clock the king came to Mile End and with him his mother in a whirlecote [a wheeled carriage] with the Earls of Buckingham, Kent, Warwick, and Oxford, Sir Thomas Percy, Sir Robert Knolles, the mayor of London, and many knights and squires; and Sir Aubrey de Vere carried the king's sword. And when he was come the commons all knelt down to him, saying; 'Welcome, our lord, King Richard, if it pleases you, and we will have no other king but you.' And Wat Tyghler, their leader and chief, prayed to him in the name of the commons that he would suffer them to take and hold all the traitors who were against him and the law; and the king granted that they should take at their wish those who were traitors and could be proved traitors by the law. And Wat and the commons were carrying two banners and many pennons and pennoncelles, while they made their petition to the king. And they required that no man should be a serf, nor do homage or any manner of service to any lord, but should give fourpence rent for an acre of land, and that no one should serve any man but at his own will, and on terms of regular covenant. And at this time the king caused the commons to arrange themselves in two lines, and caused a proclamation to be made before them that he would confirm and grant them their freedom and all their wishes generally, and that they should go through the realm of England and catch all traitors and bring them to him in safety and that he would deal with them as the law required. Under colour of this grant Wat Tyghler and the commons took their way to the Tower, to seize the archbishop and the others, the king being at Mile End.

At this time the archbishop was chanting his mass devoutly in the Tower and shrove the prior of the hospital of Clerkenwell and others, and then he heard two masses or three, and chanted the *commendation* and the *placebo* and the *dirige* and the *seven psalms* and the *litany*; and when he was at the words 'All saints, pray for us' the commons burst in and dragged him out of the chapel of the Tower, and struck and hustled him villainously, as they did the others who were with him and dragged them to Tower Hill. There they cut off the heads of Master Simon Sudbury, Archbishop of Canterbury, and of Sir Robert Hales, Prior of the Hospital of St John of Clerkenwell, Treasurer of England, Brother William Appleton, a great physician and surgeon, and one who had great influence with the king and the Duke of Lancaster. And some time afterwards they beheaded John Legge, the king's sergeant-at-arms, and with him a juror; and at the same time the commons proclaimed that anyone who could catch any Fleming or other alien of any nation might cut off his head, and so they did after this. And then they took the heads of the archbishop and the others and stuck them on wooden poles and carried them before them in procession through the city, to the shrine of Westminster Abbey, in contempt of them and of God and of Holy Church, for vengeance descended on them not long afterwards. Then they returned to London Bridge and set the head of the archbishop above the bridge and the eight other heads of those that were murdered, so that they might be seen by all who passed over the bridge. And when this was done, they went to the church of St Martin's in the Vintry, and found therein 35 Flemings, whom they dragged out and beheaded in the street. On that day were beheaded in all some 140 or 160 persons. And then they took their way to all the houses of the Lombards and other aliens, and broke into their dwellings and robbed them of all their goods which they could find. This went on throughout the day and the following night, with hideous cries and horrible tumult.

At this time, because the chancellor had been beheaded, the king made the Earl of Arundel chancellor for the day and delivered to him the great seal, and throughout the day caused various clerks to write charters and patents and protections granted to the commons touching the matters before mentioned, without taking any fines for sealing or description. And on the next day, Saturday, a great number of the commons came to the abbey of Westminster at the hour of terce and there they found John Imworth, Marshal of the Marshalsea and warden of the prisoners, a tormentor without pity; he was near the shrine of St Edward, clinging to a marble pillar, as an aid and succour to save him from his enemies. And the commons wrenched his arms away from the pillar of the shrine and brought him to Cheapside and beheaded him. And at the same time they took from Bread Street a yeoman named John Greenfield because he had spoken well of Brother William Appleton and of other murdered persons, and brought him to Cheapside and beheaded him. All this time the king caused proclamation to be made round the city that everyone should go peacefully to his own country and his own house without doing any more evil; but to this the commons paid no heed.

And on this same day, at three o'clock in the afternoon, the king came to Westminster Abbey, and some 200 persons with him. And the abbot and convent of the same abbey and the canons and vicars of the chapel of St Stephen came in procession to meet him, dressed in their copes and with bare feet, half way to Charing Cross, and they brought him to the abbey and the church and the high altar and the king made his prayer devoutly and left an offering for the altar and the relics. And afterwards he spoke to the anchorite and confessed to him and was with him for some time. And then the king caused a proclamation to be made that all those commons of the country who were still in London should come to meet him at Smithfield, and so they did. And when the king had come with his train he turned to the eastern side, near St Bartholomew's, a house of canons; and the commons arrayed themselves on the west side in battle formation, in great numbers. At this moment the mayor of London, William Walworth, came up, and the king bade him go to the commons and cause their chieftain to come to him. And when he was called by the mayor, Wat Tyghler by name, of Maidstone, he came to the king in a haughty fashion, mounted on a little horse so that he could be seen by the commons. And he dismounted, carrying in his hand a dagger which he had taken from another man, and when he had dismounted he half bent his knee, and took the king by the hand, and shook his arm forcibly and roughly, saying to him, 'Brother, be of good comfort and joyful, for you shall have within the next fortnight 40,000 more of the commons than you have now and we shall be good companions.' And the king said to Wat; 'Why will you not go back to your own country?' And the other replied with a great oath that neither he nor his fellows would depart until they had their charter such as they wished to have, and such points rehearsed in their charter as they chose to demand, threatening that the lords of the realm would rue it badly if the points were not settled to their satisfaction. And the king asked him what were the points that he wanted, and he would have them freely without contradiction written down and sealed. And then Wat rehearsed points which were to be demanded; and he asked that there should be no law except the law of Winchester, and that there should be henceforth no outlawry in any process of law, and that no lord should have any lordship, except only to be respected according to their rank among all folks, and that the only lordship should be that of the king; and that the goods of Holy Church should not remain in the hands of the religious, nor of the parsons and vicars, and other churchmen; but those who were in possession should have their sustenance from the endowments and the remainder of their goods should be divided amongst the parishioners; and no bishop should remain in England save one, nor more than one prelate, and that all the lands and tenements now held by them should be confiscated and shared amongst the commons, saving to them a reasonable substance. And he demanded that there should be no more bondmen in England, no serfdom nor villeinage, but that all should be free and of one condition. And to this the king gave an easy answer, and said that he should have all that could fairly be granted saving to himself the regality of the crown. And then he commanded him to go back to his home without further delay. And all this time that the king was speaking no lord nor any other of his council dared nor wished to give any answer to the commons in any place except the king himself.

Presently Wat Tyghler, in the king's presence, called for a flagon of water to rinse his mouth because he was in such a heat, and when it was brought he rinsed his mouth in a very rude and disgusting fashion before the king; and then he made them bring him a flagon of ale of which he drank a great deal, and in the king's presence mounted his horse. At this time a yeoman of Kent, who was among the king's retinue, asked to see Wat, the leader of the commons; and when Wat was pointed out to him, he said openly that he was the greatest thief and robber in all Kent. Wat heard these words and commanded him to come out to him, shaking his head at him in sign of malice; but the yeoman refused to go to him for fear of the mob. At last the lords made him go out to Wat, to see what he would do in the king's presence; and when Wat saw him, he ordered one of his followers, who was riding on a horse carrying his banner displayed, to dismount and cut off the yeoman's head. But the yeoman answered that he had done nothing worthy of death, for what he had said was true and he would not deny it, but in the presence of his liege lord he could not lawfully make debate without leave, except in his own defence; and that he could do without reproof, for if he was attacked he would strike back. And for these words Wat would have run him through with his dagger and killed him in the king's presence; and because of this, the mayor of London, William Walworth by name, reasoned with the said Wat for his violent behaviour and contempt done in the king's presence, and arrested him. And because he arrested him, the said Wat struck the mayor with his dagger in the stomach with great anger; but as God would have it, the mayor was wearing armour and took no harm. But like a hardy and vigorous man the said mayor drew his cutlass and struck back at the said Wat and gave him a deep cut on the neck and then a great cut on the head. And in this scuffle a yeoman of the king's household drew his sword and ran Wat two or three times through the body, mortally wounding him. And the said Wat spurred his horse, crying to the commons to avenge him, and the horse carried him some four score paces, and there he fell to the ground half dead. And when the commons saw him fall, and did not know for certain how it was, they began to bend their bows and to shoot; wherefore the king himself spurred his horse and rode out to them, commanding them that they should all come to him at the field of St John of Clerkenwell.

Meanwhile the mayor of London rode as fast as he could back to the city commanding all those who were in charge of the 24 wards to make proclamation in their wards that every man should arm himself as quickly as he could, and go to the king in St John's Fields, where the commons were, for he was in great need and necessity. And at this time nearly all the knights and squires of the king's household and many others, for fear that they had of this affray, left their liege lord and each went his own way. Afterwards when the king had reached the open fields he made the commons array themselves on the west side. And soon the aldermen came to him in a body, bringing with them the wardens of the wards, by various routes, with a fine company of people well armed in great strength and they enveloped the commons like sheep in a pen. And when the mayor had sent the wardens to the king, he returned to Smithfield with a fine company of lances to make an end of the captain of the commons abovesaid. And when he came to Smithfield he could not find the said captain Wat Tyghler, and at this he marvelled greatly and asked what had become of the traitor; and he was told that Tyghler had been carried by some of the commons to the hospital of the poorfolks near St Bartholomew's and was put to bed in the chamber of the master of the hospital. And the mayor went thither and found him and had him carried to Smithfield in the presence of his fellows and there he was beheaded. And so ended his wretched life. And the mayor caused his head to be set upon a pole and carried before him to the king who still abode in the fields. And when the king saw the head he had it brought near him to abash the commons and thanked the mayor warmly for what he had done. And when the commons saw that their leader, Wat

Tyghler, was dead in such a manner, they fell to the ground among the wheat like men discomforted, crying to the king for mercy for their misdeeds. And the king benevolently granted them mercy and many of them took to flight; and the king ordered two knights to lead the rest of the Kentishmen through London and over London Bridge without doing them any harm, so that each of them could go in peace to his own home. Then the king ordered the mayor, William Walworth, to put on his head a helmet in anticipation of what was going to happen; the mayor asked why he was to do so and the king replied that he was greatly obliged to him and therefore was going to confer on him the order of knighthood. And the mayor answered that he was not worthy nor able to have or to keep up a knight's estate, for he was but a merchant and had to live by merchandise; but at last the king made him put on the helmet and took a sword in both his hands and dubbed him knight resolutely and with great goodwill. And the same day he made three other knights from among the citizens of London on that same spot, and these are their names – John Philipot [Philpott], Nicholas Brymber [Brember] and [blank in the MS.]; and the king gave Sir William Walworth £100 in land and each of the others £40 in land for themselves and their heirs; and afterwards the king took his way towards London to his wardrobe to ease himself after his great labours.

John Ball, whose couplet 'When Adam delved and Eve span, who was then the gentleman?', became a mantra of English social protest, was hanged at St Albans on 15 July. Two months later, Richard II had the nation back under control, and revoked his promises made at Blackheath (a general pardon, abolition of villeinage, fixing of rent at fourpence per acre, and liberty to trade).

The Peasants' Revolt had been suppressed, but change in the countryside was not. Within 150 years feudalism would effectively be ended, with the English countryside a place of tenant farmers and free labourers, not serfs.

Facing down the peasant rebels at Blackheath in 1381 was Richard II's one and only hour of glory. As he matured he developed Frenchified habits (he ate with a spoon and commissioned a royal cookery book) and a worrying taste for autocratic rule. This megalomania led him to exile the late John of Gaunt's son, Henry Bolingbroke, Duke of Lancaster, and seize his estates. In response, Bolingbroke led an invasion (with an army donated by the French) to recover his inheritance, but so many defected to his cause that his ambition escalated and he seized the throne in a coup d'état. Richard II, forced to abdicate, became plain Sir Richard of Bordeaux and was imprisoned in Pontefract castle, where he died in 1400, probably through forced starvation.

Like many a usurper, Henry IV lived in a state of paranoid insecurity. It was well founded. A Welsh revolt led by Owain Glyndwr in 1400 was joined by Henry Percy, Earl of Northumberland, who also rose against the usurped crown again in 1405 and yet again in 1408. Just when Henry thought it was all over, he discovered that his own son, Prince Henry, was plotting for power. The trials of usurpation took their toll on Henry's body; he developed a disfiguring skin disease. Careworn and decrepit, he died of a fit on 20 March 1413. Three weeks later the twenty-six-year-old Prince Henry assumed the throne as Henry V.

Prince Henry had been a medieval playboy. As king, he was a revelation, serious-minded, with a political vision of England which both unified the realm and diverted from its woes: an English empire in France.

The Battle of Agincourt, 25 October 1415

ANONYMOUS PRIEST

On 11 August 1415 at the head of 10,000 soldiers, Henry V sailed to France, claiming its throne as his. After besieging and capturing Harfleur, Henry tramped across the Normandy countryside towards Calais with the intention of tempting the French to battle. At Agincourt, a French army of some 30,000 decided to oblige. Siege, disease and garrisoning duties had reduced the English force to around 5,000.

And when on the following day, Thursday, we were descending the valley towards the River of the Swords, the king was told by scouts and cavalry skirmishers that there was a powerful adversary numbering many thousands on the other side of the river, almost a league to our right. We therefore crossed the river as fast as we could, and when we reached the crest of the hill on the other side, we saw emerging from the valley about a mile from us hateful swarms of Frenchmen, who appeared to us to be an incomparable multitude in their columns, lines and divisions. They took up their position just over half a mile ahead of us, filling a broad field like an innumerable swarm of locusts, having a small valley between us and them.

Meanwhile our king was encouraging his army courteously and bravely, marshalling them into lines and wings, as if they were to go at once into battle. And then everyone who had not previously cleared his conscience by confession, put on the armour of penitence ... And among other sayings which I noted then, a certain knight, Sir Walter

Hungerford, wished to the king's face that in addition to the small band which he had there he could have had ten thousand of the better archers of England, who would have been glad to be with them. The king replied: 'Thou speakest as a fool, for by the God of Heaven in whose grace I trust and in whom is my firm hope of victory, I would not have one more than I have, even if I could. . . . Dost thou not believe that the Almighty can through this humble little band overcome the pride of these Frenchmen, who boast of their numbers and their strength?' . . .

And when the enemy in position saw and considered the disposition and fewness of our troops, they betook themselves to a field beyond a certain wood, which lay near to the left between us and them, where was our road to Calais. So our king, thinking that they might go round the wood to attack him along the road, or else might go round woods further away in the neighbourhood and surround us from all sides, at once moved his lines and he always stationed himself to face the enemy . . .

And when at last we were at the last rays of light, and darkness fell between us and them, we still stood in the field and heard our foes, everyone calling as the manner is, for his comrade, servant and friend, dispersed by chance in so great a multitude. Our men began to do the same, but the king ordered silence throughout the whole army, under penalty of the loss of horse and harness in the case of a gentleman . . . and of the right ear in the case of a yeoman or below, with no hope of pardon, for anyone who might presume to break the king's order. And he at once went in silence to a hamlet nearby, in a place where we had only a few houses; most of us had to rest in gardens and orchards, through a night of pouring rain. And when our enemies considered the quietness of our men and our silence, they thought that we were struck with fright at our small numbers and contemplated flight during the night; so they established fires and strong watches throughout the fields and routes. And as it was said they thought they were so sure of us that they cast dice that night for our king and nobles.

And on the morrow, Friday the feast of Saints Crispin and Crispinian, 25th October, the Frenchmen, at dawn, organized themselves into lines, battles, and wedges, and took up their position facing us in the field called Agincourt, through which lay our route to Calais, in terrific multitude; and they set squadrons of horsemen in many hundreds on either side of their front lines, to break our line and the strength of our archers. The front line was composed of dismounted men made up of all the noblest and choicest of their forces, who in the forest of spears

. . . were by estimation thirty times more numerous than our men. But their rear lines . . . were all on horseback . . . and compared with our men they were an innumerable multitude.

And meanwhile our king prepared himself for the field, after hearing lauds and masses and . . . arranged his small numbers in one 'battle', placing his vanguard as a wing to his right with the Duke of York in command and the rearguard as a wing to his left under Lord Camoys. Interspersed among the line were wedges of archers, whom the king ordered to affix stakes in front of them, as he had ordered earlier, to stop the attacks of the horsemen . . .

And when much of the day had been consumed . . . and both armies had stood and had not moved a foot, the king, seeing that the opposing army was abstaining from the attack which had been expected . . . either to cause us to break our order, or to strike terror into our hearts because of their numbers, or . . . because they expected more reinforcements to arrive, and knowing that our shortage of food would conquer us by hunger, ordered his men to move towards the enemy, sending orders to the baggage-train of the army to follow up close so that they should not fall as booty to the enemy . . . After the king had estimated that all his baggage had come up to his rear, he advanced towards the enemy, with his men, in the name of Jesus . . . and of the glorious Virgin and St George, and the enemy moved towards him. [The priests, including the author, then prayed hard for deliverance.]

And when they came near enough to attack, the French horsemen posted on the sides rushed against our archers on both flanks of our army; but quickly, God willing, they were compelled to retreat by the showers of arrows and to flee behind their lines . . . except the large numbers whom the points of the stakes or the sharpness of the arrows stopped from flight by piercing the horses or the horsemen. The cross-bowmen of the enemy, who were behind the men at arms and on their flanks, fell back in face of the strength of our archers after the first draw, which was too hasty and injured only a few of our men . . . But the French nobles who had first approached in line, just as they had come from their muster nearby . . . divided themselves into three columns, either for fear of the arrows . . . or to penetrate more quickly our force to the banners, attacked our forces at the three places where there were banners; and at the first clash they met our men with such a fierce impact that they were compelled to fall back for almost the distance of a lance . . . And then the battle grew hotter and our archers shot . . . their arrows through the flanks of the enemy, the battle continually renewing. And when their arrows were exhausted, they seized axes, swords and lances from those who were lying on the ground, and beat down, wounded and killed the enemy with them . . . And the just Judge who wished to strike down the proud multitude of the enemy with the thunderbolts of vengeance . . . broke their power . . . No one had time to receive them as captives, but almost all of them without distinction of persons, when they fell to the ground, struck down by our men or by those following them, I know not by what hidden judgement of God, were killed without intermission . . . For when some of them slain at the start of the engagement fell in front, such was the indisciplined violence and pressure of the host behind that the living fell on the dead, and others falling on the living were killed in turn; and so in the three places where there was a concentration of our forces, the piles of dead and those crushed in between grew so much that our men climbed on these heaps which grew higher than a man and slew those below with swords, axes, and other weapons. And when at last after two or three hours the vanguard was cut up and worn out, and the rest were forced into flight, our men began to sort these heaps and separate the living from the dead, intending to keep the living as property to be ransomed. But behold! at once, we know not by what wrath of God, a cry arose that the enemy's rearguard of cavalry, in overwhelming numbers had repaired the enemy line . . . and was coming against our small and tired band. And so they killed their prisoners with swords . . . without any distinction of persons, except for the Dukes of Orléans and Bourbon and other illustrious persons in the royal entourage, and a few others, lest the captives should be our ruin in the coming battle.

But after a little while the troops of the enemy, having tasted the bitterness of our weapons, and at our king's approach, left the field of blood to us . . .

Never before or after would England win so impossible a victory on land. Henry, a consummate communicator, ordered a battle report to be sent to England and read aloud. It was the first time that such a dispatch was written in the mother tongue.

Agincourt: Henry's Victory March, London, 23 November 1415

ANONYMOUS

He took his journey byway of the sacred thresholds of the churches of Canterbury and St Augustine's Canterbury to his manor of Eltham, proposing to honour the city of London on the following Saturday with his presence. The citizens, hearing with the greatest joy the news of his approach, prepared themselves and the city in the meanwhile. . . . And when the desired day of Saturday dawned, the citizens went out to meet the king at the brow of Blackheath, I.e. the mayor and 24 aldermen in scarlet, and the rest of the lesser citizens in red cloaks with red-and-white party-coloured hoods, to the number of about 20,000 horsemen . . . And when the king came through the midst of them about ten o'clock, and the citizens had given glory and honour to God, and congratulations to the king . . . the citizens rode before him towards the city, and the king followed . . .

When they arrived at the tower at the entrance to the bridge . . . there placed on top of the tower was an enormous figure, with . . . a great axe in his right hand and the keys of the city hanging from a staff in his left hand, like a door-keeper. On his right side stood an effigy not much smaller, of a woman dressed in a scarlet cloak and feminine ornaments, as if they were man and wife who in their best clothes were looking for the desired face of their lord and were receiving him with full honour. The tower was adorned with spears bearing the royal arms, projecting from the battlements, and trumpets and horns sounded in manifold melody; spread across the front of the tower was this elegant and convenient inscription, 'The City of the King of Justice'. And when they reached the little bridge, they found on both sides before them a lofty pillar in the manner of a tower . . . made of wood, covered with linen cloth painted the colour of white marble and green jasper, to imitate the blocks and stones of mason's work. On top of the column on the right hand side was the effigy of an antelope . . . with a splendid shield blazoned with the royal arms hanging from its neck, and bearing the royal sceptre in the right foot. On the top of the other column stood the image of a lion, which held aloft in its right claws . . . the banner of the king displayed; across . . . the road rose a turret . . . in the middle of which under a splendid canopy stood a most impressive image of St George, armed, except for his head, which was adorned with a laurel wreath sown with gems sparkling like precious stones, having behind him a scarlet tapestry gleaming with his arms in a number of shields. On his right hung a triumphal helmet, and on his left a great shield of his arms; . . . in his right hand he held the hilt of the sword with which he was girt and in his left he held a scroll extended across the battlements with the words: 'Honour and glory be to God alone'. And aloft on the tower in front was displayed this prophesy of congratulation: 'The streams of the river make glad the city of God' . . . And in a house near the tower was a great crowd of boys representing the angelic host clad in white robes, with faces gleaming with gilt paint, with shining wings and the hair of girls crowned with laurel crowns, who sang on the king's approach with sweet voices to the accompaniment of an organ a song according to the programme in English.

And when they reached the tower of the aqueduct in Cornhill they found the tower hidden under a scarlet cloth stretched in the form of a tent, on spears hidden under the cloth. Surrounding the middle of the tower in four prominent positions were the arms of St George, St Edward, St Edmund, and of England, interspersed with small shields of royal arms and inset with this pious legend:

'Since the king hopes in the Lord and in the mercy of the Highest, he shall not be moved.' . . . Under a covering was a band of venerable white-haired prophets in tunics and golden cloaks, with their heads hidden in turbans of gold and red who released, when the king came by, sparrows and other small birds in a great cloud as a sacrifice of thanksgiving to God for the victory He had given, some of the birds resting on the king's breast, some of them alighting on his shoulder, and some flying round his head, while the prophets sang in a sweet voice, according to the programme, this psalm of recognition: 'Sing to the Lord a new song, Hallelujah. For he hath done marvellous things, Hallelujah.'

Then they went on to the tower of the conduit at the entrance to Cheapside which was decked with an awning of green . . . woven with little shields of the city's arms set in florid profusion, supported on posts covered in the same colour and erected to resemble a building. The tower was decorated above with shafts of spears of arms placed on the battlements . . . and below the awning were venerable old men, twelve in number, clothed like the apostles and having the names of the twelve apostles written on their brows. With them were twelve kings, martyrs and confessors of the succession of England, with golden girdles round their loins, sceptres in their hands, and crowns on their heads . . . who sang in unison on the king's approach a sweet song. . . . And they wafted to him round foils of silver intermingled with thin round wafers, and wine from the channels and cocks of the conduit, so that they might receive him with bread and wine as Melchisedech received Abraham when he returned from the fall of the four kings.

And when they came to the cross in Cheapside . . . it was hidden by a beautiful castle of wood, very ingeniously and prettily constructed, and adorned with three beautiful columns, . . . which had . . . arches on either side projecting over the street, and stretching to the buildings on each side of the road. . . . And across the front of the arches was written, 'Glorious things of thee are spoken, O city of God'. This castle was covered with linen painted the colour of white marble, and green and red jasper, as if the whole work had been the result of the mason's art, fashioned from blocks of masonry and perfect precious stones. The top of the castle . . . was adorned with the arms of St George, flanked on one side by the arms of the king and on the other by those of the emperor; . . . on the lower turrets were the arms of the king's ancestors and of the greater magnates of the realm. From the middle of the castle . . . projected a beautiful gateway, no less cunningly contrived, from which stretched a wooden bridge almost fifteen paces in length, of good width and about the height of a man's waist . . . adorned with tapestries. When the king approached there came out on to the bridge a chorus of beautiful girls dressed in virgin white . . . and playing on tambourines as a mark of rejoicing, as if to a David rejoicing at the fall of Goliath, who . . . represented the pride of the French, and singing: 'Welcome, Henry the Fifth, King of England and of France'. From the top of the castle downwards, on the turrets, battlements, arches, and columns, were innumerable boys, dressed in white garments as angels and archangels, with shining wings and hair strewn with gems . . . who threw down on the . . . king as he passed underneath gold coins and laurel leaves, to the honour of Almighty God and as a sign of victory; and all sang together this angelic hymn as previously arranged: 'We praise thee O God, we acknowledge thee to be the Lord'.

And when they came to the tower of the conduit at the exit of Cheapside towards St Paul's, the tower had been surrounded with many . . . niches, and in each niche was a beautiful young girl, in the posture of a statue; and in their hands were golden cups from which they very lightly puffed gold leaf upon the king's head as he rode by. Above the tower was stretched a canopy sky-blue in colour decorated with clouds

and many other contrivances; and the top of the canopy was adorned
by an archangel in shining gold, and the four posts which held up the
canopy were supported by four angels equally cunning in workmanship.
Below the canopy . . . was a figure of majesty represented by a sun
darting out flashing rays. Round the top of the canopy fluttered archangels singing sweetly all kinds of music. . . . And so that this tower
might conform in its legend to the preceding praises to the honour and
glory of God, not of men, it presented to the gaze of the passers-by this
conclusion of praise: 'Thanks be to God'.

. . . Such was the dense throng of people in Cheapside from one end
to the other that horsemen had scarcely . . . room to ride through the
crowds, and the upper storeys and windows on either side were filled
with the more noble ladies and women of the realm and with honest
and honourable men, who flocked to such a delectable sight, adorned
in garments of gold and satin and scarlet, and other types of dress; so
that a bigger or more impressive crowd had never gathered before in
London.

But the king himself went along, amidst these shouts of praise and
celebrations of the citizens, dressed in a purple robe, not with a haughty
look and a pompous train . . . but with a serious countenance and a
reverend pace accompanied by only a few of his most faithful servants;
following him, guarded by knights, were the captive dukes, counts and
the marshal. From his silent face and . . . sober pace it could be inferred
that the king, silently contemplating, was giving thanks and glory to
God alone and not to man. And when he had visited the sanctuary of
SS Peter and Paul, he rode away to his palace of Westminster, escorted
by the citizens.

*By the Treaty of Troyes (1420) Henry V was made heir to the French throne.
English power in France was at its zenith.*

Some Public Nuisances, 1422

THE GENERAL COURT OF THE MAYOR OF
THE CITY OF LONDON

By the early fifteenth century the population of London had reached 50,000.

These are nuisances and defects found in the ward of Faringdon. Without, taken in the wardmoot, before Rankyn Barton, Alderman of the same ward, the year of the king abovesaid.

First, that the master of Ludgate often puts out dung in the street gutter and stops the water from flowing, to the great nuisance of all the folk passing there. Also that a mud wall in the bailey by the High Street, between the house of Shelhard, haberdasher, and Hay, spurrier, falls down piecemeal into the High Street, and makes the way foul, to the annoyance of folk passing and dwelling there. Also William Emery, horsedealer, often lays much dung in the high street and allows it to lie yet, to the great nuisance and annoyance of all folk passing and dwelling thereabout. Also the pavements before the chamber house in the bailey, and before the door of Harry Gras, barber, and of Walsh's door, are defective and need to be mended. Also the common privy of Ludgate is very defective and perilous and the filth thereof decays the stone walls, so that it is likely to be very costly and dangerous to those walls in time to come, unless it be put right as soon as possible. Also that the barriers at Shoe-Lane end are all broken with water carts, and the pavements defective in divers places of the same parish. Also that John Taverner at Bell is not a freeman of the city. Also John Whitlok at Bell at Carter Lane end and his wife are common bauds, and therefore have lately been put out of other wards. Also John Swayn and his wife are forestallers, regrators, and extortioners often, and especially lately they hired a page of the Queen's household to arrest a boatful of rushes, and brought it from Queenhithe to Fleet Bridge, and there took up from it 30 loads of rushes, and laid them in Sir Walter Beauchamp's place, and then paid to the Boatman only 26d for 30 loads, whereas he should have been paid for every burden 3d and because of this the boatman made much noise and open slander. Also the taverners of St Bride's parish set their empty tuns and pipes in the high street, to the annoyance of all folk passing there.

Also that the barriers of Chancellor Lane [Chaunselerlane] and Fetter Lane [Fayturlane] are all broken.

Of more national concern in 1422 was the premature death of Henry V from dysentery (an occupational hazard for campaigners), which left the infant Henry VI on the throne and the country governed by a regency of his paternal uncles.

Some thought Henry VI a saint – there were attempts to canonize him – and others a simpleton. John Blackman, a priest and amanuensis to the king, pictured him thus:

Concerning his humility in his walk [and] in his clothes, . . . from his youth up he had been accustomed to wear broad-toed shoes and boots like a countryman. Also he had usually a long gown with a rounded hood after the manner of a burgess, and a tunic falling below the knees, shoes, boots, hose, everything of a dark grey colour – for he would have nothing fanciful.

Moreover, on the principal feasts of the year, but chiefly when by custom he should wear his crown, he would put on next his skin a rough hair-shirt, . . . in order to keep down all arrogance or vain-glory, to which such occasions are likely to give rise.

Saint or simpleton, Henry VI's reign was disastrous for England. All the territorial gains of Henry V in France were lost to the French revival spearheaded by Joan of Arc. As the English lost their hold on France and Henry VI lost his grip on reality (he was clinically schizophrenic by August 1453), quarrelling among the leading noble factions at court became more embittered.

Open skirmishing between the Lancastrians (badge: the red rose) and Yorkists (the white rose) occurred at St Albans on 22 May 1455. The so-called Wars of the Roses which followed were of less substance than Shakespeare's Collected Works *would suggest. Both sets of protagonists would claim the right to rule England through descent from Edward III. Neither side could muster private armies ('affinities') much greater than 5,000 in number. Casualties were minimal, and few towns were besieged, because neither side dared inconvenience the populace.*

The Wars of the Roses were an unedifying misnomer; for most of their thirty years England was at peace. The Yorkist King Edward IV ruled (and had the leisure to collect books) from 1461 to 1483, save for an interruption in 1470–71 when the Lancastrians returned the bewildered Henry VI to the throne. On his return from exile in Flanders, Edward IV trounced the Lancastrians at the battle of Barnet.

The Wars of the Roses: Fog, Confusion and Treachery – the Battle of Barnet, 14 April 1471

JOHN WARKWORTH

Edward IV's Yorkist army at the battle of Barnet – which was fought in thick fog – numbered a paltry 7,000; leading the 15,000 Lancastrians was the power-broking Earl 'The Kingmaker' Warwick who, offended by gibes about his bravery, fought on foot. Like many a medieval battle, it sank into complete confusion, with the Lancastrians attacking their own centre after mistaking a private badge for Edward's 'sun and rays' insignia. Never was the expression the 'fog of war' so apposite as at Barnet in spring 1471. John Warkworth was Master of St Peter's College, Cambridge. His sympathies were Lancastrian.

And on the Wednesday next before Easter-day, King Harry, and the Archbishop of York with him, rode about London, and desired the people to be true unto him; and every man said they would. Nevertheless Urswyke, Recorder of London, and divers Aldermen, such that had rule of the city, commanded all the people, that were in harness, keeping the city, and King Harry, every man to go home to dinner; and in dinner time King Edward was let in, and so went forth to the Bishop of London's palace, and there took King Harry, and the Archbishop of York, and put them in ward, the Thursday next before Easter-day. And the Archbishop of Canterbury, the Earl of Essex, the Lord Berners, and such other as owed King Edward good will, as well in London, as in other places, made as many men as they might, in strengthening the said King Edward; so then he was a seven thousand men, and there they refreshed well themselves, all that day, and Good Friday. And upon Easter Even, he and all his host went toward Barnet, and carried King Harry with him; for he had understanding, that the Earl of Warwick, and the Duke of Exeter, the Lord Marquis Montague, the Earl of Oxford, and many other knights, squires, and commons, to the number of twenty thousand, were gathered together to fight against the King Edward. But it happened that he, with his host, were entered into the town of Barnet, before the Earl of Warwick, and his host. And so the Earl of Warwick, and his host, lay without the town all night, and each of them loosed guns at other all the night. And on Easter day in the morning, the fourteenth day of April, right early each of them came upon other; and there was such a great mist, that neither of them might see other perfectly. There they fought from four of clock in the morning, unto ten of clock the forenoon. And divers times the Earl of Warwick's party had the victory, and supposed that they had won the field. But it happened so, that the Earl of Oxford's men had upon them their lord's livery, both before and behind, which was a star with streams, which (*was*) much like King Edward's livery, the sun with streams; and the mist was so thick, that a man might not perfectly judge one thing from another; so the Earl of Warwick's men shot and fought against the Earl of Oxford's men, thinking and supposing, that they had been King Edward's men; and anon the Earl of Oxford, and his men, cried, 'treason! treason!' and fled away from the field with eight hundred men. The Lord Marquis Montague was agreed, and appointed with King Edward, and put upon him King Edward's livery; and a man of the Earl of Warwick's, saw that, and fell upon him, and killed him. And when the Earl of Warwick saw his brother dead, and the Earl of Oxford fled, he leaped on horseback and fled to a wood by the field of Barnet, where was no way forth; and one of King Edward's men had espied him, and one came upon him, and killed him, and despoiled him naked. And so King Edward got that field. And there was slain of the Earl of Warwick's party, the Earl himself, Marquis Montague, Sir William Tyrell, Knight, and many others. The Duke of Exeter fought manly there that day, and was greatly despoiled, and wounded, and left naked for dead in the field, and so lay there from seven of clock, till four afternoon, which was taken up and brought to a house by a man of his own, and a leech brought to him and so afterwards brought into sanctuary at Westminster. And (*of*) King Edward's party was slain the Lord Cromwell, son and heir to the Earl of Essex; Lord Berners (*his*) son and heir, (*Sir Humphrey Bourchier*;) Lord Say, and divers other to the number [of both parties] four thousand men. And after that the field was done, King Edward commanded both the Earl of Warwick's body, and the Lord Marquis' body, to be put in a cart, and returned himself with all his host again to London; and there commanded the said two bodies, to be laid in the church of Paul's, on the pavement, that every man might see them; and so they lay three or four days, and afterwards were buried. And King Harry being in the forward during the battle, was not hurt; but he was brought again to the Tower of London, there to be kept.

After Barnet, Edward IV marched to a decisive victory over the Lancastrians at Tewkesbury and then got on with ruling as before. Rather effectively. A French visitor to England could even claim in the 1470s – the 'worst' decade of the Wars of the Roses – that of all the countries he had visited England was the one 'where public affairs are best conducted'.

Richard III Murders the Princes in the Tower, 1483

WILLIAM SHAKESPEARE AND SIR THOMAS MORE

Made Protector when his twelve-year-old nephew Edward V inherited the throne, Richard, Duke of York, usurped power to become king in June 1483. The popular view of the great monarchical villain of English history was set for ever by the playwright and Tudor propagandist William Shakespeare in Richard III:

> But I – that am not shap'd for sportive tricks,
> Nor made to court an amorous looking-glass
> I – that am rudely stamp'd, and want love's majesty
> To strut before a wanton ambling nymph –
> I – that am curtail'd of this fair proportion,
> Cheated of feature by dissembling nature,
> Deform'd, unfinished, sent before my time
> Into this breathing world scarce half made up,
> And that so lamely and unfashionable
> That dogs bark at me as I halt by them –
> Why, I, in this weak piping time of peace,
> Have no delight to pass away the time,
> Unless to spy my shadow in the sun
> And descant on mine own deformity.

In truth Richard III may not have had the 'crouch-back' attributed to him by Shakespeare . . . but he was almost certainly guilty of the murder of Edward V and his younger brother.

Sir Thomas More (1478–1535) was Lord Chancellor under Henry VIII and the author of Utopia.

. . . I shall rehearse you the dolorous end of those babes, not after every way that I have heard, but after that way that I have so heard by such men and by such means as methinks it were hard but it should be true.

. . . forasmuch as his mind gave him that, his nephews living, men would not reckon that he could have right to the realm, (Richard) thought therefore without delay to be rid of them, as though the killing of his kinsmen could amend his cause and make him a kindly king.

Whereupon he sent one John Green, whom he specially trusted, unto Sir Robert Brackenbury, constable of the Tower, with a letter and credence also, that the same Sir Robert should . . . put the two children to death . . . who plainly answered that he would never put them to death . . . with which answer John Green, returning, recounted the same to King Richard at Warwick . . .

(On) the morrow he sent (Sir James Tyrell) to Brackenbury with a letter, by which he was commanded to deliver (to) Sir James all the keys of the Tower for one night, to the end he might there accomplish the king's pleasure . . . After which letter delivered and the keys received, Sir James appointed the night next ensuing to destroy them . . .

(Sir) James Tyrell devised that they should be murdered in their beds. To the execution whereof he appointed Miles Forest, one of the four that kept them, a fellow fleshed in murder beforetime. To him he joined one John Dighton, his own horsekeeper, a big broad square strong knave. Then, all the others being removed from them, this Miles Forest and John Dighton, about midnight, the innocent children lying in their beds, came into the chamber and suddenly lapped them up among the clothes, so bewrapped them and entangled them, keeping down by force the featherbed and pillows hard unto their mouths, that within a while smothered and stifled, their breath failing, they gave up to God their innocent souls into the joys of heaven, leaving to the tormentors their bodies dead in the bed. After the wretches perceived them, first by the struggling with the pains of death, and after long lying still, to be thoroughly dead, they laid their bodies naked out upon the bed and fetched Sir James to see them. Who, upon the sight of them, caused those murderers to bury them at the stair foot, meetly deep in the ground under a great heap of stones.

Then rode Sir James in great haste to King Richard, and showed him all the manner of the murder, who gave him great thanks and, as some say, there made him knight. But he allowed not, as I have heard, the burying in so vile a corner, saying that he would have them buried in a better place because they were a king's sons . . . Whereupon they say that a priest of Sir Robert Brackenbury took up the bodies again and secretly interred them in such place as, by the occasion of his death, who alone knew it, could never after come to light. Very truth it is and well known that at such time as Sir James Tyrell was in the Tower, for treason committed against the most famous prince King Henry the Seventh, both Dighton and he were examined, and confessed the murder in manner above-written, but whither the bodies were removed they could nothing tell.

And thus, as I have learned from them that much knew and little cause had to lie, were these two noble princes, these innocent tender children, born of most royal blood, brought up in great wealth, likely long to live to reign and rule in the realm, by traitorous tyranny taken, deprived of their estate, shortly shut up in prison, and privily slain and murdered, their bodies cast God knows where, by the cruel ambition of their unnatural uncle and his pitiless tormentors.

The Battle of Bosworth, 22 August 1485

POLYDORE VERGIL

The battle that ended the Wars of the Roses was won by the Lancastrian claimant to the throne, Henry Tudor, after Richard III was treasonably deserted mid-fight by the Stanley family.

Vergil, born in Italy, spent most of his life in England and became Archdeacon of Wells Cathedral.

At the battle of Bosworth the number of all (Henry Tudor's) soldiers, altogether, was scarcely 5,000 beside the Stanleyans, of whom about 3,000 were at the battle, under the conduct of William . . . The king's forces were twice as many and more.

. . . Henry bore the brunt (of the fighting) longer than even his own soldiers would have thought, who were now almost out of hope of victory, when, behold, William Stanley with 3,000 men came to the rescue; then truly in a very moment the residue all fled, and King Richard alone was killed fighting manfully in the thickest press of his enemies. In the meantime also the Earl of Oxford, after a little skirmishing, put to flight those that fought in the forward, whereof a great company were killed in the chase. But many more forebore to fight, who came to the field with King Richard for awe, and for no goodwill and departed without any danger, as men who desired not the safety but destruction of that prince whom they hated.

There were killed about 1,000 men, and amongst them (were) John

Duke of Norfolk, Walter Lord Ferrers, Robert Brackenbury, Richard Ratcliffe and many more. Two days after at Leicester, William Catesby, lawyer, with a few that were his fellows, were executed. And of those who took to their feet Francis Lord Lovell, Humphrey Stafford, with Thomas his brother and much more company, fled into sanctuary . . . As for the number of captives, it was very great; for when King Richard was killed, all men forthwith threw away weapon and freely submitted themselves to Henry's obedience, whereof the most part would have done the same at the beginning (but) for King Richard's scouts . . . Amongst them the chief were Henry Earl of Northumberland and Thomas Earl of Surrey . . . Henry lost in that battle scarcely a hundred soldiers . . .

The report is that King Richard might have sought to save himself by flight; for they who were about him, seeing the soldiers even from the first stroke to lift up their weapons feebly and faintly, and some of them to depart the field privily, suspected treason, and exhorted him to fly, and when the matter began manifestly to falter, they brought him swift horses; but he, who was not ignorant that the people hated him, (is) said to have answered that that very day he would make an end either of war or life . . .

Henry, after the victory obtained, gave forthwith thanks unto Almighty God for the same . . . (The) soldiers cried, 'God save King Henry, God save King Henry!', and with heart and hand uttered all the show of joy that might be; which, when Thomas Stanley did see, he set at once King Richard's crown, which was found among the spoil in the field, upon his head . . .

The body of King Richard, naked of all clothing, and laid upon a horse's back, with the arms and legs hanging down on both sides, was brought to the abbey of Franciscan monks at Leicester, a miserable spectacle in good truth, but not unworthy for the man's life, and there was buried two days after without any pomp or solemn funeral.

The legal claim of Henry Tudor (born 1457) to the English throne was tortuous; it came down an illegitimate line from Edward III's fourth son, John of Gaunt. Henry Tudor – crowned as Henry VII on 30 October 1485 – was an adventurer. What mattered was whether he had the staying power to establish a new dynasty on England's throne.

In this, Henry VII had better luck than an usurper might have hoped for. Richard III had left no heirs behind him and the Wars of the Roses had immolated a clutch of potentially troublesome magnates. Even better, his far-sighted mother

*had already betrothed him to Elizabeth of York, Edward IV's daughter; when
Henry and Elizabeth married in 1486 the Tudor–Lancastrian claim was merged
with the Yorkist, and most of the White Roses were reconciled to the new regime.*

*But not all of them. The first rebellion came in 1487 when the Yorkists dressed
up one Lambert Simnel, an Oxford joiner's son, as 'Edward VI'. Henry
captured him and put him to work as a spit-turner in the royal kitchen. A decade
later, the Yorkists advanced another impostor, Perkin Warbeck, the son of the
Controller of Tournai, who was persuaded to impersonate Richard, Duke of
York, one of the princes murdered in the Tower. Acknowledged by a mischievous
James IV of Scotland (among others), Warbeck invaded Cornwall in 1497 to
claim 'his' throne. Warbeck fared worse than Simnel; he was rounded up,
imprisoned and, insistent on escape, executed.*

*The very longevity of Henry VII's reign – it lasted until 1509 – made for
stability, which in turn allowed English commerce to flourish. (Export of woollen
cloth, the yardstick of the early Tudor economy, as it was of the medieval era,
rose by 50 per cent over the course of Henry's tenure.) Almost the monarchical
miser of myth, Henry VII ruthlessly enforced the crown's financial dues, selling
offices of state and issuing dubious 'attainders' whereby 'traitors' forfeited their
lands. The result was that Henry VII – the 'best businessman ever to sit on the
English throne' – bequeathed to his son and heir £1.5 million.*

*The first Tudor king left Henry VIII something more precious still. Security.
Henry VIII was the first king since Henry V who did not have to fight for his
throne.*

A Portrait of Henry VIII, 1519

SEBASTIAN GIUSTINIAN

*A picture of Henry VIII at the zenith of his reputation, a decade on the throne,
the successful battles of the Spurs (v. France) and Flodden (v. Scotland) behind
him, and still the extrovert, the virtual inventor of Merrie England. The admiring
Giustinian was the Venetian ambassador to London from 1515 to 1519.*

His majesty is twenty-nine years old and extremely handsome. Nature
could not have done more for him. He is much handsomer than any
other sovereign in Christendom; a great deal handsomer than the King
of France; very fair, and his whole frame admirably proportioned. On
hearing that Francis I wore a beard, he allowed his own to grow, and as
it is reddish, he has now a beard that looks like gold. He is very.

accomplished, a good musician, composes well, is a most capital horseman, a fine jouster, speaks good French, Latin, and Spanish, is very
religious, hears three masses daily when he hunts, and sometimes five
on other days. He hears the office every day in the queen's chamber,
that is to say vesper and compline. He is very fond of hunting, and never
takes his diversion without tiring eight or ten horses, which he causes
to be stationed beforehand along the line of country he means to take,
and when one is tired he mounts another, and before he gets home they
are all exhausted. He is extremely fond of tennis, at which game it is the
prettiest thing in the world to see him play, his fair skin glowing through
a shirt of the finest texture. He gambles with the French hostages, to the
amount occasionally, it is said, of from 6,000 to 8,000 ducats in a day.
He is affiable and gracious, harms no one, does not covet his neighbour's
goods, and is satisfied with his own dominions, having often said to me,
'Sir Ambassador, we want all potentates to content themselves with their
own territories; we are satisfied with this island of ours.' He seems
extremely desirous of peace.

He is very rich. His father left him ten millions of ready money in
gold, of which he was supposed to have spent one-half in the war against
France, when he had three armies on foot; one crossed the Channel
with him, another was in the field against Scotland, and the third
remained with the queen in reserve.

His revenues amount to about 350,000 ducats annually, and are
derived from estates, forests, and meres, the customs, hereditary and
confiscated property, the duchies of Lancaster, York, Cornwall and
Suffolk, the county palatine of Chester, and others, the principality of
Wales, the export duties, the wool staple, the great seal, the annates
yielded by Church benefices, the Court of Wards, and from New Year's
gifts; for on the first day of the year it is customary for his majesty to
make presents to everybody, but the value of those he receives in return
greatly exceeds his own outlay. His majesty's expenses may be estimated
at 100,000 ducats, those in ordinary having been reduced from 100,000
to 56,000 to which must be added 16,000 for salaries, 5,000 for the stable,
5,000 for the halberdiers, who have been reduced from 500 to 150, and
16,000 for the wardrobe, for he is the best dressed sovereign in the
world. His robes are very rich and superb, and he puts on new clothes
every holyday.

The Field of the Cloth of Gold, 7–24 June 1520

POLYDORE VERGIL

The 'eighth wonder of the world', the Field of the Cloth of Gold was a Brobdingnagian peace festival in France intended to bind England and France together against a common foe, Charles V's Hapsburg Empire. It was the brainchild of Henry VIII's chief minister, Thomas Wolsey (son of an Ipswich butcher; the one policy of his father's that Henry VIII did continue was promotion by merit not status). Wolsey constantly sought a role for England in Europe above her weight as a small offshore nation.

Then the king of England showed himself some deal forward in beauty and personage, the most goodliest prince that ever reigned over the realm of England. His grace was apparelled in a garment of cloth of silver, of damask ribbed with cloth of gold, so thick as might be; the garment was large and pleated very thick and cantled of very good intail, of such shape and making that it was marvellous to behold. The courser which his grace rode on was trapped in a marvellous vesture of a new devised fashion; the trapper was of fine gold in bullion, curiously wrought, pounced and set with antique work of Roman figures. Attending on the king's grace of England was the Master of the Horse, by name sir Henry Guilford, leading the king's spare horse: . . . After followed nine henchmen, riding on coursers of Naples; the same young gentlemen were apparelled in rich cloth of tissue, the coursers in harness of marvellous fashion, scaled in fine gold in bullion, and works subtle more than my sight could contrive; and all the same horse-harness was set full of trembling spangs that were large and fair. The lord marquess Dorset bare the king's sword of state before the king's grace; the reverend father lord cardinal did his attendance.

Thus in little time, abiding the coming of the French king and his, the which in short time came with great number of horsemen, freshly apparelled; the French king and his retinue put themselves in place appointed, direct against the English party, beholding every other of both nations. The Frenchmen mused much of the battle of the footmen, and every of the Frenchmen to other spake of the multitude of the Englishmen which seemed great; yet were not they so many as the French party.

When the French king had a little beholden the Englishmen, he put himself somewhat before his people, that were there on him attendant, the duke of Bourbon bearing a naked sword upright, the lord admiral of France and the count Cosmen Galias, Master of the French king's Horse; and no more persons gave their attendance in passing with the French king. When it was perceived that the French king's sword was borne naked, then the king of England commanded the lord marquess Dorset to draw out the sword of state and bare it up naked in presence; which was so done.

Then up blew the trumpets, sackbuts, clarions and all other minstrels on both sides, and the kings descended down toward the bottom of the valley of Arden, in sight of both the nations; and on horseback met and embraced the two kings each other. Then the two kings alighted and after embraced with benign and courteous manner each to other, with sweet and goodly words of greeting. And after few words these two noble kings went together into the rich tent of cloth of gold, that there was set on the ground for such purpose. Thus arm in arm went the French king Francis I of France and Henry VIII king of England and of France, together passing with communication.

When the two princes were in the tent, before rehearsed, the French king said: 'My dear brother and cousin, thus far to my pain have I travelled to see you personally; I think verily that you esteem me as I am. And that I may to you be your aid, the realms and seignories show the might of my person.' 'Sir,' said the king of England, 'neither your realms nor other the places of your power is the matter of my regard, but the steadfastness and loyal keeping of promise, comprised in charters between you and me; that observed and kept, I never saw prince with my eyes that might of my heart be more loved. And for your love I have passed the seas, into the farthest frontier of my realm to see you presently; the which doing now gladdeth me.' And then were the two kings served with a banquet, and after mirth had communication in the banquet time, and there shewed the one the other their pleasure.

The English officers went and ran with great pots of wine and bowls to the Frenchmen and them cheered the best that might be. All this season stood still the noblemen of the English party and all other, and from their places moved nothing that they were appointed unto. And the serving men in like wise not once moved from their ground or standing; but the Frenchmen suddenly brake and many of them came into the English party, speaking fair; but for all that, the court of England and the lords still kept their array.

After the two kings had ended the banquet, and spice and wine given to the Frenchmen, Ipocras was chief drink of plenty to all that would drink. In open sight then came the two kings, that is to wit the French king and the king of England, out of their tent: . . . This French king had on his head a coif of damask gold set with diamonds, and his courser that he rode on was covered with a trapper of tissue, embroidered with devise, cut in fashion mantle-wise; the skirts were embowed and fret with frieze work and knit with cordels, and buttons tusselled of Turkey making; reins and headstall answering of like work. And verily of his person the same Francis, the French king, a goodly prince; stately of countenance, merry of cheer, brown-coloured, great eyes, high-nosed, big-lipped, fair breasted and shoulders, small legs and long feet.

All the nobles of the French court were in garments of many colours, so that they were not known from the braggery. Thus as the two kings were in communication, divers noblemen of England were called to presence. And then the two kings departed with their company, the king of England to Guisnes, the French king to Arden.

Truth to tell, Henry and Francis could hardly keep up an entente cordiale for a week, let alone perpetuity. By 1523 England and France were once again at war.

The Field of the Cloth of Gold did change the course of history, but not in the way intended. It was there that Henry VIII first met Anne Boleyn.

'Mine Own Sweetheart': Henry VIII Writes to Anne Boleyn, c. 1526

HENRY VIII

By 1525 Henry VIII had tired of the charms of his ageing wife, Catherine of Aragon, and become mesmerized by those of the vital Anne Boleyn, niece of the Duke of Norfolk. Not content to become the king's mistress (unlike her famously good-time sister Mary), the ambitious Anne kept Henry dangling at arm's length – which only made him desire her more.

Mine own sweetheart, this shall be to advertise you of the great melancholy that I find here since your departing; for, I ensure you, methinketh the time longer since your departing now last than I was wont to do a whole fortnight. I think your kindness and my fervency of love causeth it; for, otherwise I would not have thought it possible that for so little a while it should have grieved me. But now I am coming towards you, methinketh my pains by half removed; and also I am right well comforted insomuch that my book maketh substantially for my matter; in looking where of I have spent above four hours this day, which causeth me now to write the shorter letter to you at this time, because of some pain in my head. Wishing myself (especially an evening) in my sweetheart's arms whose pretty duckies★ I trust shortly to kiss. Written by the hand of him that was, is, and shall be yours by his own will,

H. R.

The following year, 1527, Henry VIII determined to divorce Catherine and marry Anne. His heart was set on it; so was his head. Catherine of Aragon – now beyond child-bearing age – had not produced the male heir on which the embryonic Tudor dynasty seemingly depended.

All Henry needed was for the Pope to issue a divorce. This should have been a formality, but the Pope was a pawn of Charles V, Henry's rival and Catherine of Aragon's nephew. For three years the 'King's Great Matter' dragged on inconclusively, until Anne Boleyn herself took a dainty but deft hand in the matter and pressed upon Henry a copy of William Tyndale's On the Obedience of a Christian Man and how Christian Rulers Ought to Govern. *This asserted that the monarch was chief of both Church and State. A keen amateur Bible student, Henry now had the theological answer to his prayers: he could be Pope in his own land – and issue a do-it-yourself divorce. In a spate of statutes, Henry and Parliament – acting for the first time in English history as the supreme legislative assembly – ended the allegiance to Rome, proclaiming that 'this realm is an empire'. Under the Act of Supremacy Henry was installed as 'supreme head' of the Church of England.*

Few objected. Although Anne Boleyn was not popular in the country, most of the xenophobic English were quite content to cut free from the 'Bishop of Rome'. Henry's divorce was only the occasion for the 'Reformation' of the Church in England, not its cause.

In January 1533 Henry VIII secretly married Anne Boleyn and four months later Archbishop Cranmer pronounced the king's former marriage to Catherine of Aragon null and void. On Whit Sunday Anne was crowned Queen of England ('somewhat big with child', noted the officiating Archbishop Cranmer). However, Henry's passion for her was already cooling and was not revived by the birth of a daughter and then a still-born son. Now an encumbrance to Henry's desire for

★ Breasts.

a male heir, Anne Boleyn was beheaded on 19 May 1536 for adultery with her brother as well as four commoners. Eleven days after Boleyn's execution Henry married Jane Seymour, who at last produced the requisite live boy child, but died in the doing. The remainder of Henry's six wives were: Anne of Cleves (marriage annulled because she was too plain), Catherine Howard (beheaded for adultery) and Catherine Parr (who survived her husband).

The Dissolution of the Monasteries: Cromwell's Agents Report, 1535–8

JOHN LONDON, JOHN AP RICE, RICHARD LAYTON, GEOFFREY CHAMBER, ROGER TOWNSEND

Henry VIII's own inclination in the English Reformation was towards Catholicism without the Pope, but the times and his most able minister, Thomas Cromwell (Wolsey having died in disgrace for failing to obtain the king's divorce from Catherine of Aragon), had other, radical ideas. One of Cromwell's notions was touched by genius: it was to close and sell off all the monasteries in England and Wales. The money garnered would pay for Henry's expensive habits (wars and palaces), while those doing the purchasing, the squirearchy, would literally be buying into the new order. To convince the public that the dissolution of the monasteries was necessary, Cromwell sent out 'Visitors' to catalogue their sins.

In my most humble manner I have me commended unto your good lordship, ascertaining the same that I have pulled down the image of Our Lady at Caversham, whereunto was great pilgrimage. The image is plated over with silver, and I have put it in a chest fast locked and nailed up, and by the next barge that cometh from Reading to London it shall be brought to your lordship. I have also pulled down the place she stood in, with all other ceremonies, as lights, shrowds, crosses, and images of wax hanging about the chapel, and have defaced the same thoroughly in eschewing of any further resort thither. This chapel did belong to Notley Abbey, and there always was a canon of that monastery which was called the Warden of Caversham, and he sung in this chapel and had the offerings for his living. He was accustomed to show many pretty relics, among the which were (as he made report) the holy dagger that killed King Henry, and the holy knife that killed St Edward. All these with many other, with the coats of this image, her cap and hair, my servants shall bring unto your lordship this week, with the surrender of the friars under their convent seal, and their seal also. I have sent the canon home again to Notley, and have made fast the doors of the chapel, which is thoroughly well covered with lead, and if it be your lordship's pleasure I shall see it made sure to the King's grace's use. And if it be not so ordered, the chapel standeth so wildly that the lead will be stolen by night, as I was served at the Friars. For as soon as I had taken the Friars' surrender, the multitude of the poverty of the town resorted thither, and all things that might be had they stole away, insomuch that they had conveyed the very clappers of the bells. And saving that Mr Fachell, which made me great cheer at his house, and the Mayor did assist me, they would have made no little spoil . . .

Please it your good lordship to be advertised that . . . the Abbot of Langdon passeth all other that ever I knew in profound bawdry; the drunkennest knave living. All his canons be even as he is, not one spark of virtue amongst them; arrant bawdy knaves every man. The Abbot caused his chaplain to take an whore, and instigate him to it, brought her up into his own chapter, took one of his feather-beds off his own bed, and made his chaplain's bed in the inner chamber, within him, and there caused him to go to bed with his whore that the Abbot had provided for him. To rehearse you the whole story, it were long and too abominable to hear. The house is in utter decay and will shortly fall down. You must needs depose him and suddenly sequestrate the fruits, and take an inventory of the goods. You can do no less of justice . . .

My singular good lord, my duty remembered unto your lordship, this shall be to advertise the same that upon the defacing of the late monastery of Boxley, and plucking down the images of the same, I found in the image of the Rood called the Rood of Grace, the which heretofore hath been had in great veneration of the people, certain engines and old wire, with old rotten sticks in the back of the same, that did cause the eyes of the same to move and stare in the head thereof, like unto a living thing; and also the nether lip in like wise to move as though it should speak, which, so famed, was not a little strange to me and other that was present at the plucking down of the same, whereupon the abbot, hearing this bruit, did thither resort, whom to my little wit and cunning, with other of the old monks, I did examine of their knowledge of the premises; who do declare themselves to be ignorant of the same.

Please it your goodness to understand that on Friday 22 October I rode back with speed to take an inventory of Folkestone (priory), and from thence went to Langdon. Whereas immediately descending from my horse, I sent Bartelot your servant, with all my servants to circumcept the abbey, and surely to keep all back doors and startyng hoilles;* etc. I myself went alone to the abbot's lodging joining upon the fields and wood, even like a cony clapper† full of private ways; a good space knocking at the abbot's door, neither sound nor sign of life appearing, saving the abbot's little dog, that within his door fast locked, bayed and barked. I found a short pole-axe standing behind the door, and with it I dashed the abbot's door in pieces, and set one of my men to keep that door, and about the house I go with the pole-axe in my hand, for the abbot is a dangerous desperate knave and a hardy. But for a conclusion, his whore alias his gentlewoman bestirred her stumps towards her startyng hoilles, and there Bartelot watching the pursuit took the tender damsel, and after I had examined her, to Dover there to the mayor to set her in some cage or prison for 8 days, and I brought holy father abbot to Canterbury, and there in Christ Church (priory) I will leave him in prison. In this sudden doing extempore, to circumcept the house and to search, your servant John Antony and his men marvelled what fellow I was, and so did the rest of the abbey, for I was unknown there of all men. At last I found her apparel in the abbot's coffer. To tell you all this comedy, but for the abbot a tragedy, it were too long.

Please it your mastership, forasmuch as I suppose ye shall have suit made unto you touching Bury ere we return, I thought convenient to advertise you of our proceedings there, and also of the comperta of the same. As for the abbot, we found nothing suspect as touching his living, but it was detected that he lay much forth in his granges, that he delighted much in playing at dice and cards, and therein spent much money, and in building for his pleasure. He did not preach openly. Also that he converted divers farms into copyholds, whereof poor men doth complain. Also he seemeth to be addict to the maintaining of such superstitious ceremonies as hath been used heretofore.

As touching the convent, we could get little or no reports among them, although we did use much diligence in our examination, and thereby, with some other arguments gathered of their examinations, I firmly believe and suppose that they had conferred and compacted before our coming that they should disclose nothing. And yet it is confessed and proved, that there was here such frequence of women coming and resorting to this monastery as to no place more. Amongst the relics we found much vanity and superstition, as the coals that Saint Lawrence

---

* Private posterns.
† A rabbit's burrow.

was toasted withal, the parings of S. Edmund's nails, S. Thomas of Canterbury's penknife and his boots, and divers skills for the headache; pieces of the holy cross able to make a holy cross of . . .

Approximately 800 institutions were closed between 1536 and 1540, and their 9,000 inmates turned out. There was opposition in the North, notably the Pilgrimage of Grace, but in the more reform-minded South and East, where most of the monasteries were based, barely a squeak. Anti-clericalism ran deep in the English mind.

During the short reign of Henry's son, Edward VI (1547–53) the Reformation in England finally took on a theological aspect. The boy-king was a Protestant devotee, and the radical Archbishop of Canterbury, Thomas Cranmer, received his leave to introduce into the English Church the Act of Uniformity and the Book of Common Prayer (1549, revised 1552), which replaced Latin services with English – for the first time – and removed all reference to the Mass. The sixteen-year-old Edward VI died on 6 July 1553 (almost his last words were 'O! my Lord God, defend this realm from papistry'), having barred his Catholic half-sister, Mary, from the succession in favour of Lady Jane Grey, the virtuously Protestant daughter-in-law of the Protector, Northumberland. Alas, no one had thought to incarcerate Mary. A Tudor regent, even a Catholic one, seemed preferable to a Protestant nonentity. Besides, Mary quite duplicitously hid the degree of her Catholic fanaticism. Lady Jane Grey's 'reign' lasted nine days, before Mary marched into London in queenly triumph.

The Burning of Archbishop Cranmer, 21 March 1556

A BYSTANDER

The love affair of the English with Mary Tudor was short-lived. She insisted on marrying a foreigner (Philip of Spain, Charles V's son) and restoring Catholicism by incinerating Protestants. Among those set afire alive was Thomas Cranmer, the first Protestant Archbishop of Canterbury. He recanted his 'heresy' no fewer than seven times before publicly and dramatically affirming his Protestantism on the day of his execution in London.

But to come to the matter: on Saturday last, being 21 of March, was his day appointed to die. And because the morning was much rainy, the sermon appointed by Mr Dr Cole to be made at the stake, was made in St Mary's church: whither Dr Cranmer was brought by the mayor and aldermen, and my lord Williams: with whom came divers gentlemen of the shire, sir T. A. Bridges, sir John Browne, and others. Where was prepared, over against the pulpit, an high place for him, that all the people might see him. And, when he had ascended it, he kneeled him down and prayed, weeping tenderly: which moved a great number to tears, that had conceived an assured hope of his conversion and repentance . . .

When praying was done, he stood up, and, having leave to speak, said, 'Good people, I had intended indeed to desire you to pray for me; which because Mr Doctor hath desired, and you have done already, I thank you most heartily for it. And now will I pray for myself, as I could best devise for mine own comfort, and say the prayer, word for word, as I have here written it.' And he read it standing: and after kneeled down, and said the Lord's Prayer; and all the people on their knees devoutly praying with him . . .

And then rising, he said, 'Every man desireth, good people, at the time of their deaths, to give some good exhortation, that other may remember after their deaths, and be the better thereby. So I beseech God grant me grace, that I may speak something, at this my departing, whereby God may be glorified, and you edified . . .

'And now I come to the great thing that troubleth my conscience more than any other thing that ever I said or did in my life: and that is, the setting abroad of writings contrary to the truth. Which here now I renounce and refuse, as things written with my hand, contrary to the truth which I thought in my heart, and written for fear of death, and to save my life, if it might be: and that is, all such bills, which I have written or signed with mine own hand since my degradation: where-in I have written many things untrue. And forasmuch as my hand offended in writing contrary to my heart, therefore my hand shall first be punished: for if I may come to the fire, it shall be first burned. And as for the pope, I refuse him, as Christ's enemy and antichrist, with all his false doctrine.'

And here, being admonished of his recantation and dissembling, he said, 'Alas, my lord, I have been a man that all my life loved plainness, and never dissembled till now against the truth; which I am most sorry for it.' He added hereunto, that, for the sacrament, he believed as he had taught in his book against the bishop of Winchester. And here he was suffered to speak no more . . .

Then was he carried away; and a great number, that did run to see him go so wickedly to his death, ran after him, exhorting him, while time was, to remember himself. And one Friar John, a godly and well learned man, all the way travelled with him to reduce him. But it would not be. What they said in particular I cannot tell, but the effect appeared in the end: for at the stake he professed, that he died in all such opinions as he had taught, and oft repented him of his recantation.

Coming to the stake with a cheerful countenance and willing mind, he put off his garments with haste, and stood upright in his shirt: and a bachelor of divinity, named Elye, of Brazen-nose college, laboured to convert him to his former recantation, with the two Spanish friars. And when the friars saw his constancy, they said in Latin one to another, 'Let us go from him: we ought not to be nigh him: for the devil is with him.' But the bachelor in divinity was more earnest with him: unto whom he answered, that, as concerning his recantation, he repented it right sore, because he knew it was against the truth; with other words more. Whereby the Lord Williams cried, 'Make short, make short.' Then the bishop took certain of his friends by the hand. But the bachelor of divinity refused to take him by the hand, and blamed all others that so did, and said, he was sorry that ever he came in his company. And yet again he required him to agree to his former recantation. And the bishop answered, (shewing his hand), 'This was the hand that wrote it, and therefore shall it suffer first punishment.'

Fire being now put to him, he stretched out his right hand, and thrust it into the flame, and held it there a good space, before the fire came to any other part of his body; where his hand was seen of every man sensibly burning, crying with a loud voice, 'This hand hath offended.' As soon as the fire got up, he was very soon dead, never stirring or crying all the while.

Cranmer was one of some 300 Protestants burned at the stake in the reign of 'Bloody Queen Mary' for what Mary called their 'corrupt and naughty opinions'. Mary's brutality disgusted Englishmen and proved Protestantism's best recruiter, especially when the sufferings of the burned were turned into the eloquent propaganda of John Foxe's Acts and Monuments *(aka* Book of Martyrs*), the best-seller of Tudor England.*

Moreover, as many English feared, Mary Tudor's marriage to Philip of Spain caused England to become involved in his country's conflict with France. Mary's conduct of the war was calamitous, with the result that Calais, England's last possession in France, was captured in January 1558.

The impact of the loss of Calais on Tudor England can scarcely be under-estimated. Calais, the glittering symbol of the great wars of the Black Prince and

Henry V, Calais the wool staple port. Mary herself cried that when she died, Calais would be found written on her heart.

Only months later Mary did die, of ovarian cancer, tragically deluded that her bloated tumour was a baby. To her chagrin, the only possible successor was her half-sister, Elizabeth, daughter of Henry VIII and the 'goggle-eyed whore' Anne Boleyn.

Elizabeth I. Gloriana, Virginia, Deborah, the Faerie Queen – for her contemporaries, as well as posterity, her reign was a Golden Age of England. Like most English, Elizabeth I was only moderately religious (Calvinist John Knox described her, neatly, as 'neither a good protestant, nor yet a resolute papist'), and above everything she was the mistress of realpolitik. She understood that the future of England was Protestant, so settled upon it a mild Protestantism (near-indistinguishable from modern Anglicanism), based on the 1552 Prayer Book, which stabilized the realm for her long tenure (1558–1603). Abroad, she pursued a cautious policy of aid to the North European Protestant powers, mostly to enervate the Catholic big two, France and Spain. She was never married, save to her country, whose ring she wore in token. Elizabethan England was God's chosen land for his chosen people – who were rapidly growing in numbers, up from 2.98 million in 1561 to 4.10 million in 1601. The sense of national enchantment was perfectly caught by William Shakespeare, the era's dramatist-laureate, in Richard II: *'This precious stone set in the silver sea . . . This blessed plot, this earth, this realm, this England . . . This land of such dear souls, this dear, dear land'.*

The English, as befitted an island people, had long been sailors, but it was during Elizabeth's reign that they found their destiny on the 'silver sea'.

An Encounter with Drake at Sea, off Guatemala, 4 April 1579

FRANCISCO DE ZARATE

Francis Drake (c. 1540–96) left England in the Pelican *in December 1577 to become the first Englishman to sail around the world. Typically of the Elizabethan sea-dogs, he had little interest in exploration for exploration's sake. His intentions were all practical: to find new trading opportunities, to grab unstaked land, and to plunder Spanish gold-ships in the New World. If in the doing of these things he spited the Pope, so much the better. (Drake's favourite reading matter aboard the* Pelican *was Foxe's* Book of Martyrs, *the woodcuts of which he coloured-in in idler moments, the text of which he preached to his Spanish prisoners). The queen was one of his sponsors.*

Off Guatemala, Drake seized the ship belonging to the Spaniard Francisco de Zarate:

I sailed out of the port of Acapulco on the 23rd of March and navigated until Saturday, the fourth of April, on which date, half an hour before dawn, we saw, by moonlight, a ship very close to ours. Our steersman shouted that she was to get out of the way and not come alongside of us. To this they made no answer, pretending to be asleep. The steersman then shouted louder, asking them where their ship hailed from. They answered 'from Peru', and that she was 'of *Miguel Angel*', which is the name of a well-known captain of that route . . .

The ship of the adversary carried her bark at her prow as though she were being towed. Suddenly, in a moment, she crossed our poop, ordering us 'to strike sail' and shooting seven or eight arquebuse shots at us.

We thought this as much of a joke as it afterwards turned out to be serious.

On our part there was no resistance, nor had we more than six of our men awake on the whole boat, so they entered our ship with as little risk to themselves as though they were our friends. They did no personal harm to any one, beyond seizing the swords and keys of the passengers. Having informed themselves as to who were on board ship, they ordered me to go in their boat to where their general was – a fact I was glad of, as it appeared to me that it gave me more time in which to recommend myself to God. But in a very short time we arrived where he was, on a very good galleon, as well mounted with artillery as any I have seen in my life.

I found him promenading on deck and, on approaching him, I kissed his hands. He received me with a show of kindness, and took me to his cabin, where he bade me be seated and said: 'I am a friend of those who tell me the truth, but with those who do not I get out of humour. Therefore you must tell me (for this is the best road to my favour) how much silver and gold does your ship carry?' I said to him, 'None'. He repeated his question. I answered, 'None, only some small plates that I use and some cups – that is all that is in her.' He kept silent for a while, then renewing the conversation asked me if I knew Your Excellency, I said, 'Yes' . . .

This general of the Englishmen is a nephew of John Hawkins, and is the same who, about five years back, took the port of Nombre de Dios. He is called Francisco Drac, and is a man of about 35 years of age, low of stature, with a fair beard, and is one of the greatest mariners that sail the seas, both as a navigator and as a commander. His vessel is a galleon of nearly four hundred tons, and is a perfect sailer. She is manned with a hundred men, all of service, and of an age for warfare, and all are as practised therein as old soldiers from Italy could be. Each one takes particular pains to keep his arquebuse clean. He treats them with affection, and they treat him with respect. He carries with him nine or ten cavaliers, cadets of English noblemen. These form a part of his council, which he calls together for even the most trivial matter, although he takes advice from no one. But he enjoys hearing what they say and afterwards issues his orders. He has no favourite.

The aforesaid gentleman sits at his table, as well as a Portuguese pilot, whom he brought from England, who spoke not a word during all the time I was on board. He is served on silver dishes with gold borders and gilded garlands, in which are his arms. He carries all possible dainties and perfumed waters. He said that many of these had been given to him by the Queen.

None of these gentlemen took a seat or covered his head before him, until he repeatedly urged him to do so. This galleon of his carries about thirty heavy pieces of artillery and a great quantity of firearms with the requisite ammunition and lead. He dines and sups to the music of viols. He carries trained carpenters and artisans, so as to be able to careen the ship at any time. Beside being new, the ship has a double lining. I understood that all the men he carries with him receive wages, because, when our ship was sacked, no man dared take anything without his orders. He shows them great favour, but punishes the least fault. He also carries painters who paint for him pictures of the coast in its exact colours . . .

This corsair, like a pioneer, arrived two months before he intended to pass through and during that time for many days there were great storms. So it was that one of the gentlemen, whom he had with him, said to him: 'We have been a long while in this strait and you have placed all of us, who follow or serve you, in danger of death. It would therefore be prudent for you to give order that we return to the North Sea, where we have the certainty of capturing prizes, and that we give up seeking to make new discoveries. You see how fraught with difficulties these are.'

This gentleman must have sustained this opinion with more vigour than appeared proper to the General. His answer was that he had the gentleman carried below deck and put in irons. On another day, at the same hour, he ordered him to be taken out, and to be beheaded in presence of all.

The term of his imprisonment was no more than was necessary to substantiate the lawsuit that was conducted against him. All this he told me, speaking much good about the dead man, but adding that he had not been able to act otherwise, because this was what the Queen's service demanded. He showed me the commissions that he had received from her and carried. I tried to ascertain whether any relatives of the dead man had remained on board. They told me that there was only one, who was one of those who ate at his table. During all this time that I was on board, which was fifty-five hours, this youth never left the ship, although all the others did so, in turn. It was not that he was left to guard me. I think that they guarded him.

I managed to ascertain whether the General was well liked, and all said that they adored him.

This is what I was able to find out during the time I spent with him . . .

On returning to England, Drake was knighted by the sovereign in whose name he had claimed California for England. Unfortunately, the Spanish blithely ignored Drake's staked claim to California; the English colonization of America was fated to occur on the nearer, East Coast, beginning with Raleigh's voyage to Virginia in 1584 and the foundation of the Roanoke settlement there a year later.

The Execution of Mary, Queen of Scots, 8 February 1587

R. K. WYNKFIELDE

After fleeing the 1567 revolt of the confederated lords, Mary Stuart threw herself on the mercy of her cousin, Elizabeth I, who kept the Scottish queen in a series of velvet-lined prisons − Carlisle, Bolton, Tutbury, Wingfield, Coventry, Chatsworth, Sheffield, Buxton, Chartley and Fotheringay. The presence of Mary Stuart was a source of unease for Elizabeth's government: as a Catholic she was a natural figurehead for the minority who wanted a return to the old religion (and who, following Pope Pius V's excommunication of Elizabeth, were absolved from loyalty to her). Ministers cajoled for a pre-emptive execution, but it was only when Mary incriminated herself in the Babington plot to assassinate Elizabeth that the English queen would allow Mary Stuart to be brought to trial. She was forty-five at the time of her subsequent beheading at Fotheringay.

Her prayers being ended, the executioners, kneeling, desired her Grace to forgive them her death: who answered, 'I forgive you with all my heart, for now, I hope, you shall make an end of all my troubles.' Then they, with her two women, helping her up, began to disrobe her of her apparel: then she, laying her crucifix upon the stool, one of the executioners took from her neck the *Agnus Dei*, which she, laying hands off it, gave to one of her women, and told the executioner he should be answered money for it. Then she suffered them, with her two women, to disrobe her of her chain of pomander beads and all her other apparel most willingly, and with joy rather than sorrow, helped to make unready herself, putting on a pair of sleeves with her own hands which they had pulled off, and that with some haste, as if she had longed to be gone.

All this time they were pulling off her apparel, she never changed her countenance, but with smiling cheer she uttered these words, 'that she never had such grooms to make her unready, and that she never put off her clothes before such a company'.

Then she, being stripped of all her apparel saving her petticoat and kirtle, her two women beholding her made great lamentation, and crying and crossing themselves prayed in Latin. She, turning herself to them, embracing them, said these words in French, 'Ne crie vous, j'ay promé pour vous', and so crossing and kissing them, bad them pray for her and rejoice and not weep, for that now they should see an end of all their mistress's troubles.

Then she, with a smiling countenance, turning to her men servants, as Melvin and the rest, standing upon a bench nigh the scaffold, who sometime weeping, sometime crying out aloud, and continually crossing themselves, prayed in Latin, crossing them with her hand bade them farewell, and wishing them to pray for her even until the last hour.

This done, one of the women having a *Corpus Christi* cloth lapped up three-corner-ways, kissing it, put it over the Queen of Scots' face, and pinned it fast to the caule of her head. Then the two women departed from her, and she kneeling down upon the cushion most resolutely, and without any token or fear of death, she spake aloud this Psalm in Latin, *In Te Domine confido, non confundar in eternam*, etc. Then, groping for the block, she laid down her head, putting her chin over the block with both her hands, which, holding there still, had been cut off had they not been espied. Then lying upon the block most quietly, and stretching out her arms cried, *In manus tuas, Domine*, etc., three or four times. Then she, lying very still upon the block, one of the executioners holding her slightly with one of his hands, she endured two strokes of the other executioner with an axe, she making very small noise or none at all, and not stirring any part of her from the place where she lay: and so the executioner cut off her head, saving one little gristle, which being cut asunder, he lift up her head to the view of all the assembly and bade *God save the Queen*. Then, her dress of lawn falling from off her head, it appeared as grey as one of threescore and ten years old, polled very short, her face in a moment being so much altered from the form she had when she was alive, as few could remember her by her dead face. Her lips stirred up and down a quarter of an hour after her head was cut off.

Then Mr Dean [Dr Fletcher, Dean of Peterborough] said with a loud voice, 'So perish all the Queen's enemies', and afterwards the Earl of Kent came to the dead body, and standing over it, with a loud voice said, 'Such end of all the Queen's and the Gospel's enemies.'

Then one of the executioners, pulling off her garters, espied her little dog which was crept under her clothes, which could not be gotten forth but by force, yet afterward would not depart from the dead corpse, but came and lay between her head and her shoulders, which being imbrued with her blood was carried away and washed, as all things else were that had any blood was either burned or washed clean, and the executioners sent away with money for their fees, not having any one thing that belonged unto her. And so, every man being commanded out of the hall, except the sheriff and his men, she was carried by them up into a great chamber lying ready for the surgeons to embalm her.

The Armada: the Commander's Report,
21–29 July 1588

LORD HOWARD OF EFFINGHAM AND
JOHN HAWKINS

Save for Drake playing bowls on Plymouth Ho, the legend of the Armada's defeat is not far removed from the truth of it.

Desirous of dethroning the 'heretical' Elizabeth I, of preventing piratical English incursions into the New World, of stemming English aid to fellow Protestants in the Spanish-controlled Netherlands, Philip II of Spain (Mary I's former husband) dispatched a fleet of 130 ships from La Coruna with the intention that this 'Armada' would rendezvous with his Army of Flanders off the Netherlands. Then the combined force would invade England.

On 19 July the Armada was spotted off the Scilly Isles.

Lord Howard of Effingham was commander of the English fleet, which totalled 197 ships, smaller than their Spanish counterparts but more agile, with better guns, better gun crews. (Some Spanish galleons could hardly manage a broadside a day.) The English combat reports below were sent to Sir Francis Walsingham, principal Secretary of State.

Sir,

I will not trouble you with any long letter; we are at this present otherwise occupied than with writing. Upon Friday, at Plymouth, I received intelligence that there were a great number of ships descried off of the Lizard; whereupon, although the wind was very scant, we first warped out of harbour that night, and upon Saturday turned out very hardly, the wind being at South-west; and about three of the clock in the afternoon, descried the Spanish fleet, and did what we could to work for the wind, which by this morning we had recovered, descrying their fleet to consist of 120 sail, whereof there are four galleasses and many ships of great burden.

At nine of the clock we gave them fight, which continued until one. In this fight we made some of them to bear room to stop their leaks; notwithstanding we durst not adventure to put in among them, their fleet being so strong. But there shall be nothing either neglected or unhazarded, that may work their overthrow.

Sir, the captains in her majesty's ships have behaved themselves most bravely and like men hitherto, and I doubt not will continue, to their great commendation. And so, recommending our good success to your godly prayers, I bid you heartily farewell. From aboard the *Ark*, thwart of Plymouth the 21st of July, 1588.

Your very loving friend,

C. Howard.

Sir, the southerly wind that brought us back from the coast of Spain brought them out. God blessed us with turning us back. Sir, for the love of God and our country, let us have with some speed some great shot sent us of all bigness; for this service will continue long; and some powder with it.

★   ★   ★

My bounden duty humbly remembered unto your good lordship: – have not busied myself to write often to your lordship in this great cause, for that my lord admiral doth continually advertise the manner of all things that doth pass. So do others that understand the state of all things as well as myself. We met with this fleet somewhat to the westward of Plymouth upon Sunday in the morning, being the 21st of July, where we had some small fight with them in the afternoon. By the coming aboard one of the other of the Spaniards, a great ship, a Biscayan, spent her foremast and bowsprit, which was left by the fleet in the sea, and so taken up by sir Francis Drake the next morning. The same Sunday there was, by a fire chancing by a barrel of powder, a great Biscayan spoiled and abandoned, which my lord took up and sent away.

The Tuesday following, athwart of Portland, we had a sharp and long fight with them, wherein we spent a great part of our powder and shot, so as it was not thought good to deal with them any more till that was relieved.

The Thursday following, by the occasion of the scattering of one of the great ships from the fleet, which we hoped to have cut off, there grew a hot fray, wherein some store of powder was spent; and after that little done till we came near to Calais, where the fleet of Spain anchored, and our fleet by them; and because they should not be in peace there, to refresh their water or to have conference with that of the duke of Parma's party, my lord admiral, with firing of ships, determined to renew them; as he did, and put them to the seas; in which broil the chief galleass spoiled her rudder, and so rode ashore near the town of Calais, where she was possessed of our men, but so aground as she could not be brought away.

That morning, being Monday, the 29th of July, we followed the Spaniards; and all that day had with them a long and great fight, wherein there was great valour showed generally of our company. In this battle there was spent very much of our powder and shot; and so the wind began to blow westerly, a fresh gale, and the Spaniards put themselves somewhat the northward, where we follow and keep company with them. In this fight there was some hurt done among the Spaniards. A great ship of the galleons of Portugal, her rudder spoiled, and so the fleet left her in the sea. I doubt not but all these things are written more at large to your lordship than I can do; but this is the substance and material matter that hath passed.

Our ships, God be thanked, have received little hurt, and are of great force to accompany them, and of such advantage that with some continuance at the seas, and sufficiently provided of shot and powder, we shall be able, with God's favour, to weary them out of the sea and confound them . . .

Your lordship's humbly to command,
John Hawkyns.

The Armada: Elizabeth Addresses Her Troops, 9 August 1588

ELIZABETH I

Elizabeth's speech to her land troops gathered at Tilbury, on the Thames below London. Her love of her country and her subjects is manifest.

My Loving People:

We have been perswaded by some that are careful of our safety, to take heed how we commit ourselves to armed multitudes, for fear of treachery; but I assure you, I do not desire to live to distrust my faithful and loving people.

Let tyrants fear; I have always so behaved myself that, under God, I have placed my chiefest strength and safeguard in the loyal hearts and good will of my subjects, and therefore I am come amongst you, as you see, at this time, not for my recreation and disport, but being resolved in the midst and heat of the battle to live or die amongst you all, to lay down for my God and for my kingdoms and for my people, my honour and my blood, even in the dust.

I know I have the body but of a weak and feeble woman; but I have the heart and stomach of a king, and of a king of England, too; and think foul scorn that Parma [Duke of Parma] or Spain or any prince of Europe should dare to invade the borders of my realm; to which rather than any dishonour should grow by me, I myself will take up arms, I myself will be your general, judge, and rewarder of every one of your virtues in the field . . .

The 'famous victory' was near at hand. The Armada, beaten in battle at Gravelines on 28–29 July, had fled to the North Sea, where it escaped the English (who gave up the chase due to lack of gunpowder, food and water, the dehydrated mariners obliged to drink their own urine) only to enter the clutches of merciless weather. Slinking around Scotland and down past the coast of Donegal, the Armada lost a greater toll to gales than it had to English guns. Only eighty-six ships of the Armada reached the safety of Santander. Philip II went into mourning for the 9,000 dead.

Protestant England, meanwhile, celebrated with prayers of thanksgiving. Not one English ship had been sunk or captured in the Armada engagement. 'God breathed and they were scattered' was the motto struck on the Armada victory medal.

The Torturing of a Jesuit Priest in the Tower of London, 14–15 April 1597

FATHER JOHN GERARD

The Counter-Reformation's efforts against Protestant England were not limited to military means. English Jesuit priests, trained at Douai, were infiltrated into the country, to wage theological war. Gerard was betrayed by a servant.

On the third day the warder came to my room straight from his dinner. Looking sorry for himself, he said the Lords Commissioners had arrived with the Queen's Attorney-General and that I had to go down to them at once.

'I am ready,' I said, 'but just let me say an *Our Father* and *Hail Mary* downstairs.'

He let me go, and then we went off together to the Lieutenant's lodgings inside the walls of the Tower. Five men were there waiting for me, none of whom, except Wade, had examined me before. He was there to direct the charges against me.

The Attorney-General took out a sheet of paper and solemnly began to write out a form of juridical examination. They put no questions about individual Catholics – they were all about political matters – and I answered on the general lines I had always done before. I said that matters of state were forbidden to Jesuits and consequently I never had anything to do with them; if they wanted confirmation they had it. I had been in prison now three years and had been examined time and time again, and they had not produced a scrap of writing or a single trustworthy witness to show that I had taken part in any activities against the Government.

Then they asked me about the letters I had recently received from our Fathers abroad; and I realized for the first time why I had been removed to the Tower. I answered, 'If I have ever received any letters from abroad at any time, they have had nothing to do with politics. They were concerned merely with the financial assistance of Catholics living on the Continent.'

'Didn't you receive a packet a short time ago,' said Wade, 'and hand it over to so and so to give to Henry Garnet?'

'If I have received any such packet and forwarded it, I did what I was bound to do. But, I repeat, the only letters I have received or forwarded are those, as I have said, dealing with the despatch of money to religious and students on the Continent.'

'Very well,' they said, 'then tell us the name of the man you gave the letters to, and where he lives.'

'I don't know, and even if I did, I could not and would not tell you,' and I gave them the usual reasons for this answer.

'You say,' said the Attorney-General, 'you have no wish to obstruct the Government. Tell us, then, where Father Garnet is. He is an enemy of the state, and you are bound to report on all such men.'

'He isn't an enemy of the state,' I said. 'On the contrary, I am certain that if he were given the opportunity to lay down his life for his Queen and country, he would be glad of it. But I don't know where he lives, and if I did, I would not tell you.'

'Then we'll see to it that you tell us before we leave this place.'

'Please God, you won't,' I answered.

Then they produced a warrant for putting me to torture. They had it ready by them and handed it to me to read. (In this prison a special warrant is required for torture.)

I saw that the warrant was properly made out and signed, and then I answered, 'With God's help I shall never do anything that is unjust or act against my conscience or the Catholic faith. You have me in your power. You can do with me what God allows you to do – more you cannot do.'

Then they began to implore me not to force them to take steps they were loath to take. They said they would have to put me to the torture every day, as long as my life lasted, until I gave them the information they wanted.

'I trust in God's goodness,' I answered, 'that He will prevent me from ever committing a sin such as this – the sin of accusing innocent people. We are all in God's hands and therefore I have no fear of anything you can do to me.'

This was the sense of my answers, as far as I can recall them now.

We went to the torture room in a kind of solemn procession, the attendants walking ahead with lighted candles.

The chamber was underground and dark, particularly near the entrance. It was a vast place and every device and instrument of human torture was there. They pointed out some of them to me and said that I would try them all. Then they asked me again whether I would confess.

'I cannot,' I said.

I fell on my knees for a moment's prayer. Then they took me to a big upright pillar, one of the wooden posts which held the roof of this huge underground chamber. Driven in to the top of it were iron staples for supporting heavy weights. Then they put my wrists into iron gauntlets and ordered me to climb two or three wicker steps. My arms were then lifted up and an iron bar was passed through the rings of one gauntlet, then through the staple and rings of the second gauntlet. This done, they fastened the bar with a pin to prevent it slipping, and then, removing the wicker steps one by one from under my feet, they left me hanging by my hands and arms fastened above my head. The tips of my toes, however, still touched the ground, and they had to dig away the earth from under them. They had hung me up from the highest staple in the pillar and could not raise me any higher, without driving in another staple.

Hanging like this I began to pray. The gentlemen standing around asked me whether I was willing to confess now.

'I cannot and I will not,' I answered.

But I could hardly utter the words, such a gripping pain came over me. It was worst in my chest and belly, my hands and arms. All the blood in my body seemed to rush up into my arms and hands and I thought that blood was oozing out from the ends of my fingers and the pores of my skin. But it was only a sensation caused by my flesh swelling above the irons holding them. The pain was so intense that I thought I could not possibly endure it, and added to it, I had an interior temptation. Yet I did not feel any inclination or wish to give them the information they wanted. The Lord saw my weakness with the eyes of His mercy, and did not permit me to be tempted beyond my strength. With the temptation He sent me relief. Seeing my agony and the struggle going on in my mind, He gave me this most merciful thought: the utmost and worst they can do to you is to kill you, and you have often wanted to give your life for your Lord God. The Lord God sees all you are enduring – He can do all things. You are in God's keeping. With these thoughts, God in His infinite goodness and mercy gave me the grace of resignation, and, with a desire to die and a hope (I admit) that I would, I offered Him myself to do with me as He wished. From that moment the conflict in my soul ceased, and even the physical pain seemed much more bearable than before, though I am sure it must, in fact, have been greater with the growing strain and weariness of my body.

When the gentlemen present saw that I was not answering their questions, they went off to the Lieutenant's house, and stayed there. Every now and again they sent to find out how things were going with me.

Three or four robust men remained behind to watch and supervise the torture, and also my warder. He stayed, I think, out of kindness, for every few minutes he took a cloth and wiped the perspiration that ran in drops continuously down my face and whole body. That helped me a little, but he added to my sufferings when he started to talk. He went on and on, begging and imploring me to pity myself and tell the gentlemen what they wanted to know. And he urged so many human reasons for this that I thought that the devil instigated him to feign this affection or that my torturers had left him behind on purpose to trick me. But I felt all these suggestions of the enemy like blows in the distance: they did not seem to touch my soul or affect me in any way. More than once I interrupted him, 'Stop this talk, for heaven's sake. Do you think I'm going to throw my soul away to save my life? You exasperate me.'

But he went on. And several times the others joined in.

'You will be a cripple all your life if you live. And you are going to be tortured every day until you confess.'

But I prayed in a low voice as well as I could, calling on the names of Jesus and Mary.

Some time after one o'clock, I think, I fell into a faint. How long I was unconscious I don't know, but I don't think it was long, for the men held my body up or put the wicker steps under my feet until I came to. Then they heard me pray and immediately they let me down again. And they did this every time I fainted – eight or nine times that day – before it struck five.

After four or before five o'clock Wade returned. Coming to me he asked, 'Are you ready now to obey the Queen and her Council?'

I answered, 'You want me to do what is sinful. I will not do it.'

'All you have to say,' said Wade, 'is that you wish to speak to Cecil, Her Majesty's Secretary.'

'I have nothing to say to him,' I said, 'except what I have said to you already. If I asked to speak to him, people would be scandalized. They would think I had given way, that at last I was going to say something that I should not say.'

In a rage he suddenly turned his back on me and strode out of the room, shouting angrily in a loud voice, 'Then hang there until you rot off the pillar.'

He left. And I think all the Commissioners left the Tower then, for at five o'clock the Tower bell is rung, a signal for all to leave unless they want to have the gates locked on them. A little later they took me down. My legs and feet were not damaged, but it was a great effort to stand upright.

They led me back to my cell. On the way we met some prisoners who had the run of the Tower, and I turned to speak to my warder, intending them to overhear.

'What surprises me,' I said, 'is that the Commissioners want me to say where Father Garnet's house is. Surely they know it is a sin to betray an innocent man? I will never do it, even if I have to die.'

I said this to prevent them spreading a report, as they so often do, that I had confessed something. And I also wanted word to get round through these men that it was chiefly concerning Father Garnet that I had been questioned, so that he might get to hear and look to his own safety. I saw that the warder was not pleased at my talking in their hearing, but that made no difference to me.

When I reached my cell the man seemed really sorry for me. He laid a fire and brought me some food, as it was now nearly supper time. But I could eat only a little; and I lay down on my bed and rested quietly until the morning.

In the morning after the gates of the Tower were opened, my warder came up to say that Wade had arrived and that I had to go down and see him. I put on a cloak with wide sleeves – I could not get my swollen hands through the sleeves of my own gown – and I went down.

When I entered the Lieutenant's house, Wade said to me, 'I have been sent here in the name of the Queen and her Secretary, Cecil. They say they know for certain that Garnet meddles in politics and is a danger to the State. And this the Queen asserts on the word of a Sovereign and Cecil on his honour. Unless you choose to contradict them both, you must agree to hand him over.'

'They cannot be speaking from experience,' I answered, 'or from any reliable information; they don't know the man. I have lived with him and know him well, and I can say for certain that he is not that kind of man.'

'Come,' said Wade, 'why not admit the truth and answer our questions?'

'I cannot,' I said, 'and I will not.'

'It would be better for you if you did,' and saying this he called out to a gentleman waiting in the next room. He was a well-built man whom Wade called 'Master of Torture'. I knew such an officer existed, but I found out later that this was not the man. He was Master of the Artillery. Wade gave him this title to terrorize me.

'By order of the Queen and Council,' he addressed this gentleman, 'I hand this man over to you. You are to torture him twice today and twice every day until he confesses.'

The man took charge of me. Wade left. In the same way as before we went to the torture chamber.

The gauntlets were placed on the same part of my arms as last time. They would not fit anywhere else, because the flesh on either side had swollen into small mounds, leaving a furrow between; and the gauntlets could only be fastened in the furrow. I felt a very sharp pain when they were put on.

But God helped me and I gladly offered Him my hands and my heart. I was hung up in the same way as before, but now I felt a much severer pain in my hands but less in my chest and belly. Possibly this was because I had eaten nothing that morning.

I stayed like this and began to pray, sometimes aloud, sometimes to myself, and I put myself in the keeping of Our Lord Jesus and His blessed Mother. This time it was longer before I fainted, but when I did they found it so difficult to bring me round that they thought that I was dead, or certainly dying, and summoned the Lieutenant. I don't know how long he was there or how long I remained in a faint. But when I came to myself, I was no longer hanging but sitting on a bench with men supporting me on either side. There were many people about, and my teeth had been forced open with a nail or some iron instrument and hot water had been poured down my throat.

When the Lieutenant saw that I could speak he said, 'Don't you see how much better for you it would be if you submitted to the Queen instead of dying like this?'

God helped me and I was able to put more spirit into my answer than I had felt up to now.

'No, no I don't!' I said. 'I would prefer to die a thousand times rather than do as they suggest.'

'So you won't confess, then?'

'No, I won't,' I said. 'And I won't as long as there is breath left in my body.'

'Very well, then, we must hang you up again now, and a second time after dinner.'

He spoke as though he were sorry to have to carry out his orders.

'*Eamus in nomine Domini,*' I said. 'I have only one life, but if I had several I would sacrifice them all for the same cause.'

I struggled to my feet and tried to walk over to the pillar but I had to be helped. I was very weak now and if I had any spirit left in me it was given by God and given to me, although most unworthy, because I shared the fellowship of the Society.

I was hung up again. The pain was intense now, but I felt great consolation of soul, which seemed to me to come from a desire of death. Whether it arose from a true love of suffering for Christ, or from a selfish longing to be with Christ, God knows best. But I thought then that I was going to die. And my heart filled with great gladness as I abandoned myself to His will and keeping and condemned the will of men. Oh! that God would grant me the same spirit always, though I am sure that in His eyes it was far from a perfect spirit, for my life was to be longer than I then thought, and God gave me time to make it more perfect in His sight, since, it seems, I was not then ready.

Perhaps the Governor of the Tower realized he would gain nothing by torturing me any longer; perhaps it was his dinner hour or maybe he was moved with genuine pity for me; whatever the reason, he ordered me to be taken down. It seemed that I had been hanging only an hour in this second period today. Personally, I believe he was moved by compassion, for some time after my escape a gentleman of position told me that he had heard Sir Richard Berkeley, this same Lieutenant, say that he had freely resigned his office because he no longer wished to be an instrument in such torture of innocent men. At all events it is a fact that he did resign, and only three or four months after his appointment. His place was taken by another knight and it was under him that I escaped.

My warder brought me back to my room. His eyes seemed swollen with tears. He assured me that his wife, whom I had never seen, had wept and prayed for me all the time.

He brought me some food. I could eat little, and the little I did eat he had to cut up into small pieces. For many days after I could not hold a knife in my hands – that day I could not even move my fingers or help myself in the smallest way. He had to do everything for me. But in spite of this on orders from the authorities he took away my knife, scissors and razors. I thought they must be afraid that I would attempt suicide, but I later learned that they always do this in the Tower when a prisoner is under warrant for torture.

Gerard escaped from the Tower six months later by swinging over Tower Ditch on a rope, and became one of the Gunpowder Plotters. For the last ten years of his life he was Director of the English College in Rome.

A Meeting with Queen Elizabeth, 1598

PAUL HENTZNER

The meeting took place at Greenwich. Hentzner was a German visitor to England.

Elizabeth, the reigning Queen of England, was born at the royal palace of Greenwich, and here she generally resides, particularly in summer, for the delightfulness of its situation. We were admitted by an order, which Mr Rogers had procured from the Lord Chamberlain, into the presence-chamber hung with rich tapestry, and the floor, after the English fashion, strewed with hay, through which the Queen commonly passes in her way to chapel. At the door stood a gentleman dressed in velvet, with a gold chain, whose office was to introduce to the Queen any person of distinction that came to wait on her. It was Sunday, when there is usually the greatest attendance of nobility. In the same hall were the Archbishop of Canterbury, the Bishop of London, a great number of counsellors of state, officers of the crown, and gentlemen, who waited the Queen's coming out, which she did from her own apartment when it was time to go to prayers, attended in the following manner: –

First went gentlemen, barons, earls, knights of the Garter, all richly dressed and bareheaded; next came the Lord High Chancellor of England, bearing the seals in a red silk purse, between two, one of whom carried the royal sceptre, the other the sword of state in a red scabbard, studded with golden fleur-de-lis, the point upwards; next came the Queen, in the 65th year of her age (as we were told), very majestic; her face oblong, fair but wrinkled; her eyes small, yet black and pleasant; her nose a little hooked, her lips narrow, and her teeth black (a defect the English seem subject to, from their too great use of sugar); she had in her ears two pearls with very rich drops; her hair was of an auburn colour, but false; upon her head she had a small crown, reported to be made of some of the gold of the celebrated Luneburg table; her bosom was uncovered, as all the English ladies have it till they marry; and she had on a necklace of exceeding fine jewels; her hands were slender, her fingers rather long, and her stature neither tall nor low; her air was stately, her manner of speaking mild and obliging. That day she was dressed in white silk, bordered with pearls of the size of beans, and over it a mantle of black silk shot with silver threads; her train was very long, the end of it borne by a marchioness; instead of a chain, she had an oblong collar of gold and jewels. As she went along in all this state and magnificence, she spoke very graciously, first to one, then to another (whether foreign ministers, or those who attend for different reasons), in English, French and Italian: for besides being well skilled in Greek, Latin and the languages I have mentioned, she is mistress of Spanish, Scotch and Dutch. Whoever speaks to her, it is kneeling; now and then she raises some with her hand. While we were there, William Slawata, a Bohemian baron, had letters to present to her; and she, after pulling off her glove, gave him her right hand to kiss, sparkling with rings and jewels – mark of particular favour. Wherever she turned her face as she was going along, everybody fell down on their knees. The ladies of the court followed next to her, very handsome and well-shaped, and for the most part dressed in white. She was guarded on each side by the gentlemen pensioners, fifty in number, with gilt halberds. In the ante-chapel, next the hall where we were, petitions were presented to her, and she received them most graciously, which occasioned the acclamation of *God save the Quene Elizabeth*! She answered it with *I thancke you myn good peupel*. In the chapel was excellent music; as soon as it and the service were over, which scarcely exceeded half-an-hour, the Queen returned in the same state and order, and prepared to go to dinner. But while she was still at prayers, we saw her table set out with the following solemnity: –

A gentleman entered the room bearing a rod, and along with him another who had a table-cloth, which after they had both knelt three times, with the utmost veneration, he spread upon the table, and after kneeling again they both retired. Then came two others, one with the rod again, the other with a salt-cellar, a plate and bread; when they had knelt as the others had done, and placed what was brought upon the table, they too retired with the same ceremonies performed by the first. At last came an unmarried lady of extraordinary beauty (we were told that she was a countess) and along with her a married one, bearing a tasting-knife; the former was dressed in white silk, who, when she had prostrated herself three times, in the most graceful manner, approached the table and rubbed the plates with bread and salt with as much awe as if the Queen had been present. When they had waited there a little while, the yeomen of the guard entered, bareheaded, clothed in scarlet, with a golden rose upon their backs, bringing in at each turn a course of twenty-four dishes, served in silver most of it gilt; these dishes were received by a gentleman in the same order as they were brought and placed upon the table, while the lady-taster gave to each of the guard a mouthful to eat of the particular dish he had brought, for fear of any poison. During the time that this guard, which consists of the tallest and stoutest men that can be found in all England, 100 in number, being carefully selected for this service, were bringing dinner, twelve trumpets and two kettle-drums made the hall ring for half-an-hour together. At the end of all this ceremonial, a number of unmarried ladies appeared, who with particular solemnity lifted the meat off the table, and conveyed it into the Queen's inner and more private chamber, where after she had chosen for herself, the rest goes to the ladies of the court. The Queen dines and sups alone with very few attendants; and it is very seldom that any body, foreigner or native, is admitted at that time, and then only at the intercession of some distinguished personage.

The Age of Shakespeare: Theatregoing, 1599–1613

THOMAS PLATTER AND SIR HENRY WOTTON

William Shakespeare (1564–1616), born in Stratford-upon-Avon, joined the Lord Chamberlain's Men as an actor and playwright by 1592. In 1598 he became one of the landlords of the new Globe Theatre. Before the Elizabethan age, with its purpose-built stages, plays had been performed in the courtyards of inns.

Thomas Platter, a visitor to London from Basel, attended a performance of Shakespeare's Julius Caesar *in 1599.*

After dinner on the 21st of September, at about two o'clock, I went with my companions over the water, and in the strewn roof-house saw the tragedy of the first Emperor Julius with at least fifteen characters very well acted. At the end of the comedy they danced according to their custom with extreme elegance. Two in men's clothes and two in women's gave this performance, in wonderful combination with each other. On another occasion, I also saw after dinner a comedy, not far from our inn, in the suburb; if I remember right, in Bishopsgate. Here they represented various nations, with whom on each occasion an Englishman fought for his daughter, and overcame them all except the German, who won the daughter in fight. He then sat down with him, and gave him and his servant strong drink, so that they both got drunk, and the servant threw his shoe at his master's head and they both fell asleep. Meanwhile the Englishman went into the tent, robbed the German of his gains, and thus he outwitted the German also. At the end they danced very elegantly both in English and in Irish fashion. And thus every day at two o'clock in the afternoon in the city of London two and sometimes three comedies are performed, at separate places, wherewith folk make merry together, and whichever does best gets the greatest audience. The places are so built, that they play on a raised platform, and every one can well see it all. There are, however, separate galleries and there one stands more comfortably and moreover can sit, but one pays more for it. Thus anyone who remains on the level standing pays only one English penny: but if he wants to sit, he is let in at a further door, and there he gives another penny. If he desires to sit on a cushion in the most comfortable place of all, where he not only sees everything well, but can also be seen, then he gives yet another English penny at another door. And in the pauses of the comedy food and drink are carried round amongst the people, and one can thus refresh himself at his own cost.

The comedians are most expensively and elegantly apparelled, since it is customary in England, when distinguished gentlemen or knights die, for nearly the finest of their clothes to be made over and given to their servants, and as it is not proper for them to wear such clothes but only to imitate them, they give them to the comedians to purchase for a small sum.

What they can thus produce daily by way of mirth in the comedies, every one knows well, who has happened to see them acting or playing . . .

With such and many other pastimes besides the English spend their time; in the comedies they learn what is going on in other lands, and this happens without alarm, husband and wife together in a familiar place, since for the most part the English do not much use to travel, but are content ever to learn of foreign matters at home, and ever to take their pastime.

Sir Henry Wotton recounts the famous burning down of the Globe during a production of the Bard's Henry VIII *on 29 June 1613.*

Now to let matters of state sleep, I will entertain you at the present with what has happened this week at the Bank's side. The King's players had a new play, called *All is True*, representing some principal pieces of the reign of Henry VIII, which was set forth with many extraordinary circumstances of pomp and majesty, even to the matting of the stage; the Knights of the Order with their Georges and garters, the Guards with their embroidered coats, and the like: sufficient in truth within a while to make greatness very familiar, if not ridiculous. Now, King Henry making a masque at the Cardinal Wolsey's house, and certain chambers being shot off at his entry, some of the paper, or other stuff, wherewith one of them was stopped, did light on the thatch, where being thought at first but an idle smoke, and their eyes more attentive to the show, it kindled inwardly, and ran round like a train, consuming within less than an hour the whole house to the very grounds. This was the fatal period of that virtuous fabric, wherein yet nothing did perish but wood and straw, and a few forsaken cloaks; only one man had his breeches set on fire, that would perhaps have broiled him, if he had not by the benefit of a provident wit put it out with bottle ale.

The Death of Elizabeth, 24 March 1603

LADY SOUTHWELL

Lady Southwell was one of Elizabeth's ladies-in-waiting. The Cecil mentioned (and to whom Elizabeth directed her legendary temper) was Robert Cecil, who succeeded his father, William Cecil, as the queen's first minister. Elizabeth died at Richmond Palace, Surrey.

Now falling into extremity, she sat two days and three nights upon her stool, ready dressed, and could never be brought by any of her council, to go to bed, or eat, or drink: only, my lord admiral one time persuaded her to drink some broth. For any of the rest, she would not answer them to any question; but said softly to my lord admiral's earnest persuasions, that, if he knew what she had seen in her bed, he would not persuade her as he did. And secretary Cecil, overhearing her, asked if her majesty had seen any spirits; to which she said she scorned to answer him to so idle a question. Then he told her how, to content the people, her majesty must go to bed: to which she smiled, wonderfully contemning him, saying that the word *must* was not to be used to princes; and thereupon said, 'Little man, little man, if your father had lived, ye durst not have said so much: but thou knowest I must die, and that maketh thee so presumptuous.' And presently, commanding him and the rest to depart from her chamber, she willed my lord admiral to stay; to whom she shook her head, and, with a pitiful voice, said, 'My lord, I am tied with a chain of iron about my neck.' He alleging her wonted courage to her, she replied, 'I am tied, and the case is altered with me.'

Now being given over by all, and at the last gasp, keeping still her sense in every thing, and giving, ever, when she spake, apt answers (though she spake very seldom, having then a sore throat) she desired to wash it, that she might answer more freely to what the council demanded; which was, to know whom she would have king: – but they, seeing her throat troubled her so much, desired her to hold up her finger, when they named whom liked her. Whereupon they named the king of France – the king of Scotland – at which she never stirred. They named my lord Beauchamp; whereto she said, 'I will have no rascal's son in my seat, but one worthy to be a king.' Hereupon, instantly she died.

The Virgin Queen's appointed successor was in fact James VI of Scotland, the son of her cousin Mary and Lord Darnley. James sat on the English throne as James I.

And so started the Stuart dynasty – arguably the least successful ever to reign over England.

A Sketch of King James I, 1603–23

SIR ANTHONY WELDON

Little of his long rule in impoverished, under-populated Scotland prepared James I (born 1566) for the complexities of managing England, particularly its assertive Parliament, with whom he was soon at loggerheads over the extent of his prerogative. His habit of planting sloppy kisses on the lips of his male favourites like Buckingham ('Christ had his John and I have my George!') disgusted many. As did his coarseness, as did his reckless spending, as did his cutting dead of expansionism, overseas and in the English mind. Like the Pope, he found the new humanist learning – in the works of men like Raleigh and Bacon – seditious.

Weldon was Clerk of the Green Cloth. He was removed from his post when his satire on the Scots was found wrapped in departmental records.

He sided with Parliament in the Civil War.

He was of a middle stature, more corpulent through his clothes than in his body, yet fat enough, his clothes ever being made large and easy, the doublets quilted for stiletto proof, his breeches in great pleats and full stuffed. He was naturally of a timorous disposition, which was the reason of his quilted doublets: his eyes large, ever rolling after any stranger that came into his presence, insomuch as many for shame have left the room, as being out of countenance; his beard was very thin: his tongue too large for his mouth which ever made him speak full in the mouth, and made him drink very uncomely, as if eating his drink, which came out into the cup of each side of his mouth; his skin was as soft as taffeta sarsnet, which felt so, because he never washed his hands, only rubbed his fingers ends slightly with the wet end of a napkin. His legs were very weak, having had (as was thought) some foul play in his youth, or rather before he was born, that he was not able to stand at seven years of age, that weakness made him ever leaning on other men's shoulders: his walk was ever circular, his fingers ever in that walk fiddling about his cod-piece.

He was very temperate in his exercises and in his diet, and not intemperate in his drinking; however, in his old age, at Buckingham's jovial suppers, when he had any turn to do with him, made him sometimes overtaken, which he would the very next day remember and repent with tears; it is true he drank very often, which was rather out of a custom than any delight, and his drinks were of the kind for strength, as Frontinack, Canary, High Country Wine, Tent Wine and Scottish Ale, that, had he not had a very strong brain, might have daily been overtaken, although he seldom drank at any one time above four spoonfuls, many times not above one or two.

He was very constant in all things (his favourites excepted), in which he loved change, yet never cast down any (he once raised) from the height of greatness, though from their wonted nearness and privacy, unless by their own default . . . In his diet, apparel and journeys, he was very constant . . . that the best observing courtier of our time was wont to say, were he asleep seven years, and then awakened, he would tell where the King every day had been, and every dish he had had at table.

He was not very uxorious, though he had a very brave queen that never crossed his designs, nor intermeddled with State affairs, but ever complied with him . . . in the change of favourites; for he was ever best when furthest from his queen, and that was thought to be the first grounds of his often removes, which afterwards proved habitual . . .; he naturally loved not the sight of a soldier, nor of any valiant man . . .

He was very witty, and had as many ready witty jests as any man living, at which he would not smile himself, but deliver them in a grave and serious manner. He was very liberal of what he had not in his own grip, and would rather part with 100 *li.* he never had in his keeping than one twenty shilling piece within his own custody; he spent much, and had much use of his subjects' purses, which bred some clashings with them in parliament, yet would *always* come off, and end with a sweet and plausible close.

For the Puritans, James I committed only one virtue. Following the Hampton Court conference of 1604 he ordered the Authorized Version (or King James Version) of the Bible, a translation into English which became a work of literary art. But it was not just the Puritans James I offended in matters of religion. The Catholics despised him for retaining the penal laws.

The Gunpowder Plot, 5 November 1605

GUY FAWKES

The Gunpowder Plot was a conspiracy to advance the Catholic cause in England by blowing up the king and the Houses of Parliament. A warning given in time to Lord Monteagle foiled the plot, and led to the arrest of the plotters, who were directed by Robert Catesby and included Guy Fawkes.

I confesse, that a practise in generall was first broken unto me, against his Maiestie for reliefe of the Catholic cause, and not invented or propounded by my selfe. And this was first propounded unto me about Easter Last was twelve moneth beyond the seas, in the Lowe Countreys of the *Archdukes* obeissance, by *Thomas Winter*, who came thereupon with mee into England, and there we imparted our purpose to three other Gentlemen more, namely, *Robert Catesby*, *Thomas Percy* and *Iohn Wright*, who all five consulting together of the means how to execute the same, and taking a vow among our selves for secrecie, *Catesby* propounded to have it performed by Gunpowder, and by making a Myne under the upper House of Parliament: which place wee made a choice of the rather because Religion having been unjustly suppressed there, it was fittest that Justice and punishment should be executed there.

This being resolved amongst us, *Thomas Percy* hired an House at Westminster for that purpose, neere adioyning to the Parliament House, and there we begun to make our Myne about the II of December 1604.

The five that first entred into the worke were *Thomas Percy*, *Thomas Catesby*, *Thomas Winter*, *Iohn Wright* and myselfe: and soone after wee tooke another unto us, *Christopher Wright* having Sworne him also, and taken the Sacrament for secrecie.

When we came to the very foundation of the Wall of the House, which was about three yards thicke, and found it a matter of great difficultie, wee tooke unto us another Gentleman *Robert Winter*, in like maner with oath and sacrament as afore said.

It was about Christmas when we brought our myne unto the Wall, and about Candlemas we had wrought the wall halfe through: and whilst they were in working, I stood as Sentinell to descrie any man that came neere, whereof I gave them warning, and so they ceased until I gave notice againe to proceede.

All we seven lay in the House, and had Shot and Powder, being resolved to die in that place before we should yield or be taken. As they were working upon the wall they heard a rushing in the Cellar of remooving of Coales, whereupon we feared we had been discovered: and they sent me to go to the Cellar, who finding that the Coales were a-selling and that the Cellar was to bee let, viewing the commoditie thereof for our purpose, *Percy* went and hired the same for yeerely rent.

We had before this provided and brought into the House twentie Barrels of Powder, which we removed into the Cellar, and covered the same with Billets and Faggots, which were provided for that purpose.

About Easter, the Parliament being prorogued till October next, we dispersed ourselves and I retired into the Low countreys by advice and direction of the rest, as well to aquaint *Owen* with the particulars of the Plot, as also lest by my longer stay I might have growen suspicious, and so have come in question.

In the meantime *Percy* having the key of the Cellar, laide in more Powder and wood into it. I returned about the beginning of September next, and then receiving the key againe of Percy, we brought in more Powder and Billets to cover the same againe, and so I went for a time into the Countrey till the 30 of October.

It was a further resolve amongst us that the same day that this act should have been performed, some other of our Confederates should have surprised the person of Lady Elizabeth the King's eldest daughter, who was kept in Warwickshire at Lo. *Harrington's* house, and presently have her proclaimed as Queen, having a project of a Proclamation ready for that purpose, wherein we made no mention of altering of Religion, nor would have avowed the deede to be ours, until we should have had power enough to make our partie good and then we would have avowed both.

Concerning Duke Charles, the King's second sonne, wee had sundry consultations how to seise on his Person. But because we found no means how to compasse it (the Duke being kept neere London, where we had not Forces y-nough) we resolved to serve our turn with the Lady Elizabeth.

THE NAMES OF OTHER PRINCIPALL PERSONS, THAT WERE MADE PRIVY AFTERWARDS TO THIS HORRIBLE CONSPIRACIE

The Puritans resisted the temptation to blow King James sky-high, and instead began to break away from the Anglican Church, and then England itself.

The Pilgrims Land in New England, 11 November 1620

WILLIAM BRADFORD

On 16 September 1620 the Pilgrim Fathers, a dissident and persecuted Puritan sect, sailed from Plymouth in the Mayflower *for America. They dropped anchor near the present-day Provincetown and explored Cape Cod, before formally establishing Plymouth Colony on 21 December.*

Being thus arrived at Cap-Cod, and necessity calling them to look out a place for habitation (as well as the masters and mariners importunity), they having brought a large ship with them out of England, stowed in quarters in the ship, they now got her out, and set their carpenters to work to trim her up, but being much bruised and shattered in the ship with foul weather, they saw she would be long in mending. Whereupon a few of them tendered themselves, to go by land and discover those nearest places, while the ship was in mending. . . . It was conceived there might be some danger in the attempt, yet seeing them resolute they were permitted to go, being 16 of them well armed under the conduct of Captain Standish. . . . After some hours sailing, it began to snow and rain, and about the middle of the afternoon, the wind increased, and the sea became very rough; and they broke their rudder, and it was as much as two men could do to steer her with a couple of oars. But their pilot bade them be of good cheer for he saw the harbor, but the storm increasing, and night drawing on, they bore what sail they could to get in, while they could see; but herewith they broke their mast in three pieces and their sail fell overboard, in a very high sea . . .

But a lusty seaman which steered, bade those which rowed if they were men, about with her, or else they were all cast away; which they did with speed, so he bid them be of good cheer, and row justly for there was a fair sound before them, and he doubted not, but they should find one place or other, where they might ride in safety. And though it was very dark, and rained sore; yet in the end they got under the lee of a small island and remained there all that night in safety . . .

But though this had been a day and night of much trouble, and danger unto them; yet God gave them a morning of comfort and refreshing (as usually he does to his children) for the next day was a fair sunshining day, and they found themselves to be on an island secure from the

Indians; where they might dry their stuff, fix their pieces, and rest themselves, and gave God thanks for his mercies, in their manifold deliverances. And this being the last day of the week, they prepared there to keep the Sabbath; on Monday they sounded the harbor, and found it fit for shipping; and marched into the land, and found many cornfields, and little running brooks, a place (as they supposed) fit for situation, at least it was the best they could find, and the season, and their present necessity made them glad to accept of it. So they returned to their ship again with this news to the rest of their people, which did much comfort their hearts . . .

Afterwards [they] took better view of the place, and resolved where to pitch their dwelling; and the 25th day began to erect the first house, for common use to receive them, and their goods . . .

In these hard and difficult beginnings they found some discontents and murmurings arise amongst some, and mutinous speeches and carriages in other; but they were soon quelled, and overcome, by the wisdom, patience, and just and equal carriage of things, by the Governor and the better part which clave faithfully together in the main. But that which was most sad, and lamentable, was, that in two or three months the half of their company died, especially in January and February, being the depth of winter, and wanting houses and other comforts; being infected with the scurvy and other diseases, which this long voyage and their inaccommodate condition had brought upon them; so as there died some times two or three of a day, in the foresaid time; that of one hundred and odd persons scarce fifty remained: and of these in the time of most distress there was but six or seven sound persons; who to their great commendations, be it spoken, spared no pains, night nor day, but with abundance of toil and hazard of their own health, fetched them wood, made them fires, dressed their meat, made their beads, washed their loathsome clothes, clothed and unclothed them. In a word did all the homely, and necessary offices for them, which dainty and queasy stomachs cannot endure to hear named and all this willingly and cheerfully, without any grudging in the least, showing herein their true love unto their friends and brethren. A rare example and worthy to be remembered, two of these seven were Mr William Brewster, their Reverend Elder, and Miles Standish, their Captain and military commander (unto whom myself, and many others were much beholden in our low, and sick condition). . . . And what I have said of these, I may say of many others who died in this general visitation and others yet living; that while they had health . . . or any strength continuing they were not wanting to any that had need of them; and I [doubt] not but their recompense is with the Lord . . .

All this while the Indians came skulking about them, and would sometimes show themselves aloof, but when any approached near them, they would run away; and once they stole away their tools when they had been at work and were gone to dinner. But about the 16th of March a certain Indian came boldly amongst them, and spoke to them in broken English which they could well understand, but marveled at it; at length they understood by discourse with him, that he was not of these parts, but belonged to the eastern parts where some English ships came to fish, with whom he was acquainted, and could name sundry of them by their names, amongst whom he had got his language. He became profitable to them in acquainting them with many things concerning the state of the country in the east parts where he lived . . . of the people here, of their names, number and strength, of their situation and distance from this place, and who was chief amongst them. His name was Samasett; he told them also of another Indian whose name was Squanto, a native of this place, who had been in England and could speak better English than himself. Being after some time of entertainment, and gifts dismissed, a while after he came again, and five more with him, and they brought again all the tools that were stolen away before, and made way for the coming of their great Sachem, called Massasoyt. Who about four or five days after came with the chief of his friends, and other attendance with the aforesaid Squanto. With whom after friendly entertainment, and some gifts given him, they made a peace with him (which has now continued this 24 years) in these terms:

1. That neither he nor any of his, should injure or do hurt, to any of their people.
2. That if any of his, did any hurt to any of theirs; he should send the offender, that they might punish him.
3. That if any thing were taken away from any of theirs, he should cause it to be restored; and they should do the like to his.
4. If any did unjustly war against him, they would aide him; if any did war against them, he should aide them.
5. He should send to his neighbors confederates to certify them of this [treaty], that they might not wrong them [the Pilgrims], but might be likewise comprised in the conditions of peace.
6. That when [Massasoyt's] men came to [the Pilgrims,] they should leave their bows and arrows behind them . . .

They [the Pilgrims] began now to gather in the small harvest they had; and to fit up their houses and dwellings, against winter, being all well recovered in health and strength; and had all things in good plenty, for as some were thus employed in affairs abroad; others were exercised in fishing, about cod, and bass, other fish of which they took good store, of which every family had their portion; all the summer there was no want; and now began to come in store of fowl, as winter approached, of which this place did abound when they came first (but afterward decreased by degrees), and besides water fowl, there was great store of wild turkeys, of which they took many, besides venison etc. Besides they had about a peck of meal a week to a person, or now since harvest, Indian corn to that proportion, which made many afterwards write so largely of their plenty here to their friends in England, which were not fained, but true reports.

A Post-mortem, 1636

WILLIAM HARVEY

Harvey discovered the circulation of blood in the human body, and was physician to both James I and Charles I. Below he performs an autopsy on the body of Thomas Parr, supposedly 154 years old.

The appearance of the body was well nourished, the chest was hairy, and the hair on the forearm was still black although the shins were hairless and smooth.

The genital organs were in good condition, the penis was neither retracted nor thin, nor was the scrotum, as is usual in old persons, distended by any watery hernia, while the testicles were large and sound – so good in fact as not to give the lie to the story commonly told of him that, after reaching his hundredth year, he was actually convicted of fornication and punished. Moreover his wife, a widow, whom he had married in his hundred and twentieth year, in reply to questions, could not deny that he had had intercourse with her exactly as other husbands do, and had kept up the practice to within twelve years of his death.

The chest was broad and full; his lungs were not spongy but, particularly on the right side, were attached to the ribs by fibrous bands. The lungs also were considerably distended with blood as is usual in pulmonary consumption (peri-pneumonia), so much so that before the blood was drawn off, a quantity seemed to become black. To this cause, too, I attributed the bluish colour of the face, and, a little before death, a difficulty in breathing and orthopnoea. As a result, the armpits and chest remained warm long after death. To sum up, there were clearly visible in his dead body this and other signs customarily found in those dying from suffocation. I concluded that he was suffocated, and that death was due to inability to breathe, and a similar report was given to his most Serene Majesty by all the physicians present. Later, when the blood had been drained off and wiped away from the lungs, they were seen to have a quite white and almost milky parenchyma.

The heart was large, thick, and fibrous with a considerable mass of fat around its wall and partition. The blood in the heart was blackish, liquid, and scarcely grumous. Only in the right ventricle were some clots seen.

When the sternum was dissected, the cartilages were not more osseous than in other men, but rather were flexible and soft.

The intestines were in excellent condition, fleshy and vigorous: the stomach was the same. The small intestine appeared muscular, but had some ring-shaped constrictions due to the fact that frequently he ate any kind of food both by day and night without any rules of diet or regular hours for meals. He was quite happy with half-rancid cheese and all kinds of milk dishes, brown bread, small beer, but most usually sour milk. By living frugally and roughly, and without cares, in humble circumstances, he in this way prolonged his life. He had taken a meal about the midnight shortly before his death.

As the biographer John Aubrey, a friend of Harvey's, recalled, when The Circulation of Blood *was published Harvey 'fell mightily in his Practize, and 'twas believed by the vulgar that he was crack-brained . . . With much ado at last, in about 20 or 30 years time, it was received in all the Universities in the world; and Mr [Thomas] Hobbes says in his book* De Corpore, *he is the only man, perhaps, that ever lived to see his owne Doctrine established in his life-time . . .'*

Cromwell in the House of Commons, November 1640

SIR PHILIP WARWICK

James I died of dysentery on 27 March 1625, to be succeeded by his son, Charles I. Although mercifully free of his father's crude personal habits, Charles fatally inherited his absolutism and his Catholicism, which resulted in a head-on collision with the Puritan-tinged Parliament as it marched towards greater democratic government.

Charles would find no more stalwart Parliamentary critic than Oliver Cromwell. Born in Huntingdon in 1599, of minor gentry stock, Oliver Cromwell had undergone a damascene conversion to Puritanism after being, in his words, 'the chief of sinners'. Henceforth, like Puritans all, he believed that Charles I's Catholicism was the devil's mark on England, God's chosen country. The politically well-connected Cromwell (no fewer than nine of his cousins were MPs) was first returned to Parliament for Huntingdon, then in 1640 for Cambridge City. It was in the Long Parliament of that year that the royal courtier, Sir Philip Warwick, first clapped eyes on Farmer Cromwell.

I have no mind to give an ill character of Cromwell, for in his conversation towards me he was ever friendly, though at the latter end of the day, finding me ever incorrigible and having some inducements to suspect me a tamperer, he was sufficiently rigid. The first time that ever I took notice of him was in the very beginning of the Parliament held in November 1640, when I vainly thought myself a courtly young gentleman (for we courtiers valued ourselves much upon our good clothes). I came one morning into the House well clad, and perceived a gentleman speaking (whom I knew not) very ordinarily apparelled, for it was a plain-cloth suit, which seemed to have been made by an ill country tailor: his linen was plain and not very clean, and I remember a speck or two of blood upon his little band, which was not much larger than his collar. His hat was without a hatband. His stature was of good size, his sword stuck close to his side, his countenance swollen and reddish, his voice sharp and untunable, and his eloquence full of fervour, for the subject matter would not bear much of reason, it being in behalf of a servant of Mr Prynne's, who had dispersed libels against the Queen for her dancing and such like innocent and courtly sports: and he aggravated the imprisonment of this man by the Council-Table unto that height that one would have believed the very government itself had been in great danger by it.

Charles I had only called the Long Parliament because he had no other way to raise money. To the king's ire, the Long Parliament proved even more truculent than its forebears. It rejected ship money (a tax imposed by Charles during the Parliament-less 'eleven years' tyranny', 1629–40) as illegal, it impeached the king's ministers Strafford and Laud, and secured a bill preventing its dissolution without its own consent. The Long Parliament also abolished the jury-free Royal Courts, despotically used by Charles to imprison MPs.

In December 1641 Parliament passed by 159 votes to 148 the Grand Remonstrance, which demanded that the king remove all bishops from Parliament, replace his 'evil counsellors' (believed to be planning the reintroduction of Catholicism), and reform the Church in a more Protestant direction.

Predictably, Charles I refused the Grand Remonstrance.

The Attempted Arrest of the Five Members, 4 January 1642

JOHN RUSHWORTH

The breach between Charles I and Parliament became absolute on 4 January 1642 when the king tried to arrest five Members of the House of Commons – Pym, Hampden, Hesilrige, Holles and Strode – for treason.

Rushworth was secretary to the House of Commons and later to Oliver Cromwell.

. . . The said five accused Members this day *after dinner* came into the House, and did appear according to the special Order and Injunction of the House laid upon them yesterday, to give their attendance upon the House, *de die in diem* and their appearance was entred in the Journal.

They were no sooner sate in their places, but the House was informed by one Captain *Langrish*, lately an Officer in Arms in *France*, that he came from among the Officers, and souldiers at *White Hall*, and understanding by them, that his Majesty was coming with a Guard of Military Men, Commanders and Souldiers, to the House of Commons, he passed by them with some difficulty to get to the House before them, and sent in word how near the said Officers and Souldiers were come; Whereupon a certain Member of the House having also private Intimation from the

Countess of *Carlile*, Sister to the Earl of *Northumberland*, that endeavours would be used this day to apprehend the five Members, the House required the five Members to depart the House forthwith, to the end to avoid Combustion in the House, if the said Souldiers should use Violence to pull any of them out. To which Command of the House, four of the said Members yielded ready Obedience, but Mr *Stroud* was obstinate, till Sir *Walter Earle* (his ancient acquaintance) pulled him out by force, the King being at that time entring into the *New Pallace-yard*, in *Westminster*: And as his Majesty came through *Westminster Hall*, the Commanders, Reformadoes, &c. that attended him, made a Lane on both sides the Hall (through which his Majesty passed and came up the Stairs to the House of Commons) and stood before the Guard of Pentioners, and Halberteers, (who also attended the King Person,) and the door of the House of Commons being thrown open, his Majesty entred the House, and as he passed up towards *the Chair* he cast his eye on the Right-hand near the Bar of the House, where Mr *Pym* used to sit, but his Majesty not seeing him there (knowing him well) went up to the Chair, and said, 'By your leave, (Mr Speaker) I must borrow your Chair a little,' whereupon the Speaker came out of the Chair, and his Majesty stept up into it, after he had stood in the Chair a while, casting his Eye upon the Members as they stood up *uncovered*, but could not discern any of the five Members to be there, nor indeed were they easie to be discerned (had they been there) among so many bare Faces all standing up together.

Then his Majesty made this Speech,

'Gentlemen,

I Am sorry for this occasion of coming unto you: Yesterday I sent a Serjeant at Arms upon a very Important occasion to apprehend some that by my command were accused of High Treason, whereunto I did expect Obedience and not a Message. And I must declare unto you here, that albeit, no King that ever was in *England*, shall be more careful of your Priviledges, to maintain them to the uttermost of his power than I shall be; yet you must know that in Cases of Treason, no person hath a priviledge. And therefore I am come to know if any of these persons that were accused are here: For I must tell you Gentlemen, that so long as these persons that I have accused (for no slight Crime but for Treason) are here, I cannot expect that this House will be in the Right way that I do heartily wish it: Therefore I am come to tell you that I must have them wheresoever I find them. Well since I see all the Birds are Flown, I do expect from you, that you shall send them unto me, as soon as they return hither. But I assure you, in the word of a King, I never did intend any Force, but shall proceed against them in a legal and fair way, for I never meant any other.

And now since I see I cannot do what I came for, I think this no unfit occasion to repeat what I have said formerly, That whatsoever I have done in favour, and to the good of my Subjects, I do mean to maintain it.

I will trouble you no more, but tell you I do expect as soon as they come to the House, you will send them to me; otherwise I must take my own Course to find them.'

When the King was looking about the House, the Speaker standing below by the Chair, his Majesty ask'd him, whether any of these persons were in the House? Whether he saw any of them? and where they were? To which the Speaker falling on his Knee, thus Answered.

'*May it please your Majesty*, I Have neither Eyes to see, nor Tongue to speak in this place, but as the House is pleased to direct me, whose Servant I am here, and humbly beg your Majesties Pardon, that I cannot give any other Answer than this, to what your Majesty is pleased to demand of me.'

The King having Concluded his Speech, went out of the House again which was in great disorder, and many Members cried out, aloud so as he might hear them, 'Priviledge! Priviledge!' and forthwith Adjourned till the next Day at One of the Clock . . .

To this day, no sovereign has ever been allowed in the House of Commons.

The failure of Charles' coup, and the mass protests against him on London's streets the following day (the crowds shouted 'Privilege of Parliament!'), persuaded the king to abandon the capital. Since Charles had so readily resorted to physical force, Parliament set about defending itself by passing the Militia Ordinance, calling up country troops.

The Militia Ordinance proved a wise precaution for on 22 August 1642 Charles I raised the royal standard at Nottingham, effectively declaring war on his own country. Much is made of how the ensuing Civil War left families 'by the sword divided', and of course there were personal tragedies, but in truth the main lines of division avoided kin: they were about class, region and religion. Thus the bulk of Parliament's support came from the South and East (more commercially advanced, more populated by the sort of on-the-up gentry and merchants who subscribed literally to the Protestant work ethic), the mainstay of the King's support came from the underdeveloped, Catholic-leaning North and West. His army was heavily dependent on mercenaries.

From the outset the two sides traded inventive invective. The Royalists name-called the Parliamentarians 'Roundheads' (probably after the Puritans' pudding-basin hairstyle), the Parliamentarians insulted the Royalists as 'Malignants' and 'Cavaliers', the latter term taking its raffish and debauched connotations from the person of Prince Rupert of the Rhine, Charles' nephew and General of Horse. According to one mischievous Puritan scribbler, the Cavalier might be identified by his twenty 'Ridiculous Habits and apish Gestures':

1. His hat in fashion like a close-stoolepan.
2. Set on the top of his noddle like a coxcombe.
3. Banded with a calves tail, and a bunch of riband.
4. A feather in his hat, hanging down like a Fox taile.
5. Long haire, with ribands tied in it.
6. His face spotted.
7. His beard on the upper lip, compassing his mouth.
8. His chin thrust out, singing as he goes.
9. His band lapping over before.
10. Great band strings, with a ring tied.
11. A long wasted dubblet unbuttoned half way.
12. Little skirts.
13. His sleeves unbuttoned.
14. In one hand a stick, playing with it, in the other side his cloke hanging.
15. His breeches unhooked ready to drop off.
16. His shirt hanging out.
17. His codpiece open tied at the top with a great bunch of riband.
18. His belt about his hips.
19. His sword swapping between his legs like a Monkeys taile.
20. Many dozen points at knees.

It was a good war for trading words, a less good one in the beginning for the military arts, since the English had not fought a major land campaign for a century. Proof came in the first major engagement of the war.

Civil War: Sir Richard Bulstrode in Action at Edgehill, 23 October 1642

SIR RICHARD BULSTRODE

Bulstrode fought at Edgehill, Warwickshire, for the Royalists, commanded by Charles I and Prince Rupert; the Parliamentarians were led by the Earl of Essex. The opposing sides had about 14,000 men apiece.

Our whole army was drawn up in a body, the horse three deep in each wing, and the foot in the centre six deep. The Prince of Wales' regiment was on the right wing, which was commanded by Prince Rupert, and Colonel Washington was with his dragoons upon our right. In the centre was the infantry, commanded in chief by General Ruthven, and under him, by Sir Jacob Astley. The Earl of Lindsey marched on foot, in the head of the regiment of the royal foot guards, with his son, the Lord Willoughby, and Sir Edmund Verney carried the Royal Standard. The left wing of our horse was commanded by Commissary-General Wilmot, with Lieutenant-Colonel Edward Fielding and some other principal officers; and Lieutenant-Colonel George Lisle, with Lieutenant-Colonel John Ennis were in the left wing, with a regiment of dragoons, to defend the briars on that side, and we had a body of reserve, of six hundred horse, commanded by the Earl of Carnarvon. When our army was drawn up at the foot of the hill and ready to march, all the generals went to the King (who intended to march with the army) and desired he would retire to a rising ground, some distance from thence, on the right, with the Prince of Wales and the Duke of York (having his guard of Pensioners on horseback with him) from whence he might see the issue of the battle and be out of danger, and that otherwise the army would not advance towards the enemy. To which the King (very unwillingly) was at last persuaded.

Just before we began our march, Prince Rupert passed from one wing to the other, giving positive orders to the horse, to march as close as was possible, keeping their ranks with sword in hand, to receive the enemy's shot, without firing either carbine or pistol, till we broke in amongst the enemy, and then to make use of our firearms as need should require, which order was punctually observed.

The enemy stayed to receive us in the same posture as was formerly declared; and when we came within cannon shot of the enemy, they discharged at us three pieces of cannon from their left wing, commanded by Sir James Ramsey; which cannon mounted over our troops, without doing any hurt, except that their second shot killed a quarter-master in the rear of the Duke of York's troop. We soon after engaged each other, and our dragoons on our right beat the enemy from the briars, and Prince Rupert led on our right wing so furiously, that, after a small resistance, we forced their left wing, and were masters of their cannon; and the Prince being extremely eager of this advantage (which he better knew how to take than to keep) was not content with their cannon, and keeping their ground, but eagerly pursued the enemy, who fled on the other side of Kineton towards Warwick. And we of the Prince of Wales' regiment (who were all scattered) pursued also, till we met with two foot regiments of Hampden and Holles, and with a regiment of horse coming from Warwick to their army, which made us hasten as fast back as we had pursued.

In this pursuit I was wounded in the head by a person who turned upon me and struck me with his pole-axe, and was seconding his blow, when Sir Thomas Byron being near, he shot him dead with his pistol, by which means I came back. In fine, by meeting these three regiments, we were obliged to return back to our army and then found our great error, in leaving our foot naked who were rudely handled by the enemy's horse and foot together in our absence, who fell principally upon the King's royal regiment of foot guards, who lost eleven of thirteen colours, the King's Standard-Bearer, Sir Edmund Verney, killed, and the Royal Standard taken, which was presently retaken by Captain John Smith, who was knighted for it that night by the King, under the Standard Royal and made a banneret with the usual ceremonies; and had afterwards a large medal of gold given him, with the King's picture on the one side, and the banner on the other, which he always wore to his dying day, in a large green watered ribband, cross his shoulders . . .

Now, when we returned from following the enemy, the night came soon upon us, whereas, in all probability, we had gained the victory, and made an end of the war, if we had only kept our ground after we had beaten the enemy, and not left our foot naked to their horse and foot. And, to add to our misfortune, a careless soldier, in fetching powder (where a magazine was) clapt his hand carelessly into a barrel of powder, with his match lighted betwixt his fingers, whereby much powder was blown up and many kill'd . . .

On Monday morning, being next after the battle, several parties were sent down to view the dead, the greatest part of the enemy having retired in the night to the town of Kineton, which was near them; and Mr Adrian Scroop having seen his father fall (being much wounded) desired the Duke of Lennox to speak to the King, that one of his coaches might go with him, to bring up his father's body; which being granted, he found his father stripped, with several very dangerous wounds, and that he was alive. Whereupon he lap'd him up in his cloak, and brought him in the coach, where he was presently dressed by the King's chirurgeons, and by their care and skill was cured, and lived many years after, tho' he had seventeen wounds, and had died upon the place, but that the coldness of the weather stopp'd the bleeding of his wounds, which saved also several other men's lives that were wounded.

Prince Rupert's ill-disciplined (cavalier, even) departure from the battlefield in pursuit of the Roundheads into Kineton probably cost the Royalists a victory. As it was, Edgehill ended in a draw, and the King continued on his way towards London – a dubious objective, since the city was solid against him. At Turnham Green, on the capital's fringe, he was met by a 24,000-strong militia, the 'Trained Bands', and with little ado turned around for Oxford, which became the Royalist headquarters.

A year and a half of indecisive skirmish and siege ensued, until Prince Rupert determined to bring the Roundheads to a definitive battle at Marston Moor in Yorkshire.

Unfortunately for the inspired but luckless Rupert, the Roundhead army was bolstered by Parliament's new Scottish allies, secured by the 'Solemn League and Covenant' of 1643. Worse, the Roundheads now boasted a cavalry commander who was Rupert's peer.

Civil War: The Death of a Nephew at Marston Moor, 2 July 1644

OLIVER CROMWELL

Appointed a Captain of Horse at the outset of the Civil War, Oliver Cromwell had early showed his mettle as a soldier but, more importantly for the Parliamentary cause, as a commander of men. Singularly, he had eschewed snobbery, informing his fellow officers that he 'would rather have a plain russet-coated captain that knows what he fights for and loves what he knows, than that which you call a gentlemen and nothing else'. Disciplined and meritocratic, Cromwell's 'Ironsides' had immediately eclipsed the other Parliamentary horse units.

Below Cromwell writes to his brother-in-law, Colonel Valentine Wilson, from the battlefield of Marston Moor. It was Cromwell's surprise charge, late in the moonlit evening, that enabled Parliament to rout the Royalists. Rupert himself, his horse shot from under him, passed the latter stages of the battle hiding ignominiously in a beanfield, before high-tailing it to safety. Behind him he left his poodle dog, Boy, one of the 4,000 Royalist casualties of the day.

It's our duty to sympathize in all mercies; and to praise the Lord together in chastisements or trials, that so we may sorrow together.

Truly England and the Church of God hath had a great favour from the Lord, in this great Victory given unto us, such as the like never was since this War began. It had all the evidences of an absolute Victory obtained by the Lord's blessing upon the Godly Party principally. We never charged but we routed the enemy. The Left Wing, which I commanded, being our own horse, saving a few Scots in our rear, beat all the Prince's horse. God made them as stubble to our swords. We charged their regiments of foot with our horse, and routed all we charged. The particulars I cannot relate now; but I believe, of Twenty-thousand the Prince hath not Four-thousand left. Give glory, all the glory, to God . . .

Sir, God hath taken away your eldest Son by a cannon-shot. It brake his leg. We were necessitated to have it cut off, whereof he died.

Sir, you know my own trials this way: but the Lord supported me with this, That the Lord took him into the happiness we all pant for and live for. There is your precious child full of glory, never to know sin or sorrow any more. He was a gallant young man, exceedingly gracious. God give you His comfort. Before his death he was so full of comfort that to Frank Russel and myself he could not express it, 'It was so great above his pain.' This he said to us. Indeed it was admirable. A little after, he said, One thing lay upon his spirit. I asked him, What that was? He told me it was, That God had not suffered him to be anymore the executioner of His enemies. At his fall, his horse being killed with the bullet, and as I am informed three horses more, I am told he bid them, Open to the right and left, that he might see the rogues run. Truly he was exceedingly beloved in the Army, of all that knew him. But few knew him; for he was a precious young man, fit for God. You have cause to bless the Lord. He is a glorious Saint in Heaven; wherein you ought exceedingly to rejoice. Let this drink up your sorrow; seeing these are not feigned words to comfort you, but the thing is so real and undoubted a truth. You may do all things by the strength of Christ.

Seek that, and you shall easily bear your trial. Let this public mercy to
the Church of God make you to forget your private sorrow. The Lord
be your strength: so prays

  Your truly faithful and loving brother
My love to your Daughter, and my Cousin Perceval, Sister Desborow
and all friends with you.

After Marston Moor, the tide of the Civil War turned resolutely in Parlia-
ment's favour. Cromwell himself rose to become the cavalry commander of the
New Model Army, the Roundhead army remoulded for military efficiency
(through the centralization of command and the ejection of insufficiently resolute
aristocratic officers) and cohered by ideological purpose. Item 1 in the New Model
Army's catechism on soldierly qualities, was: 'That he is religious and godly'.

  Any lingering hope the king had of defeating Parliament in the field was
dashed to death at Naseby, Leicestershire, on 14 June 1645. Inevitably Cromwell
was there, on God's errand, his men fired up on religious fervour. After the
battle, in which Cromwell's right wing had played the key part, Cromwell
reported to William Lenthall, Speaker of the House of Commons: 'We, after
three-hours fight very doubtful routed his [the king's] Army; killed and took
about 5,000 . . . We took also about 200 carriages, all he had; and all his guns,
being 12 in number, whereof two were demi-cannon, two demi-culverins, and I
think the rest sackers. We pursued the Enemy from three miles short of Har-
borough to nine beyond, even to the sight of Leicester, whither the King fled . . .
Sir, this is none other than the hand of God; and to Him alone belongs the
glory, wherein none are to share with him.'

  Eleven months later, with the Royal game up, Charles surrendered to the
Scottish Presbyterians. There was some desultory politicking – whereby Charles
hoped to secure their support, they wanted him to establish Presbyterianism –
before the Scots tired of it and sold the king to Parliament for £400,000. 'Cheap
at the price,' Charles joked.

  Now that the victors had their illustrious man, they squabbled about what to
do. Parliament wanted a restoration of the monarchy, but with a Presbyterian
settlement to the Church; Cromwell's divines in the New Model Army wanted
greater religious toleration and limited changes to the franchise; a left wing in the
Army wanted universal manhood suffrage. (In the memorable words of the radical
'Leveller' spokesman Colonel Rainsborough: 'I think that the poorest he that in
England hath a life to live, as the greatest he . . . that every man that is to live
under a government ought first by his own consent to put himself under that
government.')

  Meanwhile, Charles escaped to the Isle of Wight, and decided that he could, after all, stomach a deal with the Scots whereby Presbyterianism was introduced and they fought for his restoration. Alas for King Charles, the Scots were no match for Cromwell's New Model Army, who sent them packing at Preston in August 1648. Unforgiving of the recaptured king's treasonable dealings with the Scots, Cromwell pressed for the trial of the 'tyrant, traitor, and murderer, Charles Stuart'.

Charles I had unsheathed the sword, and he perished by it.

The Execution of Charles I, 30 January 1649

PHILIP HENRY

Henry was an undergraduate at Christ Church, Oxford.

At the later end of the year 1648 I had leave to goe to london to see my Father, & during my stay there at that time at Whitehal it was that I saw the Beheading of King Charles the first; He went by our door on Foot each day that hee was carry'd by water to Westminster, for he took Barge at Gardenstayres where we liv'd & once he spake to my Father & sayd Art thou alive yet! On the day of his execution, which was Tuesday, Jan. 30, I stood amongst the crowd in the street before Whitehal gate, where the scaffold was erected, and saw what was done, but was not so near as to hear any thing. The Blow I saw given, & can truly say with a sad heart; at the instant whereof, I remember well, there was such a Grone by the Thousands then present, as I never heard before & desire I may never hear again. There was according to Order one Troop immediately marching from-wards charing-cross to Westm^r & another from-wards Westm^r to charing-cross purposely to masker the people, & to disperse & scatter them, so that I had much adoe amongst the rest to escape home without hurt.

In May 1649 England became a republic, with Oliver Cromwell the chairman of the Council of State.

The Storming of Drogheda, 10–11 September 1649

OLIVER CROMWELL

To protect the new Commonwealth of England, Cromwell crossed to Ireland, which was feared to be a potential launch-pad for a Royalist invasion of the mainland. His slaughter of the garrison at Drogheda, a seaport on the Boyne, was controversial then, as now.

It hath pleased God to bless our endeavours at Tredah (Drogheda). After battery, we stormed it. The enemy were about 3,000 strong in the Town. They made a stout resistance; and near 1,000 of our men being entered, the Enemy forced them out again. But God giving a new courage to our men, they attempted again, and entered; beating the enemy from their defences.

The Enemy had made three retrenchments, both to the right and left of where we entered; all which they were forced to quit. Being thus entered, we refused them quarter; having, the day before, summoned the Town. I believe we put to the sword the whole number of the defendants. I do not think Thirty of the whole number escaped with their lives. Those that did, are in safe custody for the Barbadoes. Since that time, the Enemy quitted to us Trim and Dundalk. In Trim they were in such haste that they left their guns behind them.

This hath been a marvellous great mercy. The Enemy, being not without some considerable loss; Colonel Castle being there shot in the head, whereof he presently died; and divers officers and soldiers doing their duty killed and wounded. There was a Tenalia to flanker the south Wall of the Town, between Duleek Gate and the corner Tower before mentioned; – which our men entered, wherein they found some forty or fifty of the Enemy, which they put to the sword. And this 'Tenalia' they held: but it being without the Wall, and the sally-port through the Wall into that Tenalia being choked up with some of the Enemy which were killed in it, it proved of no use for an entrance into the Town that way.

Although our men that stormed the breaches were forced to re-coil, as is before expressed; yet, being encouraged to recover their loss, they made a second attempt; wherein God was pleased so to animate them that they got ground of the enemy, and by the goodness of God, forced him to quit his entrenchments. And after a very hot dispute, the

Enemy having both horse and foot, and we only foot, within the Wall – they gave ground, and our men became masters both of their retrenchments and of the Church; which, indeed, although they made our entrance the more difficult, yet they proved of excellent use to us; so that the Enemy could not now annoy us with their horse, but thereby we had the advantage to make good the ground, that so we might let in our own horse; which accordingly was done, though with much difficulty.

Divers of the Enemy retreated into the Mill-Mount: a place very strong and difficult of access; being exceedingly high, having a good graft, and strong palisadoed. The Governor, Sir Arthur Ashton, and divers considerable Officers being there, our men getting up to them, were ordered by me to put them all to the sword. And indeed, being in the heat of action, I forbade them to spare any that were in arms in the Town; and, I think, that night they put to the sword about 2,000 men; – divers of the officers and soldiers being fled over the Bridge into the other part of the Town, where about 100 of them possessed St Peter's Church-steeple, some the west Gate, and others a strong Round Tower next the Gate called St Sunday's. These being summoned to yield to mercy, refused. Whereupon I ordered the steeple of St Peter's Church to be fired, when one of them was heard to say in the midst of the flames: 'God damn me, God confound me; I burn, I burn.'

The next day, the other two Towers were summoned; in one of which was about six or seven score; but they refused to yield themselves: and we knowing that hunger must compel them, set only good guards to secure them from running away until their stomachs were come down. From one of the said Towers, notwithstanding their condition, they killed and wounded some of our men. When they submitted, their officers were knocked on the head; and every tenth man of the soldiers killed; and the rest shipped for the Barbadoes. The soldiers in the other Tower were all spared, as to their lives only; and shipped likewise for the Barbadoes.

I am persuaded that this is a righteous judgement of God upon these barbarous wretches, who have imbrued their hands in so much innocent blood; and that it will tend to prevent the effusion of blood for the future. Which are the satisfactory grounds to such actions, which otherwise cannot but work remorse and regret. The officers and soldiers of this Garrison were the flower of their army. And their great expectation was, that our attempting this place would put fair to ruin us ... And now give me leave to say how it comes to pass that this work is wrought.

It was set upon some of our hearts, That a great thing should be done, not by power or might, but by the Spirit of God. And is it not so, clearly? That which caused your men to storm so courageously, it was the Spirit of God, who gave your men courage, and took it away again; and gave the Enemy courage, and took it away again; and gave your men courage again, and therewith this happy success. And therefore it is good that God alone have all the glory . . .

Your most obedient servant,

OLIVER CROMWELL.

After Ireland, Cromwell turned his attention to Scotland where Charles I's son had been acclaimed king as Charles II. Cromwell defeated the Scots at Dunbar, and then a Scottish invasion under Charles II at Worcester in September 1651. So ended the Civil War.

Cromwell Purges the Long Parliament, 20 April 1653

BULSTRODE WHITELOCK

By 1653 the Long Parliament had been sitting for thirteen years without re-election. When it began discussion of a law to perpetuate itself, Cromwell dismissed it.

In this manner [accompanied by a troop of soldiers] entering the house, he, in a furious manner, bid the Speaker leave his chair; told the house 'That they had sat long enough, unless they had done more good; that some of them were whoremasters, (looking then towards Henry Martyn and Sir Peter Wentworth) that others of them were drunkards, and some corrupt and unjust men, and scandalous to the profession of the Gospel; and that it was not fit they should sit as a parliament any longer, and desired them to go away.' The Speaker not stirring from his seat, col. Harrison, who sat near the chair, rose up and took him by the arm, to remove him from his seat; which when the Speaker saw, he left his chair. Some of the members rose up to answer Cromwell, but he would suffer none to speak but himself; which he did with so much arrogance in himself, and reproach to his fellow-members, that some of his priva-does were ashamed of it, but he and his officers and party would have it so; and among all the parliament men, of whom many wore swords, and would sometimes brag high, not one man offered to draw his sword against Cromwell, or to make the least resistance against him; but all of them tamely departed the house. He bid one of his soldiers to take away that fool's bauble, the mace, and stayed himself to see all the members out of the house, himself the last of them, and then caused the doors of the house to be shut up.

The ensuing Puritan Convention (the 'Barebones' Parliament') was not to Cromwell's taste either, and was soon dismissed. From 16 December 1653 Cromwell ruled as Lord Protector in what, the occasional calling of a Parliament aside, was a military dictatorship. The other options were Anarchy or the Stuarts.

    The Interregnum is invariably portrayed as a kill-joy tyranny. On the contrary, Cromwell's rule tended to benevolent tolerance ('our chief of men' wasn't fêted by the greatest poet of the age, John Milton, for the money or for want of other subjects) and more importantly it was the making of modern capitalist England. By conquering Scotland and Ireland and placing them under English hegemony, he united the Isles. And then, with the 1651 Navigation Act, he turned the Isles outwards to become a commercial world power, with a world-scale merchant marine, and a big-gun navy to protect it.

Cromwell's Funeral, 23 November 1658

JOHN EVELYN

Cromwell was defeated by bronchitis in September 1658. Evelyn was a High Church Royalist.

Saw the superb funeral of the protector. He was carried from Somerset House in a velvet bed of state, drawn by six horses, housed with the same; the pall held by his new lords; Oliver lying in effigy, in royal robes, and crowned with a crown, sceptre, and globe, like a king. The pendants and guidons were carried by the officers of the army; the imperial banners, achievements, etc., by the heralds in their coats; a rich caparisoned horse, embroidered all over with gold; a knight of honor, armed *cap-a-pie*, and, after all, his guards, soldiers, and innumerable mourners. In this equipage, they proceeded to Westminster: but it was the most joyful funeral I ever saw; for there were none that cried but dogs, which the soldiers hooted away with a barbarous noise, drinking and taking tobacco in the streets as they went.

With Cromwell dead it became starkly obvious that the republic depended almost entirely on his persona. Cromwell's son Richard ('Tumbledown Dick') tried on the mantle of Lord Protector before wisely giving it up as beyond him. A gyre widened. For the want of greater evil, the Army invited the Stuarts back to England.

The Restoration: Charles II Returns to England, 12–25 May 1660

SAMUEL PEPYS

Pepys, a Navy clerk, was appointed secretary to Sir Edward Montague on the expedition to Holland to fetch Charles II from exile. The famous diary, written in shorthand code (partly so that Pepys' wife did not discover his peccadilloes) was not deciphered until 1825.

12 May. My Lord did give order for weighing anchor; which we did, and sailed all day. In our way in the morning, coming in the midway between Dover and Callis, we could see both places very easily, and very pleasant it was to me, but the farther we went the more we lost sight of both lands.

14 May. In the morning, when I waked and rose, I saw myself out of the scuttle close by the shore, which afterwards I was told to be the Duch shore. The Hague was clearly to be seen by us. Some masty Duchmen came on board to proffer their boats to carry things from us on shore &c., to get money by us. Before noon, some gentlemen came on board from the shore to kiss my Lords hands. And by and by Mr North and Dr Clerke went to kiss the Queen of Bohemia's hands from my Lord, with a dozen of attendants from on board to wait on them; among which I sent my boy – who, like myself, is with child to see any strange thing. Mr Creed and I went in the fore-part of a coach, wherein there was two very pretty ladies, very fashionable and with black paches, who very merrily sang all the way and that very well. And were very free to kiss the two blades that were with them. I took out my flagelette and piped. The Hague is a most neat place in all respects. The houses so neat in all places and things as is possible. Here we walked up and down a great while, the town being now very full of Englishmen. We walked up and down the town and Court to see the place; and by the help of a stranger, an Englishman, we saw a great many places and were made to understand many things, as the intention of the maypoles which we saw there standing at every great man's door, of different greatness according to the quality of the person.

18 May. [Delft] is a most sweet town, with bridges and a river in every street. Observing that in every house of entertainment there hangs in every room a poor man's box and desirous to know the reason thereof, it was told me that it is their custom to confirm all bargains by putting something into the poor people's box, and that that binds as fast as anything. We saw likewise the Guesthouse, where it was very pleasant to see what neat preparation there is for the poor. We saw one poor man a–dying there. Back by water, where a pretty sober Duch lass sat reading all the way, and I could not fasten any discourse upon her.

19 May. [At Lausdune] I met my old chamberfellow Mr Ch. Anderson and a friend of his (both physicians), Mr Wright, who took me to a Duch house where there was an exceeding pretty lass and right for the sport; but it being Saturday, we could not have much of her company; but however, I stayed with them till 12 at night; by that time Charles was almost drunk; and then broke up, he resolving to go thither again (after he had seen me at my lodging) and lie with the girl, which he told me he had done in the morning. Going to my lodging, we met with the bell-man, who strikes upon a clapper, which I took in my hand and it is just like the clapper that our boys fright the birds away from the corn with in summer time in England. To bed.

23 May. The King, with the two Dukes [his brothers, the Dukes of York and Gloucester], the Queen of Bohemia [his aunt, Elizabeth, Dowager Queen], Princesse Royalle, and Prince of Orange [his sister Mary and her son, later William III of England], came on board; where I in their coming in kissed the Kings, Queen and Princesses hands, having done the other before. Infinite shooting off of the guns, and that in a disorder on purpose, which was better than if it had been otherwise. Dined in a great deal of state, the royall company by themselves in the coach, which was a blessed sight to see. We weighed ancre, and with a fresh gale and most happy weather we set sail for England – all the afternoon the King walking here and there, up and down (quite contrary to what I thought him to have been), very active and stirring. Upon the quarterdeck he fell in discourse of his escape from Worcester. Where it made me ready to weep to hear the stories that he told of his difficulties that he had passed through. As his travelling four days and three nights on foot, every step up to his knees in dirt, with nothing but a green coat and a pair of country breeches on and a pair of country shoes, that made him so sore all over his feet that he could scarce stir.

25 May. By the morning we were come close to the land and everybody made ready to get on shore. The King and the two Dukes did eat their breakfast before they went, and there being set some shipps diet before them, only to show them the manner of the shipps diet, they eat of nothing else but pease and pork and boiled beef. I spoke with the Duke of York about business, who called me Pepys by name, and upon my desire did promise me his future favour. I went, and Mr Mansell and one of the King's footmen, with a dog that the King loved (which shit in the boat, which made us laugh and me think that a King and all that belong to him are but just as others are) went in a boat by ourselfs; and so got on shore when the King did, who was received by Generall Monke with all imaginable love and respect at his entrance upon the land at Dover. Infinite the croud of people and the gallantry of the horsmen, citizens, and noblemen of all sorts. The Mayor of the town came and gave him his white staffe, the badge of his place, which the King did give him again. The Mayor also presented him from the town a very rich Bible, which he took and said it was the thing that he loved above all things in the world.

The Stuarts might have been allowed back on the throne, but the political clock had not been turned back to the days before Charles I's misuse of power. Parliament considered few, if any, matters outside its purview, especially religion. Charles II wanted toleration for Catholics (and was opportunistically willing to allow it to dissenting Protestants in a quid pro quo*), and in response Parliament passed the Clarendon Code, which set up an Anglican monopoly. When the king tried again with the Declaration of Indulgence, Parliament responded with the Test Act, which barred Catholics from public office. Parliament's suspicion of Catholicism was well-founded: it was the religion of the absolutist powers which surrounded England.*

Charles II's reign began with euphoria and descended into gloominess, as a series of disasters beset the nation.

Journal of the Plague Year, 1665

JOHN EVELYN

The Great Plague, which began in London in late 1664, was the last major outbreak of bubonic pestilence in England. Over 68,000 Londoners died.

Diary 1665, July 7. To London, to Sir William Coventrie; and so to Sion, where his Majesty sat at Council during the contagion; when business was over, I viewed that seat belonging to the Earl of Northumberland, built out of an old Nunnery, of stone, and fair enough, but more celebrated for the garden than it deserves; yet there is excellent wall-fruit, and a pretty fountain; nothing else extraordinary.

16. There died of the plague in London this week 1,100, and in the week following above 2,000. Two houses were shut up in our parish.

Aug. 2. A solemn fast through England to deprecate God's displeasure against the land by pestilence and war; our Dr preaching on 26 Levit: 41, 42. That the means to obtain remission of punishment was not to repine at it, but humbly submit to it.

8. I waited on the D. of Albemarle, who was resolved to stay at the Cock-pit in St James's Park. Died this week in London 4,000.

15. There perished this week 5,000.

28. The contagion still increasing and growing now all about us, I sent my wife and whole family (two or three necessary servants excepted) to my brother's at Wotton, being resolved to stay at my house myself and to look after my charge, trusting in the providence and goodness of God.

Sept. 5. To Chatham to inspect my charge, with £900 in my coach.

7. Came home, there perishing near 10,000 poor creatures weekly; however I went all along the City and suburbs from Kent Street to St James's, a dismal passage, and dangerous to see so many coffins exposed in the streets, now thin of people; the shops shut up, and all in mournful silence, as not knowing whose turn might be next. I went to the Duke of Albemarle for a pest-ship, to wait on our infected men, who were not a few.

October 1. This afternoon, whilst at evening prayers, tidings were brought me of the birth of a daughter at Wotton, after six sons, in the same chamber I had first took breath in, and at the first day of that month, as I was on the last, 45 years before.

4. The monthly fast.

11. To London, and went through the whole City, having occasion to alight out of the coach in several places about business of money, when I was environed with multitudes of poor pestiferous creatures begging alms; the shops universally shut up, a dreadful prospect! I dined with my Lord General; was to receive £10,000 and had guards to convey both myself and it, and so returned home, through God's infinite mercy.

31. I was this day 45 years of age, wonderfully preserved, for which I blessed God for his infinite goodness towards me.

November 23. Went home, the contagion having now decreased considerably.

The Great Fire of London, 2 September 1666

SAMUEL PEPYS

2 September. Lords Day. Some of our maids sitting up late last night to get things ready against our feast today, Jane called us up, about 3 in the morning, to tell us of a great fire they saw in the City. So I rose, and slipped on my nightgown and went to her window, and thought it to be on the back side of Markelane at the furthest; but being unused to such fires as fallowed, I thought it far enough off, and so went to bed again and to sleep. About 7 rose again to dress myself, and there looked out at the window and saw the fire not so much as it was, and further off. So to my closet to set things to rights after yesterday's cleaning. By and by Jane comes and tells me that she hears that above 300 houses have been burned down tonight by the fire we saw, and that it was now burning down all Fishstreet by London Bridge. So I made myself ready presently, and walked to the Tower and there got up upon one of the high places, Sir J. Robinsons little son going up with me; and there I did see the houses at that end of the bridge all on fire, and an infinite great fire on this and the other side the end of the bridge – which, among other people, did trouble me for poor little Michell and our Sarah on the Bridge. So down, with my heart full of trouble, to the Lieutenant of the Tower, who tells me that it begun this morning in the King's bakers house in Pudding Lane, and that it hath burned down St Magnes Church and most part of Fishstreete already. So I down to the waterside and there got a boat and through bridge, and there saw a lamentable fire. Poor Michells house, as far as the Old Swan, already burned that way and the fire running further, that in a very little time it got as far as the Stillyard while I was there. Everybody endeavouring to remove their goods, and flinging into the river or bringing them into lighters that lay off. Poor people staying in their houses as long as till the very fire touched them, and then running into boats or clambering from one pair of stair by the waterside to another. And among other things, the poor pigeons I perceive were loath to leave their houses, but hovered about the windows and balconies till they were some of them burned, their wings, and fell down.

Having stayed, and in an hour's time seen the fire rage every way, and nobody to my sight endeavouring to quench it, but to remove their goods and leave all to the fire; and having seen it get as far as the Steeleyard, and the wind mighty high and driving it into the city, and everything, after so long a drought, proving combustible, even the very stones of churches. I to Whitehall with a gentleman with me who desired to go off from the Tower to see the fire in my boat – to Whitehall, and there up to the King's closet in the chapel, where people came about me and I did give them an account dismayed them all; and word was carried in to the King, so I was called for and did tell the King and Duke of York what I saw, and that unless his Majesty did command houses to be pulled down, nothing could stop the fire. They seemed much troubled, and the King commanded me to go to my Lord Mayor from him and command him to spare no houses but to pull down before the fire every way. The Duke of York bid me tell him that if he would have any more soldiers, he shall. Here meeting with Captain Cocke, I in his coach, which he lent me, and Creed with me, to Pauls; and there walked along Watling Street as well as I could, every creature coming away loaden with goods to save – and here and there sick people carried away in beds. Extraordinary good goods carried in carts and on backs. At last met my Lord Mayor in Canning Streete, like a man spent, with a hankercher about his neck. To the King's message, he cried like a fainting woman, 'Lord, what can I do? I am spent! People will not obey me. I have been pull[ing] down houses. But the fire overtakes us faster than we can do it.' That he needed no more soldiers; and that for himself, he must go and refresh himself, having been up all night. So he left me, and I him, and walked home – seeing people all almost distracted and no manner of means used to quench the fire. The houses too, so very thick thereabouts, and full of matter for burning, as pitch and tar, in Thames Street – and warehouses of oyle and wines and brandy and other things. Here I saw Mr Isaccke Houblon, that handsome man –

prettily dressed and dirty at his door at Dowgate, receiving some of his brothers things whose houses were on fire; and as he says, have been removed twice already, and he doubts (as it soon proved) that they must be in a little time removed from his house also – which was a sad consideration. And to see the churches all filling with goods, by people who themselfs should have been quietly there at this time.

As soon as dined, I and Moone away and walked through the City, the streets full of nothing but people and horses and carts loaden with goods, ready to run over one another, and removing goods from one burned house to another – they now removing out of Canning Street (which received goods in the morning) into Lumbard Streete and further. We parted at Pauls, he home and I to Pauls Wharf, where I had appointed a boat to attend me; and took in Mr Carcasse and his brother, whom I met in the street, and carried them below and above bridge, to and again, to see the fire, which was now got further, both below and above, and no likelihood of stopping it. Met with the King and Duke of York in their barge, and with them to Queen Hith and there called Sir Rd. Browne to them. Their order was only to pull down houses apace, and so below bridge at the waterside; but little was or could be done, the fire coming upon them so fast. Good hopes there was of stopping it at the Three Cranes above, and at Buttolphs Wharf below bridge, if care be used; but the wind carries it into the City, so as we know not by the waterside what it doth there. River full of lighter[s] and boats taking in goods, and good goods swimming in the water; and only, I observed that hardly one lighter or boat in three that had the goods of a house in, but there was a pair of virginalls in it. Having seen as much as I could now, I away to Whitehall by appointment, and there walked to St James's Park, and there met my wife and Creed and Wood and his wife and walked to my boat, and there upon the water again, and to the fire up and down, it still increasing and the wind great. So near the fire as we could for smoke; and all over the Thames, with one's face in the wind you were almost burned with a shower of firedrops – this is very true – so as houses were burned by these drops and flakes of fire, three or four, nay five or six houses, one from another. When we could endure no more upon the water, we to a little alehouse on the Bankside over against the Three Cranes, and there stayed till it was dark almost and saw the fire grow; and as it grow darker, appeared more and more, and in corners and upon steeples and between churches and houses, as far as we could see up the hill of the City, in a most horrid malicious bloody flame, not like the fine flame of an ordinary fire. We stayed till, it being darkish, we saw the fire as only one entire arch of fire from this to the other side the bridge, and in a bow up the hill, for an arch of above a mile long. It made me weep to see it. The churches, houses, and all on fire and flaming at once, and a horrid noise the flames made, and the cracking of houses at their ruine.

Some 13,000 buildings were destroyed by the Fire, and 100,000 people made homeless. The cost of rebuilding was over £10 million.

Isaac Newton Experiments on Light, Cambridge, 1666

SIR ISAAC NEWTON

Principally remembered for his discoveries in mathematics and gravity, Newton (1642–1727) was also a pioneering researcher in 'Opticks'. His experiments at Cambridge refracting sunlight through a prism eventually led to the construction of reflecting telescopes.

I procured me a Triangular glass-Prisme, to try therewith the celebrated *Phaenomena of Colours*. And in order thereto having darkened my chamber, and made a small hole in my window-shuts, to let in a convenient quantity of the Suns light, I placed my Prisme at his entrance, that it might be thereby refracted to the opposite wall. It was at first a very pleasing divertisement, to view the vivid and intense colours produced thereby; but after a while applying myself to consider them more circumspectly, I became surprised to see them in an *oblong* form; which, according to the received laws of Refraction, I expected should have been *circular*.

And I saw that the light, tending to [one] end of the Image, did suffer a Refraction considerably greater than the light tending to the other. And so the true cause of the length of that Image was detected to be no other, then that *Light* consists of *Rays differently refrangible*, which, without any respect to a difference in their incidence, were, according to their degrees of refrangibility, transmitted towards divers parts of the wall.

Then I placed another Prisme . . . so that the light . . . might pass through that also, and be again refracted before it arrived at the wall. This done, I took the first Prisme in my hand and turned it to and fro slowly about its *Axis*, so much as to make the several parts of the Image

. . . successively pass through . . . that I might observe to what places on the wall the second Prisme would refract them.

When any one sort of Rays hath been well parted from those of other kinds, it hath afterwards obstinately retained its colour, notwithstanding my utmost endeavours to change it.

I have refracted it with Prismes, and reflected with it Bodies which in Day-light were of other colours; I have intercepted it with the coloured film of Air interceding two compressed plates of glass; transmitted it through coloured Mediums, and through mediums irradiated with other sorts of Rays, and diversely terminated it; and yet could never produce any new colour out of it.

But the most surprising, and wonderful composition was that of *Whiteness*. There is no one sort of Rays which alone can exhibit this. 'Tis ever compounded, and to its composition are requisite all the aforesaid primary Colours, mixed in a due proportion. I have often with Admiration beheld, that all the Colours of the Prisme being made to converge, and thereby to be again mixed, reproduced light, intirely and perfectly white.

Hence therefore it comes to pass, that *Whiteness* is the usual colour of *Light*; for, Light is a confused aggregate of Rays indued with all sorts of Colours, as they are promiscuously darted from the various parts of luminous bodies.

The Great Frost Fair, 24 January 1684

JOHN EVELYN

Before the embankment was built in the nineteenth century, the Thames froze over in severe winters. In 1676 and 1684 ice fairs were held on the river in London.

The frost continuing more and more severe, the Thames before London was still planted with boothes in formal streetes, all sortes of trades and shops furnish'd and full of commodities, even to a printing presse, where the people and ladyes tooke a fancy to have their names printed, and the day and yeare set down when printed on the Thames: this humour tooke so universally, that 'twas estimated the printer gain'd £5 a day, for printing a line onely, at sixpence a name, besides what he got by ballads, &c. Coaches plied from Westminster to the Temple, and from several other staires to and fro, as in the streetes, sleds, sliding with skeetes, a bull-baiting, horse and coach races, puppet plays and interludes, cookes, tipling, and other lewd places, so that it seem'd to be a bacchanalian triumph or carnival on the water, whilst it was a severe judgement on the land, the trees not onely splitting as if lightning-struck, but men and cattle perishing in divers places, and the very seas so lock'd up with ice, that no vessels could stir out or come in. The fowles, fish, and birds, and all our exotiq plants and greenes universally perishing. Many parkes of deer were destroied, and all sorts of fuell so deare that there were great contributions to preserve the poore alive. Nor was this severe weather much less intense in most parts of Europe, even as far as Spaine and the most southern tracts. London, by reason of the excessive coldnesse of the aire hindering the ascent of the smoke, was so filled with the fuliginous steame of the sea-coale, that hardly could one see crosse the streets, and this filling the lungs with its grosse particles, exceedingly obstructed the breast, so as one could hardly breath. Here was no water to be had from the pipes and engines, nor could the brewers and divers other tradesmen worke, and every moment was full of disastrous accidents.

The Glorious Revolution: William of Orange Enters, James II Exits, November–December 1688

JOHN EVELYN

Charles II died in 1685, after confirming his subjects' fears by professing the Catholic faith on his deathbed. He was succeeded by his brother, James II. Quite apart from his not very secret Catholicism, James II had all the old inclinations to absolutism. The English, he said, should 'follow his wishes blindly'.

Instead, the English set about finding a replacement for King James, one who could guarantee a Protestant succession and their liberties. On 30 June 1688 an invitation to become King of England was sent to the Dutchman William of Orange, the husband of James II's daughter Mary, and a definite, dyed-in the-wool Protestant. William's fleet set sail for England on 19 October.

November 5th. I went to London; heard the news of the prince [William of Orange] having landed at Torbay, coming with a fleet of near 700 sail, passing through the Channel with so favourable a wind, that our navy could not intercept, or molest them. This put the King and Court into great consternation, they were now employed in forming an army to stop their further progress, for they were got into Exeter, and the season and ways very improper for his Majesty's forces to march so great a distance.

The Archbishop of Canterbury and some few of the other Bishops and Lords in London, were sent for to Whitehall, and required to set forth their abhorrence of this invasion. They assured his Majesty they had never invited any of the Prince's party, or were in the least privy to it, and would be ready to show all testimony of their loyalty; but, as to a public declaration, being so few, they desired that his Majesty would call the rest of their brethren and Peers, that they might consult what was fit to be done on this occasion, not thinking it right to publish any thing without them, and till they had themselves seen the Prince's Manifesto, in which it was pretended he was invited in by the Lords Spiritual and Temporal. This did not please the King; so they departed.

A Declaration was published, prohibiting all persons to see or read the Prince's Manifesto, in which was set forth at large the cause of his expedition, as there had been one before from the States.

These are the beginnings of sorrow, unless God in His mercy prevent it by some happy reconciliation of all dissensions among us. This, in all likelihood, nothing can effect except a free Parliament; but this we cannot hope to see, whilst there are any forces on either side. I pray God to protect and direct the King for the best and truest interest of his people – I saw his Majesty touch for the evil, Piten the Jesuit, and Warner officiating.

14th. The Prince increases every day in force. Several Lords go in to him. Lord Cornbury carries some regiments, and marches to Honiton, the Prince's headquarters. The City of London in disorder; the rabble pulled down the nunnery newly bought by the Papists of Lord Berkeley, at St John's. The Queen prepares to go to Portsmouth for safety, to attend the issue of this commotion, which has a dreadful aspect.

18th. It was now a very hard frost. The King goes to Salisbury to rendezvous the army, and return to London. Lord Delamere appears for the Prince in Cheshire. The nobility meet in Yorkshire. The Archbishop of Canterbury and some Bishops, and such Peers as were in London, address his Majesty to call a Parliament. The King invites all foreign nations to come over. The French take all the Palatinate, and alarm the Germans more than ever.

29th. I went to the Royal Society. We adjourned the election of a

President to 23rd April, by reason of the public commotions, yet dined together as of custom this day.

2nd December. Dr Tenison preached at St Martin's on Psalm xxxvi. 5, 6, 7, concerning Providence. I received the blessed Sacrament. Afterwards, visited my Lord Godolphin, then going with the Marquis of Halifax and Earl of Nottingham as Commissioners to the Prince of Orange; he told me they had little power. Plymouth declared for the Prince. Bath, York, Hull, Bristol, and all the eminent nobility and persons of quality through England, declare for the Protestant religion and laws, and go to meet the Prince, who every day sets forth new Declarations against the Papists. The great favourites at Court, Priests and Jesuits, fly or abscond. Every thing, till now concealed, flies abroad in public print, and is cried about the streets. Expectation of the Prince coming to Oxford. The Prince of Wales and great treasure sent privily to Portsmouth, the Earl of Dover being Governor. Address from the Fleet not grateful to his Majesty. The Papists in offices lay down their commissions, and fly. Universal consternation amongst them; it looks like a revolution.

7th. My son went towards Oxford. I returned home.

9th. Lord Sunderland meditates flight. The rabble demolished all Popish chapels, and several Papist lords' and gentlemen's houses, especially that of the Spanish Ambassador, which they pillaged, and burnt his library.

13th. The King flies to sea, puts in at Feversham for ballast; is rudely treated by the people; comes back to Whitehall.

The Prince of Orange is advanced to Windsor, is invited by the King to St James's, the messenger sent was the Earl of Feversham, the General of the Forces, who going without trumpet, or passport, is detained prisoner by the Prince, who accepts the invitation, but requires his Majesty to retire to some distant place, that his own guards may be quartered about the Palace and City. This is taken heinously, and the King goes privately to Rochester; is persuaded to come back; comes on the Sunday; goes to mass, and dines in public, a Jesuit saying grace (I was present).

17th. That night was a Council; his Majesty refuses to assent to all the proposals; goes away again to Rochester.

18th. I saw the King take barge to Gravesend at twelve o'clock – a sad sight! The Prince comes to St James's, and fills Whitehall with Dutch guards. A Council of Peers meet about an expedient to call a Parliament; adjourn to the House of Lords. The Chancellor, Earl of Peterborough, and divers others taken. The Earl of Sunderland flies; Sir Edward Hales, Walker, and others, taken and secured.

All the world go to see the Prince at St James's, where there is a great Court. There I saw him, and several of my acquaintance who came over with him. He is very stately, serious, and reserved. The English soldiers sent out of town to disband them; not well pleased.

24th. The King passes into France, whither the Queen and child were gone a few days before.

26th. The Peers and such Commoners as were members of the Parliament at Oxford, being the last of Charles II, meeting, desire the Prince of Orange to take on him the disposal of the public revenue till a convention of Lords and Commons should meet in full body, appointed by his circular letters to the shires and boroughs, 22nd January. I had now quartered upon me a Lieutenant-Colonel and eight horses.

30th. This day prayers for the Prince of Wales were first left off in our church.

The Revolution of 1688 was 'Glorious' because it melded together anti-Catholic Whigs and Stuart-friendly Tories in a settlement that avoided bloodshed. (If, that is, one exempts James' slaughterous defeat two years later by William of Orange at the Battle of the Boyne, Ireland.) By the terms of the Glorious Settlement England got a Protestant monarch – two, in fact, since William III and Mary II ruled jointly – who agreed to a 'Declaration of Rights' which curtailed the royal prerogative and established a parliamentary monarchy. In an age of absolutism, this was no small achievement. Furthermore, it was the beginning of party politics, for no monarch could rule without majority support in Parliament.

William and Mary's reign brought stability, the foundation of the Bank of England, control of a standing army vested in Parliament and a widening in the freedom of the press.

But no viable heir. Of course, it probably did not help that William was syphilitic and bisexual, and Mary sapphically inclined. 'If you do not come some time today, dear husband [sic],' Mary wrote to her friend Lady Frances Apsley, 'that I may have my belly full of discourse with you, I shall take it very ill . . .'

Thus in 1702 the throne passed to Mary's sister, Anne.

Blenheim: The Victor's View, Bavaria, 13 August 1704

JOHN CHURCHILL, DUKE OF MARLBOROUGH

The Stuarts saved the best till last. Queen Anne (reigned 1702–14), memorably described as 'one of the smallest people ever set in a great place', was devoutly Protestant, self-consciously English, and had supported the Glorious Revolution against her father. In Queen Anne's name were won England's greatest victories on land since Crécy and Agincourt.

In 1701 England joined the War of the Spanish Succession, whereby Protestant Europe combined to prevent the union of France and Spain. John Churchill, Duke of Marlborough, was Captain General of the English army. At Blenheim on the river Danube, 50,000 English and Austrian troops encountered 60,000 Franco-Bavarian troops.

Sir: I gave you an account on Sunday last of the situation we were then in, and that we expected to hear the enemy would pass the Danube at Lawringen, in order to attack Prince Eugene at eleven of the clock that night. We had an express from him, that the enemy were come, and desiring he might be reinforced as soon as possible. Whereupon I ordered my Brother Churchill to advance at one of the clock in the morning with his two battalions, and by three the whole Army was in motion; for the greater expedition, I ordered part of the troops to pass over the Danube, and follow the march of the twenty battalions; and with most of the Horse and the Foot of the First Line, I passed the Lech at Rain, and came over the Danube at Donawert. So that we all joined the prince that night, intending to advance and take this Camp at Hochstet: in order whereto we went out early on Tuesday with forty squadrons to view the ground, but found the enemy had already possessed themselves of it.

Whereupon we resolved to attack them, and accordingly we marched between three and four yesterday morning from the Camp at Munster, leaving all our tents standing. About six we came in view of the enemy, who, we found, did not expect so early an onset. The cannon began to play about half an hour after eight. They formed themselves in two bodies, the Elector with Monsieur Marsin and their troops on our right, and Monsieur de Tallard with all his on our left; which last fell to my share; they had two rivulets, besides a morass before them which we were obliged to pass over in their view, and Prince Eugene was forced to take a great compass to come to the enemy, so that it was one of the clock before the battle began. It lasted with great vigour till sunset, when the enemy were obliged to retire, and by the blessing of God we obtained a complete victory.

We have cut off great numbers of them, as well in the action as in the retreat, besides upwards of twenty squadrons of the French, which I pushed into the Danube, where we saw the greater part of them perish. Monsieur Tallard, with several of his general officers being taken prisoners at the same time, and in the village of Blenheim, which the enemy had entrenched and fortified, and where they made the greatest opposition, I obliged twenty-six entire battalions, and twelve squadrons of dragoons, to surrender themselves prisoners at discretion. We took likewise all their tents standing, with their cannon and ammunition, as also a great number of standards, kettle-drums, and colours in the action, so that I reckon the greatest part of Monsieur Tallard's army is taken or destroyed.

The bravery of all our troops on this occasion cannot be expressed, the Generals, as well as the officers and soldiers, behaving themselves with the greatest courage and resolution. The horse and dragoons were obliged to charge four or five several times. The Elector and Monsieur de Marsin were so advantageously posted, that Prince Eugene could make no impression on them, till the third attack, near seven at night, when he made a great slaughter of them. But being near a woodside, a great body of Bavarians retired into it, and the rest of that army retreated towards Lawringen, it being too late, and the troops too much tired to pursue them far.

I cannot say too much in praise of that Prince's good conduct, and the bravery of his troops on this occasion. You will please to lay this before her Majesty and his Royal Highness, to whom I send my Lord Tunbridge with the good news. I pray you likewise inform yourself, and let me know her Majesty's pleasure, as well relating to Monsieur Tallard and the other general officers, as for the disposal of near one thousand two hundred other officers, and between eight and nine thousand common soldiers, who being all made prisoners by her Majesty's troops, are entirely at her disposal: but as the charge of subsisting these officers and men must be very great, I presume her Majesty will be inclined that they be exchanged for any other prisoners that offer.

I should likewise be glad to receive her Majesty's directions for the disposal of the standards and colours, whereof I have not yet the number, but guess there cannot be less than one hundred, which is more than has been taken in any battle these many years.

You will easily believe that, in so long and vigorous an action, the English, who had so great a share in it, must have suffered as well in officers as men; but I have not the particulars.

I am, Sir,

Your most obedient,

humble servant,

Marlborough.

From the camp at Hochstet

A rapturously grateful nation built Blenheim Palace in Oxfordshire for Marl-borough, who went on to back-to-back victories at Ramillies, Oudenarde and Malplaquet.

The momentous events of Queen Anne's England were not restricted to Marlborough's battles. Following the death of her only surviving son (she bore and lost seventeen children), she signed the Act of Settlement which designated the Hanoverians her successors. When the Scots objected, Scotland was brought into union with England (or, rather, under England; the Scottish Parliament was closed down) in 1707. Thus was Great Britain formed.

Bath under the Code of Beau Nash, c. 1710

OLIVER GOLDSMITH

The dandy Richard 'Beau' Nash introduced the code of exquisitely polite manners and fashion that ruled English upper-class society throughout the eighteenth century. He also established Bath as the leading English spa town. Yet the benefits of Bath were not confined to the aristocracy; they were widely enjoyed by a large middle class whose habit of conspicuous consumption would become a defining characteristic of English society.

The novelist Goldsmith was Nash's biographer.

Upon a stranger's arrival at Bath he is welcomed by a peal of the Abbey Bells, and, in the next place, by the voice and music of the city waits. For these civilities, the ringers have generally a present made them of half-a-guinea, and the waits of half-a-crown, or more, in proportion to the person's fortune, generosity, or ostentation. These customs, though disagreeable, are however, liked or they would not continue. The greatest incommodity attending them is the disturbance the bells must give the sick. But the pleasure of knowing the name of every family that comes to town recompenses the inconvenience. Invalids are fond of news, and upon the first sound of the bells everybody sends out to inquire for whom they ring.

After the family is thus welcomed to Bath, it is the custom for the master of it to go to the public places, and subscribe two guineas at the assembly-houses towards the balls and music in pump-house, for which he is entitled to three tickets every ball night. His next subscription is a crown, half-a-guinea, or a guinea, according to his rank and quality, for the liberty of walking in the private walks belonging to Simpson's assembly-house; a crown or half-a-guinea is also given to the booksellers, for which the gentleman is to have what books he pleases to read at his lodgings, and at the coffee-house another subscription is taken for pen, ink, and paper, for such letters as the subscriber shall write at it during his stay. The ladies, too, may subscribe to the booksellers, and to a house by the pump-room, for the advantage of reading the news, and for enjoying each other's conversation.

Things being thus adjusted, the amusements of the day are generally begun by bathing, which is no unpleasing method of passing away an hour or so.

The baths are five in number. On the south-west side of the Abbey Church is the King's Bath, which is an oblong square; the walls are full of niches, and at every corner are steps to descend into it: this bath is said to contain 427 tons and 50 gallons of water; and on its rising out of the ground over the springs, it is sometimes too hot to be endured by those who bathe therein. Adjoining to the King's Bath, there is another, called the Queen's Bath; this is of a more temperate warmth, as borrowing its water from the other.

In the south-west part of the city are three other baths, viz: the Hot Baths, which is not much inferior in heat to the King's Bath, and contains 53 tons, 2 hogsheads, and 11 gallons of water; the Cross Bath, which contains 52 tons, 3 hogsheads, and 11 gallons; and the Leper's Bath, which is not so much frequented as the rest.

The King's Bath (according to the best observations) will fill in about nine hours and a half; the Hot Bath in about eleven hours and a half; and the Cross Bath in about the same time.

The hours for bathing are commonly between six and nine in the morning, and the baths are every morning supplied with fresh water; for when the people have done bathing, the sluices in each bath are pulled up, and the water is carried off by drains into the River Avon.

In the morning the lady is brought in a close chair, dressed in her bathing clothes, to the bath; and, being in the water, the woman who attends presents her with a little floating dish like a basin; into which the lady puts a handkerchief, a snuff-box, and a nosegay. She then traverses the bath; if a novice, with a guide; if otherwise, by herself; and having amused herself thus while she thinks proper, calls for her chair; and returns to her lodgings.

The amusement of bathing is immediately succeeded by a general assembly of people at the pump-room; some for pleasure, and some to drink the hot waters. Three glasses at three different times is the usual portion for every drinker; and the intervals between every glass are enlivened by the harmony of a small band of music, as well as by the conversation of the gay, the witty, or the forward.

From the pump-room the ladies, from time to time, withdraw to a female coffee-house, and from thence return to their lodgings to breakfast. The gentlemen withdraw to their coffee-houses, to read the papers, or converse on the news of the day, with a freedom and ease not to be found in the metropolis.

People of fashion make public breakfasts at the assembly-houses, to which they invite their acquaintances, and they sometimes order private concerts; or, when so disposed, attend lectures on the arts and sciences, which are frequently taught there in a pretty superficial manner, so as not to tease the understanding, while they afford the imagination some amusement. The private concerts are performed in the ball-rooms; the tickets a crown each.

Concert breakfasts at the assembly-houses sometimes make also a part of the morning's amusement here, the expenses of which are defrayed by a subscription among the men. Persons of rank and fortune who can perform are admitted into the orchestra, and find a pleasure in joining with the performers.

Thus we have the tedious morning fairly over. When noon approaches, and church (if any please to go there) is done, some of the company appear upon the parade, and other public walks, where they continue to chat and amuse each other, till they have formed parties for the play, cards, or dancing for the evening. Another part of the company divert themselves with reading in the booksellers' shops, or are generally seen taking the air and exercise, some on horseback, some in coaches. Some walk in the meadows round the town, winding along the side of the River Avon and the neighbouring canal; while others are seen scaling some of those romantic precipices that overhang the city.

   When the hour of dinner draws nigh, and the company are returned from their different recreations, the provisions are generally served with the utmost elegance and plenty. Their mutton, butter, fish, and fowl, are all allowed to be excellent, and their cookery still exceeds their meat.

   After dinner is over, and evening prayers ended, the company meet a second time at the pump-house. From this they retire to the walks, and from thence go to drink tea at the assembly-houses, and the rest of the evenings are concluded either with balls, plays, or visits. A theatre was erected in the year 1705, by subscription, by people of the highest rank, who permitted their arms to be engraven on the inside of the house, as a public testimony of their liberality towards it. Every Tuesday and Friday evening is concluded with a public ball, the contributions to which are so numerous, that the price of each ticket is trifling. Thus Bath yields a continued rotation of diversions, and people of all ways of thinking, even from the libertine to the methodist, have it in their power to complete the day with employments suited to their inclinations.

Cock-fighting, London, 18 June 1710

ZACHARIAS VON UFFENBACH

Von Uffenbach was a German visitor and book-collector.

In the afternoon we went to see the cockfighting. This is a sport peculiar to the English, which appears to foreigners very foolish in spite of the pleasure this people takes in it. A special building has been made for it near 'Gras Inn'. When a fight is going to take place, printed bills are distributed and sometimes invitations to fanciers appear in the news-sheets as well as notices of the amount of the wagers and the number and species of cocks that are to fight. The building is round like a tower, and inside it resembles a 'theatrum anatomicum', for all round it there are benches in tiers, on which the spectators sit. In the middle is a round table, which is covered with mats, on which the cocks have to fight. When it is time to start, the persons appointed to do so bring in the cocks hidden in two sacks, and then everyone begins to shout and wager before the birds are on view. The people, gentle and simple (they sit with no distinction of place) act like madmen, and go on raising the odds to twenty guineas and more. As soon as one of the bidders calls 'done' (it is done or let it be thus), the other is pledged to keep to his bargain. Then the cocks are taken out of the sacks and fitted with silver spurs, such as we bought. As soon as the cocks appear, the shouting grows even louder and the betting is continued. When they are released, some attack, while others run away from, the rest, and, as we ourselves saw, are impelled by terror to jump down from the table among the people; they are then, however, driven back on the table with great yells (in particular by those who have put their money on the lively cocks which chase the others) and are thrust at each other until they get angry. Then it is amazing to see how they peck at each other, and especially how they hack with their spurs. Their combs bleed terribly and they often slit each other's crop and abdomen with the spurs. There is nothing more diverting than when one seems quite exhausted and there are great shouts of triumph and monstrous wagers; and then the cock that appeared to be quite done for suddenly recovers and masters the other. When one of the two is dead, the conqueror invariably begins to crow and to jump on the other, and it often happens that they sing their paean before the victory and the other wins after all. Sometimes, when both are exhausted and neither will attack the other again, they are removed and others take their place; in this case the wagers are cancelled. But if one of them wins, those who put their money on the losing cock have to pay immediately, so that an hostler in his apron often wins several guineas from a Lord. If a man has made a bet and is unable to pay, for a punishment he is made to sit in a basket fastened to the ceiling, and is drawn up in it amidst peals of laughter. The people become as heated about their betting as the cocks themselves. And I must confess that it is certainly more diverting if one bets oneself, though my brother and I have never wagered anything more than shillings. We watched seven couple fight in turn.

Bad King George I, 1714–1727

JOHN H. JESSE

Jesse's description of the first Hanoverian King of England, from the author's Memoirs of the Court of England, *hardly exaggerates.*

A foreigner as he was, in all his tastes and habits; ignorant, debauched, and illiterate; inelegant in his person and ungraceful in his manners, he had never condescended to acquaint himself with the laws or customs of the English, and was, indeed, utterly unacquainted with their language. In addition to these drawbacks, though he was now in his fifty-fifth year, he had the folly and wickedness to encumber himself with a seraglio of hideous German prostitutes, who rendered him equally ludicrous by their absurdities, and unpopular by their rapacity . . . It may be remarked . . . that, with the single exceptions of social pleasantry and constitutional good-humour, he seems to have been possessed of no redeeming quality which reflected dignity on him as a monarch, or rendered him amiable as a man. Profligate in his youth and libidinous in old age, he figures through life as a bad husband, a bad father, and, in as far as England is concerned, a bad king. He wanted even those graceful qualifications of the Stuarts, a love for polite literature and the fine arts; he possessed no taste for the one, and extended no patronage to the other. The only thing he seems to have had a regard for was his own ease; the only being he hated heartily was, probably, his own son. Many of these unamiable characteristics were unquestionably owing to his indifferent education; for, notwithstanding his wrong-headiness, he is said to have meant well.

Although George I (born 1660) never won the hearts of his subjects, the dismissive ease with which the 1715 and 1719 risings of the Jacobites (supporters of the line of the deposed James II) were suppressed clearly showed the English preference for the Lutheran Hanoverian monarchy.

Public Executions at Tyburn, c. 1725

C. DE SAUSSURE

César de Saussure was a Swiss tourist.

Some time after my arrival in London I witnessed a spectacle which certainly was not as magnificent or as brilliant as the Lord Mayor's Show; it is true it was quite a different kind of entertainment. I saw thirteen criminals all hanged at the same time. It will interest you, no doubt, to know something about justice in England, how it is practised, how criminals are punished, in what manner they are executed, as here it is done in quite a different way to what it is in other countries.

The day before the execution those who desire it may receive the sacrament, provided the chaplain thinks that they have sincerely repented and are worthy of it. On the day of execution the condemned prisoners, wearing a sort of white linen shirt over their clothes and a cap on their heads, are tied two together and placed on carts with their backs to the horses' tails. These carts are guarded and surrounded by constables and other police officers on horseback, each armed with a sort of pike. In this way part of the town is crossed, and Tyburn, which is a good half-mile from the last suburb, is reached, and here stands the gibbet. One often sees criminals going to their death perfectly unconcerned, others so impenitent that they fill themselves full of liquor and mock at those who are repentant. When all the prisoners arrive at their destination they are made to mount on a very wide cart made expressly for the purpose, a cord is passed round their necks and the end fastened to the gibbet, which is not very high. The chaplain who accompanies the condemned men is also on the cart; he makes them pray and sing a few verses of the Psalms. The relatives are permitted to mount the cart and take fare-well. When the time is up – that is to say about a quarter of an hour – the chaplain and the relations get off the cart, which slips from under the condemned men's feet, and in this way they remain all hanging together. You often see friends and relations tugging at the hanging men's feet so that they should die quicker and not suffer. The bodies and clothes of the dead belong to the executioner; relatives must, if they wish for them, buy them from him, and unclaimed bodies are sold to surgeons to be dissected. You see most amusing scenes between the people who do not like the bodies to be cut up and the messengers the surgeons have sent for the bodies; blows are given and returned before they can be got away, and sometimes in the turmoil the bodies are quickly removed and buried. Again, the populace often come to blows as to who will carry the bought corpses to the parents who are waiting in coaches and cabs to receive them, for the carriers are well paid for their trouble. All these scenes are most diverting, the noise and confusion is unbelievable, and can be witnessed from a sort of amphitheatre erected for spectators near the gibbet.

John Wesley Preaches, 19 March 1742

JOHN WESLEY

Wesley was the founder of Methodism, an evangelical offshoot of the Anglican Church. Following his conversion in 1738, he spent fifty-one years open-air preaching, in the process walking upwards of 250,000 miles and delivering 40,000 sermons. Wesley died in 1791, aged eighty-eight.

I rode once more to Pensford, at the earnest request of several serious people. The place where they desired me to preach was a little green spot near the town. But I had no sooner begun, than a great company of rabble, hired (as we afterwards found) for that purpose, came furiously upon us, bringing a bull which they had been baiting and now drove in among the people. But the beast was wiser than his drivers, and continually ran either on one side of us or the other, while we quietly sang praise to God and prayer for about an hour. The poor wretches finding themselves disappointed, at length seized upon the bull, now weak and tired after being so long torn and beaten both by dogs and men, and by main strength partly dragged and partly thrust him in among the people. When they had forced their way to the little table on which I stood, they strove several times to throw it down by thrusting the helpless beast against it, who of himself stirred no more than a log of wood. I once or twice put aside his head with my hand, that the blood might not drop upon my clothes, intending to go on as soon as the hurry should be a little over. But the table falling down, some of our friends caught me in their arms and carried me right away on their shoulders, while the rabble wreaked their vengeance on the table which they tore bit from bit. We went a little way off, where I finished my discourse without any noise or interruption.

Bonnie Prince Charlie Invades Manchester, 28–29 November 1745

ELIZABETH BYROM

Charles Edward Stuart ('Bonnie Prince Charlie'), grandson of James II, led the last Stuart attempt to regain the throne of England. Landing in Scotland in July 1745, he raised an army of Highlanders and Jacobites, before marching south.

28 (Thursday). About three o'clock today came into town two men in Highland dress, and a woman behind one of them with a drum on her knee, and for all the loyal work that our Presbyterians have made, they took possession of the town as one may say, for immediately after they were 'light they beat up for volunteers for Prince Charles: 'All gentlemen that have a mind to serve His Royal Highness Prince Charles with a willing mind, etc., five guineas advance,' and nobody offered to meddle with them. They were directly joined by Mr J. Bradshaw, Tom Lydall, Mr Tom Deacon, Mr Fletcher, Tom Chaddock, and several others have listed, above eighty men by eight o'clock, when my papa came down to tell us there was a party of horse come in; he took care of me to the Cross, where I saw them all; it is a very fine moonlight night; Mr Walley, Mr Foden and Deputy billeted them. They are my Lord Pitsligo's Horse, and Hugh Sterling, that was 'prentice at Mr Hibbert's, is with them, and the streets are exceeding quiet, there is not one person to be seen nor heard. One of the Highlanders that came today is a Yorkshireman, and is gone tonight to see his sister that lives at Sleat Hall; he took his drawn sword in his hand and went by himself. My papa and my uncle are gone to consult with Mr Croxton, Mr Feilden and others, how to keep themselves out of any scrape, and yet behave civilly. All the justices fled and lawyers too but Coz Clowes.

29 (Friday). They are beating up for the Prince; eleven o'clock we went up to the Cross to see the rest come in; there came small parties of them till about three o'clock, when the Prince and the main body of them came, I cannot guess how many. The Prince went straight up to Mr Dickenson's, where he lodges, the Duke of Athol at Mr Marsden's, the Duke of Perth at Gartside's. There came an officer up to us at Cross and gave us the manifests and declarations; the bells they rung, and P. Cotterel made a bonfire, and all the town was illuminated, every house except Mr Dickenson's, my papa mamma and sister, and my uncle and

I walked up and down to see it; about four o'clock the King was proclaimed, the mob shouted very cleverly, and then we went up to see my aunt Brearcliffe and stayed till eleven o'clock making St Andrew's crosses for them; we sat up making till two o'clock.

After his ludicrously easy invasion of Manchester, the Young Pretender moved on to Derby, before retreating back to Scotland, where his army was eradicated at Culloden.

The '45' failed because the Stuarts misunderstood the Jacobinism of England's Tories. The latter may have disliked the Hanoverian succession, but not to such a degree that they actually wished to upset the national apple-cart, which was doing very nicely. By a combination of naval mastery, credit expansion and mercantilist enterprise, Britain had developed a network of trading posts and colonies across the world, India included.

The Black Hole of Calcutta, 20–21 June 1756

J. Z. HOLWELL

The East India Company (formed 1600) was in the van of the British colonization of the Indian sub-continent, and was bitterly opposed by Siraj-ud-Dawlah, the Nawab of Bengal. After attacking the East India Company's fortified head-quarters in Calcutta, the nawab imprisoned his British prisoners in an 18-feet-square guardroom at Fort William. Holwell was the senior British official in Calcutta.

We had been but few minutes confined before every one fell into a perspiration so profuse, you can form no idea of it. This brought on a raging thirst, which increased in proportion as the body was drained of its moisture.

Various expedients were thought of to give more room and air. To obtain the former, it was moved to put off their cloaths; this was approved as a happy motion, and in a few minutes I believe every man was stripped (myself, Mr Court, and the two young gentlemen by me excepted). For a little time they flattered themselves with having gained a mighty advantage; every hat was put in motion to produce a circulation of air, and Mr Baillie proposed that every man should sit down on his hams. This expedient was several times put in practice, and at each time many of the poor creatures, whose natural strength was less than that of others, or who had been more exhausted and could not immediately recover their legs, as others did when the word was given to rise, fell to rise no more; for they were instantly trod to death or suffocated. When the whole body sat down, they were so closely wedged together, that they were obliged to use many efforts before they could put themselves in motion to get up again.

Before nine o'clock every man's thirst grew intolerable, and respiration difficult. Efforts were made again to force the door, but in vain. Many insults were used to the guard to provoke them to fire in upon us. For my own part, I hitherto felt little pain or uneasiness, but what resulted from my anxiety for the sufferings of those within. By keeping my face between two of the bars, I obtained air enough to give my lungs easy play, though my perspiration was excessive, and thirst commencing. At this period, so strong a urinous volatile effluvia came from the prison, that I was not able to turn my head that way, for more than a few seconds at a time.

Now every body, excepting those situated in and near the windows, began to grow outrageous, and many delirious: *Water, water*, became the general cry. And the old Jemmautdaar before mentioned, taking pity on us, ordered the people to bring some skins of water. This was what I dreaded. I foresaw it would prove the ruin of the small chance left us, and essayed many times to speak to him privately to forbid its being brought; but the clamour was so loud, it became impossible. The water appeared. Words cannot paint to you the universal agitation and raving the sight of it threw us into. I flattered myself that some, by preserving an equal temper of mind, might out-live the night; but now the reflection, which gave me the greatest pain, was, that I saw no possibility of one escaping to tell the dismal tale.

Until the water came, I had myself not suffered much from thirst, which instantly grew excessive. We had no means of conveying it into the prison, but by hats forced through the bars; and thus myself and Messieurs Coles and Scott (notwithstanding the pains they suffered from their wounds) supplied them as fast as possible. But those who have experienced intense thirst, or are acquainted with the cause and nature of this appetite, will be sufficiently sensible it could receive no more than a momentary alleviation; the cause still subsisted. Though we brought full hats within the bars, there ensued such violent struggles, and frequent contests to get at it, that before it reached the lips of any one, there would be scarcely a small tea cup full left in them. These supplies, like sprinkling water on fire, only served to feed and raise the flame.

Oh! my dear Sir, how shall I give you a conception of what I felt at the cries and ravings of those in the remoter parts of the prison, who could not entertain a probable hope of obtaining a drop, yet could not divest themselves of expectation, however unavailing! and calling on me by the tender considerations of friendship and affection, and who knew they were really dear to me! Think, if possible, what my heart must have suffered at seeing and hearing their distress, without having it in my power to relieve them: for the confusion now became general and horrid. Several quitted the other window (the only chance they had for life) to force their way to the water, and the throng and press upon the window was beyond bearing; many forcing their passage from the further part of the room, pressed down those in their way, who had less strength, and trampled them to death.

From about nine to near eleven, I sustained this cruel scene and painful situation, still supplying them with water, though my legs were almost broke with the weight against them. By this time I myself was near pressed to death, and my two companions, with Mr William Parker (who had forced himself into the window) were really so . . .

For a great while they preserved a respect and regard to me, more than indeed I could well expect, our circumstances considered; but now all distinction was lost. My friend Baillie, Messrs Jenks, Revely, Law, Buchanan, Simpson, and several others, for whom I had a real esteem and affection, had for some time been dead at my feet: and were now trampled upon by every corporal or common soldier, who, by the help of more robust constitutions, had forced their way to the window, and held fast by the bars over me, till at last I became so pressed and wedged up, I was deprived of all motion.

Determined now to give every thing up, I called to them, and begged, as the last instance of their regard, they would remove the pressure upon me, and permit me to retire out of the window, to die in quiet. They gave way; and with much difficulty I forced a passage into the centre of the prison, where the throng was less by the many dead, (then I believe amounting to one-third) and the numbers who flocked to the windows; for by this time they had water also at the other window.

In the black hole there is a platform corresponding with that in the barrack: I travelled over the dead, and repaired to the further end of it, just opposite to the other window. Here my poor friend Mr Edward Eyre came staggering over the dead to me, and with his usual coolness and good-nature, asked me how I did? but fell and expired before I had time to make him a reply. I laid myself down on some of the dead behind me, on the platform; and, recommending myself to heaven, had the comfort of thinking my sufferings could have no long duration.

My thirst grew now insupportable, and the difficulty of breathing much increased; and I had not remained in this situation, I believe, ten minutes, when I was seized with a pain in my breast, and palpitation of heart, both to the most exquisite degree. These roused and obliged me to get up again; but still the pain, palpitation, thirst, and difficulty of breathing increased. I retained my senses notwithstanding; and had the grief to see death not so near me as I hoped; but could no longer bear the pains I suffered without attempting a relief, which I knew fresh air would and could only give me. I instantly determined to push for the window opposite to me; and by an effort of double the strength I had ever before possessed, gained the third rank at it, with one hand seized a bar, and by that means gained the second, though I think there were at least six or seven ranks between me and the window.

In a few moments the pain, palpitation, and difficulty of breathing ceased; but my thirst continued intolerable. I called aloud for *Water for God's sake.* I had been concluded dead; but as soon as they found me amongst them, they still had the respect and tenderness for me, to cry out, *Give him water, give him water!* nor would one of them at the window attempt to touch it until I had drank. But from the water I had no relief; my thirst was rather increased by it; so I determined to drink no more, but patiently wait the event; and kept my mouth moist from time to time by sucking the perspiration out of my shirt sleeves, and catching the drops as they fell, like heavy rain, from my head and face; you can hardly imagine how unhappy I was if any of them escaped my mouth.

I came into the prison without coat or waistcoat; the season was too hot to bear the former, and the latter tempted the avarice of one of the guards, who robbed me of it, when we were under the Veranda. Whilst I was at this second window, I was observed by one of my miserable companions on the right of me, in the expedient of allaying my thirst by sucking my shirt-sleeve. He took the hint, and robbed me from time to time of a considerable part of my store; though after I detected him, I had even the address to begin on that sleeve first, when I thought my reservoirs were sufficiently replenished; and our mouths and noses often met in the contest. This plunderer I found afterwards was a worthy young gentleman in the service, Mr Lushington, one of the few who escaped from death, and since paid me the compliment of assuring me, he believed he owed his life to the many comfortable draughts he had from my sleeves. Before I hit upon this happy expedient, I had in an ungovernable fit of thirst, attempted drinking my urine; but it was so intensely bitter, there was no enduring a second taste, whereas no Bristol water could be more soft or pleasant than what arose from perspiration . . .

Many to the right and left sunk with the violent pressure, and were soon suffocated; for now a steam arose from the living and the dead, which affected us in all its circumstances, as if we were forcibly held by our heads over a bowl of strong volatile spirit of hartshorn, until suffocated; nor could the effluvia of the one be distinguished from the other; and frequently, when I was forced by the load upon my head and shoulders, to hold my face down, I was obliged, near as I was to the window, instantly to raise it again, to escape suffocation . . .

When the day broke, and the gentlemen found that no intreaties could prevail to get the door opened, it occurred to one of them (I think to Mr Secretary Cooke) to make a search for me, in hopes I might have influence enough to gain a release from this scene of misery. Accordingly Messrs Lushington and Walcot undertook the search, and by my shirt discovered me under the dead upon the platform. They took me from thence, and imagining I had some signs of life, brought me towards the window I had first possession of.

But as life was equally dear to every man (and the stench arising from the dead bodies was grown so intolerable) no one would give up his station in or near the window: so they were obliged to carry me back again. But soon after Captain Mills, (now captain of the company's yacht) who was in possession of a seat in the window, had the humanity to offer to resign it. I was again brought by the same gentlemen and placed in the window.

At this juncture the suba (viceroy of Bengal), who had received an account of the havock death had made amongst us, sent one of his Jemmautdaars to enquire if the chief survived. They shewed me to him; told I had appearance of life remaining; and believed I might recover if the door was opened very soon. This answer being returned to the suba, an order came immediately for our release, it being then near six in the morning.

As the door opened inwards, and as the dead were piled up against it, and covered all the rest of the floor, it was impossible to open it by any efforts from without; it was therefore necessary that the dead should be removed by the few that were within, who were become so feeble, that the task, though it was the condition of life, was not performed without the utmost difficulty, and it was twenty minutes after the order came before the door could be opened.

About a quarter after six in the morning, the poor remains of 146 souls, being no more than three and twenty, came out of the black hole alive, but in a condition which made it very doubtful whether they would see the morning of the next day; among the living was Mrs Carey, but poor Leech was among the dead. The bodies were dragged out of the hole by the soldiers, and thrown promiscuously into the ditch of an unfinished ravelin, which was afterwards filled with earth.

The task of avenging the Black Hole was given to Robert Clive (1725–74), son of a Shropshire squire and a soldier for the East India Company. At Plassey on 23 June 1757 Clive's East India Company force of 3,200 triumphed over the 50,000 soldiers (who included French gunners) led by the Nawab of Bengal. Clive wrote to the Company's directors about Plassey: 'They [the Nawab's army] made several attempts to bring out their cannon, but our advance field-pieces played so warmly and so well upon them they were always drove back. Their horse exposing themselves a good deal on this occasion, many of them were killed . . . by which the whole army being visibly dispirited and thrown into some confusion, we were encouraged to storm both the eminence and the angle of their camp, which were carried at the same instant, with little or no loss . . . On this a general rout ensued; and we pursued the enemy six miles . . .'

Plassey was the turning point in the Eastern career of the British. It checked the French and established the British Empire in India. Clive himself was elevated to the peerage.

After preventing French domination of India, the British strove to do the same in America.

The Death of General Wolfe on the Heights of Abraham, Quebec, 13 September 1759

CAPTAIN JOHN KNOX

It was of the brilliant but eccentric James Wolfe that George II remarked, 'Oh! he is mad, is he? Then I hope he will bite some other of my generals.' Wolfe's victory over the French at Quebec secured British control of Canada and eastern America. He was mortally wounded in the undertaking. Knox was one of Wolfe's officers.

Before day-break this morning we made a descent upon the north shore, about half a quarter of a mile to the eastward of Sillery; . . . we had, in this debarkation, thirty flat-bottomed boats, containing about sixteen hundred men. This was a great surprise on the enemy, who, from the natural strength of the place, did not suspect, and consequently were not prepared against, so bold an attempt. . . . As fast as we landed, the boats put off for reinforcements . . . the General, with Brigadiers Monckton and Murray, were a-shore with the first division. We lost no time here, but clambered up one of the steepest precipices that can be conceived, being almost a perpendicular, and of an incredible height. As soon as we gained the summit, all was quiet, and not a shot was heard, owing to the excellent conduct of the light infantry under Colonel Howe; it was by this time clear day-light. Here we formed again . . . we then faced to the right, and marched towards the town by files, till we came to the plains of Abraham; an even piece of ground which Mr Wolfe had made choice of, while we stood forming upon the hill. Weather showery: about six o'clock the enemy first made their appearance upon the heights, between us and the town; whereupon we halted, and wheeled to the right, thereby forming the line of battle. . . . The enemy had now likewise formed the line of battle, and got some cannon to play on us, with round and canister shot; but what galled us most was a body of Indians and other marksmen they had concealed in the corn opposite to the front of our right wing . . . but Colonel Hale . . . advanced some platoons . . . which, after a few rounds, obliged these skulkers to retire. We were now ordered to lie down, and remained some time in this position. About eight o'clock we had two pieces of short brass six-pounders playing on the enemy, which threw them into some confusion. . . . About ten o'clock the enemy began to advance briskly in three columns, with loud shouts and recovered arms, two of them inclining to the left of our army, and the third towards our right, firing obliquely at the two extremities of our line, from the distance of one hundred and thirty, until they came within forty yards; which our troops withstood with the greatest intrepidity and firmness, still reserving their fire, and paying the strictest obedience to their Officers: this uncommon steadiness, together with the havoc which the grape-shot from our field-pieces made among them, threw them into some disorder, and was most critically maintained by a well-timed, regular and heavy discharge of our small arms, such as they could no longer oppose; hereupon they gave way, and fled with precipitation, so that, by the time the cloud of smoke was vanished, our men were again loaded, and profiting by the advantage we had over them, pursued them almost to the gates of the town, and the bridge over the little river, redoubling our fire with great eagerness, making many Officers and men prisoners. The weather cleared up, with a comfortably warm sunshine. . . . Our joy at this success is inexpressibly damped by the loss we sustained of one of the greatest heroes which this or any other age can boast of – General James Wolfe, who received his mortal wound as he was exerting himself at the head of the grenadiers of Louisbourg. . . . The officers who are prisoners say that Quebec will surrender in a few days: some deserters, who came out to us in the evening, agree in that opinion, and inform us, that the Sieur de Montcalm is dying, in great agony, of a wound he received today in their retreat . . .

After our late worthy general, of renowned memory, was carried off wounded, to the rear of the front line, he desired those who were about him to lay him down; being asked if he would have a Surgeon, he replied, 'It is needless; it is all over with me'. One of them then cried out, 'They run, see how they run'. 'Who runs?' demanded our hero, with great earnestness, like a person roused from sleep. The Officer answered, 'The enemy, Sir, Egad they give way everywhere'. Thereupon the General rejoined, 'Go one of you, my lads, to Colonel Burton; tell him to march Webb's regiment with all speed down to Charles's river, to cut off the retreat of the fugitives from the bridge'. Then, turning on his side, he added, 'Now, God be praised, I will die in peace:' and thus expired.

George II Interred, 13 November 1760

HORACE WALPOLE

George the First was always reckoned
Vile, but viler George the Second

Walter Savage Landor

George II (reigned 1727–60) was unloved, unremarkable, and the dazzling expansion of Britain under Clive, Wolfe and the statesman Pitt the Elder was despite him. That said, George II gained a flicker of national respect for being the last British monarch to lead his troops into battle, at Dettingen in 1743.

Horace Walpole was the son of Sir Robert Walpole, England's first and longest-serving (1721–42) prime minister. Walpole junior's 'gothicization' of a coachman's cottage into the pseudo-castle of Strawberry Hill, Twickenham, set a national fashion, but his greatest mark on posterity was his vivid and voluminous correspondence. To one friend alone, Madame du Deffand, he sent more than 1,600 letters.

Do you know I had the curiosity to go to the burying t'other night; I had never seen a royal funeral. Nay, I walked as a rag of quality, which I found would be, and so it was, the easiest way of seeing it. It is absolutely a noble sight. The Prince's Chamber hung with purple and a quantity of silver lamps, the coffin under a canopy of purple velvet, and six vast chandeliers of silver on high stands had a very good effect: the ambassador from Tripoli and his son were carried to see that chamber. The procession through a line of footguards, every seventh man bearing a torch, the horse-guards lining the outside, their officers with drawn sabres and crape sashes, on horseback, the drums muffled, the fifes, bells tolling and minute guns, all this was very solemn. But the charm was the entrance of the Abbey, where we were received by the Dean and chapter in rich copes, the choir and almsmen all bearing torches; the whole Abbey so illuminated, that one saw it to greater advantage than by day; the tombs, long aisles, and fretted roof all appearing distinctly, and with the happiest chiaroscuro. There wanted nothing but incense, and little chapels here and there with priests saying mass for the repose of the defunct – yet one could not complain of its not being Catholic enough. I had been in dread of being coupled with some boy of ten years old – but the heralds were not very accurate, and I walked with George Grenville, taller and older enough to keep me in countenance. When we came to the chapel of Henry VII all solemnity and decorum ceased – no order was observed, people sat or stood where they could or would, the yeomen of the guard were crying out for help, oppressed by the immense weight of the coffin, the Bishop read sadly, and blundered in the prayers, the fine chapter, *Man that is born of a woman*, was chanted not read, and the anthem, besides being unmeasurably tedious, would have served as well for a nuptial. The real serious part was the figure of the Duke of Cumberland, heightened by a thousand melancholy circumstances. He had a dark brown adonis [wig] and a cloak of black cloth with a train of five yards. Attending the funeral of a father, how little reason soever he had to love him, could not be pleasant. His leg extremely bad, yet forced to stand upon it near two hours, his face bloated and distorted with his late paralytic stroke, which has affected too one of his eyes, and placed over the mouth of the vault, into which in all probability he must himself so soon descend – think how unpleasant a situation! He bore it all with a firm and unaffected countenance. This grave scene was fully contrasted by the burlesque Duke of Newcastle – he fell into a fit of crying the moment he came into the chapel and flung himself back in a stall, the Archbishop hovering over him with a smelling bottle – but in two minutes his curiosity got the better of his hypocrisy and he ran about the chapel with his glass to spy who was or was not there, spying with one hand and mopping his eyes with t'other. Then returned the fear of catching cold, and the Duke of Cumberland, who was sinking with heat, felt himself weighed down, and turning round, found it was the Duke of Newcastle standing upon his train to avoid the chill of the marble. It was very theatric to look down into the vault, where the coffin lay, attended by mourners with lights. Clavering, the Groom of the Bedchamber, refused to sit up with the body, and was dismissed by the King's order.

The late king's twenty-two-year-old grandson and heir, George III (reigned 1760–1820), made a decent fist of being English; he was affectionately nicknamed 'Farmer George' for his love of the native countryside. His popularity waned, however, as his obstinacy and his incompetence as ruler became evident during the dismal decades of 1763–83 when the American colonies were lost.

The Boston Tea Party, 16 December 1773

JOHN ANDREWS

To protect its possessions in America, the British government proposed a resident army of 10,000 and a fort-building programme. That the colonials should pay for their own defence, raised through stiff duties on imports, seemed like a good scheme in London. So too the order that money-spinning revenue stamps (courtesy of the Stamp Act, 1765) should be fixed to all printed documents circulated in America.

Antagonized, over-taxed and unrepresented, the colonists boycotted British goods – which persuaded the British government to repeal the import taxes. Save, that is, the tax on tea. Half-heartedly disguised as American Indians, colonial patriots led a protest against three British tea ships in Boston Harbor.

Andrews, a Boston selectman, wrote the account below for a relative.

The affair was transacted with the greatest regularity and despatch. . . . A general muster was assembled, from this and all the neighbouring towns, to the number of five or six thousand, at 10 o'clock Thursday morning in the Old South Meeting House, where they passed a unanimous vote that the Tea should go out of the harbour that afternoon, and sent a committee with Mr Rotch★ to the Customhouse to demand a clearance, which the Collector told them it was not in his power to give, without the duties being first paid. They then sent Mr Rotch to Milton, to ask a pass from the Governor, who sent for answer, that 'consistent with the rules of government and his duty to the King he could not grant one without they produced a previous clearance from the office'. By the time he returned with this message the candles were light in the house, and upon reading it, such prodigious shouts were made, that induced me, while drinking tea at home, to go out and know the cause of it. The house was so crowded I could get no farther than the porch, when I found the moderator was just declaring the meeting to be dissolved, which caused another general shout, outdoors and in, and three cheers. What with that, and the consequent noise of breaking up the meeting, you'd thought that the inhabitants of the infernal regions had broke loose.

For my part, I went contentedly home and finished my tea, but was soon informed what was going forward; but still not crediting it without ocular demonstration, I went and was satisfied. They mustered, I'm told, upon Fort Hill to the number of about two hundred, and proceeded, two by two, to Griffin's wharf, where *Hall, Bruce,* and *Coffin* lay, each with 114 chests of the ill-fated article on board; the two former with only that article, but the latter, arrived at the wharf only the day before, was freighted with a large quantity of other goods, which they took the greatest care not to injure in the least, and before nine o'clock in the evening every chest from on board the three vessels was knocked to pieces and flung over the sides.

They say the actors were Indians from Narragansett. Whether they were or not, to a transient observer they appeared as such, being clothed in blankets with the heads muffled, and copper-coloured countenances, being each armed with a hatchet or axe, and pair pistols, nor was their dialect different from what I conceive these geniuses to speak, as their jargon was unintelligible to all but themselves. Not the least insult was offered to any person, save one Captain Connor, a letter of horses in

★ Owner of one of the tea ships.

this place, not many years since removed from dear Ireland, who had ripped up the lining of his coat and waistcoat, under the arms, and watching his opportunity had nearly filled them with tea, but being detected, was handled pretty roughly. They not only stripped him of his clothes, but gave him a coat of mud, with a severe bruising into the bargain; and nothing but their utter aversion to make any disturbance prevented his being tarred and feathered.

Should not have troubled you with this, by this post, hadn't I thought you would be glad of a more particular account of so important a transaction than you could have obtained by common report; and if it affords my brother but a temporary amusement, I shall be more than repaid for the trouble of writing it.

After Boston, the logic towards war became hard to escape. Feeble-minded George III and his dog-loyal Prime Minister Frederick North retaliated with the 'Intolerable Acts', designed to show the colonials that Britain was boss. The intransigent colonists were not inclined to genuflect, and skirmishing between Redcoats and American militiamen broke out at Lexington and Concord in April 1775. The War of Independence – what the Americans would call the Revolutionary War – went Britain's way . . . until the British commander, Lord Cornwallis, threw away a probable win, allowing himself to become trapped between the Americans on land and a fleet – thoughtfully provided by the French – at sea.

Britain recognized America's independence in 1783.

Machine Wreckers, Lancashire, October 1779

THOMAS BENTLEY

The introduction of machine technology, as England laboured during the world's first Industrial Revolution, was widely thought to cause unemployment. There arose in response a 'wrecking' movement, which saw its eventual zenith in the Luddism of the 1810s.

I wrote to my dear friend last from Bolton, and I mention'd the mob which had assembled in that neighbourhood; but they had not done much mischief; they only destroyed a small engine or two near Chowbent. We met them on Saturday morning, but I apprehend what we saw were not the main body; for on the same day, in the afternoon, a capital engine or mill, in the manner of Arcrites, and in which he is a partner, near Chorley, was attacked; but from its peculiar situation they could approach to it by one passage only; and this circumstance enabled the owner, with the assistance of a few neighbours, to repulse the enemy and preserve the mill for that time. Two of the mob were shot dead upon the spot, one drowned, and several wounded. The mob had no fire-arms, and did not expect so warm a reception. They were greatly exasperated, and vowed revenge; accordingly they spent all Sunday and Monday morning in collecting firearms and ammunition and melting their pewter dishes into bullets. They were now join'd by the Duke of Bridgewater's colliers and others, to the number, we are told, of eight thousand, and march'd by beat of drum and with colours flying to the mill, where they met with a repulse on Saturday. They found Sir Richard Clayton guarding the place with fifty Invalids armed, but this handful were by no means a match for enraged thousands; they (the Invalids) therefore contented themselves with looking on, while the mob completely destroyed a set of mills valued at 10,000*l*.

This was Monday's employment. On Tuesday morning we heard their drum at about two miles distance from Bolton, a little, before we left the place, and their professed design was to take Bolton, Manchester, and Stockport on their way to Crumford, and to destroy all the engines not only on these places, but throughout all England. How far they will be able to put their threats into execution time alone can discover.

Machine-smashing was doomed, because the demand for the machines was insatiable. They produced goods faster and cheaper than machine-breakers and cottage-artisans could even nightmare of. And England's burgeoning population – up from 5.2 million in 1731 to 7.1 in 1780 – clamoured to be clothed, fed and heated. And not only was England's population growing, it was relocating.

Unwanted by a countryside that had improved its agricultural output but decreased its need for sons and daughters of soil-toil, many English migrated off the land; by the mid-eighteenth century 30 per cent of England's people lived in towns. England, in other words, was the most urbanized country in northern Europe.

Urbanization created a demand for goods made by machines; machines required factories and power. This sequence of impulses was a singular reason for England entering the Industrial Revolution first among nations. So was England's aggressive empire building in the mid-eighteenth century, which gave England Ltd both cheap raw materials and vast external markets. A double economic boon.

There were other reasons, too, hovering from England's past, claiming their share of praise for Albion's early industrialization: the 'blessed plot's' natural abundance of coal, essential for steam-power and iron-smelting; the reinvestment of the hyper-profits from the slave-and-sugar trade of which John Hawkins was a premier exponent; Cromwell's smoothing of the expansion of mercantilism and the securing of Protestantism, which facilitated individualism and scientific inquiry; England's long-held nationhood, which created an internal market largely free of customs barriers; and the tradition of City of London money-men for risk-taking.

Inevitably, this self-same Industrial Revolution produced incandescent social tensions.

The Gordon Riots, 8 June 1780

GEORGE CRABBE

Lord George Gordon headed a 50,000-strong London mob demanding the repeal of the 1778 Act allowing Catholics civil rights. It was not Popery that the mob objected to so much as the influx of wage-lowering Irish Catholic navvies into England. About 300 people were killed in a week of rioting in the capital city.

Yesterday, my own business being decided, I was at Westminster at about three o'clock in the afternoon, and saw the members go to the House. The mob stopped many persons, but let all whom I saw pass, excepting Lord Sandwich, whom they treated roughly, broke his coach windows, cut his face, and turned him back. A guard of horse and foot were immediately sent for, who did no particular service, the mob increasing and defeating them.

I left Westminster when all the members, that were permitted, had entered the House and came home. In my way I met a resolute band of vile-looking fellows, ragged, dirty, and insolent, armed with clubs, going to join their companions. I since learned that there were eight or ten of these bodies in different parts of the City.

About seven o'clock in the evening I went out again. At Westminster the mob were few, and those quiet, and decent in appearance. I crossed St George's Fields, which were empty, and came home again by Black-friars Bridge; and in going from thence to the Exchange, you pass the Old Bailey; and here it was that I saw the first scene of terror and riot ever presented to me. The new prison was a very large, strong, and beautiful building, having two wings, of which you can suppose the extent, when you consider their use; besides these, were the keeper's (Mr Akerman's) house, a strong intermediate work, and likewise other parts, of which I can give you no description. Akerman had in his custody four prisoners, taken in the riot; these the mob went to his house and demanded. He begged he might send to the sheriff, but this was not permitted. How he escaped, or where he is gone, I know not; but just at the time I speak of they set fire to his house, broke in, and threw every piece of furniture they could find into the street, firing them also in an instant. The engines came, but were only suffered to preserve the private houses near the prison.

As I was standing near the spot, there approached another body of men, I suppose 500, and Lord George Gordon in a coach, drawn by the mob towards Alderman Bull's, bowing as he passed along. He is a lively-looking young man in appearance, and nothing more, though just now the reigning hero.

By eight o'clock, Akerman's house was in flames. I went close to it, and never saw any thing so dreadful. The prison was, as I said, a remarkably strong building; but, determined to force it, they broke the gates with crows and other instruments, and climbed up the outside of the cell part, which joins the two great wings of the building, where the felons were confined; and I stood where I plainly saw their operations. They broke the roof, tore away the rafters, and having got ladders they descended. Not Orpheus himself had more courage or better luck; flames all around them, and a body of soldiers expected, they defied and laughed at all opposition.

The prisoners escaped. I stood and saw about twelve women and eight men ascend from their confinement to the open air, and they were conducted through the street in their chains. Three of these were to be hanged on Friday. You have no conception of the phrensy of the multitude. This being done, and Akerman's house now a mere shell of brickwork, they kept a store of flame there for other purposes. It became red-hot, and the doors and windows appeared like the entrance to so many volcanoes. With some difficulty they then fired the debtors' prison – broke the doors – and they, too, all made their escape.

Tired of the scene, I went home, and returned again at eleven o'clock at night. I met large bodies of horse and foot soldiers coming to guard the Bank, and some houses of Roman Catholics near it. Newgate was at this time open to all; anyone might get in, and, what was never the case before, anyone might get out. I did both; for the people were now chiefly lookers on. The mischief was done, and the doers of it gone to another part of the town.

But I must not omit what struck me most. About ten or twelve of the mob getting to the top of the debtors' prison, whilst it was burning, to halloo, they appeared rolled in black smoke mixed with sudden bursts of fire – like Milton's infernals, who were as familiar with flame as with each other. On comparing notes with my neighbours, I find I saw but a small part of the mischief. They say Lord Mansfield's house is now in flames.

Twenty-one of the mob were hanged. Gordon, benefiting from the expensive legal skills of the jurist Thomas Erskine, was acquitted of treason. He then adopted Judaism before libelling Marie Antoinette and dying of gaol fever in Newgate.

A Chance Meeting with Mad King George, Kew Gardens, 2 February 1789

FANNY BURNEY

George III's madness may have been caused by the burdens of monarchy and fatherhood (the Hanoverians were the original dysfunctional family), porphyria, or even lead poisoning from the plate which held his favourite food, sauerkraut.

Whatever, he suffered bouts of insanity. Here is short-sighted Fanny Burney, joint Keeper of the Queen's Robes, encountering Mad King George at Kew.

Kew Palace

What an adventure had I this morning! one that has occasioned me the severest personal terror I ever experienced in my life.

Sir Lucas Pepys still persisting that exercise and air were absolutely necessary to save me from illness, I have continued my walks, varying my gardens from Richmond to Kew, according to the accounts I received of the movements of the King. For this I had her Majesty's permission, on the representation of Sir Lucas.

This morning, when I received my intelligence of the King from Dr John Willis, I begged to know where I might walk in safety. 'In Kew Gardens,' he said, 'as the King would be in Richmond.'

'Should any unfortunate circumstance,' I cried, 'at any time, occasion my being seen by his Majesty, do not mention my name, but let me run off without call or notice.'

This he promised. Everybody, indeed, is ordered to keep out of sight.

Taking, therefore, the time I had most at command, I strolled into the gardens. I had proceeded, in my quick way, nearly half the round, when I suddenly perceived through some trees, two or three figures. Relying on the instructions of Dr John, I concluded them to be workmen and gardeners; yet tried to look sharp, and in so doing, as they were less shaded, I thought I saw the person of his Majesty!

Alarmed past all possible expression, I waited not to know more, but turning back, ran off with all my might. But what was my terror to hear myself pursued! – to hear the voice of the King himself loudly and hoarsely calling after me, 'Miss Burney! Miss Burney!'

I protest I was ready to die. I knew not in what state he might be at the time; I only knew the orders to keep out of his way were universal; that the Queen would highly disapprove any unauthorized meeting, and that the very action of my running away might deeply, in his present irritable state, offend him. Nevertheless, on I ran, too terrified to stop, and in search of some short passage, for the garden is full of little labyrinths, by which I might escape.

The steps still pursued me, and still the poor hoarse and altered voice rang in my ears: – more and more footsteps resounded frightfully behind me, – the attendants all running, to catch their eager master, and the voices of the two Doctor Willises loudly exhorting him not to heat himself so unmercifully.

Heavens, how I ran! I do not think I should have felt the hot lava from Vesuvius – at least not the hot cinders – had I so run during its eruption. My feet were not sensible that they even touched the ground.

Soon after, I heard other voices, shriller, though less nervous, call out 'Stop! Stop! Stop!'

I could by no means consent: I knew not what was purposed, but I recollected fully my agreement with Dr John that very morning, that I should decamp if surprised, and not be named.

My own fears and repugnance, also, after a flight and disobedience like this, were doubled in the thought of not escaping: I knew not to what I might be exposed, should the malady be then high, and take the turn of resentment. Still, therefore, on I flew; and such was my speed, so almost incredible to relate or recollect, that I fairly believe no one of the whole party could have overtaken me, if these words, from one of the attendants, had not reached me, 'Doctor Willis begs you to stop!'

'I cannot! I cannot!' I answered, still flying on, when he called out, 'You must, ma'am; it hurts the King to run.'

Then, indeed, I stopped – in a state of fear really amounting to agony. I turned round, I saw the two Doctors had got the King between them, and three attendants of Dr Willis's were hovering about. They all slackened their pace, as they saw me stand still; but such was the excess of my alarm, that I was wholly insensible to the effects of a race which, at any other time, would have required an hour's recruit.

As they approached, some little presence of mind happily came to my command: it occurred to me that, to appease the wrath of my flight, I must now show some confidence: I therefore faced them as undauntedly as I was able, only charging the nearest of the attendants to stand by my side.

When they were within a few yards of me, the King called out, 'Why did you run away?'

Shocked at a question impossible to answer, yet a little assured by the mild tone of his voice, I instantly forced myself forward, to meet him, though the internal sensation, which satisfied me this was a step the most proper to appease his suspicions and displeasure, was so violently combated by the tremor of my nerves, that I fairly think I may reckon it the greatest effort of personal courage I have ever made.

The effort answered: I looked up, and met all his wonted benignity of countenance, though something still of wildness in his eyes. Think, however, of my surprise, to feel him put both his hands round my two shoulders, and then kiss my cheek!

I wonder I did not really sink, so exquisite was my affright when I saw him spread out his arms! Involuntarily, I concluded he meant to crush me: but the Willises, who have never seen him till this fatal illness, not knowing how very extraordinary an action this was from him, simply smiled and looked pleased, supposing, perhaps, it was his customary salutation!

I believe, however, it was but the joy of a heart unbridled, now, by the forms and proprieties of established custom and sober reason. To see any of his household thus by accident, seemed such a near approach to liberty and recovery, that who can wonder it should serve rather to elate than lessen what yet remains of his disorder!

He now spoke in such terms of his pleasure in seeing me, that I soon lost the whole of my terror; astonishment to find him so nearly well, and gratification to see him so pleased, removed every uneasy feeling, and the joy that succeeded, in my conviction of his recovery, made me ready to throw myself at his feet to express it.

What a conversation followed! When he saw me fearless, he grew more and more alive, and made me walk close by his side, away from the attendants, and even the Willises themselves, who, to indulge him, retreated. I own myself not completely composed, but alarm I could entertain no more.

Everything that came uppermost in his mind he mentioned; he seemed to have just such remains of his flightiness as heated his imagination without deranging his reason, and robbed him of all control over his speech, though nearly in his perfect state of mind as to his opinions.

What did he not say! He opened his whole heart to me, – expounded all his sentiments, and acquainted me with all his intentions.

The heads of his discourse I must give you briefly, as I am sure you will be highly curious to hear them, and as no accident can render of much consequence what a man says in such a state of physical intoxication.

He assured me he was quite well – as well as he had ever been in his life; and then inquired how I did, and how I went on? and whether I was more comfortable?

If these questions, in their implication, surprised me, imagine how that surprise must increase when he proceeded to explain them! He asked after the coadjutrix, laughing, and saying, 'Never mind her! – don't be oppressed – I am your friend! don't let her cast you down! – I know you have a hard time of it – but don't mind her!'

Almost thunderstruck with astonishment, I merely curtseyed to his kind 'I am your friend,' and said nothing.

Then presently he added, 'Stick to your father – stick to your own family – let them be your objects.'

How readily I assented!

Again he repeated all I have just written, nearly in the same words, but ended it more seriously: he suddenly stopped, and held me to stop too, and putting his hand on his breast, in the most solemn manner, he gravely and slowly said, 'I will protect you! – I promise you that – and therefore depend upon me!'

I thanked him; and the Willises, thinking him rather too elevated, came to propose my walking on. 'No, no, no,' he cried, a hundred times in a breath; and their good humour prevailed, and they let him again walk on with his new companion.

He then gave me a history of his pages, animating almost into a rage, as he related his subjects of displeasure with them, particularly with Mr Ernst, who, he told me, had been brought up by himself. I hope his ideas upon these men are the result of the mistakes of his malady.

Then he asked me some questions that very greatly distressed me, relating to information given him in his illness, from various motives, but which he suspected to be false, and which I knew he had reason to suspect: yet was it most dangerous to set anything right, as I was not aware what might be the view of their having been stated wrong. I was as discreet as I knew how to be, and I hope I did no mischief; but this was the worst part of the dialogue.

He next talked to me a great deal of my dear father, and made a thousand inquiries concerning his 'History of Music.' This brought him to his favourite theme, Handel; and he told me innumerable anecdotes of him, and particularly that celebrated tale of Handel's saying of himself, when a boy, 'While that boy lives, my music will never want a protector.' And this, he said, I might relate to my father.

Then he ran over most of his oratorios, attempting to sing the subjects of several airs and choruses, but so dreadfully hoarse that the sound was terrible.

Dr Willis, quite alarmed at this exertion, feared he would do himself harm, and again proposed a separation. 'No! No! No!' he exclaimed, 'not yet; I have something I must just mention first.'

Dr Willis, delighted to comply, even when uneasy at compliance, again gave way.

The good King then greatly affected me. He began upon my revered old friend, Mrs Delany; and he spoke of her with such warmth – such kindness! 'She was my friend,' he cried, 'and I loved her as a friend! I have made a memorandum when I lost her – I will show it you.'

He pulled out a pocket-book, and rummaged some time, but to no purpose.

The tears stood in his eyes – he wiped them, and Dr Willis again became very anxious. 'Come, sir,' he cried, 'now do you come in and let the lady go on her walk – come, now, you have talked a long while, – so we'll go in – if your Majesty pleases.'

'No, no!' he cried, 'I want to ask her a few questions; – I have lived so long out of the world, I know nothing!'

This touched me to the heart. We walked on together, and he inquired after various persons, particularly Mrs Boscawen, because she was Mrs Delany's friend! Then, for the same reason, after Mr Frederick Montagu, of whom he kindly said, 'I know he has a great regard for me, for all he joined the opposition.' Lord Grey de Wilton, Sir Watkin Wynn, the Duke of Beaufort, and various others, followed.

He then told me he was very much dissatisfied with several of his state officers, and meant to form an entire new establishment. He took a paper out of his pocket-book, and showed me his new list.

This was the wildest thing that passed; and Dr John Willis now seriously urged our separating; but he would not consent; he had only three more words to say, he declared, and again he conquered.

He now spoke of my father, with still more kindness, and told me he ought to have had the post of Master of the Band, and not that little poor musician Parsons, who was not fit for it: 'But Lord Salisbury,' he cried, 'used your father very ill in that business, and so he did me! However, I have dashed out his name, and I shall put your father's in, – as soon as I get loose again!'

This again – how affecting was this!

'And what,' cried he, 'has your father got, at last? nothing but that poor thing at Chelsea? O fie! fie! fie! But never mind! I will take care of him! I will do it myself!'

Then presently he added, 'As to Lord Salisbury, he is out already, as this memorandum will show you, and so are many more. I shall be much better served; and when once I get away, I shall rule with a rod of iron!'

This was very unlike himself, and startled the two good doctors, who could not bear to cross him, and were exulting at my seeing his great amendment, but yet grew quite uneasy at his earnestness and volubility.

Finding we now must part, he stopped to take leave, and renewed again his charges about the coadjutrix. 'Never mind her!' he cried, 'depend upon me! I will be your friend as long as I live! I here pledge myself to be your friend!' And then he saluted me again just as at the meeting, and suffered me to go on.

Jenner Discovers Smallpox Vaccination, 1796

EDWARD JENNER

Edward Jenner (1749–1823), a Gloucestershire country physician and amateur scientist, spent twenty years investigating a cure for smallpox.

During the investigation of the casual Cow Pox, I was struck with the idea that it might be practicable to propagate the disease by inoculation, after the manner of the Small Pox, first from the Cow, and finally from one human being to another. I anxiously waited some time for an opportunity of putting this theory to the test. At length the period arrived. The first experiment was made upon a lad of the name of Phipps, in whose arm a little Vaccine Virus was inserted, taken from the hand of a young woman who had been accidentally infected by a cow. Notwithstanding the resemblance which the pustule, thus excited on the boy's arm, bore to variolous inoculation, yet as the indisposition attending it was barely perceptible, I could scarcely persuade myself the patient was secure from the Small Pox. However, on his being inoculated some months afterwards, it proved that he was secure. This Case inspired me with confidence; and as soon as I could again furnish myself with Virus from the Cow, I made an arrangement for a series of inoculations. A number of children were inoculated in succession, one from the other; and after several months had elapsed, they were exposed to the infection of the Small Pox; some by Inoculation, others by various effluvia and some in both ways; but they all resisted it. The distrust and scepticism which naturally arose in the minds of medical men, on my first announcing so unexpected a discovery has now nearly disappeared. Many hundreds of them, from actual experience, have given their attestations that the inoculated Cow Pox proves a perfect security against the Small Pox; and I shall probably be within compass if I say, thousands are ready to follow their example; for the scope that this inoculation has now taken is immense. An hundred thousand persons, upon the smallest computation, have been inoculated in these realms.

The Battle of the Nile, 1 August 1798

JOHN NICHOL

Only a decade after the conclusion of the American War of Independence in 1783 Britain was again in arms. The enemy was the old one, France, though this time in new, Revolutionary garb and keen to export its republican ideology abroad on the end of a musket. The competence and fervour of the new French army trounced Britain and her allies on land, and only the Royal Navy – at Ushant, at Camperdown – prevented an actual invasion of the island. Despite the cruelties and poverties of life in the 'wooden world' of the Georgian Navy (which provoked mutinies at Nore and Spithead), English sailors were possessed foremost by patriotism and professionalism. The Navy crowned its glory in the French Revolutionary War in the fight at Aboukir Bay, just north-east of Alexandria. The battle of the Nile was the making of British dominance in the Mediterranean. And of Horatio Nelson.

John Nichol was in the gun crew of HMS Goliath.

The sun was just setting as we went into the bay, and a red and fiery sun it was. I would, if I had had my choice, been on the deck; there I would have seen what was passing, and the time would not have hung so heavy; but every man does his duty with spirit, whether his station be in the slaughter-house or in the magazine. (The seamen call the lower deck, near the main-mast, 'the slaughter-house', as it is amidships, and the enemy aim their fire principally at the body of the ship.) My station was in the powder-magazine with the gunner. As we entered the bay we stripped to our trousers, opened our ports, cleared, and every ship we passed gave them a broadside and three cheers. Any information we got was from the boys and women who carried the powder. They behaved as well as the men, and got a present for their bravery from the Grand Signior. When the French Admiral's ship blew up, the *Goliath* got such a shake we thought the after-part of her had blown up until the boys told us what it was. They brought us every now and then the cheering news of another French ship having struck [surrendered], and we answered the cheers on deck with heartfelt joy. In the heat of the action, a shot came right into the magazine, but did no harm, as the carpenters plugged it up, and stopped the water that was rushing in. I was much indebted to the gunner's wife, who gave her husband and me a drink of wine every now and then, which lessened our fatigue much.

There were some of the women wounded, and one woman belonging to Leith died of her wounds, and was buried on a small island in the bay. One woman bore a son in the heat of the action; she belonged to Edinburgh.

When we ceased firing, I went on deck to view the state of the fleets, and an awful sight it was. The whole bay was covered with dead bodies, mangled, wounded, and scorched, not a bit of clothes on them except their trousers. There were a number of French, belonging to the French Admiral's ship, the *L'Orient*, who had swam to the *Goliath*, and were cowering under her forecastle. Poor fellows! they were brought on board, and Captain Foley ordered them down to the steward's room, to get provisions and clothing. One thing I observed in these Frenchmen quite different from anything I had before observed. In the American War, when we took a French ship, the *Duke de Chartres*, the prisoners were as merry as if they had taken us, only saying, 'Fortune de guerre – you take me today, I take you tomorrow.' Those we now had on board were thankful for our kindness, but were sullen and as downcast as if each had lost a ship of his own.

The only incidents I heard of are two. One lad who was stationed by a salt-box, on which he sat to give out cartridges, and keep the lid close – it is a trying berth – when asked for a cartridge, he gave none, yet he sat upright; his eyes were open. One of the men gave him a push; he fell all his length on the deck. There was not a blemish on his body, yet he was quite dead, and was thrown overboard. The other, a lad who had the match in his hand to fire his gun. In the act of applying it, a shot took off his arm; it hung by a small piece of skin. The match fell to the deck. He looked to his arm, and seeing what had happened, seized the match in his left hand, and fired off the gun before he went to the cockpit to have it dressed. They were in our mess, or I might never have heard of it. Two of the mess were killed, and I knew not of it until the day after. Thus terminated the glorious first of August, the busiest night in my life.

Before the battle Nelson (born 1758, son of a Norfolk clergyman) is reputed to have told his fellow officers that he would proceed from the Nile to a tomb or the House of Lords.

He was raised to the peerage as Baron Nelson of the Nile.

Nelson Sees No Signal, Copenhagen, 2 April 1801

COLONEL WILLIAM STEWART

Circumventing the order of his sixty-two-year-old commander, Admiral Hyde Parker, to withdraw, Nelson won a famous victory over the Danes, partners in an armed coalition against British interests in the Baltic.

Lord Nelson was at this time, as he had been during the whole Action, walking the starboard side of the quarter-deck; sometimes much animated, and at others heroically fine in his observations. A shot through the mainmast knocked a few splinters about us. He observed to me, with a smile, 'It is warm work, and this day may be the last to any of us at a moment'; and then stopping short at the gangway, he used an expression never to be erased from my memory, and said with emotion, 'but mark you, I would not be elsewhere for thousands.' When the signal, No. 39, was made, the Signal Lieutenant reported it to him. He continued his walk, and did not appear to take notice of it. The Lieutenant meeting his Lordship at the next turn asked, 'whether he should repeat it?' Lord Nelson answered, 'No, acknowledge it.' On the Officer returning to the poop, his Lordship called after him, 'Is No. 16 [the signal for close action] still hoisted?' The Lieutenant answering in the affirmative, Lord Nelson said, 'Mind you keep it so.' He now walked the deck considerably agitated, which was always known by his moving the stump of his right arm. After a turn or two, he said to me, in a quick manner, 'Do you know what's shown on board of the Commander-in-Chief, No. 39?' On asking him what that meant, he answered, 'Why, to leave off Action.' 'Leave off Action!' he repeated, and then added, with a shrug, 'Now, damn me if I do.' He also observed, I believe, to Captain Foley, 'You know, Foley, I have only one eye – I have a right to be blind sometimes', and then with an archness peculiar to his character, putting the glass to his blind eye, he exclaimed, 'I really do not see the signal.'

Nelson's battering of the Danes at Copenhagen (they lost seventeen warships) secured an armistice with the Baltic League and encouraged the French to agree the Peace of Amiens in March 1802. But this was no more than a buying of time; the renewed Continental aggression of the French began the Napoleonic War in May 1803. Once again the Royal Navy, like the whale, was the king of the sea.

Wellington Meets Nelson, 10 September 1805

SIR ARTHUR WELLESLEY

Wellesley had not yet found the military fortune which would elevate him to the dukedom of Wellington.

I went to the Colonial Office in Downing Street and there I was shown into the little waiting-room on the right hand, where I found, also waiting to see the Secretary of State, a gentleman whom, from his likeness to his pictures and the loss of an arm, I immediately recognized as Lord Nelson. He could not know who I was, but he entered at once into conversation with me, if I can call it conversation, for it was almost all on his side and all about himself, and in, really, a style so vain and so silly as to surprise and almost disgust me. I suppose something that I happened to say may have made him guess that I was *somebody*, and he went out of the room for a moment, I have no doubt to ask the office-keeper who I was, for when he came back he was altogether a different man, both in manner and matter. All that I had thought a charlaton style had vanished, and he talked of the state of this country, and of the aspect and probabilities of affairs on the Continent with a good sense, and a knowledge of subjects both at home and abroad that surprised me . . . in fact he talked like an officer and a statesman. The Secretary of State kept us long waiting, and certainly, for the last half or three-quarters of an hour, I don't know that I ever had a conversation that interested me more. Now, if the Secretary of State had been punctual, and admitted Lord Nelson in the first quarter of an hour I should have had the same impression of a light and trivial character that other people have had.

Six weeks later Nelson met the combined fleet of France and Spain off the Spanish coast.

Trafalgar: The Battle Opens, Morning 21 October 1805

MIDSHIPMAN BADCOCK RN

Britain's victory over the combined French and Spanish fleet at Trafalgar was the decisive naval engagement of the Napoleonic War; it also allowed Britain to rule the world's waves for two centuries. The combined fleet numbered thirty-three ships of the line and seven frigates; the Royal Navy had thirty-two ships of the line and five frigates. By the novel 'Nelson Touch' the British attacked the enemy line in two columns, at a 90-degree angle. Midshipman Badcock served aboard HMS Neptune.

At this period the enemy were forming their double line in the shape of a crescent. It was a beautiful sight when the line was completed: their broadsides turned towards us showing their iron teeth, and now and then trying the range of a shot to ascertain the distance, that they might, the moment we came within point-blank (about six hundred yards) open their fire upon our van ships – no doubt with the hope of dismasting some of our leading vessels before they could close and break their line.

Some of the enemy's ships were painted like ourselves – with double yellow sides, some with a broad single red or yellow streak, others all black; and the noble *Santissima Trinidada* (138) with four distinct lines of red, with a white ribbon between them, made her seem to be a superb man-of-war, which, indeed, she was. Her appearance was imposing, her head splendidly ornamented with a colossal group of figures, painted white, representing the Holy Trinity, from which she took her name. This magnificent ship was destined to be our opponent. She was lying to under topsails, top-gallant sails, royals, jib, and spanker; her courses were hauled up, and her lofty, towering sails looked beautiful, peering through the smoke as she awaited the onset. The flags of France and Spain, both handsome, chequered the line, waving defiance to that of Britain.

In our fleet Union Jacks and ensigns were made fast to the fore and fore-topmast-stays, as well as to the mizen rigging, besides one at the peak, in order that we might not mistake each other in the smoke, and to show the enemy our determination to conquer. Towards eleven our two lines were better formed, but still there existed long gaps in Vice-Admiral Collingwood's division. Lord Nelson's van was strong:

three three-deckers – *Victory*, *Téméraire*, and *Neptune* – and four seventy-fours, their jib-booms nearly over the others' taffrails. The bands playing 'God Save the King', 'Rule Britannia', and 'Britons, Strike Home', the crews stationed on the forecastles of the different ships, cheering the ship ahead of them when the enemy began to fire, sent those feelings to our hearts that insured victory. About ten minutes before twelve, our antagonists opened their fire upon the *Royal Sovereign* (110), Vice-Admiral Collingwood, who most nobly, and unsupported for at least ten minutes, led his division into action, steering for the *Santa Anna* (112), which was painted all black, bearing the flag of Admiral Gravina, during which time all the enemy's line that could possibly bring a gun to bear were firing at her. She was the admiration of the whole fleet.

To show the great and master-mind of Nelson, who was thinking of everything, even in the momentous hour of battle, when most minds would have been totally absorbed in other matters, it was remarked by him that the enemy had the iron hoops round their masts painted black. Orders were issued by signal to whitewash those of his fleet, that in the event of all the ensigns being shot away, his ships might be distinguished by their white masts and hoops.

Trafalgar: The Death of Nelson, Afternoon 21 October 1805

DR WILLIAM BEATTY

At Trafalgar, the Franco-Spanish combine lost twenty ships, destroyed or captured, the British none. But the British victory at Trafalgar came at high cost: the death of the forty-seven-year-old Admiral Lord Horatio Nelson.

Beatty was the surgeon aboard Nelson's flagship, HMS Victory.

About half an hour before the enemy opened their fire, the memorable telegraphic signal was made, that 'ENGLAND EXPECTS EVERY MAN WILL DO HIS DUTY,' which was spread and received throughout the fleet with enthusiasm. It is impossible adequately to describe by any language the lively emotions excited in the crew of the *Victory* when this propitious communication was made known to them: confidence and resolution were strongly portrayed in the countenance of all; and the sentiment generally expressed to each other was that they would prove to their country that day how well British seamen *could* 'do their duty' when led to battle by their revered admiral.

At fifty minutes past eleven, the enemy opened their fire on the commander in chief. They shewed great coolness in the commencement of the battle; for as the *Victory* approached their line, their ships lying immediately ahead of her and across her bows fired only one gun at a time, to ascertain whether she was yet within their range. This was frequently repeated by eight or nine of their ships, till at length a shot passed through the *Victory*'s main topgallant sail; the hole in which being discovered by the enemy, they immediately opened their broadsides, supporting an awful and tremendous fire.

In a very short time afterwards, Mr Scott, public secretary to the commander in chief, was killed by a cannon shot while in conversation with Captain Hardy. Lord Nelson being then near them; Captain Adair of the marines, with the assistance of a seaman, endeavoured to remove the body from his Lordship's sight: but he had already observed the fall of his secretary; and now said with anxiety, 'Is that poor Scott that is gone?' and on being answered in the affirmative by Captain Adair, he replied, 'Poor fellow!'

Lord Nelson and Captain Hardy walked the quarter deck in conversation for some time after this, while the enemy kept up an incessant raking fire.

A double-headed shot struck one of the parties of marines drawn up on the poop, and killed eight of them; when his Lordship, perceiving this, ordered Captain Adair to disperse his men round the ship, that they might not suffer so much from being together.

In a few minutes afterwards a shot struck the fore brace bits on the quarter deck, and passed between Lord Nelson and Captain Hardy; a splinter from the bits bruising Captain Hardy's foot, and tearing the buckle from his shoe. They both instantly stopped; and were observed by the officers on deck to survey each other with inquiring looks, each supposing the other to be wounded. His Lordship then smiled, and said: 'This is too warm work, Hardy, to last long'; and declared that 'through all the battles he had been in, he had never witnessed more cool courage than was displayed by the *Victory*'s crew on this occasion.'

The *Victory* by this time, having approached close to the enemy's van, had suffered very severely without firing a single gun: she had lost about twenty men killed, and had about thirty wounded. Her mizzen topmast, and all her studding sails and their booms on both sides were shot away;

the enemy's fire being chiefly directed at her rigging, with a view to disable her before she could close with them.

At four minutes past twelve o'clock, she opened her fire, from both sides of her decks, upon the enemy; when Captain Hardy represented to his Lordship, that 'it appeared impracticable to pass through the enemy's line without going on board some one of their ships.'

Lord Nelson answered, 'I cannot help it: it does not signify which we run on board of; go on board which you please; take your choice.'

At twenty minutes past twelve, the tiller ropes being shot away: Mr Atkinson, the master, was ordered below to get the helm put to port; which being done, the *Victory* was soon run on board the *Redoubtable* of seventy-four guns.

On coming alongside and nearly on board of her, that ship fired her broadside into the *Victory*, and immediately let down her lower deck ports; which, as has been since learnt, was done to prevent her from being boarded through them by the *Victory*'s crew. She never fired a great gun after this single broadside.

A few minutes after this, the *Téméraire* fell likewise on board of the *Redoubtable*, on the side opposite to the *Victory*; having also an enemy's ship, said to be *La Fougueux*, on board of *her* on her other side: so that the extraordinary and unprecedented circumstance occurred here, of *four* ships of the line being *on board of each other* in the heat of battle; forming as compact a tier as if they had been moored together, their heads lying all the same way. The *Téméraire*, as was just before mentioned, was between the *Redoubtable* and *La Fougueux*.

The *Redoubtable* commenced a heavy fire of musketry from the tops, which was continued for a considerable time with destructive effect to the *Victory*'s crew: her great guns however being silent, it was supposed at different times that she had surrendered; and in consequence of this opinion, the *Victory* twice ceased firing upon her by orders transmitted from the quarter deck.

At this period, scarcely a person in the *Victory* escaped unhurt who was exposed to the enemy's musketry; but there were frequent huzzas and cheers heard from between the decks, in token of the surrender of different of the enemy's ships. An incessant fire was kept up from both sides of the *Victory*: her larboard guns played upon the *Santissima Trinidada* and the *Bucentaur*; and the starboard guns of the middle and lower decks were depressed, and fired with a diminished charge of powder, and three shot each, into the *Redoubtable*. This mode of firing was adopted by Lieutenants Williams, King, Yule, and Brown, to obviate the danger of the *Téméraire*'s suffering from the *Victory*'s shot passing through the *Redoubtable*; which must have been the case if the usual quantity of powder, and the common elevation, had been given to the guns.

A circumstance occurred in this situation which showed in a most striking manner the cool intrepidity of the officers and men stationed on the lower deck of the *Victory*. When the guns on this deck were run out, their muzzles came into contact with the *Redoubtable*'s side; and consequently at every discharge there was reason to fear that the enemy would take fire, and both the *Victory* and the *Téméraire* be involved in her flames. Here then was seen the astonishing spectacle of the fireman of each gun standing ready with a bucket full of water, which as soon as his gun was discharged he dashed into the enemy through the holes made in her side by the shot.

It was from this ship (the *Redoubtable*) that Lord Nelson received his mortal wound. About fifteen minutes past one o'clock, which was in the heat of the engagement, he was walking the middle of the quarter-deck with Captain Hardy, and in the act of turning near the hatchway with his face towards the stern of the *Victory*, when the fatal ball was fired from the enemy's mizen-top; which, from the situation of the two ships (lying on board of each other), was brought just abaft, and rather below, the *Victory*'s main-yard, and of course not more than fifteen yards distant from that part of the deck where his Lordship stood. The ball struck the epaulette on his left shoulder, and penetrated his chest. He fell with his face on the deck. Captain Hardy, who was on his right (the side furthest from the enemy) and advanced some steps before his Lordship, on turning round, saw the Sergeant-Major (Secker) of Marines with two seamen raising him from the deck; where he had fallen on the same spot on which, a little before, his secretary had breathed his last, with whose blood his Lordship's clothes were much soiled. Captain Hardy expressed a hope that he was not severely wounded; to which the gallant Chief replied: 'They have done for me at last, Hardy.' 'I hope not,' answered Captain Hardy. 'Yes,' replied his Lordship, 'my backbone is shot through.'

Captain Hardy ordered the seamen to carry the Admiral to the cockpit; and now two incidents occurred strikingly characteristic of this great man, and strongly marking that energy and reflection which in his heroic mind rose superior even to the immediate consideration of his present awful condition. While the men were carrying him down the ladder from the middle deck, his Lordship observed that the tiller ropes were not yet replaced; and desired one of the midshipmen stationed there to

go up on the quarterdeck and remind Captain Hardy of that circumstance, and request that new ones should be immediately rove. Having
delivered this order, he took his handkerchief from his pocket and
covered his face with it, that he might be conveyed to the cockpit at
this crisis unnoticed by the crew . . .

The *Victory*'s crew cheered whenever they observed an enemy's ship
surrender. On one of these occasions, Lord Nelson anxiously inquired
what was the cause of it; when Lieutenant Pasco, who lay wounded at
some distance from his Lordship, raised himself up, and told him that
another ship had struck: which appeared to give him much satisfaction.
He now felt an ardent thirst; and frequently called for drink, and to be
fanned with paper, making use of these words: 'Fan, fan,' and 'Drink,
drink.' This he continued to repeat, when he wished for drink or the
refreshment of cool air, till a very few minutes before he expired . . .

His Lordship now requested the surgeon, who had been previously
absent a short time attending Mr Rivers to return to the wounded, and
give his assistance to such of them as he could be useful to; 'for,' said he,
'you can do nothing for me.' The surgeon assured him that the assistant
surgeons were doing everything that could be effected for those unfortunate men; but on his Lordship's several times repeating his injunctions
to that purpose, he left him, surrounded by Doctor Scott, Mr Burke and
two of his Lordship's domestics. After the surgeon had been absent a
few minutes attending Lieutenants Peake and Reeves of the Marines,
who were wounded, he was called by Doctor Scott to his Lordship,
who said: 'Ah, Mr Beatty! I have sent for you to say, what I forgot to
tell you before, that all power of motion and feeling below my breast
are gone; and *you*,' continued he, 'very well *know* I can live but a short
time.' The emphatic manner in which he pronounced these last words
left no doubt in the surgeon's mind, that he adverted to the case of a
man who had some months before received a mortal injury of the spine
on board the *Victory*, and had laboured under similar privations of sense
and muscular motion. The case had made a great impression on Lord
Nelson: he was accordingly explained to him; and he now appeared to
apply the situation and fate of this man to himself. The surgeon answered,
'My Lord, you told me so before': but he now examined the extremities, to ascertain the fact; when his Lordship said, 'Ah, Beatty! I am too
certain of it: Scott and Burke have tried it already. *You know* I am gone.'
The surgeon replied: 'My Lord, unhappily for our country, nothing can
be done for you', and having made this declaration he was so much
affected, that he turned round and withdrew a few steps to conceal his

emotions. His Lordship said: 'I know it. I feel something rising in my breast,' putting his hand on his left side, 'which tells me I am gone.' Drink was recommended liberally, and Doctor Scott and Mr Burke fanned him with paper. He often exclaimed, 'God be praised, I have done my duty': and upon the surgeon's inquiring whether his pain was still very great, he declared, it continued so very severe, that he wished he was dead. 'Yet,' said he in a lower voice, 'one would like to live a little longer, too': and after a pause of a few minutes, he added in the same tone, 'What would become of poor Lady Hamilton (Nelson's mistress), if she knew my situation!' . . .

Captain Hardy now came to the cockpit to see his Lordship a second time, which was after an interval of about fifty minutes from the conclusion of his first visit. Before he quitted the deck, he sent Lieutenant Hills to acquaint Admiral Collingwood with the lamentable circumstance of Lord Nelson's being wounded. Lord Nelson and Captain Hardy shook hands again: and while the Captain retained his Lordship's hand, he congratulated him, even in the arms of death, on his brilliant victory; 'which,' said he, 'was complete'; though he did not know how many of the enemy were captured, as it was impossible to perceive every ship distinctly. He was certain however of fourteen or fifteen having surrendered. His Lordship answered, 'That is well, but I bargained for twenty': and then emphatically exclaimed, '*Anchor*, Hardy, *anchor!*' To this the Captain replied: 'I suppose, my Lord, Admiral Collingwood will now take upon himself the direction of affairs.' 'Not while I live, I hope, Hardy!' cried the dying chief; and at that moment endeavoured ineffectually to raise himself from the bed. 'No,' added he; 'do *you* anchor, Hardy.' Captain Hardy then said: 'Shall *we* make the signal, sir?' 'Yes,' answered his Lordship, 'for if I live, I'll anchor.' The energetic manner in which he uttered these his last orders to Captain Hardy, accompanied with his efforts to raise himself, evinced his determination never to resign the command while he retained the exercise of his transcendent faculties, and that he expected Captain Hardy still to carry into effect the suggestions of his exalted mind; a sense of his duty overcoming the pains of death. He then told Captain Hardy, he felt that in a few minutes he should be no more; adding in a low tone, 'Don't throw me overboard, Hardy.' The Captain answered: 'Oh! no, certainly not', 'Then,' replied his Lordship, 'You know what to do: and', continued he, 'take care of my dear Lady Hamilton, Hardy: take care of poor Lady Hamilton. Kiss me, Hardy.' The Captain now knelt down, and kissed his cheek; when his Lordship said, 'Now I am satisfied. Thank

God, I have done my duty.' Captain Hardy stood for a minute or two in silent contemplation: he knelt down again, and kissed his Lordship's forehead. His Lordship said: 'Who is that?' The Captain answered: 'It is Hardy'; to which his Lordship replied, 'God bless you, Hardy!' . . . His thirst now increased; and he called for 'drink, drink,' 'fan, fan,' and 'rub, rub,' addressing himself in the last case to Doctor Scott, who had been rubbing his Lordship's breast with his hand, from which he found some relief. These words he spoke in a very rapid manner, which rendered his articulation difficult: but he every now and then, with evident increase of pain, made a greater effort with his vocal powers, and pronounced distinctly these last words: 'Thank God, I have done my duty'; and this great sentiment he continued to repeat as long as he was able to give it utterance.

As Nelson had requested, he did not suffer the usual indignity of the dead Jack Tar, to be heaved overboard. Instead his body was preserved in a cask of brandy and brought back to England for a state funeral. The outpouring of grief by the British public was unprecedented, and nothing like it would be seen again until the death of Diana, Princess of Wales, almost 200 years later.

The Peninsular War: Plundering a Dead French Soldier after the Battle of Vimeiro, 21 August 1808

RIFLEMAN HARRIS

The Peninsular War (1808–13) was the principal British contribution to the land campaign against Bonaparte. It followed a Spanish revolt against Napoleon's attempt to install his brother Joseph as King of Spain; at Spanish request the British landed an expeditionary force in Iberia under Sir Arthur Wellesley.

At Vimeiro, Portugal, Wellesley carefully selected a defensive position – and let the French attack. They sustained 2,000 casualties. Plenty of pickings, therefore, for the jackdaw-like British soldier.

Rifleman Harris served with the 95th Rifles.

After the battle I strolled about the field in order to see if there was anything to be found worth picking up amongst the dead. The first thing I saw was a three-pronged silver fork, which, as it lay by itself, had most likely been dropped by some person who had been on the look-out before me. A little further on I saw a French soldier sitting against a small rise in the ground or bank. He was wounded in the throat, and appeared very faint, the bosom of his coat being saturated with the blood which had flowed down. By his side lay his cap, and close to that was a bundle containing a quantity of gold and silver crosses, which I concluded he had plundered from some convent or church. He looked the picture of a sacrilegious thief, dying hopelessly, and overtaken by Divine wrath. I kicked over his cap, which was also full of plunder, but I declined taking anything from him. I felt fearful of incurring the wrath of Heaven for the like offence, so I left him, and passed on. A little further off lay an officer of the 50th regiment. I knew him by sight, and recognized him as he lay. He was quite dead, and lying on his back. He had been plundered, and his clothes were torn open. Three bullet-holes were close together in the pit of his stomach: beside him lay an empty pocket-book, and his epaulette had been pulled from his shoulder.

I had moved on but a few paces when I recollected that perhaps the officer's shoes might serve me, my own being considerably the worse for wear, so I returned again, went back, pulled one of his shoes off, and knelt down on one knee to try it on. It was not much better than my own; however, I determined on the exchange, and proceeded to take off its fellow. As I did so I was startled by the sharp report of a firelock, and, at the same moment, a bullet whistled close by my head. Instantly starting up, I turned, and looked in the direction whence the shot had come. There was no person near me in this part of the field. The dead and the dying lay thickly all around; but nothing else could I see. I looked to the priming of my rifle, and again turned to the dead officer of the 50th. It was evident that some plundering scoundrel had taken a shot at me, and the fact of his doing so proclaimed him one of the enemy. To distinguish him amongst the bodies strewn about was impossible; perhaps he might himself be one of the wounded. Hardly had I effected the exchange, put on the dead officer's shoes, and resumed my rifle, when another shot took place, and a second ball whistled past me. This time I was ready, and turning quickly, I saw my man: he was just about to squat down behind a small mound, about twenty paces from me. I took a haphazard shot at him, and instantly knocked him over. I immediately ran up to him; he had fallen on his face, and I heaved him over on his back, bestrode his body, and drew my sword-bayonet. There was, however, no occasion for the precaution as he was even then in the agonies of death.

It was a relief to me to find I had not been mistaken. He was a French light-infantry man, and I therefore took it quite in the way of business

— he had attempted my life, and lost his own. It was the fortune of war; so, stooping down, with my sword I cut the green string that sustained his calibash, and took a hearty pull to quench my thirst.

After I had shot the French light-infantry man, and quenched my thirst from his calibash, finding he was quite dead, I proceeded to search him. Whilst I turned him about in the endeavour at finding the booty I felt pretty certain he had gathered from the slain, an officer of the 60th approached, and accosted me.

'What! looking for money, my lad,' said he, 'eh?'

'I am, sir,' I answered; 'but I cannot discover where this fellow has hid his hoard.'

'You knocked him over, my man,' he said, 'in good style, and deserve something for the shot. Here,' he continued, stooping down and feeling in the lining of the Frenchman's coat, 'this is the place where these rascals generally carry their coin. Rip up the lining of his coat, and then search in his stock. I know them better than you seem to do.'

Thanking the officer for his courtesy, I proceeded to cut open the lining of his jacket with my sword–bayonet, and was quickly rewarded for my labour by finding a yellow silk purse, wrapped up in an old black silk handkerchief. The purse contained several doubloons, three or four napoleons, and a few dollars. Whilst I was counting the money, the value of which, except the dollars, I did not then know, I heard the bugle of the Rifles sound out the assembly, so I touched my cap to the officer, and returned towards them.

The men were standing at ease, with the officers in front. As I approached them, Major Travers, who was in command of the four companies, called me to him.

'What have you got there, sir?' he said. 'Show me.'

I handed him the purse, expecting a reprimand for my pains. He, however, only laughed as he examined it, and, turning, showed it to his brother officers.

'You did that well, Harris,' he said, 'and I am sorry the purse is not better filled. Fall in.' In saying this, he handed me back the purse, and I joined my company. Soon afterwards, the roll being called, we were all ordered to lie down and gain a little rest after our day's work.

The Peninsular War: The Storming of Badajoz, 6 April 1812

ROBERT BLAKENEY

Badajoz was a fortress in the south of French-occupied Spain. Only three months earlier British troops in the Peninsula had stormed another French stronghold, Ciudad Rodrigo.

The dreadful strife now commenced. The thundering cheer of the British soldiers as they rushed forward through the outer ditch, together with the appalling roar of all arms sent forth in defiance from within, was tremendous. Whenever an instant pause occurred it was filled by the heart-rending shrieks of the trodden-down wounded and by the lengthened groans of the dying. Three times were the breaches cleared of Frenchmen, driven off at the point of the bayonet by gallant British soldiers to the very summit, when they were by the no less gallant foe each time driven back, leaving their bravest officers and foremost soldiers behind, who, whether killed or wounded, were tossed down headlong to the foot of the breaches. Throughout this dreadful conflict our bugles were continually sounding the advance. The cry of 'Bravo! Bravo!' resounded through the ditches and along the foot of the breaches; but no British cry was heard from within the walls of Badajoz save that of despair, uttered by the bravest, who despite of all obstacles forced their way into the body of the place, and there through dire necessity abandoned, groaned forth their last stabbed by unnumbered wounds. Again and again were the breaches attacked with redoubled fury and defended with equal pertinacity and stern resolution, seconded by every resource which science could adopt or ingenuity suggest. Bags and barrels of gunpowder with short fuses were rolled down, which, bursting at the bottom or along the face of the breaches, destroyed all who advanced. Thousands of live shells, hand-grenades, fireballs and every species of destructive combustible were thrown down the breaches and over the walls into the ditches, which, lighting and exploding at the same instant, rivalled the lightning and thunder of heaven. This at intervals was succeeded by an impenetrable darkness as of the infernal regions. Gallant foes laughing at death met, fought, bled and rolled upon earth; and from the very earth destruction burst, for the exploding mines cast up friends and foes together, who in burning torture clashed and shrieked in the air. Partly burned they fell back into the inundating water, continually lighted by the incessant bursting of shells . . .

At length the bugles of the 4th and light divisions sounded the recall . . . I galloped off to where Lord Wellington had taken his station. This was easily discerned by means of two fireballs shot out from the fortress at the commencement of the attack, which continued to burn brilliantly along the water-cut. . . . Near the end of this channel, behind a rising mound, were Lord Wellington and his personal staff, screened from the enemy's direct fire, but within the range of shells. One of his staff sat down by his side with a candle to enable the general to read and write all his communications and orders . . . I stood not far from his lordship. But due respect prevented any of us bystanders from approaching so near as to enable us to ascertain the import of the reports which he was continually receiving; yet it was very evident that the information which they conveyed was far from flattering; and the recall on the bugles was again and again repeated. But about half-past eleven o'clock an officer rode up at full speed on a horse covered with foam, and announced the joyful tidings that General Picton had made a lodgment within the castle by escalade, and had withdrawn the troops from the trenches to enable him to maintain his dearly purchased hold. Lord Wellington was evidently delighted . . . I mounted my horse . . . and then made the best of my way to the walls of the castle; their height was rather forbidding, and an enfilading fire still continued. The ladders were warm and slippery with blood and brains of many a gallant soldier.

After capturing Badajoz Wellesley's 'scum of the earth' ran amok inside the town. On entering, James McGrigor, Wellington's medical officer, found: 'the whole of the soldiers appeared to be in a state of mad drunkenness. In every street, and in every corner we met them forcing their way like furies into houses . . . In passing some houses which they had entered we heard the shrieks of females, and sometimes the groans of those they were no doubt butchering . . .' It was twenty-nine hours before the troops were brought under control.

Waterloo: Taken Prisoner, 18 June 1815

ENSIGN EDMUND WHEATLEY

Waterloo was the final battle of Napoleon's Hundred Days, his last grasp at glory. He commanded an army of 80,000; the Allied Army under Wellington consisted of 67,000 men. As was the wont of Wellesley – now the Duke of Wellington – he positioned his force carefully, along a line of hills. There were two advance posts: the farms at La Haye Sainte and Hougemont.

About ten o'clock, the order came to clean out the muskets and fresh load them. Half an allowance of rum was then issued, and we descended into the plain, and took our position in solid Squares. When this was arranged as per order, we were ordered to remain in our position but, if we like, to lay down, which the battalion did [as well as] the officers in the rere.

I took this opportunity of surveying our situation. It was singular to perceive the shoals of Cavalry and artillery suddenly in our rere all arranged in excellent order as if by a magic wand. The whole of the horse Guards stood behind us. For my part I thought they were at Knightsbridge barracks or prancing on St James's Street.

A Ball whizzed in the air. Up we started simultaneously. I looked at my watch. It was just eleven o'clock, Sunday . . . morning. In five minutes a stunning noise took place and a shocking havock commenced.

One could almost feel the undulation of the air from the multitude of cannon shot. The first man who fell was five files on my left. With the utmost distortion of feature he lay on his side and shrivelling up every muscle of the body he twirled his elbow round and round in acute agony, then dropped lifeless, dying as it's called a death of glory, heaving his last breath on the field of fame. *Dieu m'engarde!*

A black consolidated body was soon seen approaching and we distinguished by sudden flashes of light from the sun's rays, the iron-cased cavalry of the enemy. Shouts of 'Stand firm!' 'Stand fast!' were heard from the little squares around and very quickly these gigantic fellows were upon us.

No words can convey the sensation we felt on seeing these heavy-armed bodies advancing at full gallop against us, flourishing their sabres in the air, striking their armour with the handles, the sun gleaming on the steel. The long horse hair, dishevelled by the wind, bore an appearance confounding the senses to an astonishing disorder. But we dashed them back as coolly as the sturdy rock repels the ocean's foam. The sharp-toothed bayonet bit many an adventurous fool, and on all sides we presented our bristly points like the peevish porcupines assailed by clamorous dogs.

The horse Guards then came up and drove them back; and although the sight is shocking 'tis beautiful to see the skirmish of Cavalry.

The French made repeated attacks of this kind. But we stood firm as the ground we stood on, and two long hours were employed in these successive attacks.

About two o'clock the cavalry ceased annoying and the warfare took a new turn. In order to destroy our squares, the enemy filled the air with shells, howitzers and bombs, so that every five or six minutes, the whole Battalion lay on its face then sprang up again when the danger was over.

The Prince of Orange gallop'd by, screaming out like a new born infant, 'Form into line! Form into line!' And we obeyed.

About this time the battle grew faint and a mutual cannonade with musketry amused us for one and a half hours, during which time I walked up and down chatting and joking with the young officers who had not until then smelt powder.

An ammunition cart blew up near us, smashing men and horses. I took a calm survey of the field around and felt shocked at the sight of broken armour, lifeless bodies, murdered horses, shattered wheels, caps, helmets, swords, muskets, pistols, still and silent. Here and there a frightened horse would rush across the plain trampling on the dying and the dead. Three or four poor wounded animals standing on three legs, the other dangling before them. We killed several of these unfortunate beasts and it would have been an equal Charity to have perform'd the same operation on the wriggling, feverish, mortally lacerated soldiers as they rolled on the ground.

About four o'clock the battle was renewed with uncommon ardour. We still stood in line. The carnage was frightful. The balls which missed us mowed down the Dutch behind us, and swept away many of the closely embattled Cavalry behind them.

I saw a cannon ball take away a Colonel of the Nassau Regiment so cleanly that the horse never moved from under him. While I was busy in keeping the men firm in their ranks, closing up the vacuities as the balls swept off the men, inspecting the fallen to detect deception or subterfuge, a regiment of Cuirassiers darted like a thunderbolt among us. At the instant a squadron of horse Guards dashed up to our rescue. In the confusion of the moment I made for the Colors to defend them. And we succeeded with infinite difficulty in rallying the men again.

I parried with great good fortune a back stroke from a horseman as he flew by me and Captain Sander had a deep slice from the same fellow on the head the instant after.

The battalion once more formed into a solid square, in which we remained the whole afternoon.

I felt the ardor of the fight increase very much within me, from the uncommon fury of the engagement.

Just then I fired a slain soldier's musket until my shoulder was nearly jellied and my mouth was begrimed with gunpowder to such a degree that I champed the gritty composition unknowingly.

Nothing could equal the splendor and terror of the scene. Charge after charge succeeded in constant succession. The clashing of swords, the clattering of musketry, the hissing of balls, and shouts and clamours produced a sound, jarring and confounding the senses, as if hell and the Devil were in evil contention.

About this time I saw the Duke of Wellington running from a charge of Cavalry towards the Horse-Guards, waving his hat to beckon them to the encounter.

All our artillery in front fell into the French power, the bombardiers skulking under the carriages. But five minutes put them again into our hands and the men creeping out applied the match and sent confusion and dismay into the retreating enemy.

Several times were these charges renewed and as often defeated. Charge met charge and all was pellmell. The rays of the sun glittered on the clashing swords as the two opposing bodies closed in fearful combat and our balls clattered on the shining breastplates like a hail shower.

As I stood in the square I looked down, I recollect, to take a pinch of snuff and thought of the old ballad, which I had seen somewhere, of the aged Nurse who describes the glorious battles of Marlborough to the child. After each relation of valor and victory, the infant says:

> 'Ten thousand slain you say and more?
> What did they kill each other for?'
> 'Indeed I cannot tell,' said she,
> 'But 'twas a famous victory.'

The field was now thickened with heaps of bodies and shattered instruments. Carcases of men and beasts lay promiscuously entwined. Aide-de-Camps scoured across with inconceivable velocity. All was hurry and indefatigable exertion. The small squares on our right kept up incessant firings and the fight was as obstinate as at the commencement.

The Duke of Wellington passed us twice, slowly and coolly.

No advantage as yet was discernible on either side. The French Cavalry were less annoying. Their brave, repeated assaults had cost them very dear.

About six o'clock a passe-parole ran down the line – not to be disheartened, as the Prussians were coming up to our left, which news we received with loud cheers. And on looking to the left I perceived at some distance a dark swarm moving out of a thick wood. In twenty minutes a fresh cannonading began as if in rere of the French and the battle raged with increased vehemence.

A French Regiment of Infantry before us opposite the Farm house called the holy hedge (La Haye Sainte) advanced considerably just then and poured a destructive fire into our Battalion.

Colonel Ompteda ordered us instantly into line to charge, with a strong injunction to 'walk' forward, until he gave the word. When within sixty yards he cried 'Charge', we ran forward huzzaing. The trumpet sounded and no one but a soldier can describe the thrill one instantly feels in such an awful moment. At the bugle sound the French stood until we just reached them. I ran by Colonel Ompteda who cried out, 'That's right, Wheatley!'

I found myself in contact with a French officer but ere we could decide, he fell by an unknown hand. I then ran at a drummer, but he leaped over a ditch through a hedge in which he stuck fast. I heard a cry of, 'The Cavalry! The Cavalry!' But so eager was I that I did not mind it at the moment, and when on the eve of dragging the Frenchman back (his iron-bound hat having saved him from a Cut) I recollect no more. On recovering my senses, I look'd up and found myself, bareheaded, in a clay ditch with a violent head-ache. Close by me lay Colonel Ompteda on his back, his head stretched back with his mouth open; and a hole in his throat. A Frenchman's arm across my leg.

So confused was I that I did not remember I was on the field of Battle at the moment. Lifting up a little, I look'd over the edge of the ditch and saw the backs of a French Regiment and all the day's employment instantly suggested itself to my mind. Suddenly I distinguished some voices and heard one say '*En voici! En voici!*'

I lay down as dead, retaining my breath, and fancied I was shot in the back of my head. Presently a fellow cries, '*Voici un autre b.*' And a tug at my epaulette bespoke his commission. A thought struck me – he would turn me round to rifle my pockets. So starting up, I leaped up the ditch; but a swimming seized me and I was half on the ground when the fellow thrust his hand in my collar, grinning, '*Ou va's tu, chien?*' I begged of him to let me pick up my cap and he dragged me into the house.

The inside of La Haye Sainte I found completely destroyed, nothing but the rafters and props remaining. The floor, covered with mortar bricks and straw, was strewed with bodies of the German Infantry and French Tirailleurs. A Major in Green lay by the door. The carnage had been very great in this place.

I was taken over these bodies out of a door on the right, through a garden to the back of the house where I found several Officers and men standing. They instantly crowded round me. One of my wings was on and the other half off. My oil skin haversac was across my shoulder, and my cap fastened to my waist, by running my sash through the internal lining.

A multitude of questions was put to me by the men and Officers while I fastened on my Cap: '*Vous êtes Chef de Battalion, Monsieur?*' . . .

It was bad luck on Wheatley to be taken prisoner mere minutes before Wellington began the advance which finally won the 'damned close run thing'.

Waterloo: The Final Attack; The Rifle Brigade Advance, 7 p.m., 18 June 1815

CAPTAIN J. KINCAID, RIFLE BRIGADE

I shall never forget the scene which the field of battle presented about seven in the evening. I felt weary and worn out, less from fatigue than anxiety.

Our division, which had stood upwards of 5,000 men at the commencement of the battle, had gradually dwindled down into a solitary line of skirmishers. The 27th regiment were lying literally dead, in square, a few yards behind us. My horse had received another shot through the leg, and one through the flap of the saddle, which lodged in his body, sending him a step beyond the pension list. The smoke still hung so thick about us that we could see nothing. I walked a little way to each flank to endeavour to get a glimpse of what was going on; but nothing met my eye except the mangled remains of men and horses, and I was obliged to return to my post as wise as I went.

I had never yet heard of a battle in which everybody was killed; but this seemed likely to be an exception, as all were going by turns . . .

Presently a cheer which we knew to be British commenced far to the right, and made everyone prick up his ears; it was Lord Wellington's long-wished-for orders to advance. It gradually approached, growing louder as it grew near. We took it up by instinct, charged through the hedge down upon the old knoll, sending our adversaries flying at the point of the bayonet. Lord Wellington galloped up to us at the instant, and our men began to cheer him; but he called out, 'No cheering, my lads, but forward, and complete our victory!'

This movement had carried us clear of the smoke; and to people who had been so many hours enveloped in darkness, in the midst of destruction, and naturally anxious about the result of the day, the scene which now met the eye conveyed a feeling of more exquisite gratification than can be conceived. It was a fine summer evening just before sunset. The French were flying in one confused mass. British lines were seen in close pursuit, and in admirable order, as far as the eye could reach to the right, while the plain to the left was filled with Prussians. The enemy made one last attempt at a stand on the rising ground to our right of La Belle Alliance; but a charge from General Adam's Brigade again threw them into a state of confusion, which was now inextricable, and their ruin was complete. Artillery, baggage, and everything belonging to them, fell into our hands. After pursuing them until dark, we halted about two miles beyond the field of battle, leaving the Prussians to follow up the victory.

Nelson and Wellington aside, the British won the 'Great War' (as contemporaries called the bull-dogged, twenty-year conflict against Boney and expansionist republican France) because the Industrial Revolution had given them a bigger wallet to spend on the conflict and an infinitely greater capacity to produce military materiel. (Ironic proof of this was provided by Napoleon himself, who resorted to furnishing his troops with British-made boots, smuggled in from Germany, when French manufacturers could not meet the Grand Army's demand.) Victory, meanwhile, allowed the uninterrupted expansion of the Empire, into the Dutch

East Indies, Ceylon, Egypt and South Africa. England was the strongest power on earth.

Not that everything in the English garden was rosy. The National Debt reached £861,000 and there was unrest in town and country, some of it violent, which was matched by counter-reaction by the authorities. As Fowell Buxton reminded the Commons in 1819, George III's reign had seen 'more crimes . . . denounced as capital [offences] . . . than in the reigns of the Plantagenets, the Tudors, and the Stuarts combined'. Thankfully, that last resort of English common sense and liberty, the jury system, hesitated to return guilty verdicts in capital cases. In this period of paradox, the English began to apply Christian ethics to social miseries. There was nothing new about the ills (there had been slums, after all, in London since medieval times); what was novel was the belief that they should and could be dealt with.

Factory Conditions, c. 1815

ELIZABETH BENTLEY

The evidence of a female mill-hand to the Parliamentary Commissioners.

What age are you?
  Twenty-three.

Where do you live?
  At Leeds.

What time did you begin work at the factory?
  When I was six years old.

At whose factory did you work?
  Mr Burk's.

What kind of mill is it?
  Flax mill.

What was your business in that mill?
  I was a little doffer.

What were your hours of labour in that mill?
From 5 in the morning till 9 at night, when they were thronged.

For how long a time together have you worked that excessive length of time?
For about a year.

What were the usual hours of labour when you were not so thronged?
From six in the morning till 7 at night.

What time was allowed for meals?
Forty minutes at noon.

Had you any time to get your breakfast or drinking?
No, we had to get it as we could.

Do you consider doffing a laborious employment?
Yes.

Explain what you had to do?
When the frames are full, they have to stop the frames, and take the flyers off, and take the full bobbins off, and carry them to the roller, and then put empty ones on, and set the frame going again.

Does that keep you constantly on your feet?
Yes, there are so many frames and they run so quick.

Your labour is very excessive?
Yes, you have not time for anything.

Suppose you flagged a little, or were late, what would they do?
Strap us.

And they are in the habit of strapping those who are last in doffing?
Yes.

Constantly?
Yes.

Girls as well as boys?
Yes.

Have you ever been strapped?
    Yes.

Severely?
    Yes.

Is the strap used so as to hurt you excessively?
    Yes it is . . . I have seen the overlooker go to the top end of the room, where the little girls hug the can to the backminders; he has taken a strap, and a whistle in his mouth, and sometimes he has got a chain and chained them, and strapped them all down the room.

What was his reason for that?
    He was very angry.

Did you live far from the mill?
    Yes, two miles.

Had you a clock?
    No, we had not.

Were you generally there in time?
    Yes, my mother has been up at 4 o'clock in the morning, and at 2 o'clock in the morning; the colliers used to go to their work at 3 or 4 o'clock, and when she heard them stirring she has got up out of her warm bed, and gone out and asked them the time; and I have sometimes been at Hunslet Car at 2 o'clock in the morning, when it was streaming down with rain, and we have had to stay till the mill was opened.

You are considerably deformed in person as a consequence of this labour?
    Yes I am.

And what time did it come on?
    I was about 13 years old when it began coming, and it has got worse since; it is five years since my mother died, and my mother was never able to get me a good pair of stays to hold me up, and when my mother died I had to do for myself, and got me a pair.

Were you perfectly straight and healthy before you worked at a mill?
    Yes, I was as straight a little girl as ever went up and down town.

Were you straight till you were 13?
  Yes, I was.

Did your deformity come upon you with much pain and weariness?
  Yes, I cannot express the pain all the time it was coming.

Do you know of anybody that has been similarly injured in their health?
  Yes, in their health, but not many deformed as I am.

It is very common to have weak ankles and crooked knees?
  Yes, very common indeed.

This is brought on by stopping the spindle?
  Yes.

Where are you now?
  In the poorhouse.

State what you think as to the circumstances in which you have been placed during all this time of labour, and what you have considered about it as to the hardship and cruelty of it.

The witness was too much affected to answer the question.

★   ★   ★

  Reformers convinced Parliament to pass the Factory Act in 1819 which banned the employment of children under nine in cotton mills; at the instigation of Lord Shaftesbury, an 1833 Factory Act fixed a maximum forty-eight-hour week for children aged nine to thirteen, and a sixty-eight-hour week for under eighteen-year-olds.

Climbing Boys, 1817

JOHN COOK

The use of climbing boys to clean chimneys had been banned by legislation as early as 1788, but this was honoured only in the breach. Cook was a master sweep called to give evidence before a House of Commons Select Committee on Climbing Boys.

Do you give more for children that are delicately formed, and who therefore are better calculated for ascending small chimneys? – The smaller they are the master generally likes them the better, because they are generally more serviceable to them.

So that a small boy bears a better price than a full grown boy? – Yes, if he is strong enough to do the duty, and is a hearty looking boy of his age.

Is it not the practice of some masters to advertise themselves as being in possession of small boys for the purpose of ascending flues? – Almost every one has got it in their bills, that they keep small boys for register stoves, and such like as that; I do not recollect ever seeing it in the newspapers, but they do it in their bills.

How do you ascertain the age of the boy when he is offered to you as an apprentice; do you take the parents' word for it? – The parents will often say that he is older than what he is.

Are you in the habit of getting any other evidence of their ages than the parents' own words? – No.

Are the boys ever washed? – Yes, I wash mine regularly; but some of the lower class are not washed for six months.

Do they receive any education? – Many do not.

Is it a general practice to attend divine worship? – Great numbers are neither washed nor attend on the Sunday.

Are not climbing boys subject to sores and bruises, and wounds and burns on their thighs and knees, in consequence of ascending chimneys? – Yes, because learning very fresh boys makes their knees and elbows very sore, but when they have properly learnt their trade these parts get very hard, and they very seldom get sore again unless they meet with an accident; sometimes they get burnt by chimneys partly on fire.

The committee understand, by use, that the extremities of the elbows and of the knees become as hard as the heel of the foot of a person who walks without shoes? – Yes, it does.

What time does it take before those parts get cartilaginous? – Six months.

Do you find many boys show great repugnance to go up at first? – Yes, most of them do.

And if they resist and reject, in what way do you force them up? – By telling them we must take them back again to their father and mother, and give them up again; and their parents are generally people who cannot maintain them.

So that they are afraid of going back to their parents for fear of being starved? – Yes; they go through a deal of hardship before they come to our trade.

Do you use any more violent means? – Sometimes a rod. When I was an apprentice, journeymen often used to keep a cat, made of rope, hard at each end and as thick as your thumb, in their pocket to flog the boys; and I think it is sometimes used now.

Have you ever known a journeyman ill-use any of the children? – Yes, for very little faults they will frequently kick them and smack them about; the boys are more afraid of them than of their masters.

You said that the elbows and knees of the boys, when they first begin the business, become very sore, and afterwards get callous; are those boys employed in sweeping chimneys during the soreness of those parts? – It depends upon the sort of master they have got; you must keep them a little at it, or they will never learn their business, even during the sores.

Is the skin broke generally? – Yes, it is . . .

Despite the findings of the Select Committee, it was not until Lord Salisbury's Chimney Sweepers Bill of 1875 that the employment of climbing boys was both forbidden and enforced.

Peterloo, 16 August 1819

SAMUEL BAMFORD

Some 60,000 people marched to the Suffrage Reform meeting at St Peter's Fields, Manchester. Eleven were killed when, on the orders of local magistrates, troops of the Cheshire volunteers, the Manchester Yeomanry, and the 15th Hussars rode into the crowd to arrest the speaker, Henry Hunt.

Bamford was a reformer and poet.

In about half an hour after our arrival the sounds of music and reiterated shouts proclaimed the near approach of Mr Hunt and his party; and in a minute or two they were seen coming from Deansgate, preceded by a band of music and several flags. On the driving seat of a barouche sat a neatly dressed female, supporting a small flag, on which were some emblematical drawings and an inscription. Within the carriage were Mr Hunt, who stood up, Mr Johnson, of Smedley Cottage; Mr Moorhouse, of Stockport; Mr Carlile, of London; Mr John Knight, of Manchester; and Mr Saxton, a sub-editor of the *Manchester Observer*. Their approach was hailed by one universal shout from probably 80,000 persons. They threaded their way slowly past us and through the crowd, which Hunt eyed, I thought, with almost as much of astonishment as satisfaction. This spectacle could not be otherwise in his view than solemnly impressive. Such a mass of human beings he had not beheld till then. His responsibility must weigh on his mind. Their power for good or evil was irresistible, and who should direct that power? Himself alone who had called it forth. The task was great, and not without its peril. The meeting was indeed a tremendous one. He mounted the hustings; the music ceased; Mr Johnson proposed that Mr Hunt should take the chair; it was seconded, and carried by acclamation; and Mr Hunt, stepping towards the front of the stage, took off his white hat, and addressed the people.

Whilst he was doing so, I proposed to an acquaintance that, as the speeches and resolutions were not likely to contain anything new to us, and as we could see them in the papers, we should retire awhile and get some refreshment, of which I stood much in need, being not in very robust health. He assented, and we had got to nearly the outside of the crowd, when a noise and strange murmur arose towards the church. Some persons said it was the Blackburn people coming, and I stood on tiptoe and looked in the direction whence the noise proceeded, and saw a party of cavalry in blue and white uniform come trotting, sword in hand, round the corner of a garden wall, and to the front of a row of new houses, where they reined up in a line.

'The soldiers are here,' I said; 'we must go back and see what this means.' 'Oh,' someone made reply, 'they are only come to be ready if there should be any disturbance in the meeting.' 'Well, let us go back,' I said, and we forced our way towards the colours.

On the cavalry drawing up they were received with a shout of goodwill, as I understood it. They shouted again, waving their sabres over their heads; and then, slackening rein, and striking spur into their steeds, they dashed forward and began cutting the people.

'Stand fast,' I said, 'they are riding upon us; stand fast.' And there was a general cry in our quarter of 'Stand fast.' The cavalry were in confusion: they evidently could not, with all the weight of man and horse, penetrate that compact mass of human beings; and their sabres were plied to hew a way through naked held-up hands and defenceless heads; and then chopped limbs and wound-gaping skulls were seen; and groans and cries were mingled with the din of that horrid confusion. 'Ah! ah!' 'For shame! for shame!' was shouted. Then, 'Break! break! they are killing them in front, and they cannot get away'; and there was a general cry of 'Break! break.' For a moment the crowd held back as in a pause; then was a rush, heavy and resistless as a headlong sea, and a sound like low thunder, with screams, prayers, and imprecations from the crowd-moiled and sabre-doomed who could not escape.

By this time Hunt and his companions had disappeared from the hustings, and some of the yeomanry, perhaps less sanguinarily disposed than others, were busied in cutting down the flag-staves and demolishing the flags at the hustings.

On the breaking of the crowd the yeomanry wheeled, and, dashing whenever there was an opening, they followed, pressing and wounding. Many females appeared as the crowd opened; and striplings or mere youths also were found. Their cries were piteous and heart-rending, and would, one might have supposed, have disarmed any human resentment; but here their appeals were in vain. Women, white-vested maids, and tender youths, were indiscriminately sabred or trampled; and we have reason for believing that few were the instances in which that forbearance was vouchsafed which they so earnestly implored.

In ten minutes from the commencement of the havoc the field was an open and almost deserted space. The sun looked down through a sultry and motionless air. The curtains and blinds of the windows within view were all closed. A gentleman or two might occasionally be seen looking out from one of the new houses before mentioned, near the door of which a group of persons (special constables) were collected, and apparently in conversation; others were assisting the wounded or carrying off the dead. The hustings remained, with a few broken and hewed flag-staves erect, and a torn and gashed banner or two dropping; whilst over the whole field were strewed caps, bonnets, hats, shawls, and shoes, and other parts of male and female dress, trampled, torn, and bloody. The yeomanry had dismounted – some were easing their horses' girths, others adjusting their accoutrements, and some were wiping their sabres. Several mounds of human beings still remained where they had fallen, crushed down and smothered. Some of these still groaning, others with staring eyes, were gasping for breath, and others would never breathe more. All was silent save those low sounds, and the occasional snorting and pawing of steeds. Persons might sometimes be noticed peeping from attics and over the tall ridgings of houses, but they quickly withdrew, as if fearful of being observed, or unable to sustain the full gaze of a scene so hideous and abhorrent.

The massacre, quickly dubbed 'Peterloo', prompted Percy Bysshe Shelley, always a subtle weathercock for social injustice, to compose the political poem 'The Mask of Anarchy', with its famous call for a mass, non-violent campaign for suffrage reform: 'Rise like lions after slumber/In unvanquishable number/ Shake your chains to earth like dew/Which in sleep had fallen on you/Ye are many, they are few'.

Samuel Bamford was arrested at Peterloo and sentenced to a year's imprisonment.

The Black Country, 1830

JAMES NASMYTH

The epicentre of the Industrial Revolution, the Midlands became known as the Black Country for its smoke-darkened patina. It was at Coalbrookdale in Shropshire that Abraham Derby developed his iron-smelting process in 1713, and the Coalbrookdale Works manufactured the cylinders of Newcomen's steam engine. The first iron bridge, cast in 1778, stands over the Severn there. Nasmyth was an engineer, the inventor of the steam hammer.

The Black Country is anything but picturesque. The earth seems to have been turned inside out. Its entrails are strewn about; nearly the entire surface of the ground is covered with cinder-heaps and mounds of scoriae. The coal, which has been drawn from below ground, is blazing on the surface. The district is crowded with iron furnaces, puddling furnaces and coalpit engine furnaces. By day and by night the country is glowing with fire, and the smoke of the ironworks hovers over it. There is a rumbling and clanking of iron forges and rolling mills. Workmen covered with smut, and with fierce white eyes, are seen moving about amongst the glowing iron and dull thud of forge-hammers.

Amidst these flaming, smoky, clanging works, I beheld the remains of what had once been happy farmhouses, now ruined and deserted. The ground underneath them had sunk by the working out of the coal, and they were falling to pieces. They had in former times been surrounded by clumps of trees but only the skeletons of them remained, dilapidated, black, and lifeless. The grass had been parched and killed by the vapours of sulphureous acid thrown out by the chimneys; and every herbaceous object was of a ghastly gray – the emblem of vegetable death in its saddest aspect. Vulcan had driven out Ceres. In some places I heard a sort of chirruping sound, as of some forlorn bird haunting the ruins of the old farmsteads. But no! the chirrup was a vile delusion. It proceeded from the shrill creaking of the coal-winding chains, which were placed in small tunnels beneath the hedgeless road.

I went into some of the forges to see the workmen at their labours. There was no need of introduction; the works were open to all, for they were unsurrounded by walls. I saw the white-hot iron run out from the furnace; I saw it spun, as it were, into bars and iron ribbands, with an ease and rapidity which seemed marvellous. There were also the ponderous hammers and clanking rolling-mills. I wandered from one to another without restraint. I lingered among the blast furnaces, seeing the flood of molten iron run out from time to time, and remained there until it was late. When it became dark the scene was still more impressive. The workmen within seemed to be running about amidst the flames as in a pandemonium; while around and outside the horizon was a glowing belt of fire, making even the stars look pale and feeble. At last I came away with reluctance, and made my way towards Dudley. I reached the town at a late hour. I was exhausted in mind and body, yet the day had been most interesting and exciting. A sound sleep refreshed me, and I was up in the morning early, to recommence my journey of inquiry.

I made my way to the impressive ruins of Dudley Castle, the remnant of a very ancient stronghold, originally built by Dud, the Saxon. The castle is situated on a finely wooded hill; it is so extensive that it more resembles the ruins of a town than of a single building. You enter through a treble gateway, and see the remnants of the moat, the court, and the keep. Here are the central hall, the guard-rooms and the chapel. It must have been a magnificent structure. In the Midlands it was known as the 'Castle of the Woods'. Now it is abandoned by its owners, and surrounded by the Black Country. It is undermined by collieries, and even penetrated by a canal. The castle walls sometimes tremble when a blast occurs in the bowels of the mountain beneath.

First Excursion on the Liverpool–Manchester Railway, 25 August 1830

FANNY KEMBLE

The world's first public steam railway, the Stockton–Darlington, opened in 1825; the second to open was the Liverpool–Manchester. The actress Fanny Kemble was among those invited to the Liverpool–Manchester's launch. The engine pulling the guests was George Stephenson's Rocket. *So successful was the* Rocket *(it was reliable, it could reach 31 mph) that within two decades of Fanny Kemble's jaunt, rail was carrying more freight and passengers than the nation's roads and canals. More than that, the railways produced a revolution in English thinking: they made the English realize that machines could be useful, exhilarating, liberating.*

A party of sixteen persons was ushered into a large court-yard, where, under cover, stood several carriages of a peculiar construction, one of which was prepared for our reception. It was a long-bodied vehicle with seats placed across it, back to back; the one we were in had six of these benches, and was a sort of uncovered *char à banc*. The wheels were placed upon two iron bands, which formed the road, and to which they are fitted, being so constructed as to slide along without any danger of hitching or becoming displaced, on the same principle as a thing sliding on a concave groove. The carriage was set in motion by a mere push, and, having received this impetus, rolled with us down an inclined plane into a tunnel, which forms the entrance to the railroad. This tunnel is four hundred yards long (I believe), and will be lighted by gas. At the end of it we emerged from darkness, and, the ground becoming level, we stopped. There is another tunnel parallel with this, only much wider and longer, for it extends from the place which we had now reached, and where the steam-carriages start, and which is quite out of Liverpool, the whole way under the town, to the docks. This tunnel is for waggons and other heavy carriages; and as the engines which are to draw the trains along the railroad do not enter these tunnels, there is a large building at this entrance which is to be inhabited by steam-engines of a stationary turn of mind, and different constitution from the travelling ones, which are to propel the trains through the tunnels to the terminus in the town, without going out of their houses themselves. The length of the tunnel parallel to the one we passed through is (I believe) two thousand two hundred yards. I wonder if you are understanding one word I am saying all this while! We were introduced to the little engine which was to drag us along the rails. She (for they make these curious little fire-horses all mares), consisted of a boiler, a stove, a small platform, a bench, and behind the bench a barrel containing enough water to prevent her being thirsty for fifteen miles, – the whole machine not bigger than a common fire-engine. She goes upon two wheels, which are her feet, and are moved by bright steel legs called pistons; these are propelled by steam, and in proportion as more steam is applied to the upper extremities (the hip-joints, I suppose) of these pistons, the faster they move the wheels; and when it is desirable to diminish the speed, the steam, which unless suffered to escape would burst the boiler, evaporates through a safety-valve into the air. The reins, bit, and bridle of this wonderful beast is a small steel handle, which applies or withdraws the steam from its legs or pistons, so that a child might manage it. The coals, which are its oats, were under the bench, and there was a small glass tube affixed to the boiler, with water in it, which indicates by its fulness or emptiness when the creature wants water, which is immediately conveyed to it from its reservoirs. There is a chimney to the stove, but as they burn coke there is none of that dreadful black smoke which accompanies the progress of a steam-vessel. This snorting little animal, which I felt rather inclined to pat, was then harnessed to our carriage, and Mr Stephenson having taken me on the bench of the engine with him, we started at about ten miles an hour. The steam-horse being ill adapted for going up and down hill, the road was kept at a certain level, and appeared sometimes to sink below the surface of the earth, and sometimes to rise above it. Almost at starting it was cut through the solid rock, which formed a wall on either side of it, about sixty feet high. You can't imagine how strange it seemed to be journeying on thus, without any visible cause of progress other than the magical machine, with its flying white breath and rhythmical, unvarying pace, between these rocky walls, which are already clothed with moss and ferns and grasses; and when I reflected that these great masses of stone had been cut asunder to allow our passage thus far below the surface of the earth, I felt as if no fairy tale was ever half so wonderful as what I saw. Bridges were thrown from side to side across the top of these cliffs, and the people looking down upon us from them seemed like pigmies standing in the sky. I must be more concise, or I shall want room. We were to go only fifteen miles; that distance being sufficient to show the speed of the engine, and to take us on to the most beautiful and wonderful object on the road. After proceeding through this rocky defile, we presently found ourselves raised upon embankments ten or twelve feet high; we then came to a moss, or swamp of considerable extent, on which no human foot could tread without sinking, and yet it bore the road which bore us. This had been the great stumbling-block in the minds of the committee of the House of Commons; but Mr Stephenson has succeeded in overcoming it. A foundation of hurdles, or as he called it, basket-work, was thrown over the morass, and the interstices were filled with moss and other elastic matter. Upon this the clay and soil were laid down, and the road *does* float, for we passed over it at the rate of five and twenty miles an hour, and saw the stagnant swamp water trembling on the surface of the soil on either side of us. I hope you understand me. The embankment had gradually been rising higher and higher, and in one place, where the soil was not settled enough to form banks, Stephenson had constructed artificial ones of wood-work, over which the mounds of earth were heaped, for he calculated that though the wood-work would rot, before it did so the banks of earth which covered it would have been sufficiently consolidated to support the road.

We had now come fifteen miles, and stopped where the road traversed a wide and deep valley. Stephenson made me alight and led me down to the bottom of this ravine, over which, in order to keep his road level, he has thrown a magnificent viaduct of nine arches, the middle one of which is seventy feet high, through which we saw the whole of this beautiful little valley. It was lovely and wonderful beyond all words. He here told me many curious things respecting this ravine: how he believed the Mersey had once rolled through it; how the soil had proved so unfavourable for the foundation of his bridge that it was built upon piles, which had been driven into the earth to an enormous depth; how, while, digging for a foundation, he had come to a tree bedded in the earth fourteen feet below the surface of the ground; how tides are caused, and how another flood might be caused; all of which I have remembered and noted down at much greater length than I can enter upon it here. He explained to me the whole construction of the steam-engine, and said he could soon make a famous engineer of me, which, considering the wonderful things he *has* achieved, I dare not say is impossible. His way of explaining himself is peculiar, but very striking, and I understood, without difficulty, all that he said to me. We then rejoined the rest of the party, and the engine having received its supply of water, the carriage was placed behind it, for it cannot turn, and was set off at its utmost speed, thirty-five miles an hour, swifter than a bird flies (for they tried the experiment with a snipe). You cannot conceive what that sensation of cutting the air was; the motion is as smooth as possible, too. I could either have read or written; and as it was, I stood up, and with my bonnet off 'drank the air before me.' The wind, which was strong, or perhaps the force of our thrusting against it, absolutely weighed my eyelids down. When I closed my eyes this sensation of flying was quite delightful, and strange beyond description; yet, strange as it was, I had a perfect sense of security, and not the slightest fear. At one time, to exhibit the power of the engine, having met another steam-carriage which was unsupplied with water, Mr Stephenson caused it to be fastened in front of ours; moreover, a waggon laden with timber was also chained to us, and thus propelling the idle steam-engine, and dragging the loaded waggon which was beside it, and our own carriage full of people behind, this brave little she-dragon of ours flew on. Farther on she met three carts, which being fastened in front of her, she pushed on before her without the slightest delay or difficulty; when I add that this pretty little creature can run with equal facility either backwards or forwards, I believe I have given you an account of all her capacities.

The Commons Pass the Reform Bill, 3 a.m., 23 March 1831

THOMAS MACAULAY

The Reform Bill, introduced by Earl Grey's Whigs, sought to transfer representation in Parliament from the rural landowners (with their 'rotten' and 'pocket' boroughs) to the new urban centres spawned by the Industrial Revolution. The Bill also called for extension of the franchise.

The poet and writer Macaulay (1800–59) was MP for Calne. Below, he recounts the Bill's second reading.

Such a scene as the division of last Tuesday I never saw, and never expect to see again . . . The crowd overflowed the House in every part. When the strangers were cleared out, and the doors locked, we had six hundred and eight members present – more by fifty-five than ever were in a division before. The ayes and noes were like two volleys of cannon from opposite sides of a field of battle. When the opposition went out into the lobby, an operation which took up twenty minutes or more, we spread ourselves over the benches on both sides of the House; for there were many of us who had not been able to find a seat during the evening. When the doors were shut we began to speculate on our numbers. Every body was desponding. 'We have lost it. We are only two hundred and eighty at most. I do not think we are two hundred and fifty. There are three hundred. Alderman Thompson has counted them. He says they are two hundred and ninety-nine.' This was the talk of our benches . . . I had no hope, however, of three hundred . . . We were all breathless with anxiety, when Charles Wood, who stood near the door, jumped up on a bench and cried out, 'They are only three hundred and one.' We set up a shout that you might have heard to Charing Cross, waving our hats, stamping against the floor, and clapping our hands. The tellers scarcely got through the crowd; for the House was thronged up to the table, and all the floor was fluctuating with heads like the pit of a theatre. But you might have heard a pin drop as Duncannon read the numbers. Then again the shouts broke out, and many of us shed tears. I could scarcely refrain. And the jaw of [Sir Robert] Peel fell; and the face of Twiss was as the face of a damned soul; and Herries looked like Judas taking his neck-tie off for the last operation. We shook hands, and clapped each other on the back, and went out laughing, crying, and huzzaing into the lobby. And no sooner were the outer doors opened than another shout answered that within the House. All the passages and the stairs into the waiting-rooms were thronged with people who had waited till four in the morning to know the issue. We passed through a narrow lane between two thick masses of them; and all the way down they were shouting and waving their hats, till we got into the open air. I called a cabriolet, and the first thing the driver asked was, 'Is the bill carried?' 'Yes, by one.' 'Thank God for it, sir!' And away I rode to Gray's Inn.

Tory opposition to the Bill in the Lords was only overcome when Earl Grey threatened to create 100 Whig peers to get the measure through.

   By the terms of the Reform Act of 1832 most rotten boroughs were eliminated, and the vote was extended to £10 copy-holders and householders. Effectively the electorate was increased by 50 per cent. The Act was received with national rejoicing, even though most of the workers who had campaigned for it were excluded from its benefit by the £10 qualification. They would go on to support the Chartist movement and the trade unions, the latter achieving full legality with the Trades Union Act of 1871.

Darwin in the Galapagos, 1835

CHARLES DARWIN

Before Darwin (1809–82) it was scientific orthodoxy that the Creator had hand-made every organism; after Darwin's On the Origin of Species by Means of Natural Selection *was published in 1859, it became stutteringly accepted that Evolution, principally Natural Selection, had some part in the development of the living world. Darwin, grandson of both pottery magnate Josiah Wedgwood and free-thinker Erasmus Darwin, attributed his scientific breakthrough to a visit paid to the Galapagos Archipelago in 1835, when he was the naturalist aboard HMS Beagle.*

. . . The natural history of these islands is eminently curious, and well deserves attention. Most of the organic productions are aboriginal creations, found nowhere else; there is even a difference between the inhabitants of the different islands; yet all show a marked relationship with those of America, though separated from that continent by an open space of ocean between 500 and 600 miles in width. The archipelago is a little world within itself, or rather, a satellite attached to America, whence it has derived a few stray colonists, and has received the general character of its indigenous productions. Considering the small size of these islands, we feel the more astonished at the number of their aboriginal beings, and at their confined range. Seeing every height crowned with its crater, and the boundaries of most of the lava-streams still distinct, we are led to believe that within a period geologically recent the unbroken ocean was here spread out. Hence, both in space and time, we seem to be brought somewhat near to that great fact – that mystery of mysteries – the first appearance of new beings on this earth . . .

Of land birds I obtained twenty-six kinds, all peculiar to the group and found nowhere else, with the exception of one lark-like finch from North America. . . . The other twenty-five birds consist, firstly, of a hawk, curiously intermediate in structure between a buzzard and the American group of carrion-feeding Polybori. . . . Secondly, there are two owls, representing the short-eared and white barn-owls of Europe. Thirdly, a wren, three tyrant-flycatchers . . ., and a dove – all analogous to, but distinct from, American species. Fourthly, a swallow. . . . Fifthly, there are three species of mocking thrush. . . . The remaining land-birds form a most singular group of finches, related to each other in the structure of their beaks, short tails, form of body and plumage: there are thirteen species . . . all . . . peculiar to this archipelago. . . . The most curious fact is the perfect gradation in the size of the beaks in the different species of Geospiza, from one as large as that of a hawfinch to that of a chaffinch, and . . . even to that of a warbler. [The *Journal* is illustrated at this point with drawings of the beaks of the finches.] . . . Seeing this gradation and diversity of structure in one small, intimately related group of birds, one might really fancy that from an original paucity of birds in this archipelago, one species had been taken and modified for different ends . . .

I have not as yet noticed by far the most remarkable feature in the natural history of this archipelago; it is, that the different islands to a considerable extent are inhabited by a different set of beings. My attention was first called to this fact by the Vice-Governor, Mr Lawson, declaring that the tortoises differed from the different islands, and that he could with certainty tell from which island any one was brought. I did not for some time pay sufficient attention to this statement, and I had already partially mingled together the collections from two of the islands. I never dreamed that islands, about 50 or 60 miles apart, and most of them in sight of each other, formed of precisely the same rocks, placed under a quite similar climate, rising to a nearly equal height, would have been differently tenanted; but we shall soon see that this is the case. It is the fate of most voyagers no sooner to discover what is most interesting in any locality, than they are hurried from it; but I ought, perhaps, to be thankful that I obtained sufficient materials to establish this most remarkable fact in the distribution of organic beings . . .

In 1871 Darwin published The Descent of Man, *which proposed that humans had descended from primates.*

The Coronation of Queen Victoria, 29 June 1838

CHARLES GREVILLE

Victoria was eighteen when she ascended the throne. Less than five feet tall, she would bear nine children, survive seven attempts on her life, reign longer than any other English monarch, and give her name to an age that saw England head the greatest empire the world had ever seen.

Greville was Clerk of the Privy Council.

The Coronation (which, thank God, is over) went off very well. The day was fine, without heat or rain – the innumerable multitude which thronged the streets orderly and satisfied. The appearance of the Abbey was beautiful, particularly the benches of the Peeresses, who were blazing with diamonds. The entry of Soult [one of Napoleon's marshals] was striking. He was saluted with a murmur of curiosity and applause as he passed through the nave, and nearly the same as he advanced along the choir. His appearance is that of a veteran warrior, and he walked alone, with his numerous suite following at a respectful distance, preceded by heralds and ushers, who received him with marked attention, more certainly than any of the other Ambassadors. The Queen looked very diminutive, and the effect of the procession itself was spoilt by being too crowded; there was not interval enough between the Queen and the Lords and others going before her. The Bishop of London (Blomfield) preached a very good sermon. The different actors in the ceremonial were very imperfect in their parts, and had neglected to rehearse them. Lord John Thynne, who officiated for the Dean of Westminster, told me that nobody knew what was to be done except the Archbishop and himself (who had rehearsed), Lord Willoughby (who is experienced in these matters), and the Duke of Wellington, and consequently there was a continual difficulty and embarrassment, and the Queen never knew what she was to do next. They made her leave her chair and enter into St Edward's Chapel before the prayers were concluded, much to the discomfiture of the Archbishop. She said to John Thynne, 'Pray tell me what I am to do, for they don't know'; and at the end, when the orb was put into her hand, she said to him, 'What am I to do with it?' 'Your Majesty is to carry it, if you please, in your hand.' 'Am I?' she said; 'it is very heavy.' The ruby ring was made for her little finger instead of the fourth, on which the rubric prescribes that it should be put. When the Archbishop was to put it on, she extended the former, but he said it must be on the latter. She said it was too small, and she could not get it on. He said it was right to put it there, and, as he insisted, she yielded, but had first to take off her other rings, and then this was forced on, but it hurt her very much, and as soon as the ceremony was over she was obliged to bathe her finger in iced water in order to get it off.

Prostitutes and Peers: Scenes from a Gin-palace, London, 1839

FLORA TRISTAN

A French socialist's view.

From the outside, these 'gin-palaces' with their carefully fastened shutters seem to be quietly slumbering; but no sooner has the doorkeeper admitted you by the little door reserved for initiates than you are dazzled by the light of a thousand gas lamps. Upstairs there is a spacious salon divided down the middle; in one half there is a row of tables separated one from the other by wooden screens, as in all English restaurants, with upholstered seats like sofas on each side of the tables. In the other half there is a dais where the prostitutes parade in all their finery, seeking to arouse the men with their glances and remarks; when a gallant gentleman responds, they lead him off to one of the tables loaded with cold meats, hams, poultry, pastries and every manner of wines and spirits.

The finishes are the temples which English materialism raises to its gods; the servants who minister in them are dressed in rich liveries, and the capitalist owners reverently greet the male guests who come to exchange their gold for debauchery.

Towards midnight the regular clients begin to arrive; several finishes are frequented by men in high society, and this is where the cream of the aristocracy gather. At first the young noblemen recline on the sofas, smoking and exchanging pleasantries with the women; then, when they have drunk enough for the fumes of champagne and Madeira to go to their heads, the illustrious scions of the English nobility, the very honourable members of Parliament, remove their coats, untie their cravats, take off their waistcoats and braces, and proceed to set up their private boudoir in a public place. Why not make themselves at home, since they are paying out so much money for the right to display their contempt? As for any contempt *they* might inspire, they do not care in the least. The orgy rises to a crescendo; between four and five o'clock in the morning it reaches its height.

At this point it takes a good deal of courage to remain in one's seat, a mute spectator of all that takes place. What a worthy use these English lords make of their immense fortunes! How fine and generous they are when they have lost the use of their reason and offer fifty, even a hundred, guineas to a prostitute if she will lend herself to all the obscenities that drunkenness engenders.

For in a finish there is no lack of entertainment. One of the favourite sports is to *ply a woman with drink* until she falls dead drunk upon the floor, then to make her swallow a draught compounded of *vinegar*, *mustard*, and *pepper*, this invariably throws the poor creature into horrible convulsions, and her spasms and contortions provoke the *honourable company* to gales of laughter and infinite amusement. Another diversion much appreciated at these fashionable gatherings is to empty the contents of the nearest glass upon the women as they lie insensible on the ground. I have seen satin dresses of no recognizable colour, only a confused mass of stains: wine, brandy, beer, tea, coffee, cream, etc., daubed all over them in a thousand fantastic shapes – the handiwork of debauchery!

Manchester Slums, 1844

FRIEDRICH ENGELS

A German socialist's view. Engels was sent to England in 1842 to learn the family business at the Ermen and Engels paper mill in Manchester. While there he gathered material for his book, The Condition of the Working Class in England in 1844.

I now proceed to describe Manchester's worker districts. First of all, there is the Old Town, which lies between the northern boundary of the commercial district and the Irk. Here the streets, even the better ones, are narrow and winding, as Todd Street, Long Millgate, Withy Grove, and Shude Hill, the houses dirty, old, and tumble-down, and the construction of the side streets utterly horrible. Going from the Old Church to Long Millgate, the stroller has at once a row of old-fashioned houses at the right, of which not one has kept its original level; these are remnants of the old pre-manufacturing Manchester, whose former inhabitants have removed with their descendants into better-built districts, and have left the houses, which were not good enough for them, to a working-class population strongly mixed with Irish blood. Here one is in an almost undisguised working-men's quarter, for even the shops and beerhouses hardly take the trouble to exhibit a trifling degree of cleanliness. But all this is nothing in comparison with the courts and lanes which lie behind, to which access can be gained only through covered passages, in which no two human beings can pass at the same time. Of the irregular cramming together of dwellings in ways which defy all rational plan, of the tangle in which they are crowded literally one upon the other, it is impossible to convey an idea. And it is not the buildings surviving from the old times of Manchester which are to blame for this; the confusion has only recently reached its height when every scrap of space left by the old way of building has been filled up and patched over until not a foot of land is left to be further occupied.

To confirm my statement I have drawn here a small section of the plan of Manchester – not the worst spot and not one-tenth of the whole Old Town.

This drawing will suffice to characterize the irrational manner in which the entire district was built, particularly the part near the Irk.

The south bank of the Irk is here very steep and between fifteen and thirty feet high. On this declivitous hillside there are planted three rows of houses, of which the lowest rise directly out of the river, while the front walls of the highest stand on the crest of the hill in Long Millgate. Among them are mills on the river, in short, the method of construction is as crowded and disorderly here as in the lower part of Long Millgate. Right and left a multitude of covered passages lead from the main street into numerous courts, and he who turns in thither gets into a filth and disgusting grime, the equal of which is not be found – especially in the courts which lead down to the Irk, and which contain unqualifiedly the most horrible dwellings which I have yet beheld. In one of these courts there stands directly at the entrance, at the end of the covered passage,

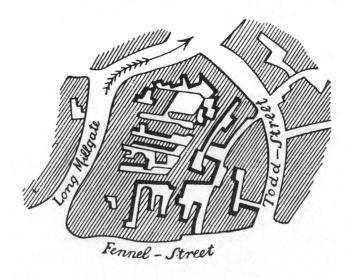

Fennel - Street

a privy without a door, so dirty that the inhabitants can pass into and out of the court only by passing through foul pools of stagnant urine and excrement. This is the first court on the Irk above Ducie Bridge – in case any one should care to look into it. Below it on the river there are several tanneries which fill the whole neighborhood with the stench of animal putrefaction. Below Ducie Bridge the only entrance to most of the houses is by means of narrow, dirty stairs and over heaps of refuse and filth. The first court below Ducie Bridge, known as Allen's Court, was in such a state at the time of the cholera that the sanitary police ordered it evacuated, swept and disinfected with chloride of lime. Dr Kay gives a terrible description of the state of this court at that time.* Since then, it seems to have been partially torn away and rebuilt; at least looking down from Ducie Bridge, the passer-by sees several ruined walls and heaps of *débris* with some newer houses. The view from this bridge, mercifully concealed from mortals of small stature by a parapet as high as a man, is characteristic for the whole district. At the bottom flows, or rather stagnates, the Irk, a narrow, coal-black, foul-smelling stream, full of *débris* and refuse, which it deposits on the shallower right bank. In dry weather, a long string of the most disgusting blackish-green slime pools are left standing on this bank, from the depths of which bubbles of miasmatic gas constantly arise and give forth a stench unendurable even on the bridge forty or fifty feet above the surface of the stream. But besides this, the stream itself is checked every few paces by high weirs, behind which slime and refuse accumulate and rot in thick masses. Above the bridge are tanneries, bonemills, and gasworks, from which all drains and refuse find their way into the Irk, which receives further the contents of all the neighbouring sewers and privies. It may be easily imagined, therefore, what sort of residue the stream deposits. Below the bridge you look upon the piles of *débris*, the refuse, filth, and offal from the courts on the steep left bank; here each house is packed close behind its neighbour and a piece of each is visible, all black, smoky, crumbling, ancient, with broken panes and window-frames. The background is furnished by old barrack-like factory buildings. On the lower right bank stands a long row of houses and mills; the second house being a ruin without a roof, piled with *débris*; the third stands so low that the lowest

---

* 'The Moral and Physical Condition of the Working-Class employed in the Cotton Manufacture in Manchester.' By James Ph. Kay, M.D. 2nd Ed. 1832. Dr Kay confuses the working-class in general with the factory workers; otherwise, an excellent pamphlet. [*Engels*]

floor is uninhabitable, and therefore without windows or doors. Here the background embraces the pauper burial-ground, the station of the Liverpool and Leeds railway, and, in the rear of this, the Workhouse, the 'Poor-Law Bastille' of Manchester, which, like a citadel, looks threateningly down from behind its high walls and parapets on the hilltop, upon the working-people's quarter below.

Above Ducie Bridge, the left bank grows more flat and the right bank steeper, but the condition of the dwellings on both banks grows worse rather than better. He who turns to the left here from the main street, Long Millgate, is lost; he wanders from one court to another, turns countless corners, passes nothing but narrow, filthy nooks and alleys, until after a few minutes he has lost all clue, and knows not whither to turn. Everywhere half or wholly ruined buildings, some of them actually uninhabited, which means a great deal here; rarely a wooden or stone floor to be seen in the houses, almost uniformly broken, ill-fitting windows and doors, and a state of filth! Everywhere heaps of *débris*, refuse, and offal; standing pools for gutters, and a stench which alone would make it impossible for a human being in any degree civilized to live in such a district. The newly-built extension of the Leeds railway, which crosses the Irk here, has swept away some of these courts and lanes, laying others completely open to view. Immediately under the railway bridge there stands a court, the filth and horrors of which surpass all the others by far, just because it was hitherto so shut off, so secluded that the way to it could not be found without a good deal of trouble. I should never have discovered it myself, without the breaks made by the railway, though I thought I knew this whole region thoroughly. Passing along a rough bank, among stakes and washing-lines, one penetrates into this chaos of small one-storied, one-roomed huts, in most of which there is no artificial floor; kitchen, living and sleeping-room all in one. In such a hole, scarcely five feet long by six broad, I found two beds – and such bedsteads and beds! – which, with a staircase and chimney-place, exactly filled the room. In several others I found absolutely nothing, while the door stood open, and the inhabitants leaned against it. Everywhere before the doors refuse and offal; that any sort of pavement lay underneath could not be seen but only felt, here and there, with the feet. This whole collection of cattle-sheds for human beings was surrounded on two sides by houses and a factory, and on the third by the river, and besides the narrow stair up the bank, a narrow doorway alone led out into another almost equally ill-built, ill-kept labyrinth of dwellings.

Enough! The whole side of the Irk is built in this way, a planless, knotted chaos of houses, more or less on the verge of uninhabitableness, whose unclean interiors fully correspond with their filthy external surroundings. And how could the people be clean with no proper opportunity for satisfying the most natural and ordinary wants? Privies are so rare here that they are either filled up every day, or are too remote for most of the inhabitants to use. How can people wash when they have only the dirty Irk water at hand, while pumps and water pipes can be found in decent parts of the city alone? In truth, it cannot be charged to the account of these helots of modern society if their dwellings are not more clean than the pig sties which are here and there to be seen among them. The landlords are not ashamed to let dwellings like the six or seven cellars on the quay directly below Scotland Bridge, the floors of which stand at least two feet below the low-water level of the Irk that flows not six feet away from them; or like the upper floor of the corner-house on the opposite shore directly above the bridge, where the ground-floor, utterly uninhabitable, stands deprived of all fittings for doors and windows, a case by no means rare in this region, when this open ground-floor is used as a privy by the whole neighbourhood for want of other facilities!

The squalor of England's workers was not only of concern to visiting socialists. The great gulf between rich and poor caused Benjamin Disraeli, a young Tory later to become Conservative Prime Minister, to coin the phrase 'Two Nations' in his 1847 novel, *Sybil*.

'Well, society may be in its infancy,' said Egremont, slightly smiling; 'but, say what you like, our Queen reigns over the greatest nation that ever existed.' 'Which nation?' asked the younger stranger, 'for she reigns over two.' 'Yes,' resumed the younger stranger after a moment's interval. 'Two nations; between whom there is no intercourse, and no sympathy; who are as ignorant of each other's habits, thoughts, and feelings, as if they were dwellers in different zones, or inhabitants of different planets; who are formed by a different breeding, are fed by a different food, are ordered by different manners, and are governed by the same laws.'
    'You speak of –', said Egremont, hesitatingly.
'THE RICH AND THE POOR.'

Only one thing fascinated Victorian England and its visitors as much as the nation's Poverty and Wealth. And that was its progress in science and technology.

Chloroform in Surgery, 1847

CHARLES GREVILLE

Medicine and surgery made rapid strides in the Victorian era. Before the discovery and application of chloroform, surgery had been at best unbearable, at worst deadly.

I went yesterday to St George's Hospital to see the chloroform tried. A boy two years and a half old was cut for a stone. He was put to sleep in a minute; the stone was so large and the bladder so contracted, the operator could not get hold of it, and the operation lasted above twenty minutes, with repeated probings by different instruments; the chloroform was applied from time to time, and the child never exhibited the slightest sign of consciousness, and it was exactly the same as operating on a dead body. A curious example was shown of what is called the *étiquette* of the profession. The operator (whose name I forget) could not extract the stone; so at last he handed the instrument to Keate, who is the finest operator possible, and he got hold of the stone. When he announced that he had done so, the first man begged to have the forceps back that he might draw it out, and it was transferred to him; but in taking it he let go the stone, and the whole thing had to be done over again. It was accomplished, but not of course without increasing the local inflammation, and endangering the life of the child. I asked Keate why, when he had got hold of the stone, he did not draw it out. He said the other man's 'dignity' would have been hurt if he had not been allowed to complete what he had begun! I have no words to express my admiration for this invention, which is the greatest blessing ever bestowed on mankind, and the inventor of it the greatest of benefactors, whose memory ought to be venerated by countless millions for ages yet to come. All the great discoveries of science sink into insignificance when compared with this. It is a great privilege to have lived in the times which saw the production of steam, of electricity, and now of ether – that is, of the development and application of them to human purposes, to the multiplication of enjoyments and the mitigation of pain. But wonderful as are the powers and the feats of the steam-engine and the electric telegraph, the chloroform far transcends them all in its beneficent and consolatory operations.

Six years later Queen Victoria used chloroform during childbirth, a royal approval ('the effect was soothing, quieting & delightful beyond measure') which massively popularized the gas.

Chartist March, 13 April 1848

CHARLES GREVILLE

So-called from The People's Charter, *the Chartist movement was born out of proletarian despair at the limitations of the 1832 Reform Act. The Charter, drafted largely by William Lovett, made six demands: universal male suffrage, annual parliaments, voting by ballot, payment of MPs, an end to property qualifications for MPs, and equal electoral districts.*

The aims were worthy (and would be realized in 1918) but the Chartist leaders, James Bronterre O'Brien and Feargus O'Connor, were demagogues. The first Chartist petition, signed by 1,200,000 people, was presented in 1839; the third, and last, was brought to London in April 1848.

Apr. 13, 1848: – Monday passed off with surprising quiet, and it was considered a most satisfactory demonstration on the part of the Government, and the peaceable and loyal part of the community. Enormous preparations were made, and a host of military, police, and special constables were ready if wanted; every gentleman in London was sworn, and during a great part of the day, while the police were reposing, they did duty. The Chartist movement was contemptible; but everybody rejoices that the defensive demonstration was made, for it has given a great and memorable lesson which will not be thrown away, either on the disaffected and mischievous, or the loyal and peaceful; and it will produce a vast effect in all foreign countries, and show how solid is the foundation on which we are resting. We have displayed a great resolution and a great strength, and given unmistakable proofs, that if sedition and rebellion hold up their heads in this country, they will be instantly met with the most vigorous resistance, and be put down by the hand of authority, and by the zealous co-operation of all classes of the people. The whole of the Chartist movement was to the last degree contemptible from first to last. The delegates who met on the eve of the day were full of valour amounting to desperation; they indignantly rejected the intimation of the Government that their procession would not be allowed; swore they would have it at all hazard, and die, if necessary, in asserting their rights. One man said he loved his life, his wife, his children, but would sacrifice all rather than give way.

In the morning (a very fine day) everybody was on the alert; the parks were closed; our office was fortified, a barricade of Council Registers was erected in the accessible room on the ground-floor, and all our guns were taken down to be used in defence of the building. However, at about twelve o'clock crowds came streaming along Whitehall, going northwards, and it was announced that all was over. The intended tragedy was rapidly changed into a ludicrous farce. The Chartists, about 20,000 in number, assembled on Kennington Common. Presently Mr Mayne appeared on the ground, and sent one of his inspectors to say he wanted to speak to Feargus O'Connor. Feargus thought he was going to be arrested and was in a terrible fright; but he went to Mayne, who merely said he was desired to inform him that the meeting would not be interfered with, but the procession would not be allowed. Feargus insisted on shaking hands with Mayne, swore he was his best of friends, and instantly harangued his rabble, advising them not to provoke a collision, and to go away quietly – advice they instantly obeyed, and with great alacrity and good-humour. Thus all evaporated in smoke. Feargus himself then repaired to the Home Office, saw Sir George Grey, and told him it was all over, and thanked the Government for their leniency, assuring him the Convention would not have been so lenient if they had got the upper hand. Grey asked him if he was going back to the meeting. He said No; that he had had his toes trodden on till he was lame, and his pocket picked, and he would have no more to do with it. The petition was brought down piecemeal and presented in the afternoon. Since that there has been an exposure of the petition itself, covering the authors of it with ridicule and disgrace. It turns out to be signed by less than two millions, instead of by six as Feargus stated; and of those, there were no end of fictitious names, together with the insertion of every species of ribaldry, indecency, and impertinence. The Chartists are very crestfallen, and evidently conscious of the contemptible figure they cut; but they have endeavoured to bluster and lie as well as they can in their subsequent gatherings, and talk of other petitions and meetings, which nobody cares about.

The Third Petition was such a fiasco that it ensured that Chartism was of no significance thereafter.

Elsewhere in Europe in 1848, revolutions swept through like storms. To the bemusement of Karl Marx, who drafted The Communist Manifesto *in London in that year, England – with the world's biggest and most advanced 'proletariat' – remained stable.*

The English preferred patriotism and pageant to Revolution.

A Visit to the Great Exhibition, 7 June 1851

CHARLOTTE BRONTË

The Great Exhibition was housed in Joseph Paxton's Crystal Palace in Hyde Park, London. ('The blazing arch of lucid glass' was run up by navvies in just six months.) The figures for attendance were staggering; more than 6 million tickets were sold.

Yesterday I went for the second time to the Crystal Palace. We remained in it about three hours, and I must say I was more struck with it on this occasion than at my first visit. It is a wonderful place – vast, strange, new, and impossible to describe. Its grandeur does not consist in *one* thing, but in the unique assemblage of *all* things. Whatever human industry has created you find there, from the great compartments filled with railway engines and boilers, with mill machinery in full work, with splendid carriages of all kinds, with harness of every description, to the glass-covered and velvet spread stands loaded with the most gorgeous work of the goldsmith and silversmith, and the carefully guarded caskets full of real diamonds and pearls worth hundreds of thousands of pounds. It may be called a bazaar or a fair, but it is such a bazaar or fair as Eastern genii might have created. It seems as if only magic could have gathered this mass of wealth from all the ends of the earth – as if none but supernatural hands could have arranged it thus, with such a blaze and contrast of colours and marvellous power of effect. The multitude filling the great aisles seems ruled and subdued by some invisible influence. Amongst the thirty thousand souls that peopled it the day I was there not one loud noise was to be heard, not one irregular movement seen; the living tide rolls on quietly, with a deep hum like the sea heard from the distance.

The Great Exhibition was a bombastic, self-confident, chauvinist symbol of the Victorian good times, based atop a booming economy that would see wages double before the end of the century.

The Census of 1851 also made for a fascinating spectacle; it confirmed the drift of the population towards the towns (indeed, more than half England and Wales's 17,927,609 total population was now urban) and also the persistent secularism of the English. Five and a quarter million of them stayed at home on Sunday, and only 5 million passed through the porches of the Church of England. Liberalism, with its doctrines of free trade, individualism and 'scientific' improvement, was the political reflection of the Census statistics. Abroad, Liberalism meant restraint, diplomacy, the peaceful maintenance of the balance of power.

Of course, sometimes the power-balance could only be maintained by the Englishman's traditional means.

The Charge of the Light Brigade, Crimea, 25 October 1854

E. A. COOK

The causes of the Crimean War (1854–6) can be reduced to British and French fear of Russian expansion into Europe.

Despite Britain's 'modernity', its Crimean army was ill-equipped and its commander, Lord Raglan, ineffective; both deficiencies were dramatically highlighted to the war-hungry crowds at home by the new medium of the tele-graphed newspaper dispatch, as pioneered by William Howard Russell of The Times.

The following account of the melancholic Charge of the Light Brigade at Balaclava is by E. A. Cook, an officer who took part.

Heights of Sebastopol
December 1st (1854)

My dear Father,

Since I wrote last nothing decisive has been done towards finishing our now truly wretched campaign, my last letter would prove from its date that I was not present at the last engagement on the Inkerman Heights, the only affair that I have not had a share in. I was in the Black Sea on board of ship at the time lying outside the bay of Varna. The account of the battle which will reach you before this you may fully believe, I don't think the papers will exaggerate, it was without exception the most sanguinary on record for the numbers engaged. I have of course heard all the accounts about it and been over the ground, where there still remain ample proofs of a desperate slaughter. It is well known here that the Russians confess to 20,000 hors de combat – they attacked us 40,000 strong led on by the two Grand Dukes at daybreak, having been allowed to bring up a great number of heavy guns during the night, a fool of an ensign hearing them all the time without reporting it, they were there, and taking the English, it was on our side, by surprise, we turned out just as we were in our great coats, the Russians came on most furiously mistaking us in the great coats for Turks, our Guards and 4 other regiments were the only troops at hand, they held their ground bravely as long as they could, but of course were obliged to fall back on the next support. The French came up about this time and enabled us to attack the serfs, on which they turned in every direction and then commenced the most horrific slaughter. Our fellows charged them with the bay right down to the bottom of the heights. The deserters say that they got such a lesson that day, that they have tried several times since to get them on without success; and I really think there is no chance of their attacking again. Now for the other massacres as of the 25th October. I have abstained from making a report about this affair, except just that I had a most wonderful escape and got slightly wounded with a spent shot as I should have unnecessarily alarmed you because it is impossible to describe it otherwise than as the most downright useless, ridiculous, except to those in it, sacrifice seen now by *The Times* of the 13th that they have described the thing truly, so I may as well confirm it. *The Times* account is so good that I shall only say what happened to myself.

Our order to charge was brought by a half madman Capt. Nolan, the order was very difficult to understand rightly. On Lord Lucan asking what he was to charge, the only information was, there is the enemy and there is your order. There the enemy consisted of 15,000 infantry, 4,000 cavalry protected by 10 guns, to reach them we had to go down a ravine between two hills with 10 guns on each besides a host of riflemen. Down we went very steadily, the fire was terrific, it seemed impossible to escape, we were well in range of grape shot on each side besides the barkers in front. I got through safe up to the guns, cut down all that came within reach and then at the cavalry behind, but to our horror the heavy brigade had not followed in support and there was an alarm that we were cut off in rear, which was true. There was nothing left for it, but to cut our way back the same way we came, the Lancers who cut us off made a very mild resistance, they seemed to be astonished at our audacity at charging them in the wretched confusion we were in, we got through them with very little loss. Just after getting through these beggars, I thought I heard a rattle behind and, by Jove, I was only just in time, we were pursued and on looking behind a Muscovite had his sword up just in my range and in the act of cutting me down, I showed him the point of my sword instantly close to his throat, he pulled his horse almost backwards and gave me an opportunity of getting more forward. I now had nothing to fear being on a good horse except going through those infernal guns again – about a quarter of a mile from the batteries I felt a tremendous blow on the calf of the leg, and instantly my poor old horse was hit on the offside and was going to fall. I jumped off in a second with the pistol in one hand and sword in the other, and had the satisfaction of seeing my old friends only ten yards behind in full pursuit. Things looked very bad indeed, but in spite of my game leg, I ran faster than ever I did before in my life and kept pace with my friends behind till their own fire got so thick that they thought fit to drop it. I was now between these two batteries and could only raise a walk. I must have been a quarter of an hour under fire on foot, and much to the astonishment of my real friends, the few who escaped, I turned up about half an hour after the rest of the stragglers. I have finished my romance, for really my escape was almost romantic, but don't on that account put it in print as some of my brave companions like.

Enough of war, in spite of living in a tent at this time of the year with 3 inches of mud inside and 12 out, I am not down in the mouth. My fortnight at sea put my leg to rights, and those two fools who command us Lucan and C. have been kind enough to place us such a distance from our supplies, the roads being very deep, that they can't feed the wretched little wreck of a brigade, the consequence is that they are dying 8 and 10 a day, now it requires no mathematician to see that this can't last, besides the horses are so weak that I don't think any one of them could trot a mile. They can't bring us into action again. Tomorrow we move down to Balaclava to be near our supplies and if we have luck get some sort of a roof for man and beast.

The Russians are worse, if possible, off than ourselves, they are beginning to starve inside and outside of Sebastopol, still they fire away as briskly as ever, we can't assault it without large reinforcements, the army outside would instantly attack us, I fancy it will not fall for some time yet, and I have also I think a chance of going home to command the depot in about two months time. So things are looking up. The newspapers arrive very irregularly, please to speak about it and have via Marseilles put upon them. I want also the Illustrated News. Don't

put any more money at the bank, but on account, and put it into the
15 per cents.

With best love,
Your affectionate son,
E. A. Cook

Of the 600 troopers who took part in the Charge 156 were reported killed or
missing, and 122 wounded. The action inspired Alfred Tennyson's poem 'Charge
of the Light Brigade', 1854.

   The Charge was a blunder; it was also the perfect illustration of the British
Victorian soldier's unquestioning sense of duty and extraordinary valour.

   Such a hash did Lord Aberdeen's government make of the Crimean War that
it was replaced in 1855 by a Liberal coalition under the nauseously self-assertive
but enormously able Lord Palmerston. A year later the defeated Russians signed
the Treaty of Paris.

Florence Nightingale in the Crimea, 1855

FLORENCE NIGHTINGALE

The daughter of Hampshire gentry, Nightingale (1820–1910) went against her
family, her class and the patriarchal mores of Victorian society to become a nurse,
an occupation usually talked of in the same breath as prostitution. She volunteered
for duty in the Crimean War, taking thirty-eight nurses to Scutari in 1854,
where her improvements in sanitation dramatically reduced the mortality rate in
the Army hospital. On returning to England, a fund of £50,000 enabled the
'lady with the lamp' to found institutions for the training of nurses at St Thomas'
and King's College Hospitals.

When I consider what the work has been this winter, what the hard-
ships, I am surprised – not that the army has suffered so much but –
that there is any army left at all, not that we have had so many through
our hands at Scutari, but that we have not had all as Sir John McNeill
says. Fancy working 5 nights out of 7 in the trenches, fancy being 36
hours in them at a stretch – as they were, all December, lying down or
half lying down – after 48 hours without food but *raw* salt pork sprinkled
with sugar – & their rum & biscuits – nothing hot – because the *exhausted*
soldier *could not* collect his own fuel, as he was expected, to cook his
own ration. And fancy, thro' all this, the army preserving their courage

& patience – as they have done – & being now eager, the old ones more than the young ones, to be led even into the trenches. There was something sublime in the spectacle. The brave 39th, whose Regimental Hospitals are the best I have ever seen, turned out & gave Florence Nightingale three times three, as I rode away. There was nothing empty in that cheer nor in the heart which received it. I took it as a true expression of true sympathy – the sweetest I have ever had. I took it as a full reward of all I have gone through. I promised my God that I would not die of disgust or disappointment, if he would let me go through this. In all that has been said against & for me, no one soul has appreciated what I was really doing, none but the honest cheer of the brave 39th.

Nothing which the 'Times' has said has been exaggerated of Hardship.

It was a wonderful sight looking down upon Sevastopol – the shell whizzing right & left. I send you a Miniè bullet I picked up on the ground which was ploughed with shot & shell – & some little flowers. For this is the most flowery place you can imagine – a beautiful little red Tormentilla which I don't know, yellow Jessamine & every kind of low flowering shrub. A Serjt of the 97th picked me a nosegay. I once saved Serjt —'s life by finding him at 12 o'clock at night lying – wounds undressed – in our Hosp*l.* with a bullet in his eye & a fractured skull. And I pulled a stray Surgeon out of bed to take the bullet out. But you must not tell this story. For I gave evidence against the missing Surgeon – & have never been forgiven.

Indian Mutiny: Cawnpore after the Massacre, July 1857

RICHARD BARTER

Rumours that the British army used Enfield rifle cartridges smeared with pig and cow fat (thus insulting both Muslims and Hindus) were enough to start the Indian Mutiny against British rule in May 1857. Within three weeks, the entire Ganges basin was afire, Lucknow and Cawnpore besieged. The Residency at Lucknow was relieved on 26 September 1857. A month later, British troops arrived at Cawnpore.

Barter was Adjutant of the 75th Gordon Highlanders, part of General Havelock's relief force.

We reached Cawnpore, the scene of the Nana Sahib's massacre of the poor defenceless European men, women and children. Just outside the place we halted near a fine house which was, however, empty, and while waiting for the order to march on, we strolled into it. Even there there had been murder if one could judge by the crimson stain where blood had spurted on the wall and by the smear of a bloody hand. Our Camp was pitched at each side of the road, and that evening we all paid the now-famous well etc. a visit as well as the house close to it in which before their massacre the women and children were confined. The house was a small one, being as well as I can now remember one long room with a verandah in front and rear and the back verandah looked into a courtyard or zenana compound, on the other three sides of which were walls with a door leading out of that on the left to the path to the well. In the courtyard itself grew a babul tree and near the well between it and the house were three or four large trees and some low scrubby thicket of thorny shrubs. The inside of the house was of course bare of furniture and there was no matting or carpet on the floor, but instead blood, thick clotted blood looking like Russia leather, with which the walls also for three or four feet from the ground were spattered, and in some places smeared as if a great spout of it had gushed out on them, while here and there were marks where the murderers had dried their bloody hands by rubbing them against the walls in which were also deep sword cuts, as if some poor victim had dodged aside from the blow. There were also several pencil inscriptions, noting the date of arrival there, and memoranda of deaths of friends or relatives, or short prayers for help. Bonnets, slippers, hats, stays and various other articles of female clothing, with tresses and plaits of hair were scattered about with fragments of books, most, if not all of them Bibles and prayer books. Some of the bonnets and hats were hanging from the beams in the back verandah, which as well as the back yard was covered thick with clotted blood. All the way to the well was marked by a regular track along which the bodies had been dragged and the thorny bushes had entangled in them scraps of clothing and long hairs. One of the large trees to the left of this track going to the well had evidently had children's brains dashed out against its trunk, for it was covered thick with blood and children's hair matted into the coarse bark, and an eye, glazed and withered could be plainly made out pasted into the trunk. A few paces on and you stood by the well itself, now the receptacle of all these poor mangled bodies. It looked old and going fast to decay for the bricks and mortar had given way and crumbled in many places round the low edge.

I think it must have been dry or very nearly so. After peering into it for some time until the eyes had become accustomed to the gloom, you could see members of human bodies, legs and arms sticking up browned and withered like those of a mummy. But there was no putrid smell or anything of that kind that I could perceive. Those dead arms of our murdered country people seemed to be making a mute appeal to us from the darkness below; far more eloquent than words they called to Heaven for vengeance on the ruthless perpetrators of untold atrocities, and many a vow was registered over that well never to spare should they be met with hand to hand in the approaching struggle for the Relief of Lucknow, but four short marches now lay between us and that city where we knew the garrison with a crowd of women and children, were daily subject to the attacks of the Cawnpore, and thousands of similar ruffians all eager to repeat the horrors of the place where we now stood; but we had to curb our impatience to go to their relief and had days still to wait the coming of Sir Colin Campbell, the new Commander-in-Chief, who with a large force was now pushing up country.

Ringleaders of the Mutiny were blown from the mouths of cannon. The possessions of the East India Company were transferred to the crown. The Westernization of India – against which the Mutiny had, at base, been a protest – continued apace, including higher-education instruction in English. This was of no small importance: it would assist the global triumph of the English language.

Queen Victoria, meanwhile, pestered Parliament until they agreed she could be Empress of India.

Samuel White Baker Discovers the Source of the Nile, 14 March 1864

SAMUEL WHITE BAKER

The quintessential English Victorian explorer (that is, a gentleman, an amateur, a patriot: 'By Englishmen alone is the glorious feeling shared of true, fair and manly sport'), Baker was accompanied throughout his explorations of Africa by his Hungarian wife, Florence von Sass, bought at a slave market. The primary source of the Nile – Lake Victoria – had been discovered by John Hanning Speke in 1858 but Baker determined to find a reputed second source, a lake known by natives as Luta Nzige.

The sun had not risen when I was spurring my ox after the guide, who, having been promised a double handful of beads on arrival at the lake, had caught the enthusiasm of the moment. The day broke beautifully clear, and having crossed a deep valley between the hills, we toiled up the opposite slope. I hurried to the summit. The glory of our prize burst suddenly upon me! There, like a sea of quicksilver, lay far beneath the grand expanse of water – a boundless sea horizon on the south and south-west, glittering in the noon-day sun; and on the west, at fifty or sixty miles' distance, blue mountains rose from the bosom of the lake to a height of about 7,000 feet above its level.

It is impossible to describe the triumph of that moment; here was the reward for all our labour – for the years of tenacity with which we had toiled through Africa. England had won the sources of the Nile! Long before I reached this spot, I had arranged to give three cheers with all our men in English style in honour of the discovery, but now that I looked down upon the great inland sea lying nestled in the very heart of Africa, and thought how vainly mankind had sought these sources throughout so many ages, and reflected that I had been the humble instrument permitted to unravel this portion of the great mystery when so many greater than I had failed, I felt too serious to vent my feelings in vain cheers for victory, and I sincerely thanked God for having guided and supported us through all dangers to the good end. I was about 1,500 feet above the lake, and I looked down from the steep granite cliff upon those welcome waters – upon that vast reservoir which nourished Egypt and brought fertility where all was wilderness – upon that great source so long hidden from mankind; that source of bounty and of blessings to millions of human beings; and as one of the greatest objects in nature, I determined to honour it with a great name. As an imperishable memorial of one loved and mourned by our gracious Queen and deplored by every Englishman, I called this great lake 'the Albert N'yanza'. The Victoria and the Albert lakes are the two sources of the Nile.

The zigzag path to descend to the lake was so steep and dangerous that we were forced to leave our oxen with a guide, who was to take them to Magungo and wait for our arrival. We commenced the descent of the steep pass on foot. I led the way, grasping a stout bamboo. My wife in extreme weakness tottered down the pass, supporting herself upon my shoulder, and stopping to rest every twenty paces. After a toilsome descent of about two hours, weak with years of fever, but for the moment strengthened by success, we gained the level plain below the cliff. A walk of about a mile through flat sandy meadows of fine turf interspersed with trees and bush, brought us to the water's edge. The waves were rolling upon a white pebbly beach: I rushed into the lake, and thirsty with heat and fatigue, with a heart full of gratitude, I drank deeply from the Sources of the Nile. Within a quarter of a mile of the lake was a fishing village named Vacovia, in which we now established ourselves. Everything smelt of fish – and everything looked like fishing; not the 'gentle art' of England with rod and fly, but harpoons were leaning against the huts, and lines almost as thick as the little finger were hanging up to dry, to which were attached iron hooks of a size that said much for the monsters of the Albert lake. On entering the hut I found a prodigious quantity of tackle; the lines were beautifully made of the fibre of the plantain stem, and were exceedingly elastic, and well adapted to withstand the first rush of a heavy fish; the hooks were very coarse, but well barbed, and varied in size from two to six inches. A number of harpoons and floats for hippopotami were arranged in good order, and the *tout ensemble* of the hut showed that the owner was a sportsman . . .

I procured a couple of kids from the chief of the village for some blue beads, and having received an ox as a present from the headman of Parkāni in return for a number of beads and bracelets, I gave my men a grand feast in honour of the discovery; I made them an address, explaining to them how much trouble we should have been saved had my whole party behaved well from the first commencement and trusted to my guidance, as we should have arrived here twelve months ago; at the same time I told them, that it was a greater honour to have achieved the task with so small a force as thirteen men, and that as the lake was thus happily reached, and Mrs Baker was restored to health after so terrible a danger, I should forgive them past offences and wipe out all that had been noted against them in my journal. This delighted my people, who ejaculated 'El hamd el Illah!' (thank God!) and fell to immediately at their beef.

At sunrise on the following morning I took the compass, and accompanied by the chief of the village, my guide Rabonga, and the woman Bacheeta, I went to the borders of the lake to survey the country. It was beautifully clear, and with a powerful telescope I could distinguish two large waterfalls that cleft the sides of the mountains on the opposite shore. Although the outline of the mountains was distinct upon the bright blue sky, and the dark shades upon their sides denoted deep gorges, I could not distinguish other features than the two great falls, which looked like threads of silver on the dark face of the mountains. No base had been visible, even from an elevation of 1,500 feet above the water-level, on my first view of the lake, but the chain of lofty mountains on the west appeared to rise suddenly from the water. This appearance must have been due to the great distance, the base being below the horizon, as dense columns of smoke were ascending apparently from the surface of the water: this must have been produced by the burning of prairies at the foot of the mountains . . .

Both the guide and the chief of Vacovia informed me that we should be taken by canoes to Magungo, to the point at which the Somerset that we had left at Karuma joined the lake; but that we could not ascend it, as it was a succession of cataracts the whole way from Karuma until within a short distance of Magungo. The exit of the Nile from the lake at Koshi was navigable for a considerable distance, and canoes could descend the river as far as the Madi.

They both agreed that the level of the lake was never lower than at present, and that it never rose higher than a mark upon the beach that accounted for an increase of about four feet. The beach was perfectly clean sand, upon which the waves rolled like those of the sea, throwing up weeds precisely as seaweed may be seen upon the English shore. It was a grand sight to look upon this vast reservoir of the mighty Nile, and to watch the heavy swell tumbling upon the beach, while far to the south-west the eye searched as vainly for a bound as though upon the Atlantic. It was with extreme emotion that I enjoyed this glorious scene. My wife, who had followed me so devotedly, stood by my side pale and exhausted – a wreck upon the shores of the great Albert Lake that we had so long striven to reach. No European foot had ever trod upon its sand, nor had the eyes of a white man ever scanned its vast expanse of water. We were the first; and this was the key to the great secret that even Julius Cæsar yearned to unravel, but in vain. Here was the great basin of the Nile that received *every drop of water*, even from the passing shower to the roaring mountain torrent that drained from Central Africa towards the north. This was the great reservoir of the Nile!

Baker was knighted in 1866.

Stanley Meets Livingstone, Ujiji, Africa, 10 November 1871

SIR HENRY MORTON STANLEY

British missionaries such as Dr Livingstone healed the sick, condemned the slave trade and preached the gospel. Stanley's expedition, paid for by the New York Herald, *to find the 'lost' Livingstone in Africa became a celebrated Victorian adventure.*

We push on rapidly, lest the news of our coming might reach the people of Bunder Ujiji before we come in sight, and are ready for them. We halt at a little brook, then ascend the long slope of a naked ridge, the very last of the myriads we have crossed. This alone prevents us from seeing the lake in all its vastness. We arrive at the summit, travel across and arrive at its western rim, and pause, reader – the port of Ujiji is below us, embowered in the palms, only five hundred yards from us! At this grand moment we do not think of the hundreds of miles we have marched, of the hundreds of hills that we have ascended and descended, of the many forests we have traversed, of the jungles and thickets that annoyed us, of the fervid salt plains that blistered our feet, of the hot suns that scorched us, nor the dangers and difficulties now happily surmounted. At last the sublime hour has arrived! – our dreams, our hopes, and anticipations are now about to be realized! Our hearts and our feelings are with our eyes as we peer into the palms and try to make out in which hut or house lives the white man with the grey beard we heard about on the Malagarazi.

We were now about three hundred yards from the village of Ujiji and the crowds are dense about me. Suddenly I hear a voice on my right side.

'Good morning, sir!'

Startled at hearing this greeting in the midst of such a crowd of black people, I turn sharply around in search of the man, and see him at my side, with the blackest of faces, but animated and joyous – a man dressed in a long white shirt, with a turban of American sheeting around his woolly head, and I ask:

'Who the mischief are you?'

'I am Susi, the servant of Dr Livingstone,' said he, smiling, and showing a gleaming row of teeth.

'What! Is Dr Livingstone here?'

'Yes, sir.'

'In this village?'

'Yes, sir.'

'Are you sure?'

'Sure, sure, sir. Why, I leave him just now.' . . .

'Now, you Susi, run, and tell the Doctor I am coming.'

'Yes, sir,' and off he darted like a madman . . .

Soon Susi came running back, and asked me my name; he had told the Doctor that I was coming, but the Doctor was too surprised to believe him, and, when the Doctor asked him my name, Susi was rather staggered.

But, during Susi's absence, the news had been conveyed to the Doctor that it was surely a white man that was coming, whose guns were firing and whose flag could be seen; and the great Arab magnates of Ujiji – Mohammed bin Sali, Sayd bin Majid, Abid bin Suleiman, Mohammed bin Gharib, and others – had gathered together before the Doctor's house, and the Doctor had come out from his veranda to discuss the matter and await my arrival.

In the meantime, the head of the Expedition had halted, and the *kirangozi* was out of the ranks, holding his flag aloft, and Selim said to me, 'I see the Doctor, sir. Oh, what an old man! He has got a white beard.' And I – what would I not have given for a bit of friendly wilderness, where, unseen, I might vent my joy in some mad freak, such as idiotically biting my hand, turning a somersault, or slashing at trees, in order to allay those exciting feelings that were well-nigh uncontrollable. My heart beats fast, but I must not let my face betray my emotions, lest it shall detract from the dignity of a white man appearing under such extraordinary circumstances.

So I did that which I thought was most dignified. I pushed back the crowds and, passing from the rear, walked down a living avenue of people, until I came in front of the semicircle of Arabs, in the front of which stood the white man with the grey beard. As I advanced slowly towards him I noticed he was pale, looked wearied, had a grey beard, wore a bluish cap with a faded gold band round it, had on a red sleeved waistcoat, and a pair of grey tweed trousers. I would have run to him, only I was a coward in the presence of such a mob – would have embraced him, only, he being an Englishman I did not know how he would receive me; so I did what cowardice and false pride suggested was the best thing – walked deliberately to him, took off my hat, and said:

'Dr Livingstone, I presume?'

'YES,' said he, with a kind smile, lifting his cap slightly.

I replace my hat on my head, and he puts on his cap, and we both grasp hands, and I then say aloud.

'I thank God, Doctor, I have been permitted to see you.'

Missionaries were the unintended point-riders of imperialism, for they stimulated interest in the 'dark continent'. Traders followed, behind them went the British flag, until by the 1880s a quarter of the world's map was pink. Imperialism was a haphazard process, not a deliberate policy. Only in the rarest instances – such as the Opium Wars with China – did British arms make the market for British merchants.

The Revolt of the Field, 7 February 1872

JOSEPH ARCH

A series of bad harvests, cheap food imports (courtesy of bigger and speedier steam shipping) and the opening up of the North American prairies to grain-growing caused 'the great depression' in the English countryside between 1872 and the end of the century. Poverty and depopulation were the result; 40 per cent of rural male labourers left the land in the thirty years before 1901. It was of this crumbling of countryside community that the novels of Thomas Hardy spoke, and Joseph Arch's foundation of the National Agricultural Labourers' Union at Wellesbourne addressed. Arch (1826–1919) was later MP for Northwest Norfolk.

The day was 7th February, 1872. It was a very wet morning, and I was busy at home on a carpentering job; I was making a box. My wife came in to me and said, 'Joe, here's three men come to see you. What for, I don't know.' But I knew fast enough. In walked the three; they turned out to be labourers from over Wellesbourne way. I stopped work, and we had a talk. They said they had come to ask me to hold a meeting at Wellesbourne that evening. They wanted to get the men together, and start a Union directly. I told them that, if they did form a Union, they would have to fight hard for it, and they would have to suffer a great deal; both they and their families. They said the labourers were prepared both to fight and suffer. Things could not be worse; wages were so low, and provisions were so dear, that nothing but downright starvation lay before them unless the farmers could be made to raise their wages. Asking was of no use; it was nothing but waste of breath; so they must join together and strike, and hold out till the employers gave in. When I saw that the men were in dead earnest, and had counted the cost and were determined to stand shoulder to shoulder till they could squeeze a living wage out of their employers, and that they were the spokesmen of others likeminded with themselves, I said I would address the meeting that evening at 7 o'clock. I told them that I had left nine shillings a week behind me years ago, and as I had got out of the ditch myself, I was ready and willing to help them out too. I said, 'If you are ready to combine, I will run all risk and come over and help you.'

I remember that evening, as if it were but yesterday. When I set out I was dressed in a pair of cord trousers, and cord vest, and an old flannel-jacket. I have that jacket at home now, and I put a high value on it. As I tramped along the wet, muddy road to Wellesbourne my heart was stirred within me, and questions passed through my mind and troubled me. Was it a false start, a sort of hole-and-corner movement, which would come to nothing, and do more harm to the men than good? If a Union were fairly set afoot, would the farmers prove too strong for it?

When I reached Wellesbourne, lo, and behold, it was as lively as a swarm of bees in June. We settled that I should address the meeting under the old chestnut tree; and I expected to find some thirty or forty of the principal men there. What then was my surprise to see not a few tens but many hundreds of labourers assembled; there were nearly two thousand of them. The news that I was going to speak that night had been spread about; and so the men had come in from all the villages round within a radius of ten miles. Not a circular had been sent out nor a handbill printed, but from cottage to cottage, and from farm to farm, the word had been passed on; and here were the labourers gathered together in their hundreds. Wellesbourne village was there, every man in it; and they had come from Moreton and Locksley and Charlecote and Hampton Lucy, and from Barford, to hear what I had to say to them. By this time the night had fallen pitch dark; but the men got bean poles and hung lanterns on them, and we could see well enough. It was an extraordinary sight, and I shall never forget it, not to my dying day. I mounted an old pig-stool, and in the flickering light of the lanterns I saw the earnest upturned faces of these poor brothers of mine – faces gaunt with hunger and pinched with want – all looking towards me and ready to listen to the words, that would fall from my lips. These white slaves of England stood there with the darkness all about them, like the Children of Israel waiting for someone to lead them out of the land of Egypt. I determined that, if they made a mistake and took the wrong turning, it would not be my fault, so I stood on my pig-stool and spoke out straight and strong for Union. My speech lasted about an hour, I believe, but I was not measuring minutes then. By the end of it the men were properly roused, and they pressed in and crowded up asking questions; they regularly pelted me with them; it was a perfect hailstorm. We passed a resolution to form a Union then and there, and the names of the men could not be taken down fast enough; we enrolled between two and three hundred members that night. It was a brave start, and before we parted it was arranged that there should be another meeting at the same place in a fortnight's time. I knew now that a fire had been kindled which would catch on, and spread, and run abroad like sparks in stubble; and I felt certain that this night we had set light to a beacon, which would prove a rallying point for the agricultural labourers throughout the country.

The news of the meeting soon spread like wildfire, and publicity gave great help to the cause. The result was that, when I got to the chestnut tree on the evening of 21st February, a fortnight later, I found a bigger crowd than before, and I think we had nearly every policeman in the county there as well. They thought there would be a disturbance, but they need not have troubled themselves on that score. I have always preached restraint, and advocated keeping within the law, if possible. Now, more than ever, did I feel called upon to plead for moderation, and I told them in the plainest terms that, if they had recourse to violence and riot and incendiarism, or if they wantonly destroyed any kind of property, they must not look to Joseph Arch to lead them. I would be a peaceable Wat Tyler of the fields, but I would be no rioting leader of the riotous. Neither I nor they should wear handcuffs and see the inside of a gaol, if I could help it. We had come there to strike off the rusty old fetters that had crippled us, and our fathers before us, not to forge new ones for ourselves. We had come there to gain our freedom by lawful means, not to lose what little we had by lawlessness. We were going to stand up for our rights, we were going to ask for our just dues, and we were resolved to have them; but from first to last we were going to act as law-abiding citizens not as red-handed revolutionaries.

Rorke's Drift, South Africa, 21 January 1879

HENRY HOOK

21 January 1879 was a graveyard and a glory for the Victorian British Army. In the morning the British camp at Isandhlwana was annihilated by 10,000 Zulus (the last order to British troops was: 'Fix bayonets and die like British soldiers do!'), who then advanced on the British hospital and garrison at Rorke's Drift, manned by 120 soldiers, including the sick inmates. For the stand at Rorke's Drift eleven soldiers were awarded the Victoria Cross, more than for any other single engagement involving the British Army. Henry Hook was one of the recipients.

The Zulu War was occasioned by the Zulus' refusal of a British protectorate.

Just before half past four we heard firing behind the conical hill at the back of the drift, called Oskarsberg Hill, and suddenly about five or six hundred Zulus swept around, coming for us at a run. Instantly the natives – Kaffirs who had been very useful in making the barricade of waggons, mealie-bags and biscuit boxes around the camp – bolted towards Helpmakaar, and what was worse their officer and a European sergeant went with them. To see them deserting like that was too much for some of us, and we fired after them. The sergeant was struck and killed. Half-a-dozen of us were stationed in the hospital, with orders to hold it and guard the sick. The ends of the building were of stone, the side walls of ordinary bricks, and the inside walls or partitions of sun-dried bricks of mud. These shoddy inside bricks proved our salvation, as you will see. It was a queer little one-storeyed building, which it is almost impossible to describe; but we were pinned like rats in a hole, because all the doorways except one had been barricaded with mealie-bags and we had done the same with the windows. The interior was divided by means of partition walls into which were fitted some very slight doors. The patients' beds were simple rough affairs of boards, raised only about half a foot above the floor. To talk of hospitals and beds gives the idea of a big building, but as a matter of fact this hospital was a mere little shed or bungalow, divided up into rooms so small that you could hardly swing a bayonet in them. There were about nine men who could not move, but altogether there were about thirty. Most of these, however could not help to defend themselves.

As soon as our Kaffirs bolted, it was seen that the fort as we had first made it was too big to be held, so Lieutenant Chard instantly reduced the space by having a row of biscuit-boxes drawn across the middle, about four feet high. This was our inner entrenchment, and proved very valuable. The Zulus came on at a wild rush, and although many of them were shot down they got to within about fifty yards of our south wall of mealie-bags and biscuit boxes and waggons. They were caught between two fires, that from the hospital and that from the storehouse, and were checked; but they gained the shelter of the cookhouse and ovens, and gave us many heavy volleys. During the fight they took advantage of every bit of cover there was, anthills, a tract of bush that we had not had time to clear away, a garden or sort of orchard which was near us, and a ledge of rock and some caves (on the Oskarsberg) which were only about a hundred yards away. They neglected nothing, and while they went on firing, large bodies kept hurling themselves against our slender breastworks.

But it was the hospital they assaulted most fiercely. I had charge with a man that we called Old King Cole of a small room with only one patient in it. Cole kept with me for some time after the fight began, then he said he was not going to stay. He went outside and was instantly killed by the Zulus, so that I was left alone with the patient, a native whose leg was broken and who kept crying out, 'Take my bandage off, so that I can come.' But it was impossible to do anything except fight, and I blazed away as hard as I could. By this time I was the only defender of my room. Poor Old King Cole was lying dead outside and the helpless patient was crying and groaning near me. The Zulus were swarming around us, and there was an extraordinary rattle as the bullets struck the biscuit boxes, and queer thuds as they plumped into the bags of mealies. Then there was the whizz and rip of the assegais, of which I had experience during the Kaffir Campaign of 1877–8. We had plenty of ammunition, but we were told to save it and so we took careful aim at every shot, and hardly a cartridge was wasted. Private Dunbar, shot no fewer than nine Zulus, one of them being a Chief.

From the very first the enemy tried to rush the hospital, and at last they managed to set fire to the thick grass which formed the roof. This put us in a terrible plight, because it meant that we were either to be massacred or burned alive, or get out of the building.

All this time the Zulus were trying to get into the room. Their assegais kept whizzing towards us, and one struck me in front of the helmet. We were wearing the white tropical helmets then. But the helmet tilted back under the blow and made the spear lose its power, so that I escaped with a scalp wound which did not trouble me much then, although it has often caused me illness since. Only one man at a time could get in at the door. A big Zulu sprang forward and seized my rifle, but I tore it free and, slipping a cartridge in, I shot him point-blank. Time after time the Zulus gripped the muzzle and tried to tear the rifle from my grasp, and time after time I wrenched it back, because I had a better grip than they had. All this time Williams was getting the sick through the hole into the next room, all except one, a soldier of the 24th named Conley, who could not move because of a broken leg. Watching for my chance I dashed from the doorway, and grabbing Conley I pulled him after me through the hole. His leg got broken again, but there was no help for it. As soon as we left the room the Zulus burst in with furious cries of disappointment and rage.

Now there was a repetition of the work of holding the doorway, except that I had to stand by a hole instead of a door, while Williams picked away at the far wall to make an opening for escape into the next room. There was more desperate and almost hopeless fighting, as it seemed, but most of the poor fellows were got through the hole.

. . . All this time, of course, the storehouse was being valiantly defended by the rest of the garrison. When we got into the inner fort, I took my post at a place where two men had been shot. While I was there another man was shot in the neck, I think by a bullet which came through the space between two biscuit boxes that were not quite close together. This was at about six o'clock in the evening, nearly two hours after the opening shot of the battle had been fired. Every now and then the Zulus would make a rush for it and get in. We had to charge them out. By this time it was dark, and the hospital was all in flames, but this gave us a splendid light to fight by. I believe it was this light that saved us. We could see them coming, and they could not rush us and take us by surprise from any point. They could not get at us, and so they went away and had ten or fifteen minutes of a war-dance. This roused them up again, and their excitement was so intense that the ground fairly seemed to shake. Then, when they were goaded to the highest pitch, they would hurl themselves at us again. We could sometimes, by the light of the flames, keep them well in sight, so well that we could take aim and fire coolly. When we could do this they never advanced as far as the barricade, because we shot them down as they ran in on us. But every now and then one or two managed to crawl in and climb over the top of the sacks. They were bayoneted off.

All this time the sick and wounded were crying for water. We had the water-cart full of water, but it was just by the deserted hospital, and we could not hope to get at it until the day broke, when the Zulus might begin to lose heart and to stop their mad rushes. But we could not bear the cries any longer, and three or four of us jumped over the boxes and ran and fetched some water in.

The long night passed and the day broke. Then we looked around us to see what had happened, and there was not a living soul who was not thankful to find that the Zulus had had enough of it and were disappearing over the hill to the south-west.

The Cup Final, Kennington Oval, London,
30 March 1882

THE *BLACKBURN TIMES*

Formerly a medieval brawl, football had been taken into the cloisters and quads of the public schools, where a game of skill and rules had been made of it. From the public schools it was carried by 'muscular Christians' to the working classes for their self-improvement. (Not a few clubs, Aston Villa among them, sprang from Sunday Schools.) The Football Association Cup was instituted in 1872, the League in 1888. Watching Association football henceforth became the regular relaxation of men in industrial England.

When the cheering which greeted the advent of the rival captains had subsided, the toss for choice of goals was made, and the Rovers' chief was unfortunate in losing. The Etonians chose to play with the wind in their favour and the sun at their backs. The ball was 'kicked off' by Strachan at eight minutes past three. A light touch to the left gave the leather to Brown, who sent it forward, but it was instantly returned, and the Etonians rushed along and in a few seconds Chevallier made a couple of corner kicks but each was followed by a kick from the goal. Of the Rovers forwards the right wing pair first became prominent. Heading back the leather, J. Hargreaves, aided by Avery, made a good run, but when the other goal was almost reached Macauley intervened and sent it back again. Suter twice relieved his goal cleverly, but Howorth was compelled to use his hands, and then the besiegers had another corner kick, which like its predecessors, proved fruitless. A free kick awarded for a handling of the ball enabled Suter to place it well to the right wing forwards, and the first kick from the corner flag for the Rovers was immediately afterwards made by Douglas. The ball was missed by all the players in the mouth of the goal, but was promptly sent in by the Rovers captain. Kinnaird relieved his side, and Macauley made a run, in which he was aided by Dunn, who passed to Anderson, and that player by a side shot scored a goal at the end of the first eight minutes' play.

Suter and McIntyre in turn interposed with good effect, and enabled Strachan, Douglas, and Duckworth to make an attack upon the Eton citadel. The leather was sent into the hands of Rawlinson, who threw it away before he could be charged through the goal. A free kick from close to the goal enabled the Etonians to return to the attack, but they were unsuccessful, a tremendous kick from Macauley sending the ball some yards above the top bar. Subsequently the ball was thrown right into the mouth of goal by Anderson, and Howorth's charge was seriously imperilled for a time.

For a breach of rule, which forbids handling, a free kick was awarded against the Etonians in their quarters, but McIntyre missed the ball when it was lightly sent to him by Fred Hargreaves and, as the penalty, the opposing forwards rushed along the ground, and Dunn by a good kick sent the leather into the hands of Howorth.

Another rush was frustrated by McIntyre and Fred Hargreaves, and Avery secured possession of the ball. Foley interposed to bar his progress, and, jumping at the ball, gave Avery a tremendous kick on the thigh, which placed him 'hors de combat' for some minutes, and partially disabled him during the remainder of the game.

Drs Porteus and Morley attended him on the grass outside the bounds of play, and soon reported that no serious injury had been sustained.

Play was transferred to the Etonians' quarters, and kept there for a few minutes, during which J. Hargreaves, Avery, and Douglas appeared to advantage, but eventually the ball was again sent over the goal line. The ball, thrown in by Anderson, was headed back from the goal mouth by Suter just as the whistle sounded 'half-time'. Play this far had been remarkably fast, and, with the strong wind against them, the Rovers could not invade their opponents' territory very often, but their defence was good, and in the circumstances they had done exceedingly well to prevent the scoring of more than one goal against them.

With the score so low the Rovers' supporters hopefully awaited the result. At four minutes to four Goodhart started the ball from the centre, but he was instantly robbed by Strachan, who passed it to the left wing, along which it was taken by J. Hargreaves and Avery. Their progress was barred, and the Etonian forwards returned, but a strong kick sent the ball considerably in advance of them, and Howorth ran out from the goal to kick the ball back. A free kick by Kinnaird was rendered of non-effect by the interposition of the head of Strachan, who played exceedingly well throughout, and the Eton quarters were again invaded.

Some combined play by the Etonian forwards enabled them to approach the Rovers' goal, but they were speedily driven back, and Douglas and Duckworth again came into prominence. The goalkeeper was forced to use his hands, but he had a place kick immediately afterwards, and Fred Hargreaves missing the ball, the Etonian forwards secured a chance which they promptly utilized, to break away, and Chevallier shot the leather behind the goal.

Macauley subsequently made a better attempt to score, but Howorth stopped the ball with his hands, while when Duckworth a few seconds later gave Douglas an opportunity he shot the leather over the bar of the Etonian citadel, and on a second attempt he sent it over the line. As the time for play gradually shortened, the supporters of the Rovers became less confident, and there were shouts from the grand stand of 'Play up Black-burn', to which admirers of their opponents responded by cries of 'E-e-ton'. But there was ominous silence amongst the Lancashire spectators. For nearly twenty minutes before the close the Etonians were practically penned in their own quarters, and the Rovers were constantly striving to score, but only to be disappointed by seeing the ball go over the line, on the wrong side of the posts or to be stopped by the goalkeeper. All the shots were high, however, and there was no opportunity of judging of Rawlinson's power with his feet. The desperate struggle was continued until the referee's whistle signalled the expiration of time, and the Etonians were hailed the victors by one goal to none. Suter played magnificently, Strachan and Duckworth did remarkably well; McIntyre rendered good service; and the other members played well, but on the whole the team did not quite reach its most brilliant form. Of the Old Etonians the captain and Foley were best, while both backs played well; Rawlinson far exceeded expectations as goalkeeper and elicited many complimentary comments; and Macauley, Dunn, Novelli, and Anderson were the pick of the forward division.

Eton may have won, but the football future belonged to industrial, professional Blackburn Rovers.

The Diamond Jubilee, 22 June 1897

QUEEN VICTORIA

Diary: 22nd June. A never-to-be-forgotten day. No one ever, I believe, has met with such an ovation as was given to me, passing through those six miles of streets, including Constitution Hill. The crowds were quite indescribable, and their enthusiasm truly marvellous and deeply touching. The cheering was quite deafening, and every face seemed to be filled with real joy. I was much moved and gratified.

. . . At a quarter-past eleven, the others being seated in their carriages long before, and having preceded me a short distance, I started from the State entrance in an open State landau, drawn by eight creams, dear Alix [the future Queen Alexandra], looking very pretty in lilac, and Lenchen [Princess Helena] sitting opposite me. I felt a good deal agitated, and had been so all these days, for fear anything might be forgotten or go wrong. Bertie [the Prince of Wales; the future King Edward VII] and George C. [the 2nd Duke of Cambridge] rode one on each side of the carriage, Arthur [the Duke of Connaught] (who had charge of the whole military arrangements) a little in the rear. My escort was formed from the 2nd Life Guards and officers of the native Indian regiments, these latter riding immediately in front of my carriage. Guard of Honour of Bluejackets, the Guards, and the 2nd Surrey Regiment (Queen's) were mounted in the Quadrangle and outside the Palace.

Before leaving I touched an electric button, by which I started a message which was telegraphed throughout the whole Empire. It was the following: 'From my heart I thank my beloved people. May God bless them!' At this time the sun burst out. Vicky [the Princess Royal] was in the carriage nearest me, not being able to go in mine, as her rank as Empress prevented her sitting with her back to the horses, for I had to sit alone. Her carriage was drawn by four blacks, richly caparisoned in red. We went up Constitution Hill and Piccadilly, and there were seats right along the former, where my own servants and personal attendants, and members of the other Royal Households, the Chelsea Pensioners, and the children of the Duke of York's and Greenwich schools had seats. St James's Street was beautifully decorated . . . Trafalgar Square was very striking. . . . The denseness of the crowds was immense, but the order maintained wonderful. The streets in the Strand are now quite wide, but one misses Temple Bar. Here the Lord Mayor received me and presented the sword, which I touched. . . . As we neared St Paul's the procession was often stopped, and the crowds broke out into singing *God Save the Queen* . . .

In front of the Cathedral the scene was most impressive. All the Colonial troops, on foot, were drawn up round the Square. My carriage, surrounded by all the Royal Princes, was drawn up close to the steps, where the Clergy were assembled, the Bishops in rich copes, with their croziers, the Archbishop of Canterbury and the Bishop of London each holding a very fine one. A *Te Deum* was sung . . .

I stopped in front of the Mansion House, where the Lady Mayoress presented me with a beautiful silver basket full of orchids. Here I took leave of the Lord Mayor. Both he and the Lady Mayoress were quite *émus*. We proceeded over London Bridge, where no spectators were allowed, only troops, and then along the Borough Road, where there is a very poor population, but just as enthusiastic and orderly as elsewhere. The decorations there were very pretty. . . . Crossed the river again over Westminster Bridge . . . The heat during the last hour was very great, and poor Lord Howe, who was riding as Gold Stick, fainted and had a bad fall, but was not seriously hurt.

Got home at a quarter to two . . . Had a quiet luncheon with Vicky, Beatrice, and her three children. Troops continually passing by. Then rested and later had tea in the garden with Lenchen. There was a large dinner in the supper-room . . . I walked into the Ball-room afterwards, and sat down in front of the dais. Felt very tired, but tried to speak to most of the Princes and Princesses . . . In the morning I wore a dress of black silk trimmed with panels of grey satin veiled with black net and steel embroideries, and some black lace, my lovely diamond chain, given me by my younger children, round my neck. My bonnet was trimmed with creamy white flowers, and white aigrette and some black lace.

Fox-hunt, Kent, November 1898

SIEGFRIED SASSOON

Fox-hunting became the chosen sport of the English aristocracy in the mid-eighteenth century. Of all the classes in English society, the upper changed its mores, lives and pleasures least over the long industrial period. 'A curiously tough substance', as the Fabian writer Beatrice Webb remarked of the aristocracy.

Sassoon was twelve at the time of his first fox-hunt, below.

The afternoon hunt was going to be a serious affair. There never appeared to be any doubt about that. The field was reduced to about forty riders, and the chattersome contingent seemed to have gone home. We all went into the covert and remained close together at one end. Dixon got off and tightened my girths, which had got very loose (as I ought to have noticed). A resolute-looking lady in a tall hat drew her veil down after taking a good pull at the flask which she handed back to her groom. Hard-faced men rammed their hats on to their heads and sat silently in the saddle as though, for the first time in the day, they really meant business. My heart was in my mouth and it had good reason to be there. Lord Dumborough was keeping an intent eye on the ride which ran through the middle of the covert.

'Cut along up to the top end, Charlie,' he remarked without turning his head, and a gaunt, ginger-haired man in a weather-stained scarlet coat went off up the covert in a squelchy canter.

'That's Mr Macdoggart,' said Dixon in a low voice, and my solemnity increased as the legendary figure vanished on its mysterious errand.

Meanwhile the huntsman was continuing his intermittent yaups as he moved along the other side of the wood. Suddenly his cheers of encouragement changed to a series of excited shoutings. 'Hoick-holler, hoick-holler, hoick-holler!' he yelled, and then blew his horn loudly; this was followed by an outbreak of vociferation from the hounds, and soon they were in full cry across the covert. I sat there petrified by my private feelings; Sheila showed no symptoms of agitation; she merely cocked her ears well forward and listened.

And then, for the first time, I heard a sound which has thrilled generations of fox-hunters to their marrow. From the far side of the wood came the long shrill screech (for which it is impossible to find an adequate word) which signifies that one of the whips has viewed the fox quitting the covert. 'Gone Away' it meant. But before I had formulated the haziest notion about it Lord Dumborough was galloping up the ride and the rest of them were pelting after him as though nothing could stop them. As I happened to be standing well inside the wood and Sheila took the affair into her own control, I was swept along with them, and we emerged on the other side among the leaders.

I cannot claim that I felt either excitement or resolution as we bundled down a long slope of meadowland and dashed helter-skelter through an open gate at the bottom. I knew nothing at all except that I was out of breath and that the air was rushing to meet me, but as I hung on to the reins I was aware that Mr Macdoggart was immediately in front of me.

My attitude was an acquiescent one. I have always been inclined to accept life in the form in which it has imposed itself upon me, and on that particular occasion, no doubt, I just felt that I was 'in for it'. It did not so much as occur to me that in following Mr Macdoggart I was setting myself rather a high standard, and when he disappeared over a hedge I took it for granted that I must do the same. For a moment Sheila hesitated in her stride. (Dixon told me afterwards that I actually hit her as we approached the fence, but I couldn't remember having done so.) Then she collected herself and jumped the fence with a peculiar arching of her back. There was a considerable drop on the other side. Sheila had made no mistake, but as she landed I left the saddle and flew over her head. I had let go of the reins, but she stood stock-still while I sat on the wet ground. A few moments later Dixon popped over a gap lower down the fence and came to my assistance, and I saw the boy on the chestnut pony come after him and gallop on in a resolute but unhurrying way. I scrambled to my feet, feeling utterly ashamed.

'What ever made you go for it like that?' asked Dixon, who was quite disconcerted.

'I saw Mr Macdoggart going over it, and I didn't like to stop,' I stammered. By now the whole hunt had disappeared and there wasn't a sound to be heard.

'Well, I suppose we may as well go on.' He laughed as he gave me a leg up. 'Fancy you following Mr Macdoggart over the biggest place in the fence. Good thing Miss Sherston couldn't see you.'

The idea of my aunt seemed to amuse him, and he slapped his knee and chuckled as he led me onward at a deliberate pace. Secretly mortified by my failure I did my best to simulate cheerfulness. But I couldn't forget the other boy and how ridiculous he must have thought me when he saw me rolling about on the ground. I felt as if I must be covered with mud. About half an hour later we found the hunt again, but I can remember nothing more except that it was beginning to get dark and the huntsman, a middle-aged, mulberry-faced man named Jack Pitt, was blowing his horn as he sat in the middle of his hounds. The other boy was actually talking to him – a privilege I couldn't imagine myself promoted to. At that moment I almost hated him for his cocksuredness.

Then, to my surprise, the Master himself actually came up and asked me how far I was from home. In my embarrassment I could only mutter that I didn't know, and Dixon interposed with 'About twelve miles, m'lord,' in his best manner.

'I hear he's quite a young thruster.' ... The great man glanced at me for a moment with curiosity before he turned away. Not knowing what he meant I went red in the face and thought he was making fun of me.

Omdurman, 2 September 1898

WINSTON CHURCHILL

A battle fought to avenge the death of General Gordon at the hands of the Pan-Islamic Mahdi and to reconquer the Sudan (and so secure the Suez Canal, the empire's lifeline to India).

Churchill fought with the 21st Lancers, as well as simultaneously holding a roving commission as a war correspondent. The British commander at Omdurman was Major-General Horatio Kitchener.

I propose to describe exactly what happened to me: what I saw and what I felt. I recalled it to my mind so frequently after the event that the impression is as clear and vivid as it was a quarter of a century ago. The troop I commanded was, when we wheeled into line, the second from the right of the regiment. I was riding a handy, sure-footed, grey Arab polo pony. Before we wheeled and began to gallop, the officers had been marching with drawn swords. On account of my shoulder I had always decided that if I were involved in hand-to-hand fighting, I must use a pistol and not a sword. I had purchased in London a Mauser automatic pistol, then the newest and the latest design. I had practised carefully with this during our march and journey up the river. This then was the weapon with which I determined to fight. I had first of all to return my sword into its scabbard, which is not the easiest thing to do at a gallop. I had then to draw my pistol from its wooden holster and bring it to full cock. This dual operation took an appreciable time, and until it was finished, apart from a few glances to my left to see what effect the fire was producing, I did not look up at the general scene.

Then I saw immediately before me, and now only half the length of a polo ground away, the row of crouching blue figures firing frantically, wreathed in white smoke. On my right and left my neighbouring troop leaders made a good line. Immediately behind was a long dancing row of lances couched for the charge. We were going at a fast but steady gallop. There was too much trampling and rifle fire to hear any bullets.

After this glance to the right and left and at my troop, I looked again towards the enemy. The scene appeared to be suddenly transformed. The blue-black men were still firing, but behind them there now came into view a depression like a shallow sunken road. This was crowded and crammed with men rising up from the ground where they had hidden. Bright flags appeared as if by magic, and I saw arriving from nowhere Emirs on horseback among and around the mass of the enemy. The Dervishes appeared to be ten or twelve deep at the thickest, a great grey mass gleaming with steel, filling the dry watercourse. In the same twinkling of an eye I saw also that our right overlapped their left, that my troop would just strike the edge of their array, and that the troop on my right would charge into air. My subaltern comrade on the right, Wormald of the 7th Hussars, could see the situation too; and we both increased our speed to the very fastest gallop and curved inwards like the horns of the moon. One really had not time to be frightened or to think of anything else but these particular necessary actions which I have described. They completely occupied mind and senses.

The collision was now very near. I saw immediately before me, not ten yards away, the two blue men who lay in my path. They were perhaps a couple of yards apart. I rode at the interval between them. They both fired. I passed through the smoke conscious that I was unhurt. The trooper immediately behind me was killed at this place and at this moment, whether by these shots or not I do not know. I checked my pony as the ground began to fall away beneath his feet. The clever animal dropped like a cat four or five feet down on to the sandy bed of the watercourse, and in this sandy bed I found myself surrounded by what seemed to be dozens of men. They were not thickly-packed enough at this point for me to experience any actual collision with them. Whereas Grenfell's troop next but one on my left was brought to a complete standstill and suffered very heavy losses, we seemed to push our way through as one has sometimes seen mounted policemen break up a crowd. In less time than it takes to relate, my pony had scrambled up the other side of the ditch. I looked round.

Once again I was on the hard, crisp desert, my horse at a trot. I had sensation of fear. I felt myself absolutely alone. I thought these riflemen would hit me and the rest devour me like wolves. What a fool I was to loiter like this in the midst of the enemy! I crouched over the saddle, spurred my horse into a gallop and drew clear of the *mêlée*. Two or three hundred yards away I found my troop all ready faced about and partly formed up.

The other three troops of the squadron were re-forming close by. Suddenly in the midst of the troop up sprung a Dervish. How he got there I do not know. He must have leaped out of some scrub or hole. All the troopers turned upon him thrusting with their lances: but he darted to and fro causing for the moment a frantic commotion. Wounded several times, he staggered towards me raising his spear. I shot him at less than a yard. He fell on the sand, and lay there dead. How easy to kill a man! But I did not worry about it. I found I had fired the whole magazine of my Mauser pistol, so I put in a new clip of ten cartridges before thinking of anything else.

I was still prepossessed with the idea that we had inflicted great slaughter on the enemy and had scarcely suffered at all ourselves. Three or four men were missing from my troop. Six men and nine or ten horses were bleeding from spear thrusts or sword cuts. We all expected to be ordered immediately to charge back again. The men were ready, though they all looked serious. Several asked to be allowed to throw away their lances and draw their swords. I asked my second sergeant if he had enjoyed himself. His answer was 'Well, I don't exactly say I enjoyed it, Sir; but I think I'll get more used to it next time.'

Twenty thousand Dervishes were killed and wounded. British losses were 500. After Omdurman, the British marched on to Khartoum, where the bones of the slain General Gordon were disinterred and given a Christian burial.

The Siege of Mafeking, South Africa, April–May 1900

J. E. NEILLY

The Boer War (1899–1902), occasioned by Afrikaner attacks on British gold-miners in South Africa, saw the 700-strong garrison at Mafeking besieged from 12 October 1899 to 17 May 1900. The garrison was commanded by Colonel Baden-Powell, later to found the Scouts (1908) and the Girl Guides (1910).

It was not pleasant to mix among the people of the kraals. Hunger had them in its grip, and many of them were black spectres and living skeletons. I saw them crawling along on legs like the stems of well-blackened 'cutties', with their ribs literally breaking through their shrivelled skin – men, women, and children. I saw them, too, fall down on the veldt and lie where they had fallen, too weak to go on their way.

The sufferers were mostly little boys – mere infants ranging in age from four or five upwards. When the famine struck the place they were thrown out of the huts by their parents to live or die, sink or swim . . .

When the Colonel got to know of the state of affairs he instituted soup kitchens, where horses were boiled in huge cauldrons, and the savoury mess doled out in pints and quarts to all comers. Some of the people – those employed on works – paid for the food; the remainder, who were in the majority, obtained it free. One of those kitchens was established in the Stadt, and I several times went down there to see the unfortunates fed.

Words could not portray the scene of misery. The best thing I can do is to ask you to fancy five or six hundred human frameworks of both sexes and all ages, from the tender infant upwards, dressed in the remains of tattered rags, standing in lines, each holding an old blackened can or beef tin, awaiting turn to crawl painfully up to the kitchen where the food was distributed. Having obtained the horse soup, fancy them tottering off a few yards and sitting down to wolf up the life-fastening mess, and lick the tins when they had finished. It was one of the most heart-rending sights I ever witnessed, and I have seen many . . .

When a flight of locusts came it was regarded as a godsend – this visitation that is looked upon by the farmer as hardly less of a curse than the rinderpest or drought. The starving ones gathered the insects up in thousands, stripped them of their heads, legs, and wings, and ate the bodies. They picked up meat-tins and licked them; they fed like outcast curs. They went farther than the mongrel. When a dog gets a bone he polishes it white and leaves it there. Day after day I heard outside my door continuous thumping sounds. They were caused by the living skeletons who, having eaten all that was outside the bones, smashed them up with stones and devoured what marrow they could find. They looked for bones on the dust-heaps, on the roads everywhere, and I pledge my word that I saw one poor fellow weakly follow a dog with a stone and with unerring aim strike him on the ribs, which caused the lean and hungry brute to drop a bone, which the Kafir carried off in triumph to the kerb, where he smashed it and got what comfort he could from it.

When Mafeking was finally relieved, Victorian England went wild with a patriotic delirium that needed a neologism to express it: 'mafficking'.

Mafeking was safe. The British had triumphed. All was right with the world.

Except, of course, it wasn't. The long public anxiety over Mafeking was a barely conscious understanding that Britain's pre-eminence was slipping. A glance at the turn-of-the-century economic statistics only confirmed this: Great Britain's share of world manufacturing output was 18.5 per cent. America's was 23 per cent.

Worse still, Germany was beginning to catch up at 13.2 per cent.

The death of Queen Victoria on 22 January 1901 at Osborne on the Isle of Wight confirmed the end of a glorious era.

Queen Victoria's Funeral Procession, Isle of Wight to London, 1–2 February 1901

THE COUNTESS OF DENBIGH

I think you will like to hear of my going down to Southampton to see the passing of our dear Queen from Osborne to Portsmouth.

I went on the *Scot*, where both Houses were embarked. We steamed out, and took up our position between the last British ship and the first foreign ships of war, on the south side of the double line down which the procession was to pass. The day was one of glorious sunshine, with the smoothest and bluest of seas. After a while a black torpedo destroyer came dashing down the line signalling that the *Alberta* was leaving Osborne and from every ship, both British and foreign, boomed out the minute guns for close on an hour before the procession reached us. The sun was now (3 p.m.) beginning to sink, and a wonderful golden pink appeared in the sky and as the smoke slowly rose from the guns it settled in one long festoon behind them, over Haslar, a purple festoon like the purple hangings ordered by the King.

Then slowly down the long line of battleships came eight Torpedo destroyers, dark gliding forms, and after them the white *Alberta* looking very small and frail next the towering battleships. We could see the motionless figures standing round the white pall which, with the crown and orb and sceptre, lay upon the coffin. Solemnly and slowly, it glided over the calm blue water, followed by the other three vessels, giving one a strange choke, and a catch in one's heart as memory flew back to her triumphal passage down her fleet in the last Jubilee review. As slowly and as silently as it came the cortège passed away into the haze: with the solemn booming of the guns continuing every minute till Portsmouth was reached. A wonderful scene and marvellously impressive, leaving behind it a memory of peace and beauty and sadness which it is impossible to forget.

Then on Saturday, Feb. 2nd, came the wonderful procession through London, which you will see fully described in the papers.

Molly, Dorothie, Lady Denbigh and I saw it from the Household Stand at Buckingham Palace, and had a very good view. The behaviour of the crowd was wonderful in its silence and reverence as the procession passed. And this was the same everywhere, the K. of P. [King of Portugal], told Denbigh that the crowd in Hyde Park was quite half a mile deep. The only thing which jarred was the harnessing of the celebrated creams, with their gold and crimson trappings to a gun carriage. The demeanour of our new King in his dignified sadness was very striking, and of course the coffin in its white pall and regalia, he and the Kaiser were the most observed. The slow solemn march of the naval men with their arms reversed, moved me much for I could not help comparing the then with the now as I thought of last year in Dublin when the naval contingent went past the Queen with heads erect and their wonderful brisk step.

Not a sound was heard from the crowd during the procession and a great hush fell upon it when the coffin came in sight.

When all was over we waited awhile for the crowd to move away and then tried unsuccessfully to get up Constitution Hill and St James, so went up Grosvenor Place only to find a line of cavalry across it near St George's Hospital, so made for Albert Gate via Belgrave Sq. only to meet such a dense crowd streaming out that we had to retreat up the steps of the French Embassy, where we waited for an hour, and then with difficulty made our way into the park, and so home.

Victoria had ruled for almost sixty-four years. She was succeeded by her eldest son, who reigned as Edward VII, but was 'Tum-tum' to his family and 'Good Old Teddy' to the racing fraternity. His reign, 1901–10, coincided with a distinct shift from 'laissez-faire' Liberalism to interventionist Liberalism. In particular, the Liberal governments of 1906–14 carried through a raft of social legislation – free school meals, old age pensions, labour exchanges, National Insurance – which laid the foundations of the later Welfare State. The motivation for the reforms was not entirely altruistic; it was intended, in part, to sate the new Labour Party (founded in 1900) and the increasingly militant trade unions (whose membership rose by two-thirds between 1910 and 1913). Industrial agitation was not the only unrest in late Edwardian England:

Force-feeding of a Suffragette, Walton Jail, Liverpool, 18 January 1910

LADY CONSTANCE LYTTON

Founded by Emmeline Pankhurst in 1903, the Women's Social and Political Union campaigned for the extension of the franchise to women. Its members were repeatedly imprisoned for attacks on property and refusal to pay taxes. Like a number of gaoled suffragettes, Constance Lytton went on hunger-strike to draw further attention to the cause.

I was visited again by the Senior Medical Officer, who asked me how long I had been without food. I said I had eaten a buttered scone and a banana sent in by friends to the police station on Friday at about midnight. He said, 'Oh, then, this is the fourth day; that is too long, I shall feed you, I must feed you at once,' but he went out and nothing happened till about six o'clock in the evening, when he returned with, I think, five wardresses and the feeding apparatus. He urged me to take food voluntarily. I told him that was absolutely out of the question, that when our legislators ceased to resist enfranchising women then I should cease to resist taking food in prison. He did not examine my heart nor feel my pulse; he did not ask to do so, nor did I say anything which could possibly induce him to think I would refuse to be examined. I offered no resistance to being placed in position, but lay down voluntarily on the plank bed. Two of the wardresses took hold of my arms, one held my head and one my feet. One wardress helped to pour the food. The doctor leant on my knees as he stooped over my chest to get at my mouth. I shut my mouth and clenched my teeth. I had looked forward to this moment with so much anxiety lest my identity should be discovered beforehand, that I felt positively glad when the time had come. The sense of being overpowered by more force than I could possibly resist was complete, but I resisted nothing except with my mouth. The doctor offered me the choice of a wooden or steel gag; he explained elaborately, as he did on most subsequent occasions, that the steel gag would hurt and the wooden one not, and he urged me not to force him to use the steel gag. But I did not speak nor open my mouth, so that after playing about for a moment or two with the wooden one he finally had recourse to the steel. He seemed annoyed at my resistance and he broke into a temper as he plied my teeth with the steel implement. He found that on either side at the back I had false teeth mounted on a bridge which did not take out. The superintending wardress asked if I had any false teeth, if so, that they must be taken out; I made no answer and the process went on. He dug his instrument down on to the sham tooth, it pressed fearfully on the gum. He said if I resisted so much with my teeth, he would have to feed me through the nose. The pain of it was intense and at last I must have given way for he got the gag between my teeth, when he proceeded to turn it much more than necessary until my jaws were fastened wide apart, far more than they could go naturally. Then he put down my throat a tube which seemed to me much too wide and was something like four feet in length. The irritation of the tube was excessive. I choked the moment it touched my throat until it had got down. Then the food was poured in quickly; it made me sick a few seconds after it was down and the action of the sickness made my body and legs double up, but the wardresses instantly pressed back my head and the doctor leant on my knees. The horror of it was more than I can describe.

The Arrest of Dr Crippen, 31 July 1910

CAPTAIN H. G. KENDALL

After murdering his wife with the exotic poison hyoscine, Crippen tried to flee to Canada aboard the liner Montrose. *Instead, Crippen and his paramour, Ethel Le Neve (dressed as a boy), became the first people to be caught by use of the wireless. Kendall was the captain of the* Montrose.

The *Montrose* was in port at Antwerp when I read in the *Continental Daily Mail* that a warrant had been issued for Crippen and LeNeve. They were reported to have been traced to a hotel in Brussels but had then vanished again.

Soon after we sailed for Quebec I happened to glance through the porthole of my cabin and behind a lifeboat I saw two men. One was squeezing the other's hand. I walked along the boat deck and got into conversation with the elder man. I noticed that there was a mark on the bridge of his nose through wearing spectacles, that he had recently shaved off a moustache, and that he was growing a beard. The young fellow was very reserved, and I remarked about his cough.

'Yes,' said the elder man, 'my boy has a weak chest, and I'm taking him to California for his health.'

I returned to my cabin and had another look at the *Daily Mail*. I studied the description and photographs issued by Scotland Yard. Crippen was fifty years of age, 5 ft 4 ins high, wearing spectacles and a moustache; Miss LeNeve was twenty-seven, 5 ft 5 ins, slim, with pale complexion. I then examined the passenger list and ascertained that the two passengers were travelling as 'Mr Robinson and son'. I arranged for them to take meals at my table.

When the bell went for lunch I tarried until the coast was clear, then slipped into the Robinsons' cabin unobserved, where I noticed two things: that the boy's felt hat was packed round the rim to make it fit, and that he had been using a piece of a woman's bodice as a face flannel. That satisfied me. I went down to the dining saloon and kept my eyes open. The boy's manners at table were ladylike. Later, when they were promenading the saloon deck, I went out and walked behind them, and called out, 'Mr Robinson!' I had to shout the name several times before the man turned and said to me, 'I'm sorry, Captain, I didn't hear you – this cold wind is making me deaf.'

In the next two days we developed our acquaintance. Mr Robinson was the acme of politeness, quiet-mannered, a non-smoker; at night he went on deck and roamed about on his own. Once the wind blew up his coat tails and in his hip pocket I saw a revolver. After that I also carried a revolver, and we often had pleasant little tea parties together in my cabin, discussing the book he was reading, which was *The Four Just Men*, a murder mystery by Edgar Wallace – and when that little fact was wirelessed to London and published it made Edgar Wallace's name ring, so agog was everybody in England over the Crippen case.

That brings me to the wireless. On the third day out I gave my wireless operator a message for Liverpool: *One hundred and thirty miles west of Lizard . . . have strong suspicions that Crippen London cellar murderer and accomplice are among saloon passengers . . . Accomplice dressed as boy; voice, manner, and build undoubtedly a girl.*

I remember Mr Robinson sitting in a deckchair, looking at the wireless aerials and listening to the crackling of our crude spark-transmitter, and remarking to me what a wonderful invention it was.

I sent several more reports, but our weak transmitting apparatus was soon out of communication with land. We could hear other ships at a great distance, however, and you may imagine my excitement when my operator brought me a message he had intercepted from a London newspaper to its representative aboard the White Star liner *Laurentic* which was also heading westward across the Atlantic: *What is Inspector*

Dew doing? Is he sending and receiving wireless messages? Is he playing games with passengers? Are passengers excited over chase? Rush reply.

This was the first I knew that my message to Liverpool had caused Inspector Dew to catch the first boat out – the *Laurentic*. With her superior speed, I knew she would reach the Newfoundland coast before me. I hoped that if she had any news for me the *Laurentic* would leave it at the Belle Island station to be transmitted to me as soon as I passed that point on my approach to Canada.

She had news indeed: *Will board you at Father Point . . . strictly confidential . . . from Inspector Dew, Scotland Yard, on board Laurentic.*

I replied: *Shall arrive Father Point about 6 a.m. tomorrow . . . should advise you to come off in small boat with pilot, disguised as pilot . . .*

This was confirmed. The last night was dreary and anxious, the sound of our fog-horn every few minutes adding to the monotony. The hours dragged on as I paced the bridge; now and then I could see Mr Robinson strolling about the deck. I had invited him to get up early to see the 'pilots' come aboard at Father Point in the River St Lawrence. When they did so they came straight to my cabin. I sent for Mr Robinson. When he entered I stood with the detective facing the door, holding my revolver inside my coat pocket. As he came in, I said, 'Let me introduce you.'

Mr Robinson put out his hand; the detective grabbed it, at the same time removing his pilot's cap, and said, 'Good morning, Dr Crippen. Do you know me? I'm Inspector Dew, from Scotland Yard.'

Crippen quivered. Surprise struck him dumb. Then he said, 'Thank God it's over. The suspense has been too great. I couldn't stand it any longer.'

Crippen was later hanged at Pentonville prison. Le Neve, charged as an accessory to murder, was acquitted.

Antarctic Expedition: Scott's Last Diary Entries, January 1912

CAPTAIN R. F. SCOTT RN

Robert Falcon Scott and four companions reached the South Pole on 18 January 1912, only to find that the Norwegian Roald Amundsen had beaten them to it by a month. The bodies of Scott and his men were found on 12 November 1912. It is generally assumed that Scott mistakenly wrote 'March' for 'January' in the diary entries below.

Friday, 16 March or Saturday 17. Lost track of dates, but think the last correct. Tragedy all along the line. At lunch, the day before yesterday, poor Titus Oates said he couldn't go on; he proposed we should leave him in his sleeping-bag. That we could not do, and induced him to come on, on the afternoon march. In spite of its awful nature for him he struggled on and we made a few miles. At night he was worse and we knew the end had come.

Should this be found I want these facts recorded. Oates' last thoughts were of his mother, but immediately before he took pride in thinking that his regiment would be pleased with the bold way in which he met his death. We can testify to his bravery. He has borne intense suffering for weeks without complaint, and to the very last was able and willing to discuss outside subjects. He did not – would not – give up hope to the very end. He was a brave soul. This was the end. He slept through the night before last, hoping not to wake; but he woke in the morning – yesterday. It was blowing a blizzard. He said, 'I am just going outside and may be some time.' He went out into the blizzard and we have not seen him since.

I take this opportunity of saying that we have stuck to our sick companions to the last. In case of Edgar Evans, when absolutely out of food and he lay insensible, the safety of the remainder seemed to demand his abandonment, but Providence mercifully removed him at this critical moment. He died a natural death, and we did not leave him till two hours after his death. We knew that poor Oates was walking to his death, but though we tried to dissuade him, we knew it was the act of a brave man and an English gentleman. We all hope to meet the end with a similar spirit, and assuredly the end is not far.

I can only write at lunch and then only occasionally. The cold is intense, −40° at midday. My companions are unendingly cheerful, but we are all on the verge of serious frostbites, and though we constantly talk of fetching through I don't think any one of us believes it in his heart.

We are cold on the march now, and at all times except meals. Yesterday we had to lay up for a blizzard and today we move dreadfully slowly. We are at No. 14 pony camp, only two pony marches from One Ton Depot. We leave here our theodolite, a camera, and Oates' sleeping-bags. Diaries, etc., and geological specimens carried at Wilson's special request, will be found with us or on our sledge.

Sunday, 18 March. Today, lunch, we are 21 miles from the depot. Ill fortune presses, but better may come. We have had more wind and drift from ahead yesterday; had to stop marching; wind NW, force 4, temp. −35°. No human being could face it, and we are worn out *nearly*.

My right foot has gone, nearly all the toes − two days ago I was proud possessor of best feet. These are the steps of my downfall. Like an ass I mixed a small spoonful of curry powder with my melted pemmican − it gave me violent indigestion. I lay awake and in pain all night; woke and felt done on the march; foot went and I didn't know it. A very small measure of neglect and have a foot which is not pleasant to contemplate. Bowers takes first place in condition, but there is not much to choose after all. The others are still confident of getting through − or pretend to be − I don't know! We have the last *half* fill of oil in our primus and a very small quantity of spirit − this alone between us and thirst. The wind is fair for the moment, and that is perhaps a fact to help. The mileage would have seemed ridiculously small on our outward journey.

Monday, 19 March. Lunch. We camped with difficulty last night and were dreadfully cold till after our supper of cold pemmican and biscuit and a half a pannikin of cocoa cooked over the spirit. Then, contrary to expectation, we got warm and all slept well. Today we started in the usual dragging manner. Sledge dreadfully heavy. We are 15½ miles from the depot and ought to get there in three days. What progress! We have two days' food but barely a day's fuel. All our feet are getting bad − Wilson's best, my right foot worst, left all right. There is no chance to nurse one's feet till we can get hot food into us. Amputation is the least I can hope for now, but will the trouble spread? That is the serious question. The weather doesn't give us a chance − the wind from N to NW and −40° temp. today.

Wednesday, 21 March. Got within 11 miles of depot Monday night; had to lay up all yesterday in severe blizzard. Today forlorn hope, Wilson and Bowers going to depot for fuel.

Thursday, 22 and 23 March. Blizzard bad as ever – Wilson and Bowers unable to start – tomorrow last chance – no fuel and only one or two of food left – must be near the end. Have decided it shall be natural – we shall march for the depot with or without our effects and die in our tracks.

Thursday, 29 March. Since the 21st we have had a continuous gale from WSW and SW. We had fuel to make two cups of tea apiece and bare food for two days on the 20th. Every day we have been ready to start for our depot *11 miles* away, but outside the door of the tent it remains a scene of whirling drift. I do not think we can hope for any better things now. We shall stick it out to the end, but we are getting weaker, of course, and the end cannot be far.

It seems a pity, but I do not think I can write more.

R. SCOTT

For God's sake look after our people.

The Titanic *Sinks, 15 April 1912*

HAROLD BRIDE

Bride was one of the Titanic*'s wireless operators. Hailed as 'unsinkable', the* Titanic *had room for only 1,178 people in its lifeboats; the passengers and crew on its maiden voyage numbered 2,224. A total of 1,513 lives were lost when the ship struck an iceberg in mid-Atlantic.*

From aft came the tunes of the band. It was a ragtime tune. I don't know what. Then there was 'Autumn' . . . I went to the place I had seen the collapsible boat on the boat deck, and to my surprise I saw the boat, and the men still trying to push it off. I guess there wasn't a sailor in the crowd. They couldn't do it. I went up to them and was just lending a hand when a large wave came awash of the deck. The big wave carried the boat off. I had hold of an oarlock and I went with it. The next I knew I was in the boat. But that was not all. I was in the boat, and the boat was upside-down, and I was under it. And I remember realizing I was wet through and that whatever happened I must not breathe, for I was under water. I knew I had to fight for it, and I did. How I got out from under the boat I do not know but I felt a breath of air at last. There were men all around me – hundreds of them. The sea was dotted with them, all depending on their lifebelts. I felt I simply had to get away from the ship. She was a beautiful sight then. Smoke and sparks were rushing out of her funnel. There must have been an explosion, but we heard none. We only saw the big stream of sparks. The ship was turning gradually on her nose – just like a duck that goes for a dive. I had only one thing on my mind – to get away from the suction. The band was still playing. I guess all of them went down. They were playing 'Autumn' then. I swam with all my might. I suppose I was 150 feet away when the *Titanic*, on her nose, with her after-quarter sticking straight up in the air, began to settle – slowly.

When at last the waves washed over her rudder there wasn't the least bit of suction I could feel. She must have kept going just so slowly as she had been . . . I felt after a little while like sinking. I was very cold. I saw a boat of some kind near me, and put all my strength into an effort to swim to it. It was hard work. I was all done when a hand reached out from the boat and pulled me aboard. It was our same collapsible. The same crowd was on it. There was just room for me to roll on the edge. I lay there not caring what happened. Somebody sat on my legs. They were wedged in between slats and were being wrenched. I had not the heart left to ask the man to move. It was a terrible sight all around – men swimming and sinking.

I lay where I was, letting the man wrench my feet out of shape. Others came near. Nobody gave them a hand. The bottom-up boat already had more men than it would hold, and it was sinking. At first the larger waves splashed over my clothing. Then they began to splash over my head, and I had to breathe when I could. As we floated around on our capsized boat and I kept straining my eyes for a ship's lights, somebody said, 'Don't the rest of you think we ought to pray?' The man who made the suggestion asked what the religion of the others was. Each man called out his religion. One was a Catholic, one a Methodist, one a Presbyterian. It was decided the most appropriate prayer for all was the Lord's Prayer. We spoke it over in chorus with the man who first suggested that we pray as the leader. Some splendid people saved us. They had a right-side-up boat and it was full to capacity. Yet they came to us and loaded us all into it.

The Drift to World War: The View from 10 Downing Street, 1–2 August 1914

HERBERT ASQUITH, PRIME MINISTER

August 1

When most of them [the Cabinet] had left, Sir W. Tyrrell arrived with a long message from Berlin to the effect that the German Ambassador's efforts for peace had been suddenly arrested and frustrated by the Tsar's decree for a complete Russian mobilization. We all set to work, Tyrrell, Bongie, Drummond and myself, to draft a direct personal appeal from the King to the Tsar. When we had settled it I called a taxi, and, in company with Tyrrell, drove to Buckingham Palace at about 1.30 a.m. The King was hauled out of bed, and one of my strangest experiences was sitting with him, clad in a dressing gown, while I read the message and the proposed answer.

There was really no fresh news this morning. Lloyd George, all for peace, is more sensible and statesmanlike for keeping the position still open. Grey declares that if an out-and-out and uncompromising policy of non-intervention at all costs is adopted, he will go. Winston [Churchill] very bellicose and demanding immediate mobilization. The main controversy pivots upon Belgium and its neutrality. We parted in fairly amicable mood, and are to sit again at 11 to-morrow, Sunday. I am still not quite hopeless about peace, though far from hopeful, but if it comes to war, I feel sure we shall have a split in the Cabinet. Of course if Grey went I should go and the whole thing would break up. On the other hand, we may have to contemplate, with such equanimity as we can command, the loss of Morley and possibly, though I do not think it, of Simon.

August 2

Things are pretty black. Germany is now in active war with both Russia and France, and the Germans have violated the neutrality of Luxembourg. We are waiting to know whether they are going to do the same with Belgium. I had a visit at breakfast from Lichnowsky, who was very *emotionné* and implored me not to side with France. He said that Germany, with her army cut in two between France and Russia, was far more likely to be crushed than France. He was very agitated, poor man, and wept. I told him that we had no desire to intervene, and that it rested largely with Germany to make intervention impossible if she would (1) not invade Belgium, and (2) not send her fleet into the Channel to attack the unprotected north coast of France. He was bitter about the policy of his Government in not restraining Austria and seemed quite heart-broken.

Then we had a long Cabinet from 11 till nearly two, which very soon revealed that we are on the brink of a split. We agreed at last with some difficulty that Grey should be authorized to tell Cambon that our fleet would not allow the German fleet to make the Channel a base of hostile operations. John Burns at once resigned, but was persuaded to hold on at any rate till the evening when we meet again. There is a strong party against any kind of intervention in any event. Grey, of course, will never consent to this, and I shall not separate myself from him. Crewe, McKenna and Samuel are a moderating intermediate body. Bonar Law writes that the Opposition will back us up in any measure we may take for the support of France and Russia. I suppose a good number of our own party in the House of Commons are for absolute non-interference. It will be a shocking thing if at such a moment we break up.

Happily I am quite clear in my mind as to what is right and wrong. (1) We have no obligation of any kind either to France or Russia to give them military or naval help. (2) The dispatch of the Expeditionary Force to help France at this moment is out of the question and would serve no object. (3) We must not forget the ties created by our long-standing and intimate friendship with France. (4) It is against British interests that France should be wiped out as a Great Power. (5) We cannot allow Germany to use the Channel as a hostile base. (6) We have obligations to Belgium to prevent it being utilized and absorbed by Germany . . .

With the German invasion of neutral Belgium on 4 August all hope of British non-intervention in the First World War was wiped away. King George V recorded: 'I held a Council at 10.45 to declare war with Germany, it is a terrible catastrophe, but it is not our fault . . . Please God it may soon be over & that he will protect dear Bertie's life'.

All over Europe, young men, flushed with excitement and patriotism, volunteered for service. Few Englishmen had any idea of what war meant: the English had not fought a major war for a century. Professional soldiers were more sanguine: Their favourite song was:

Send out the Army and the Navy,

> Send out the rank and file.
> (Have a banana!)
> Send out the brave Territorials,
> They'll face the danger with a smile.
> (I don't think!)
> Send out the boys of the girls' brigade,
> They will keep old England free;
> Send out my mother, my sister and my brother,
> But for Gawd's sake don't send me!'

Within three months of the declaration of hostilities, the First World War in the West had settled down to a muddy line of trench-fighting that stretched from the English Channel to Switzerland.

It had been an almost universal expectation that the war would be 'over by Christmas'. Instead, the troops just wished it was – and organized an impromptu Yuletide peace.

Christmas in the Trenches, 25 December 1914

CAPTAIN SIR EDWARD HAMILTON WESTROW HULSE

At 8.30 a.m. I was looking out, and saw four Germans leave their trenches and come towards us; I told two of my men to go and meet them, *unarmed* (as the Germans were unarmed), and to see that they did not pass the half-way line. We were 350–400 yards apart at this point. My fellows were not very keen, not knowing what was up, so I went out alone, and met Barry, one of our ensigns, also coming out from another part of the line. By the time we got to them, they were three quarters of the way over, and much too near our barbed wire, so I moved them back. They were three private soldiers and a stretcher-bearer, and their spokesman started off by saying that he thought it only right to come over and wish us a happy Christmas, and trusted us implicitly to keep the truce. He came from Suffolk, where he had left his best girl and a 3½ h.p. motor-bike! He told me that he could not get a letter to the girl, and wanted to send one through me. I made him write out a post card in front of me, in English, and I sent it off that night. I told him that she probably would not be a bit keen to see him again. We then entered on a long discussion on every sort of thing. I was dressed in an old stocking-cap and a man's overcoat, and they took me for a corporal, a thing which I did not discourage, as I had an eye to going as near their lines as possible. I asked them what orders they had from their officers as to coming over to us, and they said *none*; they had just come over out of goodwill . . .

I kept it up for half an hour, and then escorted them back as far as their barbed wire, having a jolly good look round all the time, and picking up various little bits of information which I had not had an opportunity of doing under fire! I left instructions with them that if any of them came out later they must not come over the half-way line, and appointed a ditch as the meeting place. We parted after an exchange of Albany cigarettes and German cigars, and I went straight to H.-qrs. to report.

On my return at 10 a.m. I was surprised to hear a hell of a din going on, and not a single man left in my trenches; they were completely denuded (against my orders), and nothing lived! I heard strains of 'Tipperary' floating down the breeze, swiftly followed by a tremendous burst of 'Deutschland über Alles', and as I got to my own Coy. H.-qrs. dug-out, I saw, to my amazement, not only a crowd of about 150 British and Germans at the half-way house which I had appointed opposite my lines, but six or seven such crowds, all the way down our lines, extending towards the 8th Division on our right. I bustled out and asked if there were any German officers in my crowd, and the noise died down (as this time I was myself in my own cap and badges of rank).

I found two, but had to talk to them through an interpreter, as they could neither talk English nor French . . . I explained to them that strict orders must be maintained as to meeting half-way, and everyone unarmed; and we both agreed not to fire until the other did, thereby creating a complete deadlock and armistice (if strictly observed) . . .

Meanwhile Scots and Huns were fraternizing in the most genuine possible manner. Every sort of souvenir was exchanged, addresses given and received, photos of families shown, etc. One of our fellows offered a German a cigarette; the German said, 'Virginian?' Our fellow said, 'Aye, straight-cut': the German said, 'No thanks, I only smoke Turkish!' (Sort of 10/- a 100 me!) It gave us all a good laugh.

A German N.C.O. with the Iron Cross – gained, he told me, for conspicuous skill in sniping – started his fellows off on some marching tune. When they had done I set the note for 'The Boys of Bonnie

Scotland, where the heather and the bluebells grow', and so we went on, singing everything from 'Good King Wenceslaus' down to the ordinary Tommies' song, and ended up with 'Auld Lang Syne', which we all, English, Scots, Irish, Prussians, Wurtembergers, etc., joined in. It was absolutely astounding, and if I had seen it on a cinematograph film I should have sworn that it was faked! . . .

Just after we had finished 'Auld Lang Syne' an old hare started up, and seeing so many of us about in an unwonted spot – did not know which way to go. I gave one loud 'View Holloa', and one and all, British and Germans, rushed about giving chase, slipping up on the frozen plough, falling about, and after a hot two minutes we killed in the open, a German and one of our fellows falling together heavily upon the completely baffled hare. Shortly afterwards we saw four more hares, and killed one again; both were good heavy weight and had evidently been out between the two rows of trenches for the last two months, well-fed on the cabbage patches, etc., many of which are untouched on the 'no-man's land'. The enemy kept one and we kept the other. It was now 11.30 a.m. and at this moment George Paynter arrived on the scene with a hearty 'Well, my lads, a Merry Christmas to you! This is d—d comic, isn't it?' . . . George told them that he thought it was only right that we should show that we could desist from hostilities on a day which was so important in both countries; and he then said, 'Well, my boys, I've brought you over something to celebrate this funny show with', and he produced from his pocket a large bottle of rum (not ration rum, but the proper stuff). One large shout went up, and the nasty little spokesman uncorked it, and in a heavy ceremonious manner, drank our healths, in the name of his 'cameraden'; the bottle was then passed on and polished off before you could say knife . . .

During the afternoon the same extraordinary scene was enacted between the lines, and one of the enemy told me that he was longing to get back to London: I assured him that 'So was I'. He said that he was sick of the war, and I told him that when the truce was ended, any of his friends would be welcome in our trenches, and would be well-received, fed, and given a free passage to the Isle of Man! Another coursing meeting took place, with no result, and at 4.30 p.m. we agreed to keep in our respective trenches, and told them that the truce was ended.

The respective high commands curtailed future Christmas fraternizations.
1915 would be a year of stalemate on the Western Front, the numerical

superiority of the Allied (British and French) Army offset by the fact that the Germans held the high ground along the front. In this year alone, the British took 300,000 casualties for mere yards of German-held mud. There were various stratagems to break the deadlock, the most inventive being that of Winston Churchill at the Admiralty, which was to land Allied troops at the entrance to the Dardanelles and open a front against Germany's ally, Turkey. Inept execution turned the subsequent Gallipoli campaign, begun in April 1915, into one of the Great War's greatest disasters. For months Allied troops were unable to break out of a narrow bridgehead on the rocky, sun-beaten peninsula.

An Infantryman at Gallipoli, June 1915

LEONARD THOMPSON

Thompson was a former farmhand.

We arrived at the Dardanelles and saw the guns flashing and heard the rifle fire. They heaved our ship, the *River Clyde*, right up to the shore. They had cut a hole in it and made a little pier, so we were able to walk straight off and on to the beach. We all sat there – on the Hellespont! – waiting for it to get light. The first things we saw were big wrecked Turkish guns, the second a big marquee. It didn't make me think of the military but of the village fêtes. Other people must have thought like this because I remember how we all rushed up to it, like boys getting into a circus, and then found it all laced up. We unlaced it and rushed in. It was full of corpses. Dead Englishmen, lines and lines of them, and with their eyes wide open. We all stopped talking. I'd never seen a dead man before and here I was looking at two or three hundred of them. It was our first fear. Nobody had mentioned this. I was very shocked. I thought of Suffolk and it seemed a happy place for the first time.

Later that day we marched through open country and came to within a mile and half of the front line. It was incredible. We were there – at the war! The place we had reached was called 'dead ground' because it was where the enemy couldn't see you. We lay in little square holes, myself next to James Sears from the village. He was about thirty and married. That evening we wandered about on the dead ground and asked about friends of ours who had arrived a month or so ago. 'How is Ernie Taylor?' – 'Ernie? – he's gone.' 'Have you seen Albert Paternoster?' – 'Albert? – he's gone.' We learned that if 300 had 'gone' but 700 were left, then this wasn't too bad. We then knew how unimportant our names were.

I was on sentry that night. A chap named Scott told me that I must only put my head up for a second but that in this time I must see as much as I could. Every third man along the trench was a sentry. The next night we had to move on to the third line of trenches and we heard that the Gurkhas were going over and that we had to support their rear. But when we got to the communication trench we found it so full of dead men that we could hardly move. Their faces were quite black and you couldn't tell Turk from English. There was the most terrible stink and for a while there was nothing but the living being sick on to the dead. I did sentry again that night. It was one – two – sentry, one – two – sentry all along the trench, as before. I knew the next sentry up quite well. I remembered him in Suffolk singing to his horses as he ploughed. Now he fell back with a great scream and a look of surprise – dead. It is quick, anyway, I thought. On June 4th we went over the top. We took the Turks' trench and held it. It was called Hill 13. The next day we were relieved and told to rest for three hours, but it wasn't more than half an hour before the relieving regiment came running back. The Turks had returned and recaptured their trench. On June 6th my favourite officer was killed and no end of us butchered, but we managed to get hold of Hill 13 again. We found a great muddle, carnage and men without rifles shouting '*Allah! Allah!*', which is God's name in the Turkish language. Of the sixty men I had started out to war from Harwich with, there were only three left.

We set to work to bury people. We pushed them into the sides of the trench but bits of them kept getting uncovered and sticking out, like people in a badly made bed. Hands were the worst; they would escape from the sand, pointing, begging – even waving! There was one which we all shook when we passed, saying, 'Good morning', in a posh voice. Everybody did it. The bottom of the trench was springy like a mattress because of all the bodies underneath. At night, when the stench was worse, we tied crêpe round our mouths and noses. This crêpe had been given to us because it was supposed to prevent us being gassed. The flies entered the trenches at night and lined them completely with a density which was like moving cloth. We killed millions by slapping our spades along the trench walls but the next night it would be just as bad. We were all lousy and we couldn't stop shitting because we had caught dysentery. We wept, not because we were frightened but because we were so dirty.

Eventually, in December 1915, the Allied survivors were evacuated from Gallipoli. Behind them they left the bodies of 46,000 compatriots. With the failure of the Gallipoli expedition, the focus of the war swung back to the Western Front, where trench raids, saturation bombing and 'Big Pushes' became an idée fixe.

Night Raid, Western Front, 25 May 1916

SIEGFRIED SASSOON

Sassoon won a Military Cross in the action described below.

Twenty-seven men with faces blackened and shiny – Christy-minstrels – with hatchets in their belts, bombs in pockets, knobkerries – waiting in a dug-out in the reserve line. At 10.30 they trudge up to Battalion H.Q. splashing through mire and water in the chalk trench, while the rain comes steadily down. The party is twenty-two men, five N.C.O.s and one officer (Stansfield). From H.Q. we start off again, led by Compton-Smith: across the open to the end of 77 street. A red flashlight winks a few times to guide us thither. Then up to the front line – the men's feet making a most unholy tramp and din; squeeze along to the starting-point, where Stansfield and his two confederates (Sergeant Lyle and Corporal O'Brien) loom over the parapet from above, having successfully laid the line of lime across the craters to the Bosche wire. In a few minutes the five parties have gone over – and disappear into the rain and darkness – the last four men carry ten-foot light ladders. It is 12 midnight. I am sitting on the parapet listening for something to happen – five, ten, nearly fifteen minutes – not a sound – nor a shot fired – and only the usual flare-lights, none very near our party. Then a few whizz-bangs fizz over to our front trench and just behind the raiders. After twenty minutes there is still absolute silence in the Bosche trench; the raid is obviously held up by their wire, which we thought was so easy to get through. One of the bayonet-men comes crawling back; I follow him to our trench and he tells me that they can't get through: O'Brien says it's a failure; they're all going to throw a bomb and retire.

A minute or two later a rifle-shot rings out and almost simultaneously several bombs are thrown by both sides: a bomb explodes right in the water at the bottom of left crater close to our men, and showers a pale spume of water; there are blinding flashes and explosions, rifle-shots, the scurry of feet, curses and groans, and stumbling figures loom up from below and scramble awkwardly over the parapet – some wounded – black faces and whites of eyes and lips show in the dusk; when I've counted sixteen in, I go forward to see how things are going, and find Stansfield wounded, and leave him there with two men who soon get him in: other wounded men crawl in; I find one hit in the leg; he says O'Brien is somewhere down the crater badly wounded. They are still throwing bombs and firing at us: the sinister sound of clicking bolts seems to be very near; perhaps they have crawled out of their trench and are firing from behind their advanced wire. Bullets hit the water in the craters, and little showers of earth patter down on the crater. Five or six of them are firing into the crater at a few yards' range. The bloody sods are firing down at me at point-blank range. (I really wondered whether my number was up.) From our trenches and in front of them I can hear the mumble of voices – most of them must be in by now. After minutes like hours, with great difficulty I get round the bottom of the crater and back toward our trench; at last I find O'Brien down a very deep (about twenty-five feet) and precipitous crater on my left (our right as they went out). He is moaning and his right arm is either broken or almost shot off: he's also hit in the right leg (body and head also, but I couldn't see that then). Another man (72 Thomas) is with him; he is hit in the right arm. I leave them there and get back to our trench for help, shortly afterwards Lance-Corporal Stubbs is brought in (he has had his foot blown off). Two or three other wounded men are being helped down the trench; no one seems to know what to do; those that are there are very excited and uncertain: no sign of any officers – then Compton-Smith comes along (a mine went up on the left as we were coming up at about 11.30 and thirty (R.E.s) men were gassed or buried). I get a rope and two more men and we go back to O'Brien, who is unconscious now. With great difficulty we get him half-way up the face of the crater; it is now after one o'clock and the sky beginning to get lighter. I make one more journey to our trench for another strong man and to see to a stretcher being ready. We get him in, and it is found that he has died, as I had feared. Corporal Mick O'Brien (who often went patrolling with me) was a very fine man and had been with the Battalion since November 1914. He was at Neuve Chapelle, Festubert and Loos.

I go back to a support-line dug-out and find the unwounded men of the raiding-party refreshing themselves: everyone is accounted for now; eleven wounded (one died of wounds) and one killed, out of twenty-eight. I see Stansfield, who is going on all right, but has several bomb-wounds. On the way down I see the Colonel, sitting on his bed in a woollen cap with a tuft on top, and very much upset at the non-success of the show, and the mine disaster; but very pleased with the way our men tried to get through the wire.

A week after Sassoon's night raid, the British and German fleets engaged together at Jutland, the major naval battle of the war. The British claimed victory because they remained in control of the North Sea; the Germans claimed victory because they sank more ships (fourteen to eleven). As not a few British sailors noticed, their ships and weaponry at Jutland were shoddy and obsolete compared to those of the enemy. Admiral Jellicoe himself was moved to comment, 'There seems to be something wrong with our damn ships today.'

England's fall from industrial grace needed no other proof.

Home Front: Death of a Brother, 15 June 1916

VERA BRITTAIN

Brittain's fiancé, Roland Leighton, had already been killed in action.

I had just announced to my father, as we sat over tea in the dining room, that I really must do up Edward's papers and take them to the post office before it closed for the weekend, when there came the sudden loud clattering at the front-door knocker that always meant a telegram.

For a moment I thought that my legs would not carry me, but they behaved quite normally as I got up and went to the door. I knew what was in the telegram – I had known for a week – but because the persistent hopefulness of the human heart refuses to allow intuitive certainty to persuade the reason of that which it knows, I opened and read it in a tearing anguish of suspense.

'Regret to inform you Captain E. H. Brittain M.C. killed in action Italy June 15th.'

'No answer,' I told the boy mechanically, and handed the telegram to my father, who had followed me into the hall. As we went back into the dining room I saw, as though I had never seen them before, the bowl of blue delphiniums on the table; their intense colour, vivid, ethereal, seemed too radiant for earthly flowers.

Then I remembered that we should have to go down to Purley and tell the news to my mother.

Late that evening, my uncle brought us all back to an empty flat. Edward's death and our sudden departure had offered the maid – at that time the amateur prostitute – an agreeable opportunity for a few hours' freedom of which she had taken immediate advantage. She had not even finished the household handkerchiefs, which I had washed that morning and intended to iron after tea; when I went into the kitchen I found them still hanging, stiff as boards, over the clothes-horse near the fire where I had left them to dry.

Long after the family had gone to bed and the world had grown silent, I crept into the dining room to be alone with Edward's portrait. Carefully closing the door, I turned on the light and looked at the pale, pictured face, so dignified, so steadfast, so tragically mature. He had been through so much – far, far more than those beloved friends who had died at an earlier stage of the interminable War, leaving him alone to mourn their loss. Fate might have allowed him the little, sorry compensation of survival, the chance to make his lovely music in honour of their memory. It seemed indeed the last irony that he should have been killed by the countrymen of Fritz Kreisler, the violinist whom of all others he had most greatly admired.

And suddenly, as I remembered all the dear afternoons and evenings when I had followed him on the piano as he played his violin, the sad, searching eyes of the portrait were more than I could bear, and falling on my knees before it I began to cry, 'Edward! Oh, Edward!' in dazed repetition, as though my persistent crying and calling would somehow bring him back.

Wounded, The Somme, 15 September 1916

BERT STEWARD

After a week's heavy shelling British troops went 'over the top' on the morning of 1 July 1916 along a fifteen-mile sector of the Western Front. They expected no opposition; instead they met a hurricane of German bullets, and 60,000 British casualties were sustained in just twenty-four hours. Their deaths secured 100,000 yards of ground. The Battle of the Somme raged until mid-November, by which time the conflagration had claimed 420,000 British killed and wounded. Bert Steward, at High Wood, was one of them.

Zero hour, and my corporal made a little gesture at me, and we got out of the ditch and started to walk. I never saw him again.

Imagine us then rather like overladen porters going slow over a shockingly ploughed field in a man-made thunder storm. Hailstones of a lethal kind zipped past our heads. From behind us the bombardment from our own guns, which I had seen massed wheel to wheel, went on. To left and right men were moving forward in uneven lines. My plan was to walk alone and not get bunched up with others. I kept away from them. I soon found this easier. On each side some had disappeared. I saw only one tank – in a ditch with a broken track, like a dying hippopotamus, with shells bursting round it. I kept walking. I walked about half a mile. I reached the shelter of an embankment. With this solid mass between me and the enemy I felt safe.

The next moment was the luckiest of my life. I had walked all the way through a hail of bullets. I had been a slowly-moving target for the machine guns. The bullets had all missed, though narrowly, for parts of my tunic were in ribbons. Then, just as I had reached safety, as I thought, what seemed like a hammer blow hit me on the top of my left shoulder. I opened my tunic. There was a clean round hole right through the shoulder. A bullet! But where from? Then I realised I was getting enfiladed by some machine-gunner to my right, on my side of the embankment. I threw myself down, but not before another bullet struck my right thigh.

In the embankment was the entrance to a dugout. I crawled into it. It was occupied by Germans. None of them spoke. They were all dead.

There was parcels from home strewn about, cigarettes, black bread, eatables, and one huge German, lying face downwards, made a good couch to sit on. Now I was joined by two friends, one less lucky, a young lad from Liverpool, with a bullet through the stomach.

Here we were, in front of our front line. About a hundred yards back I could see tin hats bobbing about. The remnants of the cast-irons were manning an improvised front line among the shellholes. Beyond them. I thought, was England, home and beauty.

I had taken High Wood, almost by myself, it seemed. I had no further territorial ambitions. Indeed, what I now had in mind was to go as quickly as possible in the opposite direction, as soon as possible. Leaving the dugout, I ran for it, zigzagging to escape bullets (two were enough) and so fast that I toppled head-first on top of a rifleman who was almost as scared as I was. After he had recovered he told me how I could work my way along the line of shellholes to a dressing station. I went, keeping my head down; I was taking no chances. I had two bullet holes. If they had been drilled by a surgeon they could not have been located more conveniently. I was incredibly lucky. But another might spoil everything. I crawled along.

The dressing station was a captured German underground hospital, with entrance big enough for an ambulance, built like a fortress, furnished with tiers of wooden bunks. It was crowded with wounded, now being sorted out by our adjutant.

'Those who can run follow me, nobody with a leg wound,' he said. 'We have to move fast,' I was the first to follow. In and out of shellholes we went – a rough but rapid journey in the right direction – until we reached a sunken lane where a horse-drawn hooded cart waited to take a dozen of us an hour's trot nearer home . . .

The Canadian doctor looked like any other in his white coat. He turned out to be a saint. 'You've been very lucky,' he said in a kindly way. Then he explained that one bullet, almost incredibly, had found a narrow gap between collar-bone and shoulder-blade, and that neither of the two had touched muscle or bone. 'How old are you and how long have you been in the trenches?' he asked and, when I told him, he wrote on a card and gave it to the nurse.

Later I looked up at the card pinned to the chart above my bed. It was marked with a big B. What did it mean? A nurse hurrying by answered my question. She smiled as she said – 'It means Blighty.'

T. E. Lawrence Blows up a Train on the Hejaz Railway, Arabia, 1917

LIEUTENANT–COLONEL T. E. LAWRENCE

Lawrence of Arabia was a British intelligence officer attached to the irregular Arab arm of the Grand Sharif of Mecca, Hussein. Not the least part of Lawrence's guerrilla war was spent disrupting the Hejaz railway, the Turks' main supply line in the desert.

Zaal and I rushed uphill and saw by its shape and volume that indeed there must be a train waiting in that station. As we were trying to see it over the hill, suddenly it moved out in our direction. We yelled to the Arabs to get into position as quick as possible, and there came a wild scramble over sand and rock. Stokes and Lewis, being booted, could not win the race; but they came well up, their pains and dysentery forgotten.

The men with rifles posted themselves in a long line behind the spur running from the guns past the exploder to the mouth of the valley. From it they would fire directly into the derailed carriages at less than one hundred and fifty yards, whereas the ranges for the Stokes and Lewis guns were about three hundred yards. An Arab stood up on high behind the guns and shouted to us what the train was doing – a necessary precaution, for if it carried troops and detrained them behind our ridge we should have to face about like a flash and retire fighting up the valley for our lives. Fortunately it held on at all the speed the two locomotives could make on wood fuel.

It drew near where we had been reported, and opened random fire into the desert. I could hear the racket coming, as I sat on my hillock by the bridge to give the signal to Salem, who danced round the exploder on his knees, crying with excitement, and calling urgently on God to make him fruitful. The Turkish fire sounded heavy, and I wondered with how many men we were going to have affair, and if the mine would be advantage enough for our eighty fellows to equal them. It would have been better if the first electrical experiment had been simpler.

However, at that moment the engines, looking very big, rocked with screaming whistles into view around the bend. Behind them followed ten box-waggons, crowded with rifle-muzzles at the windows and doors; and in little sand-bag nests on the roofs Turks precariously held on, to shoot at us. I had not thought of two engines, and on the moment decided to fire the charge under the second, so that however little the mine's effect, the uninjured engine should not be able to uncouple and drag the carriages away.

Accordingly, when the front 'driver' of the second engine was on the bridge, I raised my hand to Salem. There followed a terrific roar, and the line vanished from sight behind a spouting column of black dust and smoke a hundred feet high and wide. Out of the darkness came shattering crashes and long, loud metallic clangings of ripped steel, with many lumps of iron and plate; while one entire wheel of a locomotive whirled up suddenly black out of the cloud against the sky, and sailed musically over our heads to fall slowly and heavily into the desert behind. Except for the flight of these, there succeeded a deathly silence, with no cry of men or rifle-shot, as the now grey mist of the explosion drifted from the line towards us, and over our ridge until it was lost in the hills.

In the lull, I ran southward to join the sergeants. Salem picked up his rifle and charged out into the murk. Before I had climbed to the guns the hollow was alive with shots, and with the brown figures of the Beduin leaping forward to grips with the enemy. I looked round to see what was happening so quickly, and saw the train stationary and dismembered along the track, with its waggon sides jumping under the bullets which riddled them, while Turks were falling out from the far doors to gain the shelter of the railway embankment.

As I watched, our machine-guns chattered out over my head, and the long rows of Turks on the carriage roofs rolled over, and were swept off the top like bales of cotton before the furious shower of bullets which stormed along the roofs and splashed clouds of yellow chips from the planking. The dominant position of the guns had been an advantage to us so far.

When I reached Stokes and Lewis the engagement had taken another turn. The remaining Turks had got behind the bank, here about eleven feet high, and from cover of the wheels were firing point-blank at the Beduin twenty yards away across the sand-filled dip. The enemy in the crescent of the curving line were secure from the machine-guns; but Stokes slipped in his first shell, and after a few seconds there came a crash as it burst beyond the train in the desert.

He touched the elevating screw, and his second shot fell just by the trucks in the deep hollow below the bridge where the Turks were taking refuge. It made a shambles of the place. The survivors of the group broke out in a panic across the desert, throwing away their rifles and equipment as they ran. This was the opportunity of the Lewis gunners. The sergeant grimly traversed with drum after drum, till the open sand was littered with bodies. Mushagraf, the Sherari boy behind the second gun, saw the battle over, threw aside his weapon with a yell, and dashed down at speed with his rifle to join the others who were beginning, like wild beasts, to tear open the carriages and fall to plunder. It had taken nearly ten minutes.

I looked up-line through my glasses and saw the Mudowwara patrol breaking back uncertainly towards the railway to meet the train-fugitives running their fastest northward. I looked south, to see our thirty men cantering their camels neck and neck in our direction to share the spoils. The Turks there, seeing them go, began to move after them with infinite precaution, firing volleys. Evidently we had a half hour respite, and then a double threat against us.

I ran down to the ruins to see what the mine had done. The bridge was gone; and into its gap was fallen the front waggon, which had been filled with sick. The smash had killed all but three or four and had rolled dead and dying into a bleeding heap against the splintered end. One of those yet alive deliriously cried out the word typhus. So I wedged shut the door, and left them there, alone.

Succeeding waggons were derailed and smashed: some had frames irreparably buckled. The second engine was a blanched pile of smoking iron. Its driving wheels had been blown upward, taking away the side of the fire-box. Cab and tender were twisted into strips, among the piled stones of the bridge abutment. It would never run again. The front engine had got off better: though heavily derailed and lying halfover, with the cab burst, yet its steam was at pressure, and driving-gear intact.

Our greatest object was to destroy locomotives, and I had kept in my arms a box of gun-cotton with fuse and detonator ready fixed, to make sure such a case. I now put them in position on the outside cylinder. On the boiler would have been better, but the sizzling steam made me fear a general explosion which would sweep across my men (swarming like ants over the booty) with a blast of jagged fragments. Yet they would not finish their looting before the Turks came. So I lit the fuse, and in the half-minute of its burning drove the plunderers a little back, with difficulty. Then the charge burst, blowing the cylinder to smithers, and the axle too. At the moment I was distressed with uncertainty whether the damage were enough; but the Turks later found the engine beyond use and broke it up.

The valley was a weird sight. The Arabs, gone raving mad, were rushing about at top speed bareheaded and half-naked, screaming, shooting into the air, clawing one another nail and fist, while they burst open trucks and staggered back and forward with immense bales, which they ripped by the railside, and tossed through, smashing what they did not want. The train had been packed with refugees and sick men, volunteers for boat-service on the Euphrates, and families of Turkish officers returning to Damascus.

There were scores of carpets spread about; dozens of mattresses and flowered quilts, blankets in heaps, clothes for men and women in full variety; clocks, cooking-pots, food, ornaments and weapons. To one side stood thirty or forty hysterical women, unveiled, tearing their clothes and hair; shrieking themselves distracted. The Arabs without regard to them went on wrecking the household goods; looting their absolute fill. Camels had become common property. Each man frantic-ally loaded the nearest with what it could carry and shooed it westward into the void, while he turned to his next fancy.

Seeing me tolerably unemployed, the women rushed, and caught at me with howls for mercy. I assured them that all was going well: but they would not get away till some husbands delivered me. These knocked their wives off and seized my feet in a very agony of terror of instant death. A Turk so broken down was a nasty spectacle: I kicked them off as well as I could with bare feet, and finally broke free.

Next a group of Austrians, officers and non-commissioned officers, appealed to me quietly in Turkish for quarter. I replied with my halting German; whereupon one, in English, begged a doctor for his wounds. We had none: not that it mattered, for he was mortally hurt and dying. I told them the Turks would return in an hour and care for them. But he was dead before that, as were most of the others (instructors in the new Skoda mountain howitzers supplied to Turkey for the Hejaz war), because some dispute broke out between them and my own bodyguard, and one of them fired a pistol shot at young Rahail. My infuriated men cut them down, all but two or three, before I could return to interfere.

When Lawrence of Arabia blew up the Turkish train in the Hejaz the First World War still had a year to run, but its outcome was already determined. The Kaiser's order to his U-boats to 'sink on sight' all shipping, no matter what its nationality, in a bid to starve Britain out, had brought America into the war on the Allied side on 6 April 1917. Germany had been unable to defeat the 'thin khaki line' of the British Army; when this was reinforced by the double-sized divisions of the US Expeditionary Force and backed by the super-sized US economy she had no chance of victory.

Armistice Celebrations, London, 11 a.m., 11 November 1918

WINSTON CHURCHILL

It was a few minutes before the eleventh hour of the eleventh day of the eleventh month. I stood at the window of my room looking up Northumberland Avenue towards Trafalgar Square, waiting for Big Ben to tell that the War was over. My mind strayed back across the scarring years . . .

The minutes passed. I was conscious of reaction rather than elation . . . And then suddenly the first stroke of the chime. I looked again at the broad street beneath me. It was deserted. From the portals of one of the large hotels absorbed by Government Departments darted the slight

figure of a girl clerk, distractedly gesticulating while another stroke of
Big Ben resounded. Then from all sides men and women came scurrying
into the street. Streams of people poured out of all the buildings. The
bells of London began to clash. Northumberland Avenue was now so
crowded with people in hundreds, nay, thousands, rushing hither and
thither in a frantic manner, shouting and screaming with joy. I could
see that Trafalgar Square was already swarming. Around me in our very
headquarters, in the Hotel Metropole, disorder had broken out. Doors
banged. Feet clattered down corridors. Everyone rose from the desk and
cast aside pen and paper. All bounds were broken. The tumult grew. It
grew like a gale, but from all sides simultaneously. The street was now
a seething mass of humanity. Flags appeared as if by magic. Streams of
men and women flowed from the Embankment. They mingled with
torrents pouring down the Strand on their way to acclaim the King.
Almost before the last stroke of the clock had died away, the strict,
war-straitened, regulated streets of London had become a triumphant
pandemonium. At any rate it was clear that no more work would be
done that day. Yes, the chains which had held the world were broken.
Links of imperative need, links of discipline, links of brute force, links
of self-sacrifice, links of terror, links of honour which had held our
nation, nay, the greater part of mankind, to grinding toil, to a compulsive
cause – every one had snapped upon a few strokes of the clock. Safety,
freedom, peace, home, the dear one back at the fireside – all after
fifty-two months of gaunt distortion. After fifty-two months of making
burdens grievous to be borne and binding them on men's backs, at last,
all at once, suddenly and everywhere the burdens were cast down. At
least so for the moment it seemed.

My wife arrived, and we decided to go and offer our congratulations
to the Prime Minister, on whom the central impact of the home struggle
had fallen, in his hour of recompense. But no sooner had we entered
our car than twenty people mounted upon it, and in the midst of a
wildly cheering multitude we were impelled slowly forward through
Whitehall. We had driven together the opposite way along the same
road on the afternoon of the ultimatum. There had been the same crowd
and almost the same enthusiasm. It was with feelings which do not lend
themselves to words that I heard the cheers of the brave people who
had borne so much and given all, who had never wavered, who had
never lost faith in their country or its destiny, and who could be indulgent
to the faults of their servants when the hour of deliverance had come . . .

The First World War was over. So was the old order of things. *Returning troops were promised by Lloyd George, the Liberal Prime Minister, 'a land fit for heroes to live in'. That land could have nothing less than universal male suffrage, for all ranks of men had fought the war, all ranks required a say in the peace. By the·same token, women had helped win the war, working as nurses, munitions workers and 'land girls'.*

By the Representation of the People Act, 1918, the vote was extended to all men over twenty-one and all women over thirty. The enlarged electorate, to no one's great surprise, boosted the fortunes of the Labour Party, which formed its first government in 1924.

Whatever their hue, governments of the 1920s and 1930s were mired in problems. Ireland, brought into the Union in 1800, was in nationalist revolt, which British forces ('The Black and Tans') distinctly failed to suppress. Discretion was better than fighting De Valera and Ireland was let go (save for the Protestant-leaning Northern six counties) in 1921. There was no quick fix for the national debt, which had risen from £650,000,000 in 1914 to £7,830,000,000 in 1920. The price of freedom from the Kaiser's expansionist Germany had not been cheap. On top of the debt, Britain had definitively lost its leading role in the world's economy, and its traditional industries, especially, were antique, under-capitalized and beset by antagonistic labour relations. King Coal was the exemplar. It was the coal industry which spawned Britain's first, and last, general strike.

The General Strike, 4–12 May 1926

ARNOLD BENNETT

To support coal miners 'locked out' by their employers (as a means of forcing wage cuts), the Trades Union Congress called out workers in key industries, notably the docks, railways, gas and electricity. Much of the country came to a halt, but the TUC leaders had no stomach for constitutional conflict and called off the strike on 12 May. Almost everywhere, the strike was peaceful, coppers and strikers playing football together, with the middle classes joyfully 'black-legging' (strike-breaking) by driving buses and lorries.

To-day was the first day of the general strike. Many more motors about. I walked round Victoria, which was shut up (both stations) one small entrance guarded by policemen. I heard someone say that a train had gone somewhere during the morning. Yet in the vast empty stations

Smith's bookstalls were open. So were (outside) the cafés. The populace excited and cheery, on this 1st day of the strike. No evening paper. News from the Wireless at very short intervals, ½ hour intervals at night up to midnight. I should think that nearly all theatres would soon be closed. Already to-day there has been a noticeably increasing gravity in the general demeanour.

May 5: – Lunch at the Reform at 1.30. Upstairs, Gardiner, Tudor Walters, Hedges, Jim Currie, Sassoon, and Lord Devonport. Most people gloomy, but all uncompromising. General opinion that the fight would be short but violent. Bloodshed anticipated next week. Plenty of wireless messages, futile. Typescript-printed *Times* and *Financial News*.

May 6: – Another N.N.E. wind. Not a taxi on the streets that I saw. It is now over a week since I did anything on the novel – the last day being Thursday, 29th April. I went for a walk to Brompton Rd to spy out the land. Eleven buses passed the top of Sloane St in five minutes at 4.30. Only two of them were Generals, and both of them had a window smashed. I saw more in the evening. A policeman and a special constable on every General . . .

May 12: – The general strike now seems pitiful – a pathetic attempt of underdogs who hadn't a chance when the over-dogs really set themselves to win. Everybody, nearly, among the over-dogs seems to have joined in with grim enthusiasm to beat the strike. The Doctor called yesterday morning, and even he had been working at 'criminal investigations' for the Government. (He spoke of deaths resulting from East End rioting.) Willie Maugham was working at Scotland Yard till 8.30 of a night – I don't know what at. Special constables abounded.

May 13: – Everyone is still preoccupied with the strike, or rather with what is called 'The new strike'. Duff Tayler told great stories of his adventurous journeys on the Tube trains driven by swagger youths in yellow gloves who nevertheless now and then overran the platform with their trains, or pulled up too short. Also of University porters with gold cigarette cases and an incredible politeness and fatherliness towards you for your safety. Maugham was what he called a 'sleuth' at Scotland Yard. A police car was sent for him always. The first night he worked all night from 11 p.m. to 8.30 a.m. He said the last few hours, after dawn, were simply terrible, and he couldn't see how he would ever be able to get through them. I don't know what a 'sleuth' is.

The miners held out for another five months before trickling back to work.
   Of course, the damp-squibness of the General Strike should have come as no

surprise. England did not do class war. In the rest of Europe, governments were being toppled, workers were revolting, far-right groups were launching putsches, but in England the communitas *held together, bound by a shared understanding of Englishness, reverence for the monarchy, a sense of humour, and the long habit of parliamentary democracy.*

Body-line Bowling, Adelaide, Australia, 13–19 January 1933

W. H. FERGUSON

Cricket has been played in England since the twelfth century; in the twentieth it became the cause of fractious relations between England and the dominion of Australia. W. H. Ferguson was on the MCC's staff. Douglas Jardine was the English skipper.

This was destined to be an historic and sensational match, one of the most unpleasant exhibitions – from many aspects – it has been my misfortune to witness. I have no doubt in my mind that the Australian cricketers were terrified by Harold Larwood and his leg theory bowling, an attitude of mind fully justified by the events of the match.

One batsman after another suffered physically as Larwood relentlessly set about the job allocated to him by Jardine; Bill Ponsford, who frequently turned his back on the ball, had dozens of bruises to emphasize the folly of such attempted evasive action. Bill Woodfull, never very quick on his feet, suffered even more, and I was in full sympathy with his wife who feared for Woodfull's safety. It came as no surprise when, after receiving a severe blow on the chest from a Larwood delivery, Woodfull had to be taken to the dressing room, a very sick man.

When Bert Oldfield, always a popular figure with spectators, had to be carried to the pavilion, knocked unconscious with a fast, rising ball, the indignation of spectators was at boiling point. Maurice Tate, who was not playing for England, told me, 'Bill, I'm getting out of here. Somebody is going to get seriously hurt, and the people will start a riot,' I felt sure some hotheads in the crowd would jump the rails and try to assault the English cricketers, but, thank Heaven, it did not come to that.

'Plum' Warner, in an effort to do the right thing, looked into the Australian dressing room which, by that time, resembled a casualty clearing station, and expressed his regret for the injuries caused by the tourists' fast bowling. He received a snub which made front page news all over the world, when Woodfull told him, 'I don't want to speak to you, Mr Warner. There are two teams out there and one is playing cricket. If these tactics are persevered with, it may be better if I do not play the game. Good afternoon.'

Then followed an historic cable from the Australian Cricket Board of Control to the MCC in London. Dated 18th January, 1933, it was worded:

'Bodyline bowling has assumed such proportions as to menace the best interests of the game, making the protection of his body by a batsman his main consideration. It is causing intensely bitter feeling between the players as well as injury to them. In our opinion it is unsportsmanlike. Unless it is stopped at once it is likely to upset the friendly relations existing between Australia and England.'

Larwood was dropped from future Test teams on the insistence of J. H. Thomas, the Dominions Secretary.

Down and Out: A Night in a Doss-house, c. 1931

GEORGE ORWELL

Turning his back on his upper-middle-class upbringing (prep school, Eton), George Orwell donned tramp's clothes to go and explore impoverished England – as related in Down and Out in Paris and London. *By 1931 the Great Depression was at its zenith and unemployment in England had reached 3 million.*

At about eleven I began looking for a bed. I had read about doss-houses (they are never called doss-houses, by the way), and I supposed that one could get a bed for fourpence or thereabouts. Seeing a man, a navvy or something of the kind, standing on the kerb in the Waterloo Road, I stopped and questioned him. I said that I was stony broke and wanted the cheapest bed I could get.

'Oh,' said he, 'you go to that 'ouse across the street there, with the sign "Good Beds for Single Men". That's a good kip [sleeping place], that is. I bin there myself on and off. You'll find it cheap *and* clean.'

It was a tall, battered-looking house, with dim lights in all the windows, some of which were patched with brown paper. I entered a stone passage-way, and a little etiolated boy with sleepy eyes appeared from a door leading to a cellar. Murmurous sounds came from the cellar, and a wave of hot air and cheese. The boy yawned and held out his hand.

'Want a kip? That'll be a 'og, guv'nor.'

I paid the shilling, and the boy led me up a rickety unlighted staircase to a bedroom. It had a sweetish reek of paregoric and foul linen; the windows seemed to be tight shut, and the air was almost suffocating at first. There was a candle burning, and I saw that the room measured fifteen feet square by eight high, and had eight beds in it. Already six lodgers were in bed, queer lumpy shapes with all their own clothes, even their boots, piled on top of them. Someone was coughing in a loathsome manner in one corner.

When I got into the bed I found that it was as hard as a board, and as for the pillow, it was a mere hard cylinder like a block of wood. It was rather worse than sleeping on a table, because the bed was not six feet long, and very narrow, and the mattress was convex, so that one had to hold on to avoid falling out. The sheets stank so horribly of sweat that I could not bear them near my nose. Also, the bedclothes only consisted of the sheets and a cotton counterpane, so that though stuffy it was none too warm. Several noises recurred throughout the night. About once in an hour the man on my left – a sailor, I think – woke up, coughed vilely, and lighted a cigarette. Another man, victim of bladder disease, got up and noisily used his chamber pot half a dozen times during the night. The man in the corner had a coughing fit once in every twenty minutes, so regularly that one came to listen for it as one listens for the next yap when a dog is baying the moon. It was an unspeakably repellent sound; a foul bubbling and retching, as though the man's bowels were being churned up within him. Once when he struck a match I saw that he was a very old man, with a grey, sunken face like that of a corpse, and he was wearing his trousers wrapped round his head as a nightcap, a thing which for some reason disgusted me very much. Every time he coughed or the other man swore, a sleepy voice from one of the other beds cried out:

'Shut up! Oh, for Christ's – *sake* shut up!'

I had about an hour's sleep in all. In the morning I was woken by a dim impression of some large brown thing coming towards me. I opened my eyes and saw that it was one of the sailor's feet, sticking out of bed close to my face. It was dark brown, quite dark brown like an Indian's, with dirt. The walls were leprous, and the sheets, three weeks from the wash, were almost raw umber colour. I got up, dressed and went downstairs. In the cellar were a row of basins and two slippery roller towels. I had a piece of soap in my pocket, and I was going to wash, when I noticed that every basin was streaked with grime – solid, sticky filth as black as boot-blacking. I went out unwashed. Altogether, the lodging-house had not come up to its description as cheap *and* clean. It was however, as I found later, a fairly representative lodging-house.

I crossed the river and walked a long way eastward, finally going into a coffee-shop on Tower Hill. An ordinary London coffee-shop, like a thousand others, it seemed queer and foreign after Paris. It was a little stuffy room with the high-backed pews that were fashionable in the 'forties, the day's menu written on a mirror with a piece of soap, and a girl of fourteen handling the dishes. Navvies were eating out of newspaper parcels, and drinking tea in vast saucerless mugs like china tumblers. In a corner by himself a Jew, muzzle down in the plate, was guiltily wolfing bacon.

'Could I have some tea and bread and butter?' I said to the girl.

She stared. 'No butter, only marg,' she said, surprised. And she repeated the order in the phrase that is to London what the eternal *coup de rouge* is to Paris: 'Large tea and two slices!'

On the wall beside my pew there was a notice saying 'Pocketing the sugar not allowed,' and beneath it some poetic customer had written:

> He that takes away the sugar,
> Shall be called a dirty —

but someone else had been at pains to scratch out the last word. This was England. The tea-and-two-slices cost threepence halfpenny, leaving me with eight and twopence.

The Battle of Cable Street, 7 October 1936

PHIL PIRATIN

To steer England out of the Depression doldrums, there were calls from the sidelines for drastic change. On the far left, the pro-Russian Communist Party of Great Britain (maximum membership 10,000) dominated a fractious political allsorts. On the far right, Sir Oswald Mosley founded the British Union of

Fascists in 1932, whose 20,000 members wore the uniform of Mussolini's Black-shirts. At Cable Street, in London's East End, the CPGB determined to stop the Blackshirts from marching.

　Piratin was an official of the Communist Party of Great Britain.

It was obvious that the Fascists and the police would now turn their attention to Cable Street. We were ready. The moment this became apparent the signal was given to put up the barricades. We had prepared three spots. The first was near a yard where there was all kinds of timber and other oddments, and also an old lorry. An arrangement had been made with the owner that this old lorry could be used as a barricade. Instructions had been given about this, but when someone shouted 'Get the lorry!' evidently not explaining that it was in the nearby yard, some of the lads, looking up the street, saw a stationary lorry about 200 yards away. They went along, brought it back, and pushed it over on its side before anyone even discovered that it was not the lorry meant to be used. Still it was a lorry, and supplemented by bits of old furniture, mattresses, and every kind of thing you expect to find in boxrooms, it was a barricade which the police did not find it easy to penetrate. As they charged they were met with milk bottles, stones, and marbles. Some of the housewives began to drop milk bottles from the roof tops. A number of police surrendered. This had never happened before, so the lads didn't know what to do, but they took away their batons, and one took a helmet for his son as a souvenir.

Cable Street was a great scene. I have referred to 'the lads'. Never was there such unity of all sections of the working class as was seen on the barricades at Cable Street. People whose lives were poles apart, though living within a few hundred yards of each other; bearded Ortho-dox Jews and rough-and-ready Irish Catholic dockers – these were the workers that the Fascists were trying to stir up against each other. The struggle, led by the Communist Party, against the Fascists had brought them together against their common enemies, and their lackeys.

Meanwhile, charges and counter-charges were taking place along 'the front' from Tower Hill to Gardner's Corner. Many arrests were made, many were injured. It was the police, however, who were carrying on the battle, while the Fascists lurked in the background, protected by a 'fence' of police. Mosley was late. As soon as he arrived, in a motor-car, a brick went clean through the window.

It was later rumoured that Sir Philip Game had been on the telephone to the Home Secretary, and had pleaded with Sir John Simon to forbid the march. Sir John was adamant. Sir Philip Game, however, made up his own mind. He forbade the march and told Mosley to argue it out with Sir John Simon. The Fascists lined up, saluted their leader, and marched through the deserted City to the Embankment, where they dispersed. The working class had won the day.

The Jarrow March, October 1936

ROY CHADWICK

Much the most dramatic gesture drawing attention to the plight of the impoverished and unemployed of the 1930s was the hunger march; the most celebrated was from Jarrow ('the town they killed') to London, and was led by Jarrow's Labour MP, 'Red' Ellen Wilkinson. Two hundred Jarrow shipyard workers walked with her.

Roy Chadwick was a Guardian *journalist.*

There can be no doubt that as a gesture the march is a bounding success. I fell in with it this morning on the Ripon road. Under its two banners ('Jarrow Crusade'), with its harmonicas, its kettle-drum, and its four hundred feet, it was going strong. The marchers have with them two doctors, a barber, a group of pressmen, a Labrador dog mascot, and for a great deal of the time so far the Mayor of Jarrow (Alderman J. W. Thompson), who keeps travelling back to Jarrow to maintain touch with his civic duties and then south again to maintain touch with the marchers. It is an example of civic spirit probably without parallel anywhere else in the country. With him at the head of the procession is its marshal, County Councillor D. F. Riley, the inspirer and organizer of the march.

This is not a hunger-march, but a protest march. The unanimity of the protest that Jarrow is making to the rest of the country is indicated in the fact that the political parties represented on the Jarrow Town Council have agreed to bury the political hatchet to the extent of holding no elections this November. Further, although the town cannot by law spend a farthing of the rate-payers' money on this demonstration, the labours of its Mayor in dispatching about 200,000 letters to other corporations, trade unions, co-operative societies and similar bodies at the expense of the march fund has raised that fund to £850, and it is hoped to have the round £1,000 before the marchers reach the Marble Arch on 31 October.

The more fortunate classes of Jarrow, where not fifteen per cent of the employable population is at work, have contributed, but the bulk of the fund has come from the country at large, and more than money. I, for one, had no conception of the cost of organizing such a march until I heard about the value of the gifts in kind that ease the drain on the march fund so considerably. Take cigarettes, for instance, and calculate the cost of distributing two twopenny packets per day per man to 200 men. I will not vouch that 'fags' are among the gifts, but it illustrates the point. Any little article costing sixpence means five pounds when distributed to 200 men, and soap, tobacco, and all sorts of things have been given. Before the men set out they all had their boots soled and heeled, and two pairs of socks and two iodine soles were also issued.

With eggs and salmon and such sandwiches as I saw to-day being consumed on the menu it is emphatically not a hunger-march. The men are doing well on it, and only two of them have fallen out for reasons of health in nearly ninety miles of marching. All the time communication is maintained with Jarrow, and if work turns up for a man on the march back he will go to it.

The organization seems well nigh perfect. It includes a transport wagon – a 'bus bought for £20 and converted – which goes ahead with the sleeping kit, waterproofs for every man worn bandolero fashion, 1s. 6d. pocket-money and two 1½d. stamps a week, medical attention, haircutting (and shaving for the inexpert), cobbling, accommodation at night in drill halls, schools, church institutes, and even town halls, and advance agents in the persons of the Labour agent at Jarrow, Mr Harry Stoddert, and the Conservative agent, Mr R. Suddick, who work together in arranging accommodation and getting halls for meetings.

There is no political aspect to this march. It is simply the town of Jarrow saying 'Send us work'. In the ranks of the marchers are Labour men, Liberals, Tories, and one or two Communists, but you cannot tell who's who. It has the Church's blessing; in fact, it took the blessing of the Bishop of Ripon (Dr Lunt) and a subscription of £5 from him when it set out to-day. It also had the blessing of the Bishop of Jarrow (Dr Gordon).

With the marchers goes, prominently carried, the Jarrow petition for work, a huge book with about 12,000 signatures, which, after a meeting at the Memorial Hall, London, the previous day, Miss Ellen Wilkinson, MP for Jarrow, is to present at the bar of the House of Commons on 4 November. Miss Wilkinson met us outside Killinghall this afternoon and became the only woman in the procession. She had motored from

Manchester to-day but had met with petrol trouble and had been delayed. It was interesting to watch motorists who passed us on the road recognize her and lean out of windows as they went by. Like us all she made friends with Paddy, the Labrador dog who accompanied the procession uninvited for five miles from Jarrow before anyone realized that he intended to go all the way.

The Abdication, 11 December 1936

SIR HENRY CHANNON

Above the trials of England in the 1930s sat the monarchy, more comfortable than ever. It proved adept at the common touch (George V attending the Cup Final), traditional pageantry (George V's Silver Jubilee), and new means of communication (radio broadcasts). Even the abdication of Edward VIII left it undented. Edward VIII ('David' to the family), wished to marry the twice-divorced American, Wallis Simpson; the Cabinet, Church and Commonwealth maintained that he could not then remain king. He chose the 'woman I love'.

Channon was a Conservative MP and minister.

11 December 1936: 'The King is gone, Long live the King.' We woke in the reign of Edward VIII and went to bed in that of George VI. Honor [Lady Honor Channon, Chips's wife] and I were at the House of Commons by eleven o'clock . . . When the Bill came it was passed into law with the minimum of time . . . Then the Royal Commission was sent for, and the Lords Onslow, Denman and one other, filed out of the Chamber, and returned in full robes and wigs. Black Rod was sent to summon the Speaker, who, followed by his Commons, appeared at the bar. The Clerk read the Royal Commission. The three Lords bowed, and doffed their hats. The Bill was read. The King was still King Edward. The Clerk bowed, 'Le Roi le veult' [It is the King's will] and Edward, the beautiful boy King with his gaiety and honesty, his American accent and nervous twitching, his flair and glamour, was part of history. It was 1.52.

We went sadly home, and in the street we heard a woman selling newspapers saying, 'The Church held a pistol to his head.' In the evening we dined at the Stanleys' cheerless, characterless house, and at ten o'clock turned on the wireless to hear 'His Royal Highness Prince Edward' speak his farewell words in his unmistakable slightly Long Island voice. It was a manly, sincere farewell . . . There was a stillness in the Stanleys' room. I wept, and I murmured a prayer for he [*sic*] who had once been King Edward VIII.

Then we played bridge.

According to Sir Eric Mieville, one of George VI's secretaries, Edward VIII was 'quite unmoved' throughout the abdication drama: 'His last act prior to broadcasting his message and then leaving the country was to sit in his bedroom with a whisky and soda having his toe-nails seen to.'

World War II: Children Evacuated, London, 1 September 1939

HILDE MARCHANT

The Second World War opened at 04.45 hours on 1 September 1939, when German tanks rolled into Poland. Britain was not yet in the conflict, but prudence dictated that London's children were evacuated anyway.

The office had told me to cover the evacuation of some of London's schoolchildren. There had been great preparations for the scheme – preparations that raised strong criticism. Evacuation would split the British home, divide child and parent, break that domestic background that was our strength.

I went to a block of working-class flats at the back of Gray's Inn Road and in the early morning saw a tiny, frail, Cockney child walking across to school. The child had a big, brown-paper parcel in her hand and was dragging it along. But as she turned I saw a brown box banging against her thin legs. It bumped up and down at every step, slung by a thin string over her shoulder.

It was Florence Morecambe, an English schoolchild, with a gas mask instead of a satchel over her shoulder.

I went along with Florence to her school. It was a big Council school and the classrooms were filled with children, parcels, gas masks. The desks and blackboards were piled up in a heap in one corridor. They were not going to school for lessons. They were going on a holiday. The children were excited and happy because their parents had told them they were going away to the country. Many of them, like my little Florence, had never seen green fields. Their playground was the tarmac or a sandpit in the concrete square at the back.

I watched the schoolteachers calling out their names and tying luggage labels in their coats, checking their parcels to see there were warm and clean clothes. On the gates of the school were two fat policemen. They were letting the children through but gently asking the parents not to come farther. They might disturb the children. So mothers and fathers were saying goodbye, straightening the girls' hair, getting the boys to blow their noses, and lightly and quickly kissing them. The parents stood outside while the children went to be registered in their classrooms. There was quite a long wait before this small army got its orders through from the LCC [London County Council] to move off. In the meantime I sat in the school playground, watching these thin, wiry little Cockneys playing their rough-and-push games on the faded netball pitch. It was disturbing, for through the high grille their mothers pressed their faces, trying to see the one child that resembled them. Every now and then the policeman would call out a child's name and a mother who had forgotten a bar of chocolate or a toothbrush had a last chance to tell a child to be good, to write and to straighten her hat.

Labelled and lined up, the children began to move out of the school. I followed Florence, her live tiny face bobbing about, white among so many navy-blue school caps. She was chattering away to an older school-girl, wanting to know what the country was like, where they were going, what games they would play on the grass.

On one side of Gray's Inn Road this ragged crocodile moved towards the tube station. On the other, were mothers who were waving and running along to see the last of their children. The police had asked them not to follow, but they could not resist.

The children scrambled down into the tube.

Late on the morning of 3 September, Prime Minister Neville Chamberlain informed the nation that it was at war with Nazi Germany. (There was irony in this: Chamberlain had been an arch appeaser of Hitler and supposedly brokered 'peace in our time' only the year before.) For six months little happened – people talked of the 'Phoney War' – until April 1940, when Hitler launched his 'Blitzkrieg' on Norway and Denmark. A month later, the Germans invaded the Low Countries and France. England's patience with the irresolute, discredited Chamberlain broke, and Parliament replaced him on 13 May with Winston Churchill. So began Churchill's 'walk with destiny'. The most immediate problem on the path was the British Expeditionary Force in France which had retreated to the port of Dunkirk.

Dunkirk: The Beach, 30 May 1940

CAPTAIN RICHARD AUSTIN, BEF

Evacuation of the British Expeditionary Force was authorized by Churchill on 26 May. Over the next nine days 224,585 British and 112,546 Franco-Belgian troops were saved. Aiding the armada of 222 naval units were 665 craft – ranging from sailing dinghies to merchantmen – commanded by their civilian volunteers.

We were now in the region of the dunes, which rose like humps of a deeper darkness. And these in their turn were dotted with the still blacker shapes of abandoned vehicles, half-sunk in the sand, fantastic twisted shapes of burned-out skeletons, and crazy-looking wreckage that had been heaped up in extraordinary piles by the explosions of bombs. All these black shapes were silhouetted against the angry red glare in the sky, which reflected down on us the agony of burning Dunkirk.

Slowly we picked our way between the wreckage, sinking ankle-deep in the loose sand, until we reached the gaunt skeletons of what had once been the houses on the promenade. The whole front was one long continuous line of blazing buildings, a high wall of fire, roaring and darting in tongues of flame, with the smoke pouring upwards and disappearing in the blackness of the sky above the roof-tops. Out seawards the darkness was as thick and smooth as black velvet, except for now and again when the shape of a sunken destroyer or paddle-steamer made a slight thickening on its impenetrable surface. Facing us, the great black wall of the Mole stretched from the beach far out into the sea, the end of it almost invisible to us. The Mole had an astounding, terrifying background of giant flames leaping a hundred feet into the air from blazing oil tanks. At the shore end of the Mole stood an obelisk, and the high-explosive shells burst around it with monotonous regularity.

Along the promenade, in parties of fifty, the remnants of practically all the last regiments were wearily trudging along. There was no singing, and very little talk. Everyone was far too exhausted to waste breath. Occasionally out of the darkness came a sudden shout:

'A Company, Green Howards . . .'

'C Company, East Yorks . . .'

These shouts came either from stragglers trying to find lost units, or guides on the look-out for the parties they were to lead on to the Mole for evacuation.

The tide was out. Over the wide stretch of sand could be dimly discerned little oblong masses of soldiers, moving in platoons and orderly groups down towards the edge of the sea. Now and again you would hear a shout:

'Alf, where are you? . . .'

'Let's hear from you, Bill . . .'

'Over this way, George . . .'

It was none too easy to keep contact with one's friends in the darkness, and amid so many little masses of moving men, all looking very much alike. If you stopped for a few seconds to look behind you, the chances were you attached yourself to some entirely different unit.

From the margin of the sea, at fairly wide intervals three long thin black lines protruded into the water, conveying the effect of low wooden breakwaters. These were lines of men, standing in pairs behind one another far out into the water, waiting in queues till boats arrived to transport them, a score or so at a time, to the steamers and warships that were filling up with the last survivors. The queues stood there, fixed and almost as regular as if ruled. No bunching, no pushing, nothing like the mix-up to be seen at the turnstiles when a crowd is going to a football match. Much more orderly, even than a waiting theatre queue.

About this time, afraid that some of our men might be trailing off, I began shouting, '2004th Field Regiment . . . 2004th Field Regiment . . .' A group of dead and dying soldiers on the path in front of us quickened our desire to quit the promenade. Stepping over the bodies we marched down the slope to a dark beach.

We tacked ourselves on to the rear of the smallest of the three queues, the head of which was already standing in water up to the waist. Half an hour passed. Suddenly a small rowing boat appeared. The head of the queue clambered in and was rowed away into the blackness . . .

Along the entire queue not a word was spoken. The men just stood there silently staring into the darkness, praying that a boat would soon appear, and fearing that it would not. Heads and shoulders only showing above the water. Fixed, immovable, as though chained there. It was, in fact, practically impossible to move, even from one foot to another. The dead-weight of water-logged boots and sodden clothes pinned one down. My breeches seemed to be ballooned out with water as heavy as mercury. I was filled with a dread that when the time did come I should be unable to move.

Suddenly out of the blackness, rather ghostly, swam a white shape which materialized into a ship's lifeboat, towed by a motorboat. It moved towards us and came to a stop twenty yards in front of the head of our queue.

'Hi! Hi!' we all hailed, dreading they hadn't seen us.

'Ahoy! Ahoy!' came the lusty response.

'Come in closer,' we shouted.

'We can't. It's unsafe. Might upset the boat.' But they risked a few more yards . . .

Four sailors in tin-hats began hoisting the soldiers out of the water. It was no simple task. Half the men were so weary and exhausted that they lacked strength to climb into the boat unaided. The sailors judged the situation perfectly, as being one for rough words, threats, and bullying methods. The only spur sufficient to rouse our worn-out bodies to one last supreme effort.

'Come on you bastards . . .'

'Wake up, blast you . . .'

'Get a move on, Dopey . . .'

The gunwhale of the lifeboat stood three feet above the surface of the water. Reaching up, I could just grasp it with the tips of my fingers. When I tried to haul myself up I couldn't move an inch. The weight of my waterlogged clothes, especially my cherished greatcoat, beat me completely, desperately though I fought. I might have been a sack of lead. A great dread of being left behind seized me.

Two powerful hands reached over the gunwhale and fastened themselves into my arm-pits. Another pair of hands stretched down and hooked-on to the belt at the back of my greatcoat. Before I had time to realise it I was pulled up and pitched head-first into the bottom of the boat.

'Come on, you b—. Get up and help the others in,' shouted a sailor, as I hit the planks with a gasp. It was rough medicine. But the right medicine for the moment.

The moment came when the lifeboat could not hold another soul.

'Carry on, Mr Jolly. Carry on,' cried the sailor at our helm to someone in the motor-boat. And we got under weigh, leaving the rest of the queue behind to await the next boat.

'Bloody marvellous' said the Daily Mirror *of the 'miracle' of Dunkirk.*

Churchill's War Speeches, June 1940

WINSTON CHURCHILL, PRIME MINISTER

With the Fall of France only Britain remained standing against Nazi Germany. The country's determination to fight on was due in no small part to the bulldog oratory of Churchill himself. Below are excerpts from two of his war speeches of June 1940.

. . . I have, myself, full confidence that if all do their duty, if nothing is neglected, and if the best arrangements are made, as they are being made, we shall prove ourselves once again able to defend our island home, to ride out the storm of war, and to outlive the menace of tyranny, if necessary for years, if necessary alone. At any rate, that is what we are going to try to do. That is the resolve of His Majesty's Government – every man of them. That is the will of Parliament and the nation. The British Empire and the French Republic linked together in their cause and in their need, will defend to the death their native soil, aiding each other like good comrades to the utmost of their strength. Even though large tracts of Europe and many old and famous States have fallen or may fall into the grip of the Gestapo and all the odious apparatus of Nazi rule, we shall not flag or fail. We shall go on to the end. We shall fight in France, we shall fight on the seas and oceans, we shall fight with growing confidence and growing strength in the air, we shall defend our island, whatever the cost may be. We shall fight on the beaches, we shall fight on the landing grounds, we shall fight in the fields and in the streets, we shall fight in the hills; we shall never surrender, and even if, which I do not for a moment believe, this island or a large part of it were subjugated and starving, then our Empire beyond the seas, armed and guarded by the British Fleet, would carry on the struggle, until, in God's good time, the new world, with all its power and might, steps forth to the rescue and the liberation of the old.

★   ★   ★

. . . What General Weygand called the 'Battle of France' is over. I expect that the battle of Britain is about to begin. Upon this battle depends the survival of Christian civilization. Upon it depends our own British life and the long continuity of our institutions and our Empire. The whole fury and might of the enemy must very soon be turned on us. Hitler knows that he will have to break us in this island or lose the war. If we can stand up to him all Europe may be free, and the life of the world may move forward into broad, sunlit uplands; but if we fail then the whole world, including the United States, and all that we have known and cared for, will sink into the abyss of a new dark age made more sinister, and perhaps more prolonged, by the lights of a perverted science. Let us therefore brace ourselves to our duty and so bear ourselves that if the British Commonwealth and Empire lasts for a thousand years men will still say, 'This was their finest hour.'

The Battle of Britain: A Spitfire Pilot in Action, 2 September 1940

RICHARD HILLARY RAF

France defeated, Hitler turned his attention to a seaborne invasion of England. As the Führer realized full well, this could only be achieved if the RAF was swept from the skies above the Channel. Göring, the Luftwaffe chief, assured the Führer that it would take his pilots a mere four days to achieve this. The Luftwaffe certainly had the numerical advantage, but the operational value of its main fighter aircraft, the Messerschmitt Bf109, was limited to about ten minutes over the main battlefield, the south-east corner of England.

The Battle of Britain began on 'Eagle Day', 13 August, with the Luftwaffe raiding RAF airfields.

We made a dash for our machines and within two minutes were off the ground. Twice we circled the aerodrome to allow all twelve planes to get in formation. We were flying in four sections of three: Red Section leading, Blue and Green to right and left, and the three remaining planes forming a guard section above and behind us.

I was flying No. 2 in the Blue Section.

Over the radio came the voice of the controller, 'Hullo, Red Leader', followed by instructions on course and height.

As always, for the first few minutes we flew on the reciprocal of the course given until we reached fifteen thousand feet. We then turned about and flew on 110° in an all-out climb, thus coming out of the sun and gaining height all the way.

During the climb Uncle George was in constant touch with the ground. We were to intercept about twenty enemy fighters at twenty-five thousand feet. I glanced across at Stapme and saw his mouth moving. That meant he was singing again. He would sometimes do this with his radio set on 'Send', with the result that, mingled with our instructions from the ground, we would hear a raucous rendering of *Night and Day*. And then quite clearly over the radio I heard the Germans excitedly calling to each other. This was a not infrequent occurrence and it made one feel that they were right behind, although often they were some distance away. I switched my set to 'Send' and called out '*Halts Maul!*' and as many other choice pieces of German invective as I could remember. To my delight I heard one of them answer, 'You feelthy Englishmen, we will teach you how to speak to a German.' I am aware that this sounds a tall story, but several others in the Squadron were listening out and heard the whole thing.

I looked down. It was a completely cloudless sky and way below lay the English countryside, stretching lazily into the distance, a quite extraordinary picture of green and purple in the setting sun.

I took a glance at my altimeter. We were at twenty-eight thousand feet. At that moment Sheep yelled 'Tally-ho' and dropped down in front of Uncle George in a slow dive in the direction of the approaching planes. Uncle George saw them at once.

'OK. Line astern.'

I drew in behind Stapme and took a look at them. They were about two thousand feet below us, which was a pleasant change, but they must have spotted us at the same moment, for they were forming a protective circle, one behind the other, which is a defence formation hard to break.

'Echelon starboard,' came Uncle George's voice.

We spread out fanwise to the right.

'Going down!'

One after the other we peeled off in a power dive. I picked out one machine and switched my gun-button to 'Fire'. At three hundred yards I had him in my sights. At two hundred I opened up in a long four-second burst and saw the tracer going into his nose. Then I was pulling out, so hard that I could feel my eyes dropping through my neck. Coming round in a slow climbing turn, I saw that we had broken them up. The sky was now a mass of individual dog-fights. Several of them had already been knocked down. One I hoped was mine, but on pulling up I had not been able to see the result. To my left I saw Peter Pease make a head-on attack on a Messerschmitt. They were headed straight for each other and it looked as though the fire of both was striking home. Then at the last moment the Messerschmitt pulled up, taking Peter's fire full in the belly. It rolled on to its back, yellow flames pouring from the cockpit, and vanished.

Bombing the RAF's airfields proved too slow a way of winning the battle for Hitler's taste, and on 7 September he switched the 'Schwerpunkt' to a terror-attack on London: what Cockneys ironically called 'the Blitz'.

The Blitz on London, 7–8 September 1940

DESMOND FLOWER

Suddenly we were gaping upwards. The brilliant sky was criss-crossed from horizon to horizon by innumerable vapour-trails. The sight was a completely novel one. We watched, fascinated, and all work stopped. The little silver stars sparkling at the heads of the vapour trails turned east. This display looked so insubstantial and harmless; even beautiful. Then, with a dull roar which made the ground across London shake as one stood upon it, the first sticks of bombs hit the docks. Leisurely, enormous mushrooms of black and brown smoke shot with crimson climbed into the sunlit sky. There they hung and slowly expanded, for there was no wind, and the great fires below fed more smoke into them as the hours passed.

On Friday and Saturday morning the sky grew darker and darker as the oily smoke rose and spread in heavy, immobile columns, shutting out the sun.

At the barracks, drill quickly became monotonous. We had work to do, and we weren't the target. But we couldn't keep our eyes off those sickening, solid columns climbing up like the convolutions of a lazy snake into a torpid sky.

I suppose our masters felt that, although the Battle of Britain had begun, the worst might already be over – I don't know; but they decided to put us recruits in the hat and draw out three for week-end leave. My name came out of the hat first, and I sent a wire to my parents in Sevenoaks to say that I was coming home. My pass was from midday on Saturday, and I got down to the centre of London by Underground. Bombers were coming over at monotonously regular intervals. I walked down to Charing Cross. There was a lot of noise still, and a lot of smoke. As I entered the station the loudspeakers were ordering everyone out because planes were overhead and they were frightened of casualties if the place were hit. I strolled out to the top of that long flight of stone steps down into Villiers Street and sat on the balustrade watching.

Up in the lonely sky there was still one bomber, gleaming silver, and then he dropped a stick just across the Thames from us. Back in the station the loudspeaker announced that the main line was gone and that there wouldn't be any more trains out for hours. Hundreds of people stood around like a flock of sheep which is frightened and can't make up its mind which way to turn. You could see the dead mask of indecision on their faces as they looked about, hoping someone would tell them what to do. I walked out of the station and decided to hitch-hike home. I was lucky; somewhere on the south bank of the river I met a man on a motor-cycle who was going through Blackheath, and he took me on his pillion.

Now we were nearer to the docks. The columns of smoke merged and became a monstrous curtain which blocked the sky; only the billows within it and the sudden shafts of flame which shot up hundreds of feet made one realize that it was a living thing and not just the backdrop of some nightmare opera. There were fire-hoses along the side of the road, climbing over one another like a helping of macaroni, with those sad little fountains spraying out from the leaks, as they always seem to do from all fire-hoses. Every two or three minutes we would pull into the gutter as a fire-bell broke out stridently behind us and an engine in unfamiliar livery tore past at full tilt: chocolate or green or blue, with gold lettering – City of Birmingham Fire Brigade, or Sheffield, or Bournemouth. The feeling was something you had never experienced before – the excitement and dash of fire-engines arriving to help from so far away, and the oily, evil smell of fire and destruction, with its lazy, insolent rhythm.

It looked terrible and hopeless, but there was a kind of *Götterdämmerung* grandeur about it.

I got home in one piece, and my parents welcomed me with a splendid dinner. But that night the *Luftwaffe*, already working round the clock, came again and dropped a stick of bombs straight down our quiet Sevenoaks road. They hit the town centre just by the historic Vine cricket ground with the first bomb. The last but one landed opposite our gate, and the last by the street corner. Apart from the destruction of the town hall, no damage was done, and I wonder why that particular pilot chose that particular target; I suppose he must have seen the main London–Dover railway line and his bomb-aimer let go too soon.

Sunday in Sevenoaks was the same as Sunday throughout Kent, Surrey, Sussex and Essex. The hot summer air throbbed with the steady beat of the engines of bombers which one could not see in the dazzling blue. Then the RAF would arrive; the monotonous drone would be broken by the sudden snarl of a fighter turning at speed, and the vapour trails would start to form in huge circles. I lay on my back in the rose garden and watched the trails forming; as they broadened and dispersed a fresh set would be superimposed upon them. Then, no bigger than a pin's head, a white parachute would open and come down, growing slowly larger; I counted eight in the air at one time.

I had to be back in barracks on the Sunday night, and set off after supper. The twenty-three-mile journey took well over two hours, and no one could tell us what station we would be taken to. When we finally got there, it turned out to be Holborn. I stepped out into the darkness of the street, or what would have been darkness but for the fires; but as I did so a stick whistled down on the other side of the road and I ducked back inside. After a while I knew I had to begin to move. Hanging about in the station shelter wasn't doing me any good, so I started out on foot up Holborn. When I reached Gamages I was turned back: everything was cascaded down into the road as though two landslides had started simultaneously from opposite sides. There was utter silence, except for the crunch and crackle of my own feet treading a carpet of broken glass.

On 15 September 1940, the Luftwaffe lost sixty bombers raiding London. Two days later Hitler cancelled the invasion of England. 'The Few', the 2,500 pilots of Fighter Command, deserved their plaudits; they had shot down 1,268 aircraft for the loss of 832, and inflicted upon Nazi Germany its first defeat.

Britain stood alone against Hitler. And would do so for a year, until the entry of the USSR and then the USA into the war in 1941.

The Japanese Sink the Repulse *and the* Prince of Wales, *off the Coast of Malaya, 10 December 1941*

CECIL BROWN

On 7 December 1941, the Second World War spread to the Far East, with the Japanese attack on Pearl Harbor. Three days later the two finest battleships in the Royal Navy, HMS Prince of Wales *and HMS* Repulse, *were intercepted sailing out of Singapore by Japanese aircraft. The British ships had no air cover. Cecil Brown was a war reporter aboard the* Repulse.

10.45 – One twin-engined Jap is reported shadowing us. It is the same type that bombed Singapore the first night of the war. It is a type 96 Mitsubishi of the Naval Air Service.

The clouds have gone now, and the sky is a robin's-egg blue and the sun is bright yellow. Our ships plough through pea-green water, white where the hulls cleave it.

11.07 – The communications loudspeaker announces: 'Enemy aircraft approaching – action stations!'

I see them: one – two – three – four – five – six – seven – eight – nine. There are nine, flying line astern, one behind the other.

I would judge them about twelve thousand feet, coming straight over the *Repulse*.

11.14 – And here they come.

11.15 – The guns of the *Prince of Wales* just let go. At the same instant I see the flame belching from the guns of the *Wales*, ours break into a chattering, ear-splitting roar. The nine Japanese aircraft were stretched out across the bright blue, cloudless sky like star sapphires of a necklace.

I gape open-mouthed at those aircraft coming directly over us, flying so that they will pass from bow to stern over the *Repulse*. The sky is filled with black puffs from our ack-ack. They seem a discordant profanation of that beautiful sky. But the formation of Japanese planes, coming over one behind the other, is undisturbed.

Now they are directly overhead. For the first time I see the bombs coming down, materializing suddenly out of nothingness and streaming towards us like ever-enlarging tear-drops. There's a magnetic, hypnotic, limb-freezing fascination in that sight.

It never occurs to me to try and duck or run. Open-mouthed and rooted, I watch the bombs getting larger and larger. Suddenly, ten yards from me, out in the water, a huge geyser springs out of the sea, and over the side, showering water over me and my camera.

I instinctively hunch over, sort of a semi-crouch, and at the same instant there is a dull thud. The whole ship shudders. Pieces of paint fall from the deck over the flag deck.

11.17 – 'Fire on the boat deck. Fire below!' That just came over the loudspeakers. There are fountains of water all around the ship. Some are near misses. Most of the bombs are hitting the water ten to thirty yards off the port side. Beautiful fountains of thick white at the base and then tapering up into fine spray.

That first bomb was a direct hit. Someone on the flag deck says, 'Fire in marines' mess and hangar.'

That bomb struck the catapult deck, penetrated, exploded underneath. The bomb hit twenty yards astern of my position on the flat deck. A number of men [fifty] were killed.

11.45 – . . . The torpedo-carrying bombers are coming in. We are putting up a beautiful barrage, a wall of fire. But the bombers come on, in a long glide, from all angles, not simultaneously but alternately. Some come head-on, some astern and from all positions on both sides of the ship. They level out.

About three hundred yards distant from the ship and a hundred yards above the water they drop their torpedoes.

The torpedoes seem small, dropping flat into the water, sending up splashes, then streaking towards us. Those bombers are so close you can almost see the colour of the pilot's eyes. The bombers are machine-gunning our decks as they come in.

11.51½ – Captain Tennant is sending a message to the *Wales*: 'Have you sustained any damage?'

The answer comes back: 'We are out of control. Steering gear is gone.'

The decks of the *Repulse* are littered with empty shell-cases. Upon the faces of the sailors there's a mixture of incredulity and a sort of sensuous pleasure, but I don't detect fear. There's an ecstatic happiness, but strangely, I don't see anything approaching hate for the attackers. For the British this is a contest. The facial expression is interpreted by an officer. He turns to me and says, 'Plucky blokes, those Japs. That was as beautiful an attack as ever I expect to see.'

Less than an hour later, the Repulse *and the* Prince of Wales *were finished. 'In all the war,' Churchill wrote, 'I never received a more direct shock.' Singapore fell two months later.*

El Alamein: The Afrika Korps Retreat, North Africa, 4 November 1942

GENERAL FRITZ BAYERLEIN, AFRIKA KORPS

The German view of the decisive engagement in the Western Desert.

The battle of El Alamein began at 21.40 on the still, moonlit night of 23 October, with a 1,000-gun British barrage. The Germans had other problems; they were pathetically short of diesel and ammunition, and within a week were reduced to ninety operative tanks. The British had over 800. On 2 November, General Montgomery 'directed two hard punches at the hinges' of the German position – and forced a gap. Hitler forbade retreat on the 3rd. By the following day Rommel could do nothing else.

On the morning of November 4th the remnants of the German Africa Corps, together with the 90th Light Division, held a thin front line on either side of the wide sand dune called Tel el Mampsra: though only some twelve feet high, this dune was a commanding feature. To the south was the equally weakened Italian armoured corps. Towards dawn I reported to General Ritter von Thoma, the commander of the Africa Corps, that I was about to set off for the area south of El Daba, where I was to establish a rear command post. For the first time Thoma was wearing a proper uniform, with his general's insignia, orders and decorations, which hitherto in the desert he had never bothered to put on. He now said to me:

'Bayerlein, Hitler's order [not to withdraw] is a piece of unparalleled madness. I can't go along with this any longer. Go to the El Daba command post. I shall stay here and personally take charge of the defence of Tel el Mampsra.'

I could see that Thoma was utterly disheartened and foresaw no good. His ADC, Lieutenant Hartdegen, remained with the General: he had a wireless transmitter. The General put on his greatcoat and picked up a small canvas bag. I wondered whether the General intended to die. Then I left Tel el Mampsra and drove to the rear.

It was eight o'clock before the British attacked, after approximately one hour's artillery preparation. Their main effort was directed against Tel el Mampsra. By committing all its forces the Africa Corps was able to hold attacks by two hundred British tanks.

At eleven o'clock Lieutenant Hartdegen appeared at my command post and said, 'General von Thoma has sent me back, with the radio transmitter. He doesn't need it any more. All our tanks, anti-tank guns and ack-ack have been destroyed on Tel el Mampsra. I don't know what has happened to the general.'

I immediately climbed into a small armoured reconnaissance car and drove off eastwards. Suddenly a hail of armour-piercing shot was whistling all about me. In the noontime haze I could see countless black monsters far away in front. They were Montgomery's tanks, the 10th Hussars. I jumped out of the armoured car and beneath the burning midday sun ran as fast as I could towards Tel el Mampsra. It was a place of death, of burning tanks and smashed flak guns, without a living soul. But then, about two hundred yards away from the sandhole in which I was lying, I saw a man standing erect beside a burning tank, apparently impervious to the intense fire which criss-crossed about him. It was General von Thoma. The British Shermans which were closing up on Tel el Mampsra had halted in a wide half-circle. What should I do? The General would probably regard it as cowardice on my part were I not to go forward and join him. But to run through the curtain of fire which lay between General von Thoma and myself would have been to court certain death. I thought for moment or two. Then the British tanks began to move forward once again. There was now no fire being put down on Tel el Mampsra. Thoma stood there, rigid and motionless as a pillar of salt, with his canvas bag still in his hand. A Bren carrier was driving straight towards him, with two Shermans just behind. The British soldiers signalled to Thoma. At the same time one hundred and fifty fighting vehicles poured across Tel el Mampsra like a flood.

I ran off westwards as fast as my legs could carry me. My car had vanished. After a while I met a staff car which took me to the command post at El Daba. There I found Rommel. I told him what I had seen. Huge dust clouds were now visible both south-east and south of the command post. The Italian tanks of the 20th Corps were fighting their last, desperate battle with some hundred heavy British tanks that had punched into the Italians' open right flank. After putting up a brave resistance, the Italian corps was annihilated.

The Africa Corps signals officer brought Rommel a decoded message, from the 10th Hussars to Montgomery, which our people had intercepted. It read: 'We have just captured a General named Ritter von Thoma.'

The Field-Marshal took me aside, and said:

'Bayerlein, what we tried with all our might to prevent has now happened. Our front is smashed and the enemy is pouring through into our rear area. There can no longer be any question of obeying Hitler's order. We're withdrawing to the Fuka position so as to save what still can be saved.

. . . 'Bayerlein,' Rommel went on, 'I'm putting you in command of the Afrika Korps. There's no one else to whom I can entrust it. And if it should happen later on that the Führer court-martials us for our disobedience, we'll both have to answer squarely for our decision today. Do your duty as best you can. All your orders to the troops carry my authority. You may say this to the senior commanders, in the event of your having any trouble with them.'

'I shall do my best, sir,' I replied. Then Rommel got into his armoured command vehicle, to visit the other units of his beaten army and to give the orders for the retreat.

With only slight exaggeration, Churchill later commented, 'Before El Alamein we never had a victory, after El Alamein we never had a defeat.'

The Dambusters Destroy the Mohne Dam, Ruhr Valley, 16 May 1943

WING COMMANDER GUY GIBSON RAF

Nineteen Lancaster bombers took part in the celebrated 'bouncing-bomb' raid on the dams of the Ruhr Valley; eight of the Lancasters failed to return. Two dams, the Mohne and Eder, were destroyed, bringing widespread flooding to Germany's industrial heartland.

Down below, the Möhne Lake was silent and black and deep, and I spoke to my crew.

'Well boys, I suppose we had better start the ball rolling.' This with no enthusiasm whatsoever. 'Hello, all Cooler aircraft. I am going to attack. Stand by to come in to attack in your order when I tell you.'

Then to Hoppy: 'Hello, "M Mother". Stand by to take over if anything happens.'

Hoppy's clear and casual voice came back. 'OK, Leader. Good luck.'

Then the boys dispersed to the pre-arranged hiding-spots in the hills, so that they should not be seen either from the ground or from the air, and we began to get into position for our approach. We circled wide and came around down moon, over the high hills at the eastern end of the lake. On straightening up we began to dive towards the flat, ominous water two miles away. Over the front turret was the dam silhouetted against the haze of the Ruhr Valley. We could see the towers. We could see the sluices. We could see everything. Spam, the bomb-aimer, said, 'Good show. This is wizard.' He had been a bit worried, as all bomb-aimers are, in case they cannot see their aiming points, but as we came in over the tall fir trees his voice came up again rather quickly. 'You're going to hit them. You're going to hit those trees.'

'That's all right, Spam. I'm just getting my height.'

To Terry: 'Check height, Terry.'

To Pulford: 'Speed control, Flight-Engineer.'

To Trevor: 'All guns ready, gunners.'

To Spam: 'Coming up, Spam.'

Terry turned on the spotlights and began giving directions – 'Down – down – down. Steady – steady.' We were then exactly sixty feet.

Pulford began working the speed; first he put on a little flap to slow us down, then he opened the throttles to get the air-speed indicator exactly against the red mark. Spam began lining up his sights against the towers. He had turned the fusing switch to the 'ON' position. I began flying.

The gunners had seen us coming. They could see us coming with our spotlights on for over two miles away. Now they opened up and the tracers began swirling towards us; some were even bouncing off the smooth surface of the lake. This was a horrible moment: we were being dragged along at four miles a minute, almost against our will, towards the things we were going to destroy. I think at that moment the boys did not want to go. I know I did not want to go. I thought to myself, 'In another minute we shall all be dead – so what?' I thought again, 'This is terrible – this feeling of fear – if it is fear.' By now we were a few hundred yards away, and I said quickly to Pulford, under my breath, 'Better leave the throttles open now and stand by to pull me out of the seat if I get hit.' As I glanced at him I thought he looked a little glum on hearing this.

The Lancaster was really moving and I began looking through the special sight on my windscreen. Spam had his eyes glued to the bomb-sight in front, his hand on his button; a special mechanism on board had already begun to work so that the mine would drop (we hoped) in the right spot. Terry was still checking the height. Joe and Trev began to raise their guns. The flak could see us quite clearly now. It was not exactly inferno. I have been through far worse flak fire than that; but we were very low. There was something sinister and slightly unnerving about the whole operation. My aircraft was so small and the dam was so large; it was thick and solid, and now it was angry. My aircraft was very small. We skimmed along the surface of the lake, and as we went my gunner was firing into the defences, and the defences were firing back with vigour, their shells whistling past us. For some reason, we were not being hit.

Spam said, 'Left – little more left – steady – steady – steady – coming up.' Of the next few seconds I remember only a series of kaleidoscopic incidents.

The chatter from Joe's front guns pushing out tracers which bounced off the left-hand flak tower.

Pulford crouching beside me.

The smell of burnt cordite.

The cold sweat underneath my oxygen mask.

The tracers flashing past the windows – they all seemed the same colour now – and the inaccuracy of the gun positions near the power-station; they were firing in the wrong direction.

The closeness of the dam wall.

Spam's exultant, 'Mine gone.'

Hutch's red Very lights to blind the flak-gunners.

The speed of the whole thing.

Someone was saying over the RT, 'Good show, leader. Nice work.'

Then it was all over, and at last we were out of range, and there came over us all, I think, an immense feeling of relief and confidence.

Trevor said, 'I will get those bastards,' and he began to spray the dam with bullets until at last he, too, was out of range. As we circled round we could see a great 1,000-feet column of whiteness still hanging in the air where our mine had exploded. We could see with satisfaction that Spam had been good, and it had gone off in the right position. Then, as we came closer, we could see that the explosion of the mine had caused a great disturbance upon the surface of the lake and the water had become broken and furious, as though it were being lashed by a gale.

Guy Gibson was killed in action a year later.

Tenko: An Englishwoman in a Japanese Prison Camp, Kuching, Borneo, 1942–5

AGNES NEWTON KEITH

Our barrack was one big room with a loft above it, and no partitions. Each person occupied about five square feet. If the guard wanted to occupy it with you, there wasn't much you could do except roll over. Not that the guards spent all their time lying down near us; a lot of the time they were drunk in the guardhouse.

Some of it was good clean fun, and boys will be boys. But some-times boys are dirty boys, and one doesn't like being frisked, frolicked, bullied, chased, back-slapped or face-slapped by a young man with a gun. The gun removes the element of light-hearted gaiety from the game.

Because there were buns, rice, and privileges to be had from tolerating and encouraging the guards, and no means with which to discourage them, the fact that they treated us like tarts was sometimes justified. One good argument against collaborating was the fact that the guards had bedbugs.

They were not sadistic, or masochistic; they were not Oriental, or Occidental; they were just a gang of lowdown young hoodlums who had complete power over a hundred people who could not strike back.

Once a week a worn-out officer arrived in a worn-out motorboat, and both made a loud noise coming. He searched the guards, and us, with equal suspicion. Warned by the motor, the guards could just get their trousers on in time to reach the wharf's end and stand at attention. We could just get our forbidden diaries, books, and food hidden in the grass and the latrines. When the officer departed, everybody relaxed.

Life on Berhala was according to the whims of the guards – and they were whimsical. They could be very kind. One guard gave his own buns to the children daily, another distributed loaves of bread to them. They frequently fed us their own surplus, commenting that our food was terrible. Sometimes they let us meet our husbands openly, and sometimes they beat us for smiling at them secretly.

The first guard we had in Berhala made a speech to us after one week, on the eve of their departure. Before making it, they dictated their sentiments to me in broken English and told me to write them out in 'literary' style. The result of our effort was this:

GENTLEMEN, LADIES AND WOMEN: Nipponese soldiers are very kindly. We will pray for your health until we meet again. To-morrow we go back to Sandakan. We are very sorry for you. However, if you get conceited we will knock you down, beat you, kick you, and kill you.

I suggested that the last sentence was a trifle harsh, but they were particularly attached to it.

. . . In Kuching we learned to bow seriously. We had printed instructions, demonstrations and practice. The Nipponese orders for bowing were: Incline the body from the waist to a fifteen-degree angle, with head uncovered, hands at the side, and feet together: remain thus to the count of five (silent); then recover. (If not knocked down.)

The first time we were instructed in bowing in the Kuching camp, we were being trained to present a good appearance for the visiting lieutenant-general for whom we had planted potatoes.

The day came, we were all assembled in ranks, the Sisters in front, the women and children behind, where it was hoped we could do the least harm by our frivolous ways. The order was given to bow. The Sisters had wonderful behinds, the bow made the behinds spring into sudden prominence; by standing too close and bowing too swiftly we managed to meet the behinds with our heads. Confusion and concussion reigned, and order was not restored. The lieutenant-general was hastened away to review the pigs, who had more respect for lieutenant-generals than we did, or else did not understand the meaning of the phrase 'dumb insolence', as we did. We were never again assembled together in one group to bow to a visiting general.

. . . Every change was for the worse. Rules increased, food decreased, work, increased, and strength decreased. Disappointments multiplied, and optimism was never verified. Hope itself seemed only a refuge for those who would not face facts.

Our food ration, then, as supplied by the Japanese per person per day, was as follows: one cupful of thin rice gruel, five tablespoons of cooked rice, sometimes a few greens, a little sugar, sometimes a little salt and tea. This was what the Japanese expected us to live on. Or did they expect us to live on it?

Additions to this diet were sweet-potato tops, which we grew ourselves. We used the tops because we were too hungry to wait for the potatoes to mature. Every square foot of the camp was in use for gardens, but the soil was exhausted, and we were exhausted. The last eight months of imprisonment it was almost impossible for us to do heavy work, but we did it. We arose before sunrise to finish the work inside camp, and then went outside the camp to work for the Japanese. By nine o'clock in the morning we were worn out.

By now soldiers were trading for and buying skinned cats and rats, people were eating snails and worms, all of us were eating weeds and grass, and plenty of us would have liked to eat each other.

Newton Keith and her family survived the war.

D-Day: A British Paratrooper Lands in Normandy, 1 a.m., 6 June 1944

JAMES BYROM, PARACHUTE MEDICAL SERVICE

The Allied invasion of Normandy was the greatest amphibious invasion in history. Some 160,000 troops – British, American, French, Polish and Canadian – embarked in 5,000 craft and sailed from southern England to occupied France. The seaborne invasion was preceded by an airborne assault, with the British 6th Airborne division tasked to protect the eastern flank of the invasion beaches. The first British paratroopers began dropping out of the sky over Normandy early in the morning of D-Day.

A shadow darted from a nearby tree, and I was joined in the open by the huge sten-gunner with the black face. The whites of his eyes gleamed in the moonlight, and for all my weariness I found myself on the verge of giggles.

'You speak the lingo, tosh? All right, then, you go up and knock on the door, and we'll give you coverin' fire. I'll stay 'ere and my mate'll creep round the other side of the yard so's to cover you proper.'

A dog barked at my approach. From the corner of my eye I could see a stealthy figure flit from behind a haystack into the shadow of the barn door. There was no answer to my first knock. The household was obviously fast asleep. I knocked louder, and this time I heard a scurrying on the stairs and a sudden clamour of French voices. Footsteps approached the door, withdrew, hesitated, then approached again. The door opened.

On the way I had been searching for suitable words with which to introduce ourselves – some calming, yet elegant phrase worthy of the French gift of expression and of their infallible flair for the dramatic moment. But at the sight of the motherly, middle-aged peasant the gulf of the years disappeared, and I might have been back in 1939, an English tourist on a walking tour dropping in to ask for a glass of cider and some camembert.

'*Excusez-nous, Madame. Nous sommes des parachutistes anglais faisant partie du Débarquement Allié.*'

There was a moment of scrutiny, then the woman folded me in her arms. The tears streamed down her face, and in between her kisses she was shouting for her husband, for lamps, for wine. In a moment I was carried by the torrent of welcome into the warm, candle-lit kitchen. Bottles of cognac and Calvados appeared on the table, children came clattering down the wooden stairs, and we found ourselves – an evil-looking group of camouflaged cut-throats – surrounded and over-whelmed by the pent-up emotions of four years. The farmer and his wife wanted us to stay and drink, to laugh and cry and shake hands over and over again. They wanted to touch us, to tell us all about the Occupation, and to share with us their implacable hatred of the Boche. It seemed that the moment so long awaited could not be allowed to be spoilt by realities, till every drop of emotion was exhausted. I was nearly as much affected as they were. Warmed by the fiery trickle of Calvados, I rose to this – certainly one of the greatest occasions of my life – so completely that I forgot all about the Drop, all about the marshes and the battery. It was the sight of my companions, bewildered by all this emotion and talk, automatically drinking glass after glass, that suddenly reminded me of what we had come for. I began politely to insist on answers to questions which had already been brushed aside more than once: Where were we? How far away were the nearest Germans? Once more the questions were ignored. '*Ah, mon Dieu, ne nous quittez pas maintenant! Ah, les pauvres malheureux! Ils sont tous mouillés!*'

It was moving and exasperating. At last I managed to get what we wanted – a pocket compass and a promise of escort to the hard road through the marshes to Varaville.

Four years after Dunkirk, the British sailed back to France, touching down at 7.30 a.m. on 6 June on Sword, Gold and Juno beaches.

An Infantryman in Normandy, 6–24 June 1944

SERGEANT G. E. HUGHES, ROYAL HAMPSHIRE REGIMENT

Diary, 6 June 1944
06.00 Get in LCA [Landing Craft Assault]. Sea very rough. Hit the beach at 7.20 hours. Murderous fire, losses high. I was lucky T[hank] God. Cleared three villages. Terrible fighting and ghastly sights.

June 7. Still going. Dug in at 02:00 hrs. Away again at 05.30. NO FOOD. Writing few notes before we go into another village. CO out of action, adjutant killed. P Sgt lost. I do P Sgt['s job]. More later.

June 8. 07.30, fire coming from village. Village cleared. Prisoners taken. Night quite good but German snipers lurking in wood. Had 2 hrs' sleep. Second rest since the 6th.

June 9. 06.30 hrs went on wood clearing. Germans had flown. Only one killed for our morning's work. We are now about 8 to 10 miles inland. Promoted to Sgt.

June 10. Joan darling, I have not had you out of my thoughts. T[hank] God I have come so far. We have lost some good men. Our brigade was only one to gain objectives on D-Day.
  The French people give us a good welcome. Had wine.

June 11. Contact with enemy. Lost three of my platoon. Very lucky T[hank] God. Only had 5 hours sleep in 3 days.

June 12. This day undescrible [sic] mortar fire and wood fighting. Many casualties. T[hank] God I survived another day.

June 13. Just had my first meal since Monday morning. Up all night. Everyone in a terrible state. I keep thinking of u.

June 14. Counter-attack by Jerry from woods. Mortar fire. 13 of my platoon killed or missing. After heavy fighting yesterday CSM also wounded, also Joe. O[fficer] C[ommanding] killed. I am one mass of scratches. Advanced under creeping barrage for 3 miles. Drove Jerry back. It is hell. 3 Tiger tanks came here, up to lines during night.

June 16. [resting] Received letter from home. Wrote to Joan and Mum.

June 17. [resting]

June 18. Day of Hell. Counter-attack.

June 19. Day of Hell. Counter-attack.

June 20. Day of Hell. Advanced. Counter-attacked.

June 21. Quiet day. We have been fighting near Tilley [Tilly]. Bayonet charge. Shelled all day. Letters from home.

June 22. Out on patrol. Got within 35 yards of Tiger before spotting it. Got back safely T[hank] God. Shelled to blazes. Feeling tired out.

June 23. No sleep last night. Exchanged fire, out on patrols all day, went on OP for 4 hours. Stand-to all night. Casualties.
　　Just about had enough.

June 24. Had to go back to CCS [Casualty Clearing Station]. Malaria.

Sergeant Hughes was hospitalized with malaria for most of the rest of the Normandy campaign.

Doodlebugs, 12 June 1944

LIONEL KING

The first German FZG-76 flying bomb ('doodlebug' or 'buzz bomb' to the English) landed on England on 12 June 1944. Another 9,000 followed. King was an eight-year-old schoolboy in 1944.

On the night of 12 June the first of Hitler's V1s fell on London and the South East. News spread in from the Kent and Sussex coasts of aircraft with 'jet nozzles', 'fire exhausts' and odd engine sounds. Over Kent some of these craft had suddenly stopped and fallen with a devastating explosion to follow. Bombing of course was familiar to our family. We had moved from West Ham earlier in the war. I'd spent endless nights in the dugout in the garden unable to sleep because of Nanny's snoring. Now it was happening in the daytime too.

　　The first came over one afternoon. Our windows and doors were open in those fine June days and the drone of the approaching flying bomb was quite unmistakable. It gave us little warning. Ten seconds and the engine cut out directly overhead. There was an oddly resounding explosion about half a mile away.

　　The Boy Foot, as my mother called him, cycled up there and reported back: 'King Edward Road – there's debris everywhere. Fire brigade and wardens are there, still digging 'em out. I saw it coming. I was up on the roof.' I was envious of his roof. You could have seen anything from there.

'Where's King Edward Road, Mum?' asked Doug.

'By the County Ground. It's where Mr Gibbons lives – you know, he's in the Home Guard with Dad.'

Next day we took to the shelter when we heard the drone. Again the engine cut out, again seemingly over the house. Then it spluttered into life again. Doug and I laughed out loud. It was all rather a joke. Mum told us to duck. The droning engine had stopped. Eight second wait. A disappointing, unspectacular bang.

'I'll find out where it dropped when I go up the shops in a minute,' said Mum. 'Don't open the door to any knocks.' Later she told us it had fallen on a railway siding behind the dust destructor. Three old railway trucks were destroyed, a railwayman had told her.

Soon so many V1s were coming over the authorities gave up air-raid warnings. They would have been sounding the siren all the time. When a bomb announced its approach, Doug and I dived for the shelter, not forgetting to grab our cat Jimmy if he was in sight. Sometimes Mum was out shopping and we went to the shelter alone. We were never worried or afraid. It was all over in ten seconds anyway.

One such afternoon a V1 fell further up the road. We jumped out of the shelter and saw a huge mushroom of dust and rubble rising above the rooftops. You could see individual bricks and planks of wood sailing up into the clear sky. It looked after a few seconds like a ragged umbrella. The traffic picked up again in the road. We ran through the house to the front door. Droves of people were rushing up the road, some on bicycles, many in great distress, towards the scene. Many we knew by sight.

'There goes that man from the oil shop,' exclaimed Doug. We'd never seen him this side of the counter before. The dust cloud had settled now. The first ambulances were pulling up at the Rest Centre at the church opposite. Scruffy-looking people, some shaking, were being helped in. Mum appeared. 'Back into the house!' she barked. 'Nanny will be home from work soon. She'll tell you all about it.'

Nanny came in later. The buzz bomb had fallen by her factory. 'Mrs Lea has copped it. It fell on her house in Lea Hall Road. It's in a state round there. When it exploded the foreman told her she could go round and see if her place was all right. I went with her. We went through it two or three minutes after it happened . . .' The incident was not without humour for Doug and me. 'A spotter on Jenkins's roof saw it coming. He just threw himself over the edge. It's eighty feet off the ground.'

Despite Hitler's hi-tech terror weapons, there was to be no escape for Nazi Germany, ground between the Russian steamroller in the East and the Allied offensive in the West. On 3 May 1945 Field Marshal Montgomery received a Wehrmacht delegation at his HQ on Luneberg Heath, Germany:

They were brought to my caravan site and were drawn up under the Union Jack, which was flying proudly in the breeze. I kept them waiting for a few minutes and then came out of my caravan and walked towards them. They all saluted, under the Union Jack. It was a great moment; I knew the Germans had come to surrender and that the war was over.

The instrument of surrender was signed on 7 May 1945.

VE Day, London, 8 May 1945

MOLLIE PANTER-DOWNES

The view of the New Yorker's *correspondent in London.*

When the day finally came, it was like no other day that anyone can remember. It had a flavour of its own, an extemporaneousness which gave it something of the quality of a vast, happy village fete as people wandered about, sat, sang, and slept against a summer background of trees, grass, flowers, and water. It was not, people said, like the 1918 Armistice Day, for at no time was the reaction hysterical. It was not like the Coronation, for the crowds were larger and their gaiety, which held up all through the night, was obviously not picked up in a pub. The day also surprised the prophets who had said that only the young would be resilient enough to celebrate in a big way. Apparently the desire to assist in London's celebration combusted spontaneously in the bosom of every member of every family, from the smallest babies, with their hair done up in red-white-and-blue ribbons, to beaming elderly couples who, utterly without self-consciousness, strolled up and down the streets arm in arm in red-white-and-blue paper hats. Even the dogs wore immense tricoloured bows. Rosettes sprouted from the slabs of pork in the butcher shops, which, like other food stores, were open for a couple of hours in the morning. With their customary practicality, housewives put bread before circuses. They waited in the long bakery queues, the string bags of the common round in one hand and the Union Jack of the glad occasion in the other. Even queues seemed tolerable that morning. The bells had begun to peal and, after the night's storm, London was having that perfect, hot, English summer's day which, one sometimes feels, is to be found only in the imaginations of the lyric poets.

The girls in their thin, bright dresses heightened the impression that the city had been taken over by an enormous family picnic. The number of extraordinarily pretty young girls, who presumably are hidden on working days inside the factories and government offices, was astonishing. They streamed out into the parks and streets like flocks of twittering, gaily plumaged cockney birds. In their freshly curled hair were cornflowers and poppies, and they wore red-white-and-blue ribbons around their narrow waists. Some of them even tied ribbons around their bare ankles. Strolling with their uniformed boys, arms candidly about each other, they provided a constant, gay, simple marginal decoration to the big, solemn moments of the day. The crowds milled back and forth between the Palace, Westminster, Trafalgar Square, and Piccadilly Circus, and when they got tired they simply sat down wherever they happened to be – on the grass, on doorsteps, or on the kerb – and watched the other people or spread handkerchiefs over their faces and took a nap. Everybody appeared determined to see the King and Queen and Mr Churchill at least once, and few could have been disappointed. One small boy, holding on to his father's hand, wanted to see the trench shelters in Green Park too. 'You don't want to see shelters today,' his father said. 'You'll never have to use them again, son.' 'Never?' the child asked doubtfully. 'Never!' the man cried, almost angrily. '*Never!* Understand?' In the open space before the Palace, one of the places where the Prime Minister's speech was to be relayed by loudspeaker at three o'clock, the crowds seemed a little intimidated by the nearness of that symbolic block of grey stone. The people who chose to open their lunch baskets and munch sandwiches there among the flower beds of tulips were rather subdued. Piccadilly Circus attracted the more demonstrative spirits.

By lunchtime, in the Circus, the buses had to slow to a crawl in order to get through the tightly packed, laughing people. A lad in the black beret of the Tank Corps was the first to climb the little pyramidal Angkor Wat of scaffolding and sandbags which was erected early in the war to protect the pedestal of the Eros statue after the figure had been removed to safekeeping. The boy shinnied up to the top and took a tiptoe Eros pose, aiming an imaginary bow, while the crowd roared. He was followed by a paratrooper in a maroon beret, who, after getting up to the top, reached down and hauled up a blonde young woman in a very tight pair of green slacks. When she got to the top, the Tank Corps soldier promptly grabbed her in his arms and, encouraged by ecstatic cheers from the whole Circus, seemed about to enact the classic role of Eros right on the top of the monument. Nothing came of it, because a moment later a couple of GIs joined them and before long the pyramid was covered with boys and girls. They sat jammed together in an affectionate mass, swinging their legs over the sides, wearing each other's uniform caps, and calling down wisecracks to the crowd. 'My God,' someone said, 'think of a flying bomb coming down on this!' When a firecracker went off, a hawker with a tray of tin brooches of Monty's head happily yelled that comforting, sometimes fallacious phrase of the blitz nights, 'All right, mates, it's one of ours!'

All day long, the deadly past was for most people only just under the surface of the beautiful, safe present, so much so that the Government decided against sounding the sirens in a triumphant 'all clear' for fear that the noise would revive too many painful memories. For the same reason, there were no salutes of guns – only the pealing of the bells, and the whistles of tugs on the Thames sounding the doot, doot, doot, dooooot of the 'V', and the roar of the planes, which swooped back and forth over the city, dropping red and green signals toward the blur of smiling, upturned faces.

It was without any doubt Churchill's day. Thousands of King George's subjects wedged themselves in front of the Palace throughout the day, chanting ceaselessly, 'We want the King' and cheering themselves hoarse when he and the Queen and their daughters appeared, but when the crowd saw Churchill there was a deep, full-throated, almost reverent roar. He was at the head of a procession of Members of Parliament, walking back to the House of Commons from the traditional St Margaret's Thanksgiving Service. Instantly, he was surrounded by people – people running, standing on tiptoe, holding up babies so that they could be told later they had seen him, and shouting affectionately the absurd little nurserymaid name, 'Winnie, Winnie!' One of two happily sozzled, very old, and incredibly dirty cockneys who had been engaged in a slow, shuffling dance, like a couple of Shakespearean clowns, bellowed, 'That's 'im, that's 'is little old lovely bald 'ead!' The crowds saw Churchill again later, when he emerged from the Commons and was driven off in the back of a small open car, rosy, smiling, and looking immensely happy. Ernest Bevin, following in another car, got a cheer too. One of the throng, an excited East Ender, in a dress with a bodice concocted of a Union Jack, shouted, 'Gawd, fancy me cheering Bevin, the chap who makes us work!' Herbert Morrison, sitting unobtrusively in a corner of a third car, was hardly recognized, and the other Cabinet Ministers did no better. The crowd had ears, eyes, and throats for no one but Churchill, and for him everyone in it seemed to have the hearing, sight, and lungs of fifty men. His slightly formal official broadcast, which was followed by buglers sounding the 'cease firing' call, did not strike the emotional note that had been expected, but he hit it perfectly in his subsequent informal speech ('My dear friends, this is your victory . . .') from a Whitehall balcony.

A revered leader for war, the Conservative Churchill was not the man for the peace. During the 'People's War', the country had experienced an egalitarianism never known before, where 'fair shares' (ration books, gas masks, identity cards) were the rule, suffering was communal (the Blitz) and the country had pulled together and mixed together in the same boat. Shortly after VE Day Labour refused to continue the wartime coalition. The parties went to the polls in July: the result was a Labour landslide: 393 seats to the Conservatives' 213. Led by the understated Clement Attlee the Labour government installed a Welfare State (crowned by the National Health Service) and nationalized the major industries and institutions – coal, civil aviation, electricity, cable and wireless, railways, even the Bank of England.

A new Jerusalem, but not full-blooded socialism. Private enterprise continued quite happily in Attlee's brave new England, as did private schools, and even the NHS accepted paying beds. The Attlean compromise of welfare-statism and mixed economy proved remarkably effective, or, at least, remarkably enduring. Most Conservatives became adherents. Not until the late 1970s was it seriously challenged. In the meantime, the country groaned under a huge post-war debt and commodity shortages which meant that rationing of petrol, food, clothes and many domestic items remained until 1954. There was no shortage of work, however. Among those seeking employment were colonial subjects from the West Indies.

Passage to England: A Boy Aboard the Empire Windrush, *May–June 1948*

VINCE REID

Vince Reid was thirteen when he accompanied his parents from Jamaica to England on the Windrush; *there had been black people in England for centuries (if you think about it, there were blacks in the Roman army) but the 500 aboard the* Windrush *were the first of the large-scale black immigrations to the country.*

I was thirteen when my parents brought me. My father worked the railway as a labourer, and my mother worked in a match factory. They were church people, those thrifty people. And one of the ways in which you could accumulate large sums of money was something that they called 'pardner'. You put in so much money, and you've had a draw. I think that's how a lot of people were able to get that £28. It was an awful lot of money. And I think a lot of people, because of the opportunities they perceived were going to open up to them, would sell what they had, and, of course, they had 'pardner' schemes, where a lot of people were in churches, you had credit unions, you know, so you'd partner. That's how they got the money. I suppose he thought, well, you know, being a labourer in England couldn't be any worse than being a labourer in Jamaica. In fact, it would be better, because at least you would get more money for doing the work. And that's why they came.

For me it was a massive adventure. I mean, I'd never been outside of Kingston, let alone, you know, this massive journey to England. I had no idea where England was or how long, you know, it would take to get there. I'd never been on a train, I'd never been out of Kingston. And here I was stepping on this huge ship which was going to bring me to this place called England. I was thirteen years old and, I remember, you know, all these people on the ship and the officers on the ship were white and, you know, the crew were white. And it was fairly exciting, because I'd never been anywhere before. And going to undertake this journey I had no idea what's going to happen to me and my parents. As far as I was concerned, I didn't have any idea about how long we're going to be in England or anything like that.

It was single men. I think there might have been a couple of children but, no, they were overwhelmingly adults. In fact, off hand, I can't think of any other person of my age on the boat. I think the next youngest person to me must have been about nineteen. Obviously, some people had been to the UK before and they would talk about England and, you know, people were also looking forward to work, because, of course, in Jamaica there was not a great deal of work for people. So a lot of people were looking forward to coming. There were carpenters coming, people with all kind of different skills who were coming, and were looking forward to, you know, earning money and working and earning money to look after their people back in Jamaica. So there was a kind of general excitement and optimism.

One of the things that I liked on the boat, they had some boxers that came over – like Leftie Flynn, who was a very good fighter, Pal Silver, Brendon Solus – I used to like to watch them box, you know. And that was exciting, because I quite liked the idea of myself being a fighter. But a white guy was bringing them over, called Dale Martin. Dale Martin Promotions. And that was about the most exciting thing on the ship, except when we went to Bermuda. And we disembarked and went in the cinema and we were told we had to sit in a particular place, you know. And, of course, Jamaicans, although you had this kind of hierarchy of colour in Jamaica, this was a new experience, to be told that you couldn't sit where you bought your ticket to sit, you had to sit in a particular place. And, of course, this led to a fight, and we were, you know, told to leave the cinema and sent back to the ship. And, of course, the other thing was people were saying that there's a British warship that was shadowing the *Windrush*, and there was talk that they might blow us out of the water, that they might sink the ship. Because there was some people didn't want black people coming to England. And there was this fear that they might very well sink the ships, so that there was an element of danger. Whether it was real or not I don't know, but that's what people said, that there were certain hostilities and there was this warship that was shadowing the *Windrush*.

When the Windrush *docked at Tilbury on 21 June, the* Daily Express *recorded:*

450 ARRIVE – GET PEP TALK: 'THINGS WILL NOT BE TOO EASY'. Four hundred and fifty Jamaicans crowded the rails of the *Empire Windrush* as she anchored in the Thames last night. They sailed as refugees from their island's unemployment problem, and have

provided a new problem to the Colonial Office and the Ministry of Labour here. Loudspeakers called the 450 work-seekers to a pep talk by Mr Ivor Cummings, a principal officer of the Colonial Office, who welcomed them. They were told: Things will not be too easy.

There were other Imperial 'problems' confronting Attlee's government. With the Indian Independence Act of 1947, Britain began the long retreat from Empire. Pakistan, Burma, Ceylon and the African states followed into freedom until, by the 1960s, only a handful of scattered outposts remained from the Empire on which 'the sun never sets'. Even a veteran imperialist like Churchill accepted decolonization of 500,000,000 'subjects' with good grace, because anything else would have corroded the English belief in liberty and self-government. And, after all, why was the Second World War fought, if not for freedom? Moreover, compared to the bloodbath the French managed in Algeria and the Dutch in Indonesia, Britain removed the 'White Man's Burden' with tact and even local benefit (if democracy is the measure). Few things have become the English quite so well as the leaving of Empire. But, inevitably, a de-Empired Britannia was a smaller, more uncertain figure on the international scene. Increasingly, Britain looked to her 'special relationship' with the anglophone USA. What this meant in practice was that, Labour or Tory, the government played follow-my-American-leader.

The Korean War: Lieutenant Curtis Wins the VC, Imjin River, 22 April 1951

ANTHONY FARRAR-HOCKLEY

At the end of the Second World War, Korea had been divided (along the 38th Parallel) between the Communist North and the US-backed South. After diplomatic spats and the rattling of bayonets – the Cold War was hotting up – Kim Il-sung's Communists invaded the South in June 1950. Sixteen UN nations accorded the South military support, led by the Americans (to the tune of 2 million troops) but also including a substantial British contingent, comprised of National Service conscripts and professionals. On 22 April 1951, the Communists broke through the UN line west of Chungpyong Reservoir, and it was only the stand of the Gloucesters at Imjin River that saved the day.

The dawn breaks. A pale, April sun is rising in the sky. Take any group of trenches here upon these two main hill positions looking north across the river. See, here, the weapon pits in which the defenders stand: unshaven, wind-burned faces streaked with black powder, filthy with sweat and dust from their exertions, look towards their enemy with eyes red from fatigue and sleeplessness; grim faces, yet not too grim that they refuse to smile when someone cracks a joke about the sunrise. Here, round the weapons smeared with burnt cordite, lie the few pathetic remnants of the wounded, since removed: cap comforters; a boot; some cigarettes half-soaked with blood; a photograph of two small girls; two keys; a broken pencil stub. The men lounge quietly in their positions, waiting for the brief respite to end.

'They're coming back, Ted.'

A shot is fired, a scattered burst follows it. The sergeant calls an order to the mortar group. Already they can hear the shouting and see, here and there, the figures moving out from behind cover as their machine-guns pour fire from the newly occupied Castle Site. Bullets fly back and forth; overhead, almost lazily, grenades are being exchanged on either side; man meets man; hand meets hand. This tiny corner of the battle that is raging along the whole front, blazes up and up into extreme heat, reaches a climax and dies away to nothingness – another little lull, another breathing space.

Phil is called to the telephone at this moment; Pat's voice sounds in his ear.

'Phil, at the present rate of casualties we can't hold on unless we get the Castle Site back. Their machine-guns up there completely dominate your platoon and most of Terry's. We shall never stop their advance until we hold that ground again.'

Phil looks over the edge of the trench at the Castle Site, two hundred yards away, as Pat continues talking, giving him the instructions for the counter attack. They talk for a minute or so; there is not much more to be said when an instruction is given to assault with a handful of tired men across open ground. Everyone knows it is vital: everyone knows it is appallingly dangerous. The only details to be fixed are the arrangements for supporting fire; and, though A Company's Gunners are dead, Ronnie will support them from D Company's hill. Behind, the machine-gunners will ensure that they are not engaged from the open eastern flank. Phil gathers his tiny assault party together.

It is time, they rise from the ground and move forward up to the barbed wire that once protected the rear of John's platoon. Already two men are hit and Papworth, the Medical Corporal, is attending to them. They are through the wire safely – safely! – when the machine-gun in the bunker begins to fire. Phil is badly wounded: he drops to the ground. They drag him back through the wire somehow and seek what little cover there is as it creeps across their front. The machine-gun stops, content now it has driven them back; waiting for a better target when they move into the open again.

'It's all right, sir,' says someone to Phil. 'The Medical Corporal's been sent for. He'll be here any minute.'

Phil raises himself from the ground, rests on a friendly shoulder, then climbs by a great effort on to one knee.

'We must take the Castle Site,' he says; and gets up to take it.

The others beg him to wait until his wounds are tended. One man places a hand on his side.

'Just wait until Papworth has seen you, sir –'

But Phil has gone: gone to the wire, gone through the wire, gone towards the bunker. The others come out behind him, their eyes all on him. And suddenly it seems as if, for a few breathless moments, the whole of the remainder of that field of battle is still and silent, watching amazed, the lone figure that runs so painfully forward to the bunker holding the approach to the Castle Site: one tiny figure, throwing grenades, firing a pistol, set to take Castle Hill.

Perhaps he will make it – in spite of his wounds, in spite of the odds – perhaps this act of supreme gallantry may, by its sheer audacity, succeed. But the machine-gun in the bunker fires directly into him: he staggers, falls, is dead instantly; the grenade he threw a second before his death explodes after it in the mouth of the bunker. The machine-gun does not fire on three of Phil's platoon who run forward to pick him up, it does not fire again through the battle: it is destroyed; the muzzle blown away, the crew dead.

Back home, in the new self-contained, insular Britain, the public was shrugging off the grey weariness of the war years. If the new mood had a definite beginning it was the Labour-inspired Festival of Britain, a conscious commemoration of the Great Exhibition of 1851. Harold Nicolson, the veteran diplomat and broadcaster (and husband of the writer and gardener Vita Sackville-West), recorded in his diary:

I go to Waterloo and meet Viti. We then enter the South Bank Exhibition [the central feature of the Festival of Britain]. We are entranced from the first moment. It is rather a bore as we keep getting caught by the King and Queen, but nonetheless we enjoy it uproariously.

It is the most intelligent exhibition I have ever visited. I have never seen people so cheered up or so amused, in spite of a fine drizzle of rain and a Scotch mist.

Things were definitely on the up.

Everest Conquered, Himalayas, 29 May 1953

EDMUND HILLARY

Mount Everest, at 29,028 feet the highest peak in the world, was finally conquered in 1953 by a British team led by Sir John Hunt. Edmund Hillary and Tenzing Norgay made the final assault.

I lay on the little rock ledge panting furiously. Gradually it dawned on me that I was up the step, and I felt a glow of pride and determination that completely subdued my temporary feelings of weakness. For the first time on the whole expedition I really knew I was going to get to the top. 'It will have to be pretty tough to stop us now' was my thought. But I couldn't entirely ignore the feeling of astonishment and wonder that I'd been able to get up such a difficulty at 29,000 feet even with oxygen.

When I was breathing more evenly I stood up and, leaning over the edge, waved to Tenzing to come up. He moved into the crack and I gathered in the rope and took some of his weight. Then he, in turn, commenced to struggle and jam and force his way up until I was able to pull him to safety – gasping for breath. We rested for a moment. Above us the ridge continued on as before – enormous overhanging cornices on the right and steep snow slopes on the left running down to the rock bluffs. But the angle of the snow slopes was easing off. I went on chipping a line of steps, but thought it safe enough for us to move together in order to save time. The ridge rose up in a great series of snakelike undulations which bore away to the right, each one concealing the next. I had no idea where the top was. I'd cut a line of steps around the side of one undulation and another would come into view. We were getting desperately tired now and Tenzing was going very slowly. I'd been cutting steps for almost two hours, and my back and arms were starting to tire. I tried cramponing along the slope without cutting steps, but my feet slipped uncomfortably down the slope. I went on cutting.

We seemed to have been going for a very long time and my confidence was fast evaporating. Bump followed bump with maddening regularity. A patch of shingle barred our way, and I climbed dully up it and started cutting steps around another bump. And then I realized that this was the last bump, for ahead of me the ridge dropped steeply away in a great corniced curve, and out in the distance I could see the pastel shades and fleecy clouds of the highlands of Tibet.

To my right a slender snow ridge climbed up to a snowy dome about forty feet above our heads. But all the way along the ridge the thought had haunted me that the summit might be the crest of a cornice. It was too late to take risks now. I asked Tenzing to belay me strongly, and I started cutting a cautious line of steps up the ridge. Peering from side to side and thrusting with my ice-axe, I tried to discover a possible cornice, but everything seemed solid and firm. I waved Tenzing up to me. A few more whacks of the ice-axe, a few very weary steps, and we were on the summit of Everest.

It was 11.30 a.m. My first sensation was one of relief – relief that the long grind was over; that the summit had been reached before our oxygen supplies had dropped to a critical level; and relief that in the end the mountain had been kind to us in having a pleasantly rounded cone for its summit instead of a fearsome and unapproachable cornice. But mixed with the relief was a vague sense of astonishment that I should have been the lucky one to attain the ambition of so many brave and determined climbers. It seemed difficult at first to grasp that we'd got there. I was too tired and too conscious of the long way down to safety really to feel any great elation. But as the fact of our success thrust itself more clearly into my mind, I felt a quiet glow of satisfaction spread through my body – a satisfaction less vociferous but more powerful than I had ever felt on a mountain top before. I turned and looked at Tenzing. Even beneath his oxygen mask and the icicles hanging from his hair, I could see his infectious grin of sheer delight. I held out my hand, and in silence we shook in good Anglo-Saxon fashion. But this was not enough for Tenzing, and impulsively he threw his arm around my shoulders and we thumped each other on the back in mutual congratulations.

But we had no time to waste! First I must take some photographs and then we'd hurry down. I turned off my oxygen and took the set off my back. I remembered all the warnings I'd had of the possible fatal consequences of this, but for some reason felt quite confident that nothing serious would result. I took my camera out of the pocket of my windproof and clumsily opened it with my thickly gloved hands. I clipped on the lens-hood and ultra-violet filter and then shuffled down the ridge a little so that I could get the summit into my viewfinder. Tenzing had been waiting patiently, but now, at my request, he unfurled the flags wrapped around his ice-axe and, standing on the summit, held them above his head. Clad in all his bulky equipment and with the flags flapping furiously in the wind, he made a dramatic picture, and the thought drifted through my mind that this photograph should be a good one if it came out at all. I didn't worry about getting Tenzing to take a photograph of me – as far as I knew, he had never taken a photograph before and the summit of Everest was hardly the place to show him how.

The news of Hillary and Tenzing's summiting of Everest arrived in London in time for the Coronation of the new queen.

The Coronation of Queen Elizabeth II, 2 June 1953

JOAN REEDER

Elizabeth Windsor was twenty-six when she succeeded to the crown.
Reeder was correspondent for the Daily Mirror.

It was just 10.15. In came the Princess Royal, the Duchess of Gloucester, her two small sons stepping slowly each side of her. The Duchess of Kent, her three children pacing behind her.

Then Princess Margaret, looking like a fairy princess. Queen Elizabeth the Queen Mother, gently regal, and all their colourful, aristocratic retinues.

More music. And a Prince with sculptured features, resplendent in the gold and dark blue of the Royal Navy, a robe of magnificent scarlet velvet over it, moved slowly to his place. Admiral of the Fleet, HRH the Duke of Edinburgh, KG, KT – the husband of the Queen, the father of the King to come, four-year-old Prince Charles.

The 8,000 of us here were standing now. We felt odd, tense. Violins and organ filled the Abbey with sound. Clearly, surely came the wonderful ringing cry of the Queen's Scholars of Westminster: 'Vivat, Regina Elizabetha. Vivat, vivat, vivat.'

And suddenly we didn't want to see her.

★

Not yet. This would be a stranger to us. Not the happy girl we knew, laughing with her children, waving from a car, fishing in waders in a Scottish river. This would be a Queen.

But relentlessly the tremendous procession of might and majesty moved nearer. The great dignitaries of Church, remote, unbending. The Officers of State bearing the Regalia of this day with which to burden and bow the girl we, as a nation, had known as 'Lillibet'.

And then – at last – she came – THE QUEEN.

On her head a diadem of precious stones. . . . From her shoulders a Royal robe of crimson velvet trimmed with ermine, bordered with gold lace, its long and heavy train carried by six Maids of Honour gowned in white and gold.

The Archbishop led her to our sight.

I do not know how our voices came. Yet together, we shouted. '*God Save Queen Elizabeth.*'

She moved to her Chair of Estate, just below her mother and her family. She sat with a book between her hands; the Archbishop administered the Coronation oath:

'*Will you solemnly promise and swear to govern the Peoples of the United Kingdom of Great Britain and Northern Ireland, Canada, Australia, New Zealand, the Union of South Africa, Pakistan and Ceylon, and your Possessions and the other territories to any of them belonging or pertaining, according to their respective laws and customs?*'

And in unwavering voice came her reply: '*I solemnly promise so to do.*'

How was she feeling – that lovely creature in the midst of that small golden field, with the eyes and ears and jumbled thoughts of a nation and a world centred on her? Could she feel anything except as a person in a dream? Was her heart thudding in her ears? Were her hands slightly moist, her lips quivering?

The glory of Handel's music swelled about us. The Lord Great Chamberlain and the Mistress of the Robes went to the Queen, and took from her her crimson robes, her diadem, her jewels.

Her jewelled and patterned gown they covered with a garment of plain linen. They left her unadorned.

Suddenly there she stood, the Elizabeth we knew.

Gowned in simple white, her light brown hair softly curling about her young and serious face, waiting to be taken from us, alone, into the supreme religious moment of this service – to be anointed, blessed, and consecrated.

★

Now this was a church. Now we could pray. It was all we could do. For we wanted to put out our own hands to touch her, to comfort her, to tell her she was not alone. She looked so defenceless.

Her husband, her mother, her sister, watched her move to that ancient highbacked chair. They, too, felt her loneliness. It was upon their faces.

Four Knights of the Garter each grasped a silver staff at the four corners of the canopy of cloth of gold, and moved to hold it over the chair.

None could see her face except the bishops and archbishops.

We could see one face clearly. That of Geoffrey, Archbishop of Canterbury, as he received from the Dean of Westminster the holy oil from the golden Ampulla poured into the Spoon.

We watched him, grave and intent, dip his fingers in the oil, and anoint first the hands of Elizabeth II, then her breast, then her head, and heard him speak the solemn mystery.

'. . . *Be thy head anointed with holy oil: as kings, priests, and prophets were anointed: And as Solomon was anointed king by Zadok the Priest and Nathan the Prophet, so be thou anointed, blessed, and consecrated Queen over the People who the Lord thy God hath given thee to rule and govern . . .*'

All you could say, all you wanted to say, was: 'Please God, help her, and us.'

It was over. The white-clad figure of the girl, looking something like Joan of Arc, knelt, was blessed, and then upon her was fastened like a surplice the white Colobium Sindonis, and over it a golden coat with long sleeves, the Supertunica, and a girdle.

The Sword of State was received and given back by her – she touched the golden spurs.

She held out her small wrists for the Armills to be fastened around them – 'the bracelets of sincerity and wisdom'. She was cloaked entirely in the Robe Royal.

We stood, waiting. The Archbishop had taken the great glittering crown, and placed it on the altar. She, in her golden cloak, sitting hidden in the huge wooden chair, bareheaded, her hands laden, waited, too.

High, high, the crown rose in the Archbishop's hands above her head.

His hands gently lowered. There was a rustling as of a sudden wind stirring scattered leaves. The thousand noblemen and their ladies had lifted their coronets.

The heavy crown – for her life on earth – was upon the head of our Queen. A forest of lilies bloomed high into the air, and gently sank – it was the white arms of the peeresses putting on coronets.

And there was a great sound wrung from the heart of a nation. 'God Save the Queen.'

Two years later, the more prosaic throne of the Conservative Party enjoyed its own smooth succession, from the retiring Churchill to his heir apparent, Anthony Eden. Previously famous for his urbanity and common sense, Eden oversaw Britain's biggest post-war folie de grandeur, *when Egypt's nationalization of the part-British-owned Suez Canal prompted an old political reflex in London (and Paris): the sending in of the troops. Airborne forces landed at Port Said on 5 November 1956, seaborne troops a day later. A military success, Suez was a diplomatic fiasco. Eden, the British Prime Minister, had failed to see that in the new post-war order Britain was one of the 'Big Three' in name only. The United States disliked the Suez adventure – and so ordered Britain home like a naughty schoolboy.*

6 November 1956 was the day that Britain ceased to be a world power. Eden, humiliated and ill, resigned the premiership on 9 January 1957.

The Suez expedition had also met widespread opposition in England, where the 'angry young man' (and woman) immortalized by John Osborne's Look Back in Anger *attended the new universities, listened to skiffle music, and protested for peace.*

Banning the Bomb: Aldermaston March, 4 April 1958

ANONYMOUS

The Campaign for Nuclear Disarmament was founded in 1958. In its early years CND held annual marches from Trafalgar Square to Aldermaston in Berkshire, site of the Atomic Weapons Research Establishment. The first march took place at Easter, 1958.

Some five hundred men, women, and children were spreading out sleeping-bags and thankfully washing their feet in various church halls in Hounslow last night after marching the eleven miles from Trafalgar Square on the first lap of their descent upon Aldermaston. About a thousand more had returned to their homes in London, perhaps to march again to-day. A lamplight meeting in the well-named Treaty Road, Hounslow, had evoked the first really lusty cheers of the day as Mr Michael Foot denounced the recent Defence White Paper as 'the most shameful statement ever made by a British Government'.

It was Mr Foot who had cried from the plinth on Nelson's Column in the morning, as a cold sun played on some four thousand faces: 'This can be the greatest march in English history.' Whatever the march may turn out to be, it had already by then called out a splendid array of English faces, most of them intent on making clear their conviction that nuclear weapons are evil and should be controlled or done away with.

It was a happy crowd, a London holiday crowd, in benign mood – as benign as the weather that favoured it until the afternoon grey chill came down, no more combative than the empty London streets through which the long procession made its way across Trafalgar Square to the Albert Memorial and then to Chiswick and Hounslow, the first stop in the four-day march to the Atomic Energy Authority's weapons establishment at Aldermaston. The nearest thing to an incident was the cheerful booing as a policeman stopped a troop of folk-dancers from entertaining the lunch-time picnickers with an eightsome reel in front of Albert's statue.

The march bore the signs of careful planning. The column with its banners – 'Which is to be banned, the H-bomb or the human race?' – got off on time, and the long snake that slid down Piccadilly, Kensington High Street, and Chiswick High Road, managed with only discreet help from the police, not to obstruct what little traffic there was. Mothers wheeled children in prams, while Mr Kenneth Tynan, cigarette authoritatively held at the ready, towered above his neighbours. Behind came a troop of some fifty cars and coaches, one of them bearing that essential morale builder, the tea-urn. 'We've got 500 mattresses behind there,' said Miss Pat Arrowsmith, a pretty large-eyed girl in a white pea-jacket and carrying a rucksack, the organiser of the whole well-mannered outing.

In the morning, though, the march was supposed to be silent, so as not to break in on religious thoughts. Somewhere in Knightsbridge this proved too much for a gay band of young people from Bermondsey, the boys in bowlers and camouflaged jackets and jeans, the girls in pony-tails and high heels and men's bright shirts hanging over their skirts. They struck up 'Tannenbaum' on a handy trumpet and banjo.

Miss Arrowsmith dropped back and explained about the silence. 'We should be delighted to have any sort of music after lunch, but meanwhile we should be obliged if you would conform with us.' 'Never mind, never mind,' cried one of the elegant ones in bowler hats. 'The music's in our hearts.' They were there, it turned out, as fans of the jazz band which was going to play the march through Kensington and Chiswick.

Mrs Anne Collins, of Gillingham, encumbered with a pack and with her small daughter in a push-chair. 'I've been thinking about this for ten years,' she said, a humble yet fixed light in her eye. 'If I become a grandmother I don't want a bomb to drop on her and her children – I don't want to drop bombs on the Russians, either. I'd rather let the Communists take over.' A trifle falteringly she walked on. The same sentiment came, gently and tentatively from Miss Jean King, a doe-eyed sixth-former from Enfield with a pack on her back, and bubblingly from Mrs Frank Manning, of Barnet, a housewife with a white angora beret on her head, a firm intention of marching all the way in her heart, and a husband and two small children in a car behind. They had all seen some revelation, it seemed – some two years ago. Miss King only on Tuesday. 'Normally I'm very lazy; I stay in and read,' she said apologetically. 'We feel nothing else matters,' proclaimed Mrs Manning, who is secretary of the Barnet Committee for Nuclear Disarmament and was surrounded by three other purposeful women, all of whom had been seen off by their friends that morning from Barnet car-park.

Yet others had a more carefully shaded view of things. A King's College lecturer in geography thought we should merely offer to renounce the bomb and use this as a means of inducing other nations to do so. He was non-violently contradicted in this by the young conscientious objector who squatted next to him at Chiswick, but upheld by a passing group that chanted, 'One, two, three, four, we don't want war; five, six, seven, eight, Negotiate.' 'One, two, three, four, we don't want war,' echoed two urchins up in a tree.

By the time the marchers had left Chiswick they numbered less than two thousand. Above them bobbed the signs of the Campaign for Nuclear Disarmament, a sort of formalised white butterfly which, it appeared, was the semaphore sign for 'ND'. Skiffle groups burst here and there. At Hyde Park Corner a counter-service, held by a Lutheran minister (a former inmate of a Russian prison camp) by the Artillery war memorial, had drawn only some thirty people, and his words never reached the marchers at all. More successful was a passing car driver in Chiswick who leaned out and cried 'Ostriches! Ostriches!'

The idealism and optimism of the Ban the Bombers would soon spill into a larger wind of change sweeping across England: the Swinging Sixties.

Lady Chatterley's Trial, The Old Bailey, November 1960

KENNETH TYNAN

Looking back, the 'permissive' society in England had a definite beginning. Sexual liberation started in November 1960 at the Old Bailey, when a jury decided in favour of Penguin Books, publishers of D. H. Lawrence's supposedly obscene novel, Lady Chatterley's Lover.

Now that the case is over, and Lady Chatterley's adventures are speeding two-hundred-thousand-fold to every outpost of literacy in the country, it seems suddenly unthinkable that the jury could have brought in any other verdict. But it was desperately thinkable right up to three o'clock on Thursday afternoon, as anyone knows who sat through the six days of the trial, and sweated out the dragging hours of the jury's retirement: more than most people, Gerald Gardiner, counsel for the defence knew it, and looked the reverse of optimistic as he prowled up and down like a wounded lion, waiting for those twelve inscrutable citizens to come to their conclusion. How we had all stared at them, seizing on each smile, each sniffle, each sign of inattentiveness as evidence of sympathy or hostility to Lawrence's cause! The lean, middle-aged man at the right-hand end of the back row seemed prematurely grey: did this betoken sensitivity or hyper-sensitivity? And the quietly eccentric behaviour of the woman, upstage right, left many of us baffled; she was given to strange, secret smiles, and would take notes at inexplicable moments.

In front of her sat a younger woman, sedate and pretty, perhaps a teacher; some of us pictured her as the Henry Fonda character whose gentle persistence would finally win over her colleagues, as in *Twelve Angry Men*.

In all our ears there still rang the voice of Mervyn Griffith-Jones, counsel for the prosecution, high-cheek-boned and poker-backed, a veteran of Eton, Trinity Hall (Cambridge), the Coldstream Guards and many previous obscenity cases; a voice passionate only in disdain, but barbed with a rabid belief in convention and discipline: a slow scaly voice, listening to which one almost felt that if Penguin Books were acquitted, the prostitutes would dance in the streets, as they did after Oscar Wilde's conviction.

On Lawrence as a literary artist, the voice (for so I think of Mr Griffith-Jones, since from where I sat only his head was visible) – the voice had done some dedicated homework. 'Is that expert, artistic writing?' it would ask, having cited a passage in which a phrase was several times repeated. The mind's eye saw a man holding up one brick after another and demanding, 'Is that expert, artistic architecture?' The voice marked Lawrence as if he were an examination paper, and its interrogations had much in common with *vivas*.

It exhaled class-consciousness as effortlessly as air. Would the jury wish their servants to read Lawrence's novel? And was it natural for the lady of a great house to 'run off and copulate with her husband's game-keeper?' The voice took on a positively vengeful rasp when cross-examining people who distinguished between sex as Lawrence saw it and sex as a trivial diversion. Wasn't it true that by 'tenderness' the book actually meant tenderness towards the genital organs? (One wondered how else the voice would want them treated.) And could anyone deny that in the 'bouts' of love-making the emphasis was on the 'pleasure and satisfaction' involved? Leisurely and deadly, the voice hounded Connie Chatterley, a traitress to her class in that she not only enjoyed sex, but enjoyed it with a quasi-peasant. *A propos* of a passage in which she removed her nightdress before making love, the voice enquired why this 'striptease' was necessary; one assumed, charitably, that the question had been carelessly phrased.

Throughout the trial, one longed for a witness who might challenge Mr Griffith-Jones in Lionel Trilling's words: 'I see no reason in Morality (or in aesthetic theory) why literature should not have as one of its intentions the arousing of thoughts of lust. It is one of the effects, perhaps one of the functions, of literature to arouse desire, and I can discover no grounds for saying that sexual pleasure should not be among the objects of desire which literature presents to us, along with heroism, virtue, peace, death, food, wisdom, God, etc.'

But nobody made that answer; and we, anxious in the corridors, had all but persuaded ourselves that no jury could withstand the impact of Mr Griffith-Jones when the verdict was returned and Lawrence exonerated.

Looking back, I think I can isolate the crucial incident, the exchange wherein the case was psychologically won. It occurred on the third morning during the testimony of Richard Hoggart, who had called Lawrence's novel 'puritanical'. Mr Hoggart is a short, dark, young Midland teacher of immense scholarship and fierce integrity. From the witness box he uttered a word that we had formerly heard only on the lips of Mr Griffith-Jones: he pointed out how Lawrence had striven to cleanse it from its furtive, contemptuous and expletive connotations, and to use it in the most simple, neutral way: one fucks. There was no reaction of shock anywhere in the court, so calmly was the word pronounced and so literally employed.

'Does it gain anything,' asked Mr Gardiner, counsel for the defence, 'by being printed "f — "?' 'Yes,' said Mr Hoggart, 'it gains a dirty suggestiveness.'

Rising in cross-examination, Mr Griffith-Jones wanted to know what Mr Hoggart meant by 'puritanical', receiving an answer to the effect that a puritan was a man who felt a profound sense of responsibility to his own conscience. Counsel then read out a series of excerpts from the novel. It must have been by chance that he chose the most impressive passages, the most solemnly ecstatic, the ones about 'the primeval roots of true beauty' and 'the sons of men and the daughters of women' but slowly, as he recited them, one realized that he genuinely thought them impure and revolting.

With every defiling inflection he alienated some part of his audience, seemingly unaware that what he had intended for our scorn was moving us in a way he had never foreseen; yet still he continued, bland and derisive, utterly unconscious of his increasing loneliness. Having finished, he triumphantly asked the witness whether a puritan would feel such 'reverence for a man's balls'. 'Indeed, yes,' said Mr Hoggart, almost with compassion.

I remembered his earlier reply to the suggestion that Lady Chatterley's affair with Mellors was due solely to her husband's impotence. '*It is not*,' he said: and in those words we heard, for the first time in the trial, the stubborn, uncompromising voice of the radical English moralist.

Its volume and assurance grew as the cross-examination proceeded; and before long both jury and audience knew that the real battle had at last been joined – between all that Hoggart stood for, and all that Griffith-Jones stood for; between Lawrence's England and Sir Clifford Chatterley's England; between contact and separation; between freedom and control; between love and death.

Curiously enough, one of the main architects of the Swinging Sixties was distinctly 'square'. This was the Conservative Prime Minister Harold Macmillan, whose 'You've never had it so good!' was almost a call to pleasure. It was Macmillan who abolished National Service (giving every male in England two years of extra living) and it was Macmillan who introduced the contraceptive pill in 1961.

Macmillan's hedonistic tolerance brought him few favours; his government was brought low by sexual scandal, the liaison between Tory War Minister John Profumo and prostitute Christine Keeler. Not only did Profumo mislead Parliament about his relationship with Keeler, it transpired that she was also entertaining one Captain Ivanov, a Russian spy. Dogged by the Profumo scandal and ill-health, Macmillan resigned in 1963.

The Beatles in Performance, Cavern Club, Liverpool, 9 November 1961

BRIAN EPSTEIN

A diffident Liverpool record-shop owner, Brian Epstein was the first manager of the Beatles – John Lennon, Paul McCartney, George Harrison and Pete Best (later replaced by Ringo Starr, aka Richard Starkey). The 'Fab Four' were the vanguard of Sixties pop and permissiveness: irreverent, long-haired, drug-fuelled and libidinous.

One interesting feature of the Beatles' entry into my life was that without being conscious of it, I had seen them many times in the store.

I had been bothered a little by the frequent visits of a group of scruffy lads in leather and jeans who hung around the store in the afternoons, chatting to the girls and lounging on the counters listening to records. They were pleasant enough boys, untidy and a little wild and they needed haircuts.

I mentioned to the girls in the shop that I thought the youth of Liverpool might while their afternoons away somewhere else, but they assured me that the boys were well behaved, and amusing and they occasionally bought records. Also, said the girls, they seemed to know good discs from bad.

Though I didn't know it, the four lads were the Beatles, filling in part of the long afternoon between the lunchtime and evening shows in the best cellars.

On October 28 Raymond Jones left the store after I had taken a note of his request. I wrote on a pad: ' "My Bonnie". The Beatles. Check on Monday.'

But before I had had time to check on Monday, two girls came into the store and they too asked for a disc by this curiously-spelled group. And this, contrary to legend, was the sum total of demand for the Beatles' disc at this time in Liverpool. It is untrue that there was a milling fighting crowd around NEMS waiting for the disc to arrive.

That afternoon I telephoned a few of the agents who imported discs, told them what I was looking for and found that no one had heard of the thing, let alone imported it. I might have stopped bothering there and then if I hadn't made it a rigid rule never to turn any customer away.

And I was sure there was something very significant in three queries for one unknown disc in two days.

I talked to contacts in Liverpool and found, what I hadn't realised, that the Beatles were in fact a Liverpool group, that they had just returned from playing in clubs in the seamy, seedy end of Hamburg where they were well known, successful and fairly impoverished. A girl I know said: 'The Beatles? They're the greatest. They're at the Cavern this week' . . . The Cavern. Formerly a jazz club which had been a huge success in the mid-1950s, it was now owned by Raymond McFall, an ex-accountant who was filling some of his jazz programmes with raw 'Made in Liverpool' beat music played, usually, on loudly amplified guitars and drums. The Cavern was a disused warehouse beneath Mathew Street, Liverpool and I remember that I was apprehensive at the thought of having to march in there among a lot of teenagers who were dressed as if they belonged, talking teenage talk and listening to music only they understood. Also, I was not a member.

So I asked a girl to have a word with the Cavern, to say that I would like to pop in on November 9th at lunchtime and to ensure that I wasn't stopped at the door. I have never enjoyed scenes on doors with bouncers and people asking for 'your membership card, sir,' or that sort of thing.

I arrived at the greasy steps leading to the vast cellar and descended gingerly past a surging crowd of beat fans to a desk where a large man sat examining membership cards. He knew my name and he nodded to an opening in the wall which led into the central of the three tunnels which make up the rambling Cavern.

Inside the club it was as black as a deep grave, dank and damp and smelly and I regretted my decision to come. There were some 200 young people there jiving, chatting or eating a 'Cavern lunch' – soup, roll, cokes and things. Over all the speakers were loudly-amplified current hit discs, then mainly American, and I remember considering the possibility of some 'tie' between NEMS and the Cavern in connection with the Top Twenty.

I started to talk to one of the girls. 'Hey,' she hissed. 'The Beatles're going on now.' And there on a platform at the end of the cellar's middle tunnel stood the four boys. Then I eased myself towards the stage, past rapt young faces and jigging bodies and for the first time I saw the Beatles properly.

They were not very tidy and not very clean. But they were tidier and cleaner than anyone else who performed at that lunchtime session or, for that matter, at most of the sessions I later attended. I had never seen anything like the Beatles on any stage. They smoked as they played and they ate and talked and pretended to hit each other. They turned their backs on the audience and shouted at them and laughed at private jokes.

But they gave a captivating and honest show and they had very considerable magnetism. I loved their ad libs and I was fascinated by this, to me, new music with its pounding bass beat and its vast engulfing sound. There was quite clearly an excitement in the otherwise unpleasing dungeon which was quite removed from any of the formal entertainments provided at places like the Liverpool Empire or the London Palladium, though I learned later that the response to the Beatles was falling off a little in Liverpool – they, like me, were becoming bored because they could see no great progress in their lives.

I hadn't appreciated it but I was something of a figure in the Liverpool Pop Scene as a Director of NEMS, and I was surprised when after the Beatles had finished, Bob Wooler, the Cavern Disc jockey, who later became a great friend of mine, announced over the loudspeaker that Mr Epstein of NEMS was in the Cavern and would the kids give me a welcome.

This sort of announcement then, as now, embarrassed me and I was a little diffident when I reached the stage to try to talk to the Beatles about 'My Bonnie'.

George was the first to talk to me. A thin pale lad with a lot of hair and a very pleasant smile. He shook hands and said 'Hello there. What brings Mr Epstein here?' and I explained that I'd had queries about their German disc.

He called the others over – John, Paul and Peter Best – and said 'this man would like to hear our disc.'

Paul looked pleased and went into the tiny band-room next to the stage to get it played. I thought it was good, but nothing very special. I stayed in the Cavern and heard the second half of the programme and found myself liking the Beatles more and more. There was some indefinable charm there. They were extremely amusing and in a rough 'take it or leave way' very attractive.

Never in my life had I thought of managing an artiste or representing one, or being in any way involved in behind the scenes presentation, and I will never know what made me say to this eccentric group of boys that I thought a further meeting might be helpful to them and to me.

But something must have sparked between us, because I arranged a meeting at the Whitechapel store at 4.30 p.m. on December 3rd, 1961, 'just for a chat,' I explained, without mentioning management because nothing as precise as that had yet formed in my mind.

Ronnie Kray Murders George Cornell, 9 March 1966

RONNIE KRAY

At the Blind Beggar Public House, London.

The Kray twins, Ronnie and Reggie, ran a criminal gang in the East End of London. George Cornell was a member of the rival Richardson gang, and had been implicated in the shooting of the Krays' associate, Richard Hart.

Richard Hart had to be avenged. No one could kill a member of the Kray gang and expect to get away with it. The problem was, both of the Richardsons and Mad Frankie Fraser were in custody and likely to remain so. That left Cornell. He would have to be the one to pay the price. And, let's face it, who better? All I had to do was find him. The next night, 9 March, I got the answer. He was drinking in the Blind Beggar.

Typical of the yobbo mentality of the man. Less than twenty-four hours after the Catford killing and here he was, drinking in a pub that was officially on our patch. It was as though he wanted to be killed.

I unpacked my 9mm Mauser automatic. I also got out a shoulder holster. I called Scotch Jack Dickson and told him to bring the car round to my flat and to contact Ian Barrie, the big Scot, and to collect him on the way. As we drove towards the Blind Beggar, I checked that Barrie was carrying a weapon, just in case.

At eight-thirty p.m. precisely we arrived at the pub and quickly looked around to make sure that this was not an ambush. I told Dickson to wait in the car with the engine running, then Ian Barrie and I walked into the Blind Beggar. I could not have felt calmer, and having Ian Barrie alongside me was great. No general ever had a better right-hand man.

It was very quiet and gloomy inside the pub. There was an old bloke sitting by himself in the public bar and three people in the saloon bar: two blokes at a table and George Cornell sitting alone on a stool at the far end of the bar. As we walked in the barmaid was putting on a record. It was the Walker Brothers and it was called 'The Sun Ain't Gonna Shine Any More'. For George Cornell that was certainly true.

As we walked towards him he turned round and a sort of sneer came over his face. 'Well, look who's here,' he said.

I never said anything. I just felt hatred for this sneering man. I took out my gun and held it towards his face. Nothing was said, but his eyes told me that he thought the whole thing was a bluff. I shot him in the forehead. He fell forward on to the bar. There was some blood on the counter. That's all that happened. Nothing more. Despite any other account you may have read of this incident, that was what happened.

It was over very quickly. There was silence. Everyone had disappeared – the barmaid, the old man in the public and the blokes in the saloon bar. It was like a ghost pub. Ian Barrie stood next to me. He had said nothing.

I felt fucking marvellous. I have never felt so good, so bloody alive, before or since. Twenty years on and I can recall every second of the killing of George Cornell. I have replayed it in my mind millions of times.

After a couple of minutes we walked out, got into the car and set off for a pub in the East End run by a friend called Madge. On the way there we could hear the screaming of the police car sirens. When we got to the pub I told a few of my friends what had happened. I also told Reg, who seemed a bit alarmed.

Then we went to a pub at Stoke Newington called the Coach and Horses. There I gave my gun to a trusted friend we used to call the Cat and told him to get rid of it. I suddenly noticed my hands were covered in gunpowder burns, so I scrubbed them in the washroom. I showered and put on fresh clothing – underwear, a suit, a shirt and tie. (We had spare sets of 'emergency' clothes at several places.) All my old clothing was taken away to be burned. Upstairs in a private room I had a few drinks with some of the top members of the firm – Reg, Dickson, Barrie, Ronnie Hart and others. We listened to the radio and heard that a man had been shot dead in the East End. As the news was announced I could feel everyone in the room, including Reg, looking at me with new respect. I had killed a man. I had got my button, as the Yanks say. I was a man to be feared. I was now the Colonel.

England Win the World Cup, Wembley, 30 July 1966

DAVID MILLER

The England team: Banks, Cohen, Charlton, J., Moore, Wilson, Stiles, Charlton, R., Peters, Ball, Hunt, Hurst. The West German team: Tilkowski, Hoettges, Schulz, Weber, Schnellinger, Beckenbauer, Haller, Overath, Seeler, Held, Emmerich.

As the crowd stood in ovation, Greaves looked on wistfully. Injury had cost him his place, and though he recovered, Ramsey had resisted the almost overpowering temptation to change a winning side. This, too, was vindication, his whole aim since 1963 having been to prepare not a team but a squad, so that at any moment he might replace an out of form or injured man without noticeable deterioration in the side. When the time came, the luckless Greaves's omission caused hardly a stir of pessimism.

At the start of the tournament, I had written that if England were to win, it would be with the resolution, physical fitness and cohesion of West Germany in 1954, rather than with the flair of Brazil in the two succeeding competitions. And so it proved, with the added coincidence that it was the Germans themselves, as usual bristling with all these same characteristics in profusion, who were the unlucky and brave victims of England's methodical rather than brilliant football. Before the semi-finals I said that the deciding factor of this World Cup, when all others had cancelled out in the modern proficiency of defensive systems, would be character, and now the character of every England player burned with a flame that warmed all those who saw it. The slightest weakening, mentally or physically, in any position, could have lost this match a hundred times over, but the way in which Ball, undoubtedly the man of the afternoon, Wilson, Stiles, Peters, Bobby Charlton and above all Moore, impelled themselves on, was something one would remember long after the tumult of excitement and the profusion of incidents had faded. Justifiably, Moore was voted the outstanding player of the competition; his sudden, surging return to form on tour beforehand had helped cement the castle at the critical hour.

All assessments of great events should be measured by absolute standards along with the quality of contemporaries, and therefore one had to say that England were not a great team, probably not even at that moment the best team in the world, depending on what you mean by best.

What matters is that they were the best there at Wembley in July, on that sunny, showery afternoon, best when the chips were down in open combat, and that, after all, is what counts – the result, rather than its manner, goes into the record books. Besides, Ramsey had not set about producing the most entertaining but the most successful team. Could he afford to be the one romantic in a world of hard-headed, win-at-all-costs efficiency? Could he favour conventional wingers who promised much and produced little? A manager is ultimately only as good as the players at his disposal; handicapped by a shortage of world class, instinctive players of the calibre of the South Americans, Italians, Hungarians, or his own Bobby Charlton, and by an over-abundance of average competence, Ramsey had slowly eliminated all those who lacked what he needed for cohesion. What greater demonstration of unity of purpose could there have been than the insistence of the winners, for all the emotion of the moment, that the eleven reserves join them on the lap of honour, and after share equally the £22,000 bonus.

Some complained England were helped by playing all their matches at Wembley, yet certainly in that mood and form they could and would have won anywhere in the country. Besides, under Ramsey, England had had more success abroad than ever before. If nothing else, this World Cup, penetrating almost every home in the land, should have persuaded the doubters, the detractors and the cynics that this is the greatest spectator sport there is, and the Final was a fitting climax.

At the start England asserted themselves – Bobby Charlton exerting a telling influence in midfield, even though closely watched by Beckenbauer sent Peters streaming through with fine anticipation, into spaces behind the German midfield trio. Suddenly, however, in the thirteenth minute, England found themselves a goal down for the first time in the competition. It was not an error under pressure, it was unforced. As a centre from the left came over, Wilson stood alone, eyes riveted on the dropping ball. He made to head it down to Moore, but his judgement betrayed him, sending it instead straight to Haller, who whipped in a low skidding shot past an unsighted, helpless Banks.

The strapping Germans and their flag-waving supporters bounced with joy, but within six minutes England were level. Midway inside the German half, on the left, Overath tripped Moore, and even before the referee had finished wagging his finger at Overath, Moore had spotted a gaping hole in the German rearguard. He placed the ball and took the kick almost in one move, a dipping floater that carried thirty-five yards and was met by Hurst, streaking in from the right, with another graceful, expertly-timed header like that which beat Argentina.

The pattern swung once more in the ten minutes before half-time. The three German strikers, nosing in and out like carnivorous fish, began to create havoc that was only averted after extreme anxiety. In between, Hunt, from a glorious pass by Bobby Charlton, hammered a thundering shot, a difficult one running away to his left, straight at Tilkowski. On the stroke of half-time, it was England who were desperately lucky, when a fast dipper by Seeler was tipped over by Banks, arched in mid-air like a stalling buzzard.

Little happened for nearly twenty-five minutes after half-time, the lull punctuated only by 'Oh, oh, what a referee,' as Mr Dienst went fussily about his business. Then, with twenty minutes to go, England's rhythm began to build up again, Bobby Charlton, Ball and Peters stretching the Germans to the extreme of their physical endurance with passes that again and again almost saw Hurst and Hunt clear. With eleven minutes to go, Ball won a corner, put it across, the ball was headed out, and hit back first-time by Hurst. It struck a defender, fell free, and Peters swooped to lash it home.

England, sensing victory, played it slow, slow, but Hunt wasted a priceless chance when it was three red England shirts to one white German on the edge of the penalty area, by misjudging his pass. With a minute left, all was disaster as Jack Charlton was most harshly penalized for 'climbing' over the top of Held. Emmerich blasted the free kick. A German in the penalty area unquestionably pulled the ball down with his hand, and after a tremendous scramble, Weber squeezed the ball home to level the match.

You could see England's spirits sink as the teams changed over for extra time but, quickly calmed and reassured by the emotionless Ramsey, they rallied themselves instantly. Ball, still unbelievably dynamic, going like the wind right to the finish, had a shot tipped over, Bobby Charlton hit a post and with twelve minutes gone, England were once more in front as Stiles slipped the ball up the wing to Ball, whose cross was thumped hard by Hurst. The ball hit the bar, bounced down and came out, and after consultation with the Russian linesman, Bakhramov, a goal was given. I had my doubts, doubled after later seeing television, but that surely had to be the winner, for now, socks rolled down, both teams were physically in distress. Again England sought economy with gentle passes, keeping precious possession, wearing the Germans down yet further. Poor Wilson hardly knew where he was after a blow on the head. Slowly the minutes ticked away, agonizingly, until with the referee looking at his watch, Hurst staggered on alone from yet one more of Moore's perceptive passes, to hit the ball into the roof of the net with what little strength he had left, and make England's victory, like their football, solid and respectable.

Grosvenor Square, 17 March 1968

DICK POUNTAIN AND MICK FARREN

It wasn't quite Paris or Berkeley, but the Vietnam Solidarity Committee demonstration in London's Grosvenor Square – site of the US Embassy – was the height of '68 student protest in England.

Mick Farren was the leather-trousered lead singer with the cult Sixties band, Social Deviants, and journalist for the radical new sheet, IT (International Times). Dick Pountain was a member of the International Situationists, political agitators of the Absurd.

DICK POUNTAIN: The first one [Grosvenor Square demonstration], in March, turned into a real free-for-all afterwards – running down Park Lane, trashing cars and bank windows, very very heavy. We, the Situationists, actually had a presence on the march and made this huge banner that said 'Storm the Reality Studio and Retake the Universe'. Yellow letters on blue ... it was very professionally done. We joined the march amidst all these Trots, all chanting 'Ho, Ho, Ho Chi Minh!' and we were chanting 'Hot chocolate, drinking chocolate!' and getting lots and lots of aggravation from all the Trots around us. And as we went past Hyde Park Corner this figure clad in black leather from head to foot came out of the crowd and joined us and it was Micky Farren and it was the first time I ever spoke to him.

MICK FARREN: Saturday night, we'd been playing somewhere like Mother's Club in Birmingham and we were coming back down the M1 and ran into these humungous police roadblocks and they pulled out all our equipment. We said, 'What the fuck do you want?' and they said, 'We're looking for weapons.' And we get back to London and me and Sandy plan to go to the riot the next day. So we got up about lunch-time, two o'clock as was our wont, and got our shit together. Nobody else could be bothered to go because they were still asleep. We went downstairs and there were maybe 50 motorcycle cops at the top of Endell Street and buses full of these geezers who look like they feed on vodka and raw meat and don't get let out except on riots. I thought, 'Mother-fucker! what's goin on here?' There weren't exactly tanks on the boulevards but . . . shit, it was like Chile or something. So we went marching up to Centrepoint where we ran into Miles and we hooked up with the march somewhere by Tottenham Court Road and Oxford Street.

We were marching along and there were reports that Mick Jagger had been seen and this was happening and that was happening and it was all very sort of aggressive. There were all sorts of Germans who were a real nuisance because they kept linking arms and getting into that run that the Japanese had invented. We didn't really want to go that fast – we'd just got up and we didn't feel too good and we didn't need a lot of mad Krauts doing the Japanese run, very disruptive, like Zulu impis getting wound up, and they kept doing these flurries of running on the spot which got people very excited to the point that somebody tried to nose his car out of somewhere like Berwick Street through the crowd and Miles kicked in his headlamps! I thought, 'Jesus!' Me and Sandy were coming down off speed and we weren't as rambunctious as a lot of people around us. We had just meandered along.

So we got to South Audley Street and started streaming down there and everything halts and nobody knows what's going on and there's all these rumours that they're tear-gassing people here and there (in fact they weren't). We hadn't seen the US Embassy yet, although there was another rumour that there were armed marines who'd kill you if you actually got inside. Then everything started to move and we went charging down Audley Street and it seemed like the police had given way, that's what everybody assumed. We arrived on the grass in Grosvenor Square, where, although I didn't know it at the time, we had immediately been surrounded. So there we have these thousands of people boxed in on the grass, though it's not that crowded, there's room to stroll around, except down the end by the Embassy where it's so crowded you can't see anything. And we just started wandering about and I remarked to Sandy, 'It's like a fucking love-in.' Then there was a thunder of hooves and there we were in the middle of the charge of the Light Brigade, which was fucking scary. What little I knew, basically from Napoleonic history, was get under a tree, because it's very hard to swing one of those truncheons when you're on a horse and the other guy is under a tree. So the first charge goes through and they're sort of whacking people and one geezer on a white horse, who became quite notorious, whacked this girl on the head – at which point everybody became exceedingly annoyed and dragged him off his horse and kicked him. He got away a couple of times but then he was surrounded and when everyone closed ranks he was just left there. And then people were hurling bits of turf and rocks and stuff and then they'd retreat and charge again and retreat and charge and people were getting hit and hurt and injured and then we went home. Just like that. And watched it on TV.

The Grosvenor Square protests were reflections of a malaise growing under the superficial satisfactions of Sixties England. Inflation was beginning to rise; so was unemployment. The incoming 1970 Conservative government of Edward Heath grabbed at one financial fix after another, to no avail. Faced with declining living standards, the trade unions replied with muscle-power. And the miners had the biggest biceps of the lot. National miners' strikes were called in 1972 and 1974. Heath responded with an election on the theme of 'Who runs Britain?' Not Edward Richard George Heath of Sidcup, it turned out. The electorate narrowly returned a Labour government under Harold Wilson, who snake-charmed the unions with a deal ('the social contract') whereby they moderated their wage demands in return for vague promises to do something about their grievances. Despite Wilson's hypnosis of the unions, inflation and unemployment continued at historically high levels. Outsiders spoke of the UK as the new 'sick man of Europe'. Inside England the era's nihilism was perfectly lyricized, if screechingly sung, by the harbingers of punk rock:
'No future/No future/There's no future for you.'

*Never Mind the B******S: The Sex Pistols,*
November 1975–April 1976

JOHN LYDON AND PAUL COOK

It is a matter of dispute whether the Sex Pistols were manufactured – or not – by svengali Malcolm McLaren as a means of publicizing Sex, the clothes shop he ran with designer Vivienne Westwood. John Lydon is the given name of Johnny Rotten. Paul Cook was the drummer in the band.

PAUL COOK: Glen Matlock attended St Martin's College, and he set up our first gig there in November of 1975. We rehearsed across the road and wheeled all the equipment down Charing Cross Road about six in the afternoon. We set up and played for twenty minutes. Total chaos. None of us knew what we were doing. We were very nervous and all over the place. We played cover versions like 'No Lip', 'Satellite', 'Substitute', 'Seventeen', 'What'cha Gonna Do About It'. We were all still learning our trade.

JOHN LYDON: There was not one single hand clap.

COOK: People yelled at us to get off because they wanted their Bazooka Joe. We nearly had a fight with them. They thought we were an oddity because of our attitudes.

LYDON: The college audience had never seen anything like it. They couldn't connect with where we were coming from because our stance was so anti-pop, so anti-everything that had gone on before. Adam may look back on it all rather sweetly by saying he split up his band after seeing us play, but the reality was that he was very bitter and annoyed with us – as indeed most bands were that played with us. Adam Ant's band was furiously jealous because they spent so much time sewing up those silly silver jackets.

COOK: We weren't being nice. That was the main difference between us and them.

LYDON: I didn't care. We didn't do it to be loved.

COOK: That was outrageous for 1975. You have to understand what it was like at the time. Everything was so conventional –

LYDON: So English. Nobody wanted to offend anybody, and everybody was bemoaning their sorry lot, but never doing anything about it. If you stood up to express an opinion, that would be offending someone, and therefore that wouldn't be British, a terrible thing to have to fight

England: The Autobiography

against. Quite frankly, looking at Britain right now, that's what it's all reverted to. Everybody wants to be nice again.

COOK: We used to turn up at college gigs opening up for hippie bands. We weren't booked at a lot of those gigs because they wouldn't have us on. We would play unannounced at places like Central School of Art and Design in Holborn. Holborn was arranged by Glen's friend, Al MacDonald. Then there was Finchley, Queen Elizabeth College, Chelsea School of Art, Chislehurst Raven, St Albans, Aldgate, and Kensington. These were just learning gigs around Christmastime of 1975. The strange thing was that people latched on to us straight away. We got a reaction wherever we went; a lot of it was positive.

LYDON: We were terrified doing these gigs because of the fear of it all being totally new. It worked a lot better this way than if we would have spent six months to a year learning our craft in a studio, then coming out and just being musos. We had to learn our skills from a live perspective. It wouldn't have worked any other way. That's what was wrong with most of those bands then – and still is. They were too much into the perfection of it all.

COOK: There were a lot of gigs where once we started playing, they just wanted to get us off.

LYDON: Usually for an opening act, the worse they are, the better it was for the headliner. In our case, as bad as we were, it was too fucking good by far. We had something none of these people had – energy and sheer, brazen honesty. We couldn't give a fuck what people thought because we felt what we were saying was much more relevant. And that sometimes became a threat. We showed up at a couple of Andrew Logan's parties. We had done a gig there some months before. The second time I turned up was to a party I wasn't invited to. Malcolm rang me up at my old man's to invite me while I was in the pub across the street. When I got to the party, Malcolm had since decided it was a bad idea inviting me because Vivienne decided she didn't want me there. I didn't know what it was all about, but they wouldn't let me in. I was considered too uncouth, so I kicked up a huge stink. Something was going on between Malcolm and Vivienne. They thought my image should be one of mystery. That was fucking shit: Malcolm rang me up, got me there, and then I was told that I wouldn't be let in. He wouldn't even come to the door.

COOK: The Marquee Club gig in February of 1976 with Eddie and the Hot Rods was a lot of nervous energy. They thought it would be a good idea to put the Pistols on the bill because they thought we had something in common.

LYDON: From what I could gather, Eddie and the Hot Rods were show-casing for a record company that night. They knew we had a reputation, and they wanted us there. 'Sure you can use our monitors.' Since we never had our own stage monitors, we had to rely on others for their equipment, and if they bugger you about, that's the end for you. If you can't hear what you're doing, you're fucked. But when it came to the actual gig, somehow the monitors were turned off. I call that industrial sabotage or a major mistake and didn't take kindly to it. That's when things started to go sadly wrong for Eddie and the Hot Rods. I put a mike stand through one of their monitors.

COOK: Bands like Eddie and the Hot Rods thought there was going to be some great movement, so they wanted everyone to huddle together into this cozy little alliance. Being totally selfish, we weren't into that at all. It was all the other bands that had this idea of a great big movement together.

LYDON: Eddie and the Hot Rods to me was everything that was wrong with live music. Instead of fighting all this big stadium nonsense, they would narrow themselves into this tiny clique by playing in pubs. It was all about denim and plaid shirts, tatty jeans and long droopy hair. Looking awful and like nothing . . . looking like Nirvana! That was the look then. It really annoys me now fifteen or so years later when these bands say they were influenced by the Sex Pistols. They clearly can't be. They missed the point somewhere. You don't wear the tattered uniform of blandness – not if you're interested in the Pistols at all. It's all about being yourself! Be a fucking individual. As a band, the Sex Pistols were all completely different as people – the way we dressed, everything. We didn't give up our individuality just to be a Sex Pistol. That's what made the Pistols, that difference.

The Pistols' iconoclastic 'God Save Queen' ('It's a fascist regime/She's a moron/ A potential H-bomb') topped the record charts in 1977 but was kept at No. 2 by the BBC, so that the Corporation avoided embarrassing Elizabeth II in her Silver Jubilee Year. Or so conspiracy theory has it.

There was no Anarchy in the UK (like nearly every other cultural protest, punk rock became gathered to the bosom of the established order: to be a staple image on tourist postcards in this case), but there were still strawberries and cream for tea at Wimbledon.

Wade Wins Wimbledon, 1 July 1977

FRANK KEATING

Virginia Wade is the Wimbledon champion at last – and it didn't matter one jot that it was one of the worst finals in memory. The day will be long recalled for the ecstatic scenes at the very end when the Queen gave her the trophy and even starchy All England men and matrons relaxed upper lips and thunderously let go with 'For she's a jolly good fellow'. Whether the anthem was addressed to the Queen or Miss Wade they cared not a fig. And nor did England.

But, by jove, Miss Wade made the nation sweat as ever. She has been trying to win the thing for 16 years now and it was not until well into the afternoon that nails stopped being bitten. She beat the mountainous Dutch girl, Betty Stove, 4–6, 6–3, 6–1.

Miss Wade's first year at Wimbledon was in 1962 and coincided with the Queen's first visit. Afterwards Virginia said it had been so joyously noisy that she had not heard all the Queen had said to her at the end. 'It didn't matter, it was just great to see her lips moving.'

Rampant patriotism apart, it must be said that it was an awfully dank, dull match full of terrible unforced bloomers by both girls. The Queen's long-known aversion to lawn tennis cannot have been changed. Indeed she had pulled on her white gloves, was straightening her skirt, glancing at the clock and looking to get away to the tea-time racing results mid-way through the third set.

From the start both players were as nervous as field mice at harvesting, the Dutch girl seemingly the less so, for she won the first set – at the end of which you could probably hear the silence a mile away. It looked as if we were in for the biggest anti-climax since the *Titanic* similarly came across something large and unexpected all those years ago.

It was 3–3 in the second set before the despairing, muttered prayers of 14,000 people got through to their girl in the cathedral. It worked! Virginia reeled off seven games on the trot to take the second set and squat, unassailable, on a 4–0 lead in the last.

The power of prayer! Miss Wade's father, a retired archdeacon, also did his stuff. 'Yes,' he admitted before the match, 'I did pray for Virginia this morning.' Though he added after some meditative thought: 'But then I always pray for everyone each morning.'

During the 'winter of discontent' of 1978/9, the Labour contract with the unions broke down in acrimony, and an epidemic of public service strikes saw rubbish uncollected and graves undug. Inflation was edging towards 20 per cent. Labour wasn't working. The electorate agreed, and the Conservatives won the 1979 election.

Margaret Thatcher Becomes Prime Minister, 4 May 1979

MARGARET THATCHER

Margaret Hilda Thatcher, born 1925, was elected leader of the Conservative Party in 1975, the first woman party leader in British politics.

We knew we had won by the early hours of Friday 4 May, but it was not until the afternoon that we gained the clear majority of seats we needed – 44 as it eventually turned out. The Conservative Party would form the next government.

There were many friends with me as we waited for the results to come in during those long hours in Conservative Central Office. But I can remember an odd sense of loneliness as well as anticipation when I received the telephone call which summoned me to the Palace. I was anxious about getting the details of procedure and protocol right; it is extraordinary how on really important occasions one's mind often focuses on what in the cold light of day seem to be mere trivia. But I was haunted by tales of embarrassing episodes as one prime minister left and his successor entered office: Ted Heath's departure from No. 10 was a case in point. I now could not help feeling sorry for James Callaghan, who just a little earlier had conceded victory in a short speech, both dignified and generous. Whatever our past and indeed future disagreements, I believed him to be a patriot with the interests of Britain at heart, whose worst tribulations had been inflicted by his own party.

At about 2.45 p.m. the call came. I walked out of Central Office through a crowd of supporters and into the waiting car, which drove Denis and me to the Palace on my last journey as Leader of the Opposition.

The Audience at which one receives the Queen's authority to form a government comes to most prime ministers only once in a lifetime. The authority is unbroken when a sitting prime minister wins an election, and so it never had to be renewed throughout the years I was in office. All audiences with the Queen take place in strict confidence – a confidentiality which is vital to the working of both government and constitution. I was to have such audiences with Her Majesty once a week, usually on a Tuesday, when she was in London and sometimes elsewhere when the royal family were at Windsor or Balmoral.

Perhaps it is permissible to make just two points about these meetings. Anyone who imagines that they are a mere formality or confined to social niceties is quite wrong; they are quietly businesslike and Her Majesty brings to bear a formidable grasp of current issues and breadth of experience. And, although the press could not resist the temptation to suggest disputes between the Palace and Downing Street, especially on Commonwealth affairs, I always found the Queen's attitude towards the work of the government absolutely correct.

Of course, under the circumstances, stories of clashes between 'two powerful women' were just too good not to make up. In general, more nonsense was written about the so-called 'feminine factor' during my time in office than about almost anything else. I was always asked how it felt to be a woman prime minister. I would reply: 'I don't know: I've never experienced the alternative.'

After the audience, Sir Philip Moore, the Queen's Secretary, took me to his office down what are called 'the Prime Minister's stairs'. I found my new principal private secretary, Ken Stowe, waiting there, ready to accompany me to Downing Street. Ken had come to the Palace with the outgoing prime minister, James Callaghan, barely an hour before. The civil service already knew a good deal about our policies because they carefully scrutinize an Opposition's manifesto with a view to the hasty preparation of a new administration's legislative programme. Of course, as I quickly learnt, some senior civil servants would need more than a conscientious reading of our manifesto and a few speeches truly to grasp the changes we firmly intended to make. Also, it takes time to build up relationships with staff which reach beyond the formal level of respect to trust and confidence. But the sheer professionalism of the British civil service, which allows governments to come and go with a minimum of dislocation and a maximum of efficiency, is something other countries with different systems have every cause to envy.

Denis and I left Buckingham Palace in the prime ministerial car: my previous car had already gone to Mr Callaghan. As we drove out through the Palace gates, Denis noticed that this time the Guards saluted me. In those innocent days before security had to become so much tighter for fear of terrorism, crowds of well-wishers, sightseers, press and camera crews were waiting for us in Downing Street itself. The crowds extended all the way up Downing Street and out into Whitehall. Denis and I got out of the car and walked towards them. This gave me the opportunity to run through in my mind what I would say outside No. 10.

When we turned to the cameras and reporters, the cheers were so deafening that no one in the street could hear what I was saying. Fortunately, the microphones thrust in front of me picked it up and carried it over the radio and television.

I quoted a famous prayer attributed to St Francis of Assisi, beginning, 'where there is discord, may we bring harmony.' Afterwards a good deal of sarcasm was expended on this choice, but the rest of the quotation is often forgotten. St Francis prayed for more than peace; the prayer goes on: 'Where there is error, may we bring truth. Where there is doubt, may we bring faith. And where there is despair, may we bring hope.' The forces of error, doubt and despair were so firmly entrenched in British society, as the 'winter of discontent' had just powerfully illustrated, that overcoming them would not be possible without some measure of discord.

It was Margaret Thatcher who broke the political consensus forged by Clement Attlee back in 1945. She resolutely moved the Conservative Party rightwards – to nakedly embrace free-market economics and the shedding of the public sector through privatization. Thatcherism, in a word. There would be plenty of discord, but more than once Margaret Thatcher's standing would benefit from the feel-good factor generated by British troops in victorious action.

The SAS Relieve the Siege at Prince's Gate, London, 5 May 1980

ANONYMOUS SAS TROOPER

The Iranian Embassy and its staff were seized by terrorists on 30 April 1980. Five days later, when Iran refused their demand for the liberation of Khuzestan, the gunmen commenced shooting their hostages. A waiting unit of the 22nd Special Air Service Regiment was ordered to storm the Embassy building.

We took up a position behind a low wall as the demolition call sign ran forward and placed the explosive charge on the Embassy french windows. It was then that we saw the abseiler swinging in the flames on the first floor. It was all noise, confusion, bursts of submachine-gun fire. I could hear women screaming. Christ! It's all going wrong, I thought. There's no way we can blow that charge without injuring the abseiler. Instant change of plans. The sledge-man ran forward and lifted the sledge-hammer. One blow, just above the lock, was sufficient to open the door. They say luck shines on the brave. We were certainly lucky. If that door had been bolted or barricaded, we would have had big problems.

'Go. Go. Go. Get in at the rear.' The voice was screaming in my ear. The eight call signs rose to their feet as one and then we were sweeping in through the splintered door. All feelings of doubt and fear had now disappeared. I was blasted. The adrenalin was bursting through my bloodstream. Fearsome! I got a fearsome rush, the best one of my life. I had the heavy body armour on, with high-velocity plates front and back. During training it weighs a ton. Now it felt like a T-shirt. Search and destroy! We were in the library. There were thousands of books. As I adjusted my eyes to the half-light – made worse by the condensation on my respirator eyepieces – the thought occurred to me that if we had blown that explosive charge we might have set fire to the books. Then we would really have had big problems: the whole Embassy would have been ablaze in seconds.

The adrenalin was making me feel confident, elated. My mind was crystal clear as we swept on through the library and headed for our first objective. I reached the head of the cellar stairs first, and was quickly joined by Sek and two of the call signs. The entry to the stairs was blocked by two sets of step-ladders. I searched desperately with my eyes for any signs of booby-traps. There wasn't time for a thorough check. We had to risk it. We braced ourselves and wrenched the ladders out of the way.

Mercifully there was no explosion. The stairs were now cleared and we disappeared into the gloom of the basement. I fished a stun grenade out of my waistcoat and pulled the pin. Audio Armageddon, I thought as I tossed the grenade down into the darkness. We descended the stairs, squinting into the blinding flashes for any unexpected movement, any sign of the enemy, and then we were into the corridor at the bottom. We had no sledge, no Remington with us, so we had to drill the locks with 9-milly, booting the doors in, clearing the rooms methodically as we went along. Minutes turned into seconds; it was the fastest room clearance I'd ever done.

It was when I entered the last room that I saw the dark shape crouched in the corner. Christ! This is it, I thought. We've hit the jackpot. We've found a terrorist. I jabbed my MP5 into the fire position and let off a burst of twenty rounds. There was a clang as the crouched figure crumpled and rolled over. It was a dustbin!

Nothing, not a thing. The cellars were clear. I was now conscious of the sweat. It was stinging my eyes, and the rubber on the inside of the respirator was slimy. My mouth was dry and I could feel the blood pulsing through my temples. And then we were off again, no time to stop now, up the cellar stairs and into the Embassy reception area. As we advanced across the hallway, there was smoke, confusion, a tremendous clamour of noise coming from above us. The rest of the lads, having stormed over the balcony at the front and blasted their way into the first floor of the building with a well-placed explosive charge, were now systematically cleaving the upper rooms, assisted by a winning combination of the stunning effect of the initial explosion, the choking fumes of CS gas, the chilling execution of well-practised manoeuvres and the sheer terror induced by their sinister, black-hooded appearance. We were intoxicated by the situation. Nothing could stop us now.

Through the gloom I could see the masked figures of the other team members forming into a line on the main staircase. My radio earpiece crackled into life. 'The hostages are coming. Feed them out through the back. I repeat, out through the back.'

I joined a line with Sek. We were six or seven steps up from the hallway. There were more explosions. The hysterical voices of the women swept over us. Then the first hostages were passed down the line. I had my MP5 on a sling around my neck. My pistol was in its holster. My hands were free to help the hostages, to steady them, to reassure them, to point them in the right direction. They looked shocked and disorientated. Their eyes were streaming with CS gas. They stumbled down the stairs looking frightened and dishevelled. One woman had her blouse ripped and her breasts exposed. I lost count at fifteen and still they were coming, stumbling, confused, heading towards the library and freedom.

'This one's a terrorist!' The high-pitched yell cut through the atmosphere on the stairs like a screaming jet, adding to the confusion of the moment. A dark face ringed by an Afro-style haircut came into view; then the body, clothed in a green combat jacket, bent double, crouched in an unnatural pose, running the gauntlet of black-hooded figures. He was punched and kicked as he made his descent of the stairs. He was running afraid. He knew he was close to death.

He drew level with me. Then I saw it – a Russian fragmentation grenade. I could see the detonator cap protruding from his hand. I moved my hands to the MP5 and slipped the safety-catch to 'automatic'. Through the smoke and gloom I could see call signs at the bottom of the stairs in the hallway. Shit! I can't fire. They are in my line of sight, the bullets will go straight through the terrorist and into my mates. I've got to immobilize the bastard. I've got to do something. Instinctively, I raised the MP5 above my head and in one swift, sharp movement brought the stock of the weapon down on the back of his neck. I hit him as hard as I could. His head snapped backwards and for one fleeting second I caught sight of his tortured, hate-filled face. He collapsed forward and rolled down the remaining few stairs, hitting the carpet in the hallway, a sagging, crumpled heap. The sound of two magazines being emptied into him was deafening. As he twitched and vomited his life away, his hand opened and the grenade rolled out. In that split second my mind was so crystal clear with adrenalin it zoomed straight in on the grenade pin and lever. I stared at the mechanism for what seemed like an eternity, and what I saw flooded the very core of me with relief and elation. The pin was still located in the lever. It was all over, everything was going to be okay.

But this was no time to rest, this was one of the most vulnerable periods of the operation, the closing stages. This is where inexperienced troops would drop their guard. The radio crackled into life. 'You must abandon the building. The other floors are ablaze. Make your way out through the library entrance at the rear. The Embassy is clear. I repeat, the Embassy is clear.'

I joined Sek and we filed out through the library, through the smoke and the debris. We turned left and headed back for number 14, past the hostages, who were laid out and trussed up on the lawn ready for documentation, past the unexploded explosive charge, past the discarded sledgehammer and other pieces of assault equipment – all the trappings of battle in the middle of South Kensington. It was 8.07 p.m.

As we made our way through the french windows of number 14, the Gonze, ex-Para, a new boy in the regiment from one of the other call signs, removed his respirator and asked the Irish police sergeant on duty at the door what the Embassy World snooker score was. A look of total disbelief spread across the policeman's face and he just stood there shaking his head from side to side.

I crossed the room to my holdall and as I began pulling off my assault equipment I could feel the tiredness spreading through my limbs. It wasn't just the energy expended on the assault, it was the accumulation of six days of tension and high drama, of snatched sleep in a noisy room, of anxiety and worry over the outcome of the operation. I looked to my left. The Toad had just returned. He looked tired, his face was flushed and he was out of breath. He looked at me and shook his head. 'I'm getting too old for this sort of thing.'

'So am I,' I replied.

Within fifteen minutes most of the team members had stripped off their assault kit, packed it into their holdalls and parcelled their MP5s into plastic bags to be taken away for forensic examination. Before moving out through the front door of number 14 to the waiting Avis hire van, we had a dramatic visit from Home Secretary William Whitelaw, old Oyster Eyes himself. He stood before us, tears of joy unashamedly running down his cheeks, wringing his hands in relief. He thanked the assembled team members for what they had done for the country that day. 'This operation will show that we in Britain will not tolerate terrorists. The world must learn this.' It was a fine personal gesture and rounded the operation off perfectly.

Falklands War: The First Man into Port Stanley, 14 June 1982

MAX HASTINGS

One of Britain's last remnants of Empire, the barren and remote Falklands Islands, were invaded by Argentina on 2 April 1982. Pride, if not the rule of international law, required a resolute response, and the Conservative government of Margaret Thatcher accordingly dispatched a task force to the South Atlantic. Despite the furiousness of Argentine resistance at Fitzroy, at Goose Green, at Mount Harriet, at Wireless Ridge, at Tumbledown, at Two Sisters, at Longdon, the British campaign in the Falklands yomped to success. By 14 June British troops had reached the Falklands capital.

Max Hastings was war correspondent for the Evening Standard.

British forces are in Port Stanley. At 2.45 p.m. British time today [14 June], men of the 2nd Parachute Regiment halted on the outskirts at the end of their magnificent drive on the capital pending negotiations.

There, we sat on the racecourse until, after about twenty minutes I was looking at the road ahead and there seemed to be no movement. I thought, well I'm a civilian so why shouldn't I go and see what's going on because there didn't seem to be much resistance.

So I stripped off all my combat clothes and walked into Stanley in a blue civilian anorak with my hands in the air and my handkerchief in my hand.

The Argentinians made no hostile movement as I went by the apparently undamaged but heavily bunkered Government House.

I sort of grinned at them in the hope that if there were any Argentinian soldiers manning the position they wouldn't shoot at me.

Nobody took any notice so I walked on and after a few minutes I saw a group of people all looking like civilians a hundred yards ahead and I shouted at them.

I shouted: 'Are you British?' and they shouted back: 'Yes, are you?' I said 'Yes.'

They were a group of civilians who had just come out of the civil administration building where they had been told that it looked as if there was going to be a ceasefire.

We chatted for a few moments and then I walked up to the building and I talked to the senior Argentinian colonel who was standing on the steps. He didn't show any evident hostility.

They were obviously pretty depressed. They looked like men who had just lost a war but I talked to them for a few moments and I said: 'Are you prepared to surrender West Falkland as well as East?'

The colonel said: 'Well, maybe, but you must wait until four o'clock when General Menendez meets your general.'

I said: 'May I go into the town and talk to civilians?' He said: 'Yes,' so I started to walk down the main street past Falklanders who were all standing outside their houses.

They all shouted and cheered and the first person I ran into was the Catholic priest, Monsignor Daniel Spraggon, who said: 'My God, it's marvellous to see you.'

That wasn't directed at me personally but it was the first communication he had had with the British forces.

I walked on and there were hundreds, maybe thousands, of Argentinian troops milling around, marching in columns through the streets, some of them clutching very badly wounded men and looking completely like an army in defeat with blankets wrapped around themselves.

There were bits of weapons and equipment all over the place and they were all moving to central collection points before the surrender or ceasefire.

Eventually I reached the famous Falklands hotel, the Upland Goose. We had been dreaming for about three months about walking into the Upland Goose and having a drink, and I walked in and again it was marvellous that they all clapped and cheered.

They offered me gin on the assumption that this is the traditional drink of British journalists, but I asked if they could make it whisky instead and I gratefully raised my glass to them all.

Owner of the Upland Goose Desmond King said: 'We never doubted for a moment that the British would turn up. We have just been waiting for the moment for everybody to come.'

The last few days had been the worst, he said, because Argentinian guns had been operating from among the houses of Stanley and they had heard this terrific, continuous battle going on in the hills.

They were afraid that it was going to end up with a house-to-house fight in Stanley itself. The previous night when I had been with the Paras we were getting a lot of shell fire coming in on us and eventually we sorted out the coordinates from which it was firing. Our observation officer tried to call down to fire on the enemy batteries and the word came back that you could not fire on them because they are in the middle of Stanley.

So the battalion simply had to take it and suffer some casualties.

Anyway, there we were in the middle of the Upland Goose with about twenty or thirty delighted civilians who said that the Argentinians hadn't done anything appalling. It depends what one means by appalling, but they hadn't shot anybody or hung anybody up by their thumbs or whatever.

They had looted a lot of houses that they had taken over. At times they got very nervous and started pushing people around with submachine guns in their backs and the atmosphere had been pretty unpleasant.

Robin Pitaleyn described how he had been under house arrest in the hotel for six weeks, since he made contact by radio with the *Hermes*. He dismissed criticism of the Falkland Island Company representatives who had sold goods to the occupiers.

'We were all selling stuff,' he said. 'You had a simple choice – either you sold it or they took it. I rented my house to their air force people. They said – either you take rent or we take the house. What would you have done?'

Adrian Monk described how he had been compulsorily evicted from his own house to make way for Argentinian soldiers who had then totally looted it. There appears to have been widespread looting in all the houses of Stanley to which the Argentinians had access.

The houses on the outskirts of the town in which the Argentinians had been living were an appalling mess full of everything from human excrement all over the place to just property lying all over the place where soldiers had ransacked through it. But they were all alive and they all had plenty of food and plenty to drink and they were all in tremendous spirits.

It wasn't in the least like being abroad. One talks about the Falklanders and yet it was as if one had liberated a hotel in the middle of Surrey or Kent or somewhere.

It was an extraordinary feeling just sitting there with all these girls and cheerful middle-age men and everybody chatting in the way they might chat at a suburban golf club after something like this had happened.

There were other enemies without.

Long committed to blowing the British out of Northern Ireland, the Provisional IRA took the war across the sea to target the English in their beds. The Tory MP Airey Neave was an early assassination victim. In October 1984 the IRA sprang its most audacious attack on the mainland to that date.

The Brighton Bomb, 12 October 1984

NORMAN TEBBIT

The Grand Hotel, Brighton, was the venue for the 1984 Conservative Party conference. Norman Tebbit was the Conservative Trade and Industry Secretary.

There was the usual round of too many parties and receptions to attend but skipping most of them we went to the Party Treasurer, Alistair McAlpine's soirée, as it was always known. Alistair is an excellent host offering exceptionally good food and drink, and company too – provided one was selective about all three. There were always journalists aplenty (as Alistair's relations with the 'hacks' were excellent), a good number of parliamentary and Government colleagues and most of the Party establishment. I have never discovered at what time Alistair's parties ended but my wife and I drew stumps around midnight and, walking down to our room, encountered the BBC political correspondent, John

Cole, on his way upstairs. As John and I chatted, Margaret excused herself saying she was tired and would head for bed. We gossiped on for a while before I said, 'John, if I wake my wife just as she's gone to sleep I'll be in terrible trouble so I'd best be off to bed,' and we retired to our rooms.

It seldom takes me long to go to sleep and that night was no exception and we were both sleeping soundly when the bomb exploded.

We were woken by the blast which I recognized at once for what it was. There was just time for Margaret to call out in alarm and for me to reply, 'It's a bomb!' before the ceiling came crashing down on us and then, in a hail of debris, the floor collapsed, catapulting us down under an avalanche of bricks, timber and plaster. The force of the impact was indescribable – blow after blow as the debris smashed on to my left side. Something tore into my abdomen with a terrible blow and I heard my very guts sloshing inside me. There was a colossal impact tearing a great hole in my side, then I stopped falling – with no idea where, nor even which way up I was, as the debris cascaded down. The hammer blows eventually stopped and the sounds of falling masonry died away. It was pitch black and, at first, silent, then came screams and groans – some rattling and choking into silence. I called for Margaret and miraculously she replied from somewhere quite close. I found I could move my left arm and reaching out, our fingers touched and we grasped each other. Like me she was trapped, but bent almost double under a great weight of debris that had fallen on to her shoulders and neck. My head was trapped as in a vice. I could neither move nor feel my right arm which I feared I might have lost. Nor could my left hand reach my face which was half wrapped in bedding forming a trap for dust and grit threatening to fill up and cover my mouth. As I reached down my hand encountered a great sticky bleeding mess, in the gaping hole in my side.

I found Margaret's hand again. At first we assured each other we were all right, each lying to comfort the other. Then Margaret began to shout for help. 'Don't shout yet, wait until you hear them digging, or you'll exhaust yourself – it may be a long time yet.'

My mind had already constructed a picture of the scene. I assumed the whole hotel had collapsed like the American building that had been bombed in Beirut and that it might take days to reach us. I could hear water cascading down through the wreckage and hoped that we would neither be drowned, nor burned to death if fire broke out.

We had no sense of time. Gradually the cries of other victims fell silent as they died, and we comforted each other. I wondered how bad it was. How many other survivors there were. What was to be done if the Prime Minister and other members, perhaps even most of the Cabinet, were dead? We listened waiting for the rescuers without any sense of time. Great waves of pain came and went and I could feel my life ebbing away as I bled. With each new fall of debris I feared that the crushing weight on my skull might simply crush it like an eggshell. I had begun to fear that I would not last until we were rescued when suddenly my whole body was galvanized with searing pain. So this is death – how strange, what a waste, I thought – then it stopped and I was still alive. Again the pain rose to a crescendo then suddenly stopped. I realized that it had been caused by massive electric shocks but only afterwards did I discover that the rescue workers had inadvertently cut through the live main. Somehow we lost our grip on each other's hands. It may have been another fall of debris which moved Margaret or, although she did not tell me, it may have been the paralysis which was creeping through her body. Nor did I mention what I thought was the cold dead limb of a corpse I found near me in the debris. In fact it was my right arm which I thought I had lost but was merely crushed. At times I felt myself losing consciousness in the great waves of pain, and as we continued to comfort each other, I gave Margaret a message for our children if I died before rescue came.

Then suddenly there were voices. We shouted – or croaked as loud as we could. They called back, 'Who are you?' We told them. 'Can you move?' they asked. We exchanged names and told them how we were trapped. They reached Margaret first. I could see their lights and then I felt a rough hand touch mine. I grabbed it – holding on foolishly like a child begging its owner not to let go. It was Fred. He found that I was under my mattress which had probably saved my life as the masonry fell down on me, and they began to dig me out. A doctor came and tried to see what injuries I had. Then as they dug they found what they too thought was the arm of a corpse until Fred realized it was mine. Painfully, carefully, brick by brick, they cleared the debris – but I was still trapped by a great timber which they dared not cut for fear of bringing down a whole mass of wreckage precariously balanced above us. 'Can you struggle free?' they asked me. With the pain deadened I tried to lift myself over the timber. Fred leaned over to help. My shout of, 'Get off my bloody foot!' seemed to break the tension. We laughed and with another great heave they had hold of me – in minutes I was strapped on to a stretcher and swung clear of the wreckage, into the light of the blazing arc lamps and the cold air of the seafront.

The IRA later issued a communiqué:

The IRA claim responsibility for the detonation of 100 pounds of gelignite in Brighton, against the British cabinet and the Tory war-mongers. Thatcher will now realize that Britain cannot occupy our country, torture our prisoners and shoot our people on their own streets and get away with it.

Today we were unlucky, but remember, we have only to be lucky once. You will have to be lucky always. Give Ireland peace and there will be no war.

After enemies without, Thatcher faced enemies within.

The 1984–5 Miners' Strike: Scenes from a Yorkshire Pit Village, South Elmsall, 19 December 1984

PETER JENKINS, THE *GUARDIAN*

The bitter miners' strike began in March 1984 with a National Coal Board announcement of pit closures in Kent. It spread contagiously through a demoralized, declining British coalfield, with the exception of the 'super pits' in the Midlands. Their 'scabbing' was bitterly resented by union loyalists, and violent clashes followed. Yorkshire was the heartland of the strike, the HQ of the 80,000-strong National Union of Mineworkers, the home turf of the NUM president, Arthur Scargill. King Arthur.

At the Miners' Welfare Club old couples are dancing the Anniversary Waltz. Bill introduces me to some friends including local NUM branch officials. They are back from court in Pontefract giving evidence on behalf of pickets. If they were witnesses they had attended a mass picket, said the Stipendiary, and bound the lot of them over for 'besetting'.

They were full of complaints about the police and the media. Frank's children had seen the recent *World in Action* programme. 'They wanted to know "were you there, Dad?" They're going to think I'm some kind of law-breaker.'

'His father's either a thug or television's wrong,' said Roy.

Reg said, 'I'm thirty-six and I've never been in trouble with police all my life. Now I'm enemy within. Some kind of criminal. My kids know that's not me. So does my wife. They resent it.'

Nothing is more resented, I discovered, than the Prime Minister's remark. A typical comment from a much older miner was 'they didn't call us enemy within when we were digging for fucking victory.' Margaret Thatcher's insult to the miners of Great Britain will not be soon forgotten. She will be remembered like Churchill for Tonypandy.

The president of the branch, Tony, was as bald as Kojak and wore his dark glasses. He tried to sum up what it was they were fighting for. 'It's such a broad issue,' he said. 'It's like chucking a stone in a pond and the ripples spreading. You're fighting for your pit first of all. But you're fighting for your village and your kids' future. And you're fighting, I hope to God, for a police force that don't get out of hand, 'cos we've got to have a police force. And you're fighting for the trade union movement because this union has only been loaned to us by my grandfather.'

Then as an afterthought, he added: 'It's brought us closer as a community, this strike. It's done a Falklands on us.'

We move on. If miners don't like travelling far to work they'll drive miles for a pint. At another club, Jack, who's a management man but with a great deal more sympathy for the miners than for Ian MacGregor or Margaret Thatcher, says, 'It's only loyalty to the branches that's keeping them out now.'

That loyalty is immensely strong and is much more of a factor than the intimidation which has been going on. At the three local pits the number of men 'going in' is two, four and six. The strike is going to die hard in these parts.

The next morning the pickets are out as usual. At four o'clock, Bill and I walk up to Frickley through cold, wet, orange-lit streets. Nothing happens; there's a shove and a shout and the two men go in. I go back to a warm bed.

When men first went in to Frickley a few weeks ago there were riot shields and horses and broken windows and arrests, and the usual mutual accusations of violence. The pattern, at least in this part of West Yorkshire, seems to be a flare of violent anger when a pit reopens after which things settle down to a routine morning ritual, usually without incident. Low profile policing is the general order round here, and it does seem to keep the level of violence down.

The wives who run the meal centre have been dubbed the 'Frickley Wonder Women'. They have escaped from their own kitchens to cook 200 dinners and breakfasts a day for the men on strike. Brenda was managing on £32 a week from the DHSS and £13 in family allowance but her mortgage was £20 a week and there was the water rates and the phone and a video which couldn't go back. Barbara, with one son, was also 'managing' on £13.65 plus £6.85.

Her boy was having free school dinners and her husband coming into the centre for his breakfast and dinner. 'At night we have toast and a few chips,' she says with a cheerful laugh. 'It's the kids you feel sorry for isn't it?'

'It's the kids' clothes are the main problem,' says another Brenda. 'There's an allowance from council, which we appreciate, but it's not enough for coat and shoes.'

'We didn't miss our summer holidays at all,' says the first Brenda with a happy smile.

'We did,' says Merle, who is married to one of Bill's many cousins.

'I mean we knew no one else was having a holiday, didn't we?' says Brenda.

Two of their sons are 'considering army'. There hasn't been a pit job in the villages for some years, or so they claim. Bill says: 'We've got lads of twenty-two who've never worked and never will.'

'The cold's the real thing. We're freezing,' says Merle. 'Aye, you should see the rubbish we put on fires.' We leave them complaining about the police chasing their men off the tips and merrily discussing the uses of bricks in grates.

Outside a man stops Bill to inquire about a turkey dinner which is planned. There's a problem about money and turkeys. He listens to the latest and says, 'We'll be having corn beef dinner then.' Off he goes, laughing.

In the shadow of the tip (which is a phrase I heard a miner use) men are digging muddy holes as deep as themselves, sieving dirt for scraps of coal to burn. Last week someone found an 1806 penny and today it's a George V Coronation mug but the handle is broken off.

The miners were finally defeated in March 1985, after a whole year 'out'. Only twenty years before, the miners had brought down Heath. The Conservatives secured their revenge; over the next few years the British coal industry was reduced to a straggled handful of pits. Which were then privatized.

Margaret Thatcher's firm hand in dealing with unruly Argentines and British miners, coupled with an evidently growing prosperity ('yuppies', the spread of home ownership to two-thirds of the population) and disorder amongst the Labour Party enabled her to win three elections in a row. Not since Lord Liverpool in the early nineteenth century had such a thing occurred. Yet by the late 1980s her tight-faced imperial style was beginning to grate on England's sensibilities. More substantially, her implementation of the Poll Tax caused revolt (just as it had amongst England's peasantry in 1381), her party was divided pro- and con-Europe, and Nigel Lawson's apparent 'revival' of the economy had come with a £20 billion balance-of-payments-deficit. Sensing the disapproving mood of the electorate, the Conservative Party's centre-Left, under Michael Heseltine, made their move on the beleaguered Mrs Thatcher.

Thatcher Falls, 21–22 November 1990

ALAN CLARK MP

Margaret Thatcher won the first ballot against leadership contender Michael Heseltine (204 to 152 votes) but struggled to find votes for a convincing win in the second round. Alan Clark, the Defence Minister, was amongst Thatcher's staunchest supporters.

Ministry of Defence
No work is being done in Whitehall today, whatsoever. My 'In'-tray is about an inch deep. I don't think a single Minister in the Govt will be at his desk; or if he is, it will be only so as to telephone to a colleague or to a journalist. The civil servants (all of whom, down to Principal level, I suspect, were terrified of the Lady) just cannot believe their eyes.

Yet still she won't return. There is talk of a 'fighting statement' later. But this wastage of time in Paris is sheer lunacy. Harold at Stamford Bridge.

It is the general sense of disintegration now affecting everything, that is so damaging to her. Unless MH is slaughtered in the final ballot – impossibly unlikely – she herself is going to find it highly difficult to reassert her authority, even if eventually she emerges as the victor. Short, that is, of giving them the full coup-loser's treatment – arrest, manacles, beaten up in the interrogation room, shot while trying to escape. Real blood, in other words. Fun, but a bit *Angolan*.

Before walking over to the House I called Andrew MacKay into my room and we had a long talk about Tom [King]. Earlier, we had both lingered after Ministers and sounded him.

Tom likes the idea, preened himself, straightened his jacket; but he is cautious. He would need to be sure of at least thirty votes to even 'put down a marker'. And in any case, convention obliges that no member of the Cabinet puts his name forward while she is still standing. (I hear rumours that that pudgy puff-ball Kenneth Clarke is considering breaching this, but am keeping that in reserve.)

'Look,' I told him. 'If the Lady is doomed, our Number One priority is to find, and instal a leader who will win the next General Election. And we haven't got long. Who is best suited to do this?'

I told him that Heseltine would burn out very quickly. His rhetoric pleased Party Conference, but was less reliable in the national context. Anyway people are sick of passion, they want reassurance.

The only two figures who can do this are Tom and John Major. Douglas is now past it; is thought rightly or wrongly to be a buffer and a bureaucrat. John is more engaging than Tom in some ways, with a lovely grin, but seems really too youthful. There is no time to project him. Even in the House he is barely known, has never been seen under fire. Tom, on the other hand, does have gravitas. Also he's good on the stump, in small groups, canteens and so on.

Andrew was in broad agreement. But:

'Tom won't make a move while she's still in the field.'

'So what do we do?'

'I tell you what I'm doing, if she stands second time round – voting for Michael.'

I was appalled. Here was this good, intelligent man, tough and (in so far as it still means anything) right wing . . . More than any other experience this conversation has made me realize that she will lose, finally, head-to-head against Heseltine. But if she does stand again we are in a log-jam; the only people who will join in the contest are wankers like Clarke who are not worth twenty-five votes.

Andrew said that he would, very quietly, take soundings for Tom. The immediate priority is to find a way, tactfully and skilfully, to talk her out of standing a second time.

Now I must close this entry and walk over to the House.

House of Commons

I was greeted with the news that there had been an announcement. 'I fight, and I fight to win.' God alive!

Tebbit is holding an impromptu press conference in the Members' lobby.

Fifty feet away, down the tea-room corridor that mad ninny Hampson is dancing around on his tippy-toes calling out to passers-by, 'Tee-hee, she's standing. We've made it. We can't lose now, etc.'

I came back here, to my room. I kept the door open and an endless succession of visitors trooped in and out. No one seems to have any idea of what we should do. Her 'Campaign' is a shambles now. John Moore (who he?) is running around with bits of paper – 'draft statements' – asking people what they think. He seems to have a temporary HQ in Portillo's room, which is next door to mine. First I heard that Norman Fowler was going to take charge; then John Wakeham. Or was it the other way round? Gamelin's been sacked, Weygand is on the way out; Pétain's in the wings. '*Où est la masse de manoeuvre? – Aucune.*'

Every time I trawl the corridors I run into another batch of chaps who say they're going to switch, or abstain, or when-are-there-going-to-be-some-more-candidates-to-choose-from? The only visitor who has made any real sense is Francis Maude. He claims, forcefully, that John Major has a better chance than we all realize. But John won't make a move while the Lady remains in the field. 'I must get to see her. Can you help?' Apparently Peter stands sentinel, and is outside her door the whole time.

I have closed the door. These random conversations are too discursive. Tomorrow is the last day for nominations. I must clear my head.

1) If she fights head on, she loses.

2) Therefore, the opposition vote has got to be diluted by a candidate from the left – preferably Patten, making it triangular. Besides dilution, this has the advantage that it will crack Cabinet 'solidarity' open and others may lose their scruples. Therefore:

3) Try and talk Patten into standing. QED.

Archie Hamilton's just been in. Didn't make any sense. One minute he says she 'could still' win; the next that we've all 'had it'. I'm off now, upstairs.

Later
Kundan Restaurant
It is very late, and finally I have withdrawn here for a vegetable curry, and to write up the traumatic happenings of this evening.

I made first for Chris's room. On the way I passed her outer door and said to Peter that I must have a minute or so. He looked anxious, almost rattled, which he never does normally. 'I'll do my best. She's seeing every member of the Cabinet in turn . . .'

'Francis wants to see her too.'

'I'm doing my best.'

Chris wasn't in his room. The Secretary of State's corridor was deserted. Hushed, but you could feel the static.

The policeman by the lift said he was 'in with Mr Rifkind'.

I knocked and went in without waiting for an answer. Also in there, loathesomely conspiring, was little Kenneth Clarke. Her three great ill-wishers! Clarke wasn't friendly at all. If he'd said anything to me, I'd have answered 'Fuck you', so just as well.

Chris was quite amiable.

'How many votes she got at the moment?'

'It's a rout. She's down to ninety.'

'*Ninety?*'

'You've got to stand. You can't let Michael corner the left.'

He was diplomatic. A discussion was impossible. God knows what they were talking about, but it stank. Never mind, I have sowed the seed; or watered what was already there.

I went down the stairs and rejoined the group outside her door. After a bit Peter said, 'I can just fit you in now – but only for a split second, mind.'

She looked calm, almost beautiful. 'Ah, Alan . . .'

'You're in a jam.'

'I know that.'

'They're all telling you not to stand, aren't they?'

'I'm going to stand. I have issued a statement.'

'That's wonderful. That's heroic. But the Party will let you down.'

'I am a fighter.'

'Fight, then. Fight right to the end, a third ballot if you need to. But you lose.'

There was quite a little pause.

'It'd be so terrible if Michael won. He would undo everything I have fought for.'

'But what a way to go! Unbeaten in three elections, never rejected by the people. Brought down by nonentities!'

'But Michael . . . as *Prime Minister*.'

'Who the fuck's Michael? No one. Nothing. He won't last six months. I doubt if he'd even win the Election. Your place in history is towering . . .'

Outside, people were doing that maddening trick of opening and shutting the door, at shorter and shorter intervals.

'Alan, it's been so good of you to come in and see me . . .'

★

Afterwards I felt empty. And cross. I had failed, but I didn't really know what I wanted, except for her still to be Prime Minister, and it wasn't going to work out.

I sat on the bench immediately behind the Speaker's chair, watching the coming and going. After a bit Tristan [Garel-Jones] came and sat beside me. But he had little to say. What is there to say? She's still seeing visitors. Then, along came Edwina.

'Hullo, aren't you Edwina Currie?'

'Now then, Alan, there's no need to be objectionable.'

'If that is who you are, I must congratulate you on the combination of loyalty and restraint that you have shown in going on television to announce your intention to vote against the Prime Minister in the Leadership Election.'

'Alan, I'm perfectly prepared to argue this through with you, if you'll listen.'

'Piss off.'

Which she did.

Tristan said, 'She's not a bad girl really.'

At half past eight I left to come over here. The archway exit from Speaker's Court was blocked by the PM's Jaguar. She had just taken her seat, and as the detective's door slammed the interior light went out and the car slid away. I realized with a shock that this was in all probability her last night as Prime Minister. I came in with her. I go out with her, and a terrible sadness envelops me – of unfinished duties and preoccupations; of dangers and injustices remaining, of the greed, timidity and short-sightedness of so many in public life.

Albany Thursday, 22 November

Very early this morning the phone rang. It was Tristan.

'She's going.'

There will be an official announcement immediately after a short Cabinet, first thing. Then the race will be on. Apparently Douglas *and* John Major are going to stand. I said I thought it was crazy, Heseltine will go through between them. I could sense him shrugging. 'There you go.'

Anyway, would I come over to his room at the Foreign Office and watch it from there?

Afterwards, very *triste* and silent, I walked back to the MoD and sat in on a late (and unnecessary) Ministers' meeting. Tom told us that it had been 'awful'. She started to read a prepared statement to them, then broke down, and the text had to be finished by the Lord Chancellor.

Listless, I drifted over to the House. I had a word with Charles, drafted a couple of valedictory passages for her speech this afternoon, did I don't know how many impromptu TV bites.

Heseltine is meant to be coming to Plymouth tomorrow, for a fund-raising dinner. I rang Judith [Roberts, Chairman of the Sutton Division], told her we couldn't possibly allow him to use us as a platform to plug his own candidature. She only half agreed, so I immediately tele-phoned to the *Western Morning News* and told them that I had 'instructed' that the invitation be withdrawn. (Not unrich, considering I was not the host, and had long ago told everyone that I wanted nothing to do with it.)

I didn't think I could bear it, but curiosity drew me into the Chamber for the Lady's last performance. It would have been too macabre to have sat in my habitual place, next to her PPS, so I watched and listened first from behind the Chair, then from the Bar of the House. She was brilliant. Humorous, self-deprecating, swift and deadly in her argument and in her riposte. Even Dennis Skinner, her oldest adversary, was feeding her lines; and at one point Michael Carttiss shouted, 'You could wipe the floor with the lot of 'em.'

Too bloody true.

Like Lloyd George and Neville Chamberlain before her, Margaret Thatcher was removed by the backbenchers, not the voters. To replace her, the Tories chose not Michael Heseltine (as big and as divisive a beast as Thatcher in his way) but the compromise candidate, the hardly recognized Chancellor of the Exchequer, John Major. He had barely moved his furniture into 10 Downing Street before the country was again at war.

The Gulf War: Interrogation of a Captured British RAF Navigator, Iraq, February 1991

JOHN NICHOL RAF

John Nichol, a navigator in a RAF Tornado, was shot down on 17 January 1991, the opening day of Operation Desert Storm, the Allied campaign to remove the Iraqis from their illegal occupation of Kuwait. Both Nichol and the pilot were captured by Iraqi troops.

In the evening they came for me. They unshackled me, put the blindfold on, hauled me upright, dragged me down the stairs, round the streets, back into the interrogation centre; the familiar journey, almost routine by now. The chair: they threw me down into it. One guy was holding my arm on one side, one on the other. I knew in my heart of hearts that this was the time, I knew that it was going to get really rough now.

I was sitting with the solid fist of my own fear in my stomach.

'What squadron are you from?'

'I cannot answer that . . .'

Bang! somebody punched me in the face. Blood came pouring out of my face onto my lap, dripping. I could feel it warm on my thighs. On my lower half, I was wearing a flying-suit, a chemical-warfare suit, long-johns underneath all that, but I could still feel the blood dripping warm onto the upper part of my legs. Someone was hitting me in the face, over and over again. Question. Then somebody standing just to one side hit me hard across the skull with a solid piece of wood. Thwack! My head rang to the blow like some kind of bell. There were brilliant aching lights flashing behind the blindfold. You really do see stars. I was in the middle of the Milky Way. Question.

'I cannot answer . . .' A kick in the stomach – how he got to my stomach I don't know, they were still holding me down on the chair. I fell over to one side in the chair, my gorge rising; they dragged me up by the hair. Question.

'I cannot . . .' Whack! Someone punched me again, someone hit me with the wood, dazzling bright lights and the sudden downward spiral into blackness. Now I was disorientated, my brain was really starting to shut down, but still I thought, 'It's going to take more than this, it's going to take more than this. I'm not breaking down without good cause.' Somebody dragged my boot off, tearing it away with a furious wrench. 'What on earth? What are they going to do to me now?' Whack! A plastic pipe filled with something hard hit me across the shins. A biting agony across the shins, on and on, biting. Question.

And now, somebody grabs the hair at the nape of my neck, and begins stuffing tissue-paper down the back of my T-shirt. That is appalling. This is terrifying now. I am sitting in a darkened room in the middle of enemy territory, and somebody has just stuffed tissue-paper down the back of my neck. 'What are they doing that for?' I know straightaway what they are doing that for, I can imagine only too well. 'Shit, they are going to set me on fire!' Now I really want him to ask me another question, I *am* sorry, I want to say something, I want to tell him something, anything. But he doesn't ask me a question. He just sets fire to the paper.

I throw my head violently from side to side, to try to escape from the burning, to try to shake the tissue-paper clear of my neck. They are still whacking my shins. Quite soon, mercifully soon, somebody behind me slaps out the flames.

'What squadron are you from?'

'Fifteen.'

I had had enough.

The Body of Diana, Princess of Wales, Is Flown Home, RAF Northolt, 31 August 1997

JONATHAN FREEDLAND

The English icon of the latter half of the twentieth century, Diana Spencer, ex-wife of the Prince of Wales, was killed in a car crash in Paris on 30 August 1997.

In the end, they let her go quietly. No drum, no funeral note – only a dumb silence as the body of Diana, Princess of Wales, returned to the land she might have ruled as queen.

There was no crowd to meet her, none of the hordes of flagwavers she so delighted in life. Instead the flat, grey tarmac of RAF Northolt, windy as a prairie, a line-up of dignitaries – and a hearse.

She had made the journey from Paris by plane, on an RAF BAe 126. They kept the coffin in the passenger cabin, within sight of her two sisters, Lady Jane Fellowes and Lady Sarah McCorquodale, and her former husband, the Prince of Wales.

The skies themselves seemed to make way for her arrival, the clouds parting like an honour guard. Once the plane had landed, it nudged toward the welcoming party hesitantly, as if weighted down by its tragic cargo. Waiting there was the kind of receiving line Diana met every day. In the middle, arms by his sides, fists clenched tight, the Prime Minister. A cleric stood close by, bright in scarlet cassock. None of them said a word.

Eventually the plane door opened, and the Prince appeared head down, hands clasped behind his back. He was guided by the Lord

Chamberlain, the Earl of Airlie. In another context it might have been a standard royal visit: Charles shown round a new factory or hospital wing. But he had come on a more baleful duty. He took his place in line – as he has done so often.

By now, the team of coffin bearers, each one in the crisp uniform of the Queen's Colour Squadron, had completed its precise march toward the other side of the aircraft. At the stroke of seven o'clock, the hatch opened revealing a glimpse of colour, the Royal Standard clinging to the hard, square outline of the coffin. It seemed an unforgiving shape: just a box, with none of the curve or sparkle of the woman whose body lay within.

The silence of the air was cut, and not just by the sound of distant traffic – which rumbled on, as if to prove that the clocks never stop, even for the death of a princess.

The air was filled with the *chickageev, chickageev* of the thousand camera lenses pointed at the scene ahead. Even now the world's telephoto eye was still staring at her, more focused than ever. Despite everything, everyone still wanted a piece of Diana. The cameras kept up their din, but there was an eerie silence from the men who held them. Once they would cry out, 'Diana! Diana!' – urging her to look their way or to flash just one more of those million-dollar smiles. But there was no shouting yesterday. And no smiles either.

The bearers of the body inched their way to the hearse. They stood, swivelled on their heels, and clasping tight with their white gloved hands, lowered the coffin as smoothly as a hydraulic pump. They were about to turn away, but a bit of the flag was still spilling out; it had to be tucked in, just like the train of one of Diana's more lavish ball gowns.

The sisters stepped forward, each one turning to curtsy for the man whom Diana had once loved. Charles kissed each one before they stepped into the royal Daimler. The next car was filled with bouquets.

The Prince himself did his duty, talking to each one of the VIPs who had stood beside him. Tony Blair clasped both royal hands in a double handshake, nodding intently. Charles made a gesture with upturned palms, as if to say What Can I Do? He thanked the RAF guard and disappeared back inside the plane, heading for Balmoral and his newly bereaved young sons. 'He's going back to the boys,' said his spokesman.

And then, on the final day of August, the sky darkened, and the wind whipped harder. It felt like the last day of summer, and the beginning of a long winter.

Rugby World Cup: Jonny Wilkinson Kicks It Over, Telstar Stadium, Sydney, Australia, 22 November 2003

JONNY WILKINSON

Near exhaustion and despair, I look up at the clock. We have three minutes – one shot, one opportunity.

Field position is everything so we make a quick decision to kick off long, knowing Rogers will clear his lines and that we will have the lineout throw inside their half. I call 'Zig-zag' to Dawson and he relays the code word to Ben Kay, who will then call an appropriate lineout to enable us to activate the move. 'Zig-zag' is a move we have rehearsed many times, setting up the ideal position for a dropped goal. It has been in the back of my mind all through the final; now it is right at the front.

We need a secure set-piece – by no means guaranteed in a final where neither side have been able to dominate their own ball. Steve Thompson hits the button, picking out Lewis Moody at the tail, the hardest part of the lineout to find, but obligatory for this attack. It allows us to launch Catty [Mike Catt] on to the ball and immediately over the gain-line. Australia know what we are planning and concentrate on getting up fast to charge down the dropped goal but, in doing so, they leave a hole for Dawson to burst through the ruck. He is hauled down, having made a crucial 20 metres – an awesome run for the team, but don't mistake the fact that he was trying to score himself! He has put us in range and, back in the pocket, I scream for the ball 30 metres out, readying myself for the kick.

I'm to the left of the posts, so I line it up with my right foot to open up the angle and to avoid the charge-down. But Daws is buried and Backy [Neil Back] is waiting to deliver the pass at scrum half. Johnno sees this and, critically, takes the ball up one more time, making the Australia forwards defend again and allowing Daws to return to his station. The Wallabies go offside in their keenness to come through, but the referee only warns them. Then I see Daws picking up the ball. I lift my hands to receive it and he fires back the perfect pass. This is it.

The knack with a dropped goal is to connect with the ball as it makes contact with the ground, turning it into a place-kick in effect. But when I drop the ball it lands slightly off-centre, bouncing fractionally towards me as I strike it. This reduces the power I can put through the ball, but it actually makes accuracy easier. I know it doesn't have to go far, just straight.

When I connect it feels good. Phil Waugh tries to block the kick, but he can't get there – it's up and away into the sky. I look up, I see the posts and I know it is going between them. It does. After all the pain, all the sacrifice and all the hardship it might just be that England are going to win the World Cup.

Then I am seized by a moment of panic. Can the referee deny us again? I look at Watson. He raises his arm and signals the dropped goal. Everything is OK. We still have to deal with the kick-off, but Trevor Woodman catches it and the ball is fed back to Catty to deliver the laziest yet most beautiful touch-kick in the history of English rugby.

Then the match is over. We've done it. My head is spinning like a tumble dryer. I jump up and down with Will Greenwood, shouting like a mad man, 'World Cup, World Cup'. In the emotion of the moment, I am unable to come up with anything more profound. It says it all, though – we are world champions.

Personal Acknowledgements

I have many people to thank for their help in the making of this book.

First and foremost my wife, Penny Lewis-Stempel, without whom it would simply not have been done.

They also served: my agent Julian Alexander; Kate Barker at Penguin; Helen Campbell; Tracey Pallant; Emma Daffern (for sanity-saving research); Betty and Alan Jessop; Bernard and Alan Samuels (for, literally, where I am today); Bob Pitt, Matt Pitt and Mark Williams (ditto); Sarah and David and Ollie and Emma Jones; Joyce and Eric Lewis; Julie Long and John Shurvington; John and Frances Harvey-Fishenden; the staff of the British Library; the staff of Hereford Library.

Sources and Permissions Acknowledgements

The author gratefully acknowledges permission to reproduce copyright material in this book. If any material has been inadvertently included without permission, please contact the author c/o the publishers.

Andrews, John ('The Boston Tea Party'), from *Letters of John Andrews, Esq., of Boston. 1772–1775*, Winthrop Sargent (ed.), Massachusetts Historical Society Proceedings, 1864–1865, 1866

Anglo-Saxon Chronicle ('The Vikings Raid England'; 'An Estimate of William the Conqueror at his Death'), from *The Anglo-Saxon Chronicle*, trans. G. N. Garmonsway, J. M. Dent, 1953. Copyright © 1953 G. N. Garmonsway.

Anglo-Saxon Chronicle ('The Anarchy'), in *The Saxon Chronicle*, trans. J. A. Giles, Bohn, 1849

Anglo-Saxon Chronicle ('The Domesday Inquisition'), in *Anglo-Saxon Chronicle*, trans. James Ingram, Everyman Library, J. M. Dent, 1912

Anonimalle Chronicle ('The Peasants' Revolt'), from *The Anonimalle Chronicle*, V. H. Galbraith (ed.), Manchester University Press, 1927. Reprinted by permission

Anonymous ('A Saxon Warrior at the Battle of Maldon'), in *English and Norse Documents*, trans. M. Ashdown, Cambridge University Press, 1930. Copyright © CUP 1930. Reprinted by permission of CUP

Anonymous ('The Domesday Assessment of Cumnor'), from *Domesday Book*, vol. I, 1783

Anonymous ('Agincourt: Henry's Victory March'), quoted in *English Historical Documents 1327–1585*, A. R. Myers (ed.), Eyre & Spottiswoode, 1969

Anonymous ('Banning the Bomb'), from www.century.guardian.uk. Copyright © Guardian Newspapers Limited

Anonymous Court Recorder ('Sex in the Country'), quoted in *English Historical Documents 1189–1327*, H. Rothwell (ed.), Eyre & Spottiswoode, 1975

Anonymous Monk ('The Age of Chivalry: A Mass Knighting'), from *Flores Historiarum, per Matthaeum Westmonasteriensem collecti*, vol. III, H. R. Luard (ed.), Rolls series, 1890

Anonymous Priest ('The Battle of Agincourt'), quoted in *English Historical Documents 1327–1585*, A. R. Myers (ed.), Eyre & Spottiswoode, 1969

Anonymous SAS Trooper ('The SAS Relieve the Siege at Prince's Gate'), from *Soldier 'I' SAS*, Paul Kennedy, 1989. Copyright © 1989 Michael Paul Kennedy

Arch, Joseph ('The Revolt of the Field'), from *The Autobiography of Joseph Arch*, John Gerard O'Leary (ed.), MacGibbon & Kee, 1966

Asquith, Herbert ('The Drift to World War: The View from 10 Downing Street'), from *Memories and Reflexions*, vol. II, The Earl of Oxford and Asquith, Little Brown and Co., 1928

Asser ('The Viking Invasion: Alfred Saves *Angelcynn* from the Danes'), from *De Rebus Gestis Aelfredi Magni*, trans. J. A. Giles, Henry G. Bohn, 1848

Austin, Richard, BEF ('Dunkirk: The Beach'), from *Return Via Dunkirk*, Richard Austin ('Gun Buster'), Hodder & Stoughton, 1940

Badcock, Midshipman (Trafalgar: The Battle Opens'), from *Sailors Whom Nelson Led*, E. Fraser (ed.), Methuen, 1913

Baker, Geoffrey le ('The Murder of Edward II'), from *Chronicon Galfridi le Baker de Swynebroke*, ed. E. M. Thompson, Clarendon Press, 1889

Baker, Geoffrey le ('The Hundred Years War: Sea Fight at Sluys'), quoted in *Chaucer's World*, E. Rickert, OUP, 1948. Copyright © 1948 E. Rickert.

Baker, Samuel White ('Samuel White Baker Discovers the Source of the Nile'), quoted in *The Faber Book of Exploration*, Benedict Allen (ed.), Faber and Faber, 2002

Bamford, Samuel ('Peterloo'), from *Passages in the Life of a Radical*, Samuel Bamford, Simpkin Marshall & Co., 1893

Barter, Richard ('Indian Mutiny: Cawnpore after the Massacre'), from *The Siege of Delhi – Mutiny Memories of an Old Officer*, Richard Barter, Folio Society, 1984

Bayerlein, Fritz ('El Alamein: The Afrika Korps Retreat'), from *The Fatal Decisions*, W. Richardson and S. Freidin (eds), trans. Constantine Fitzgibbon, Michael Joseph, 1956

Beatty, William ('Trafalgar: The Death of Nelson'), from *Despatches and Letters of Nelson*, Nicholas Harris Nicolas (ed.), Henry Colburn, 1845

Bede ('King Edwin of Northumbria Is Converted to Christianity'), from *Bede's Ecclesiastical History of the English People*, Bertram Colgrave and R. A. B. Mynors (eds), Oxford University Press, 1969. Reprinted by permission of OUP

Beha-ed-Din, ('Richard I Massacres His Muslim Prisoners After Seizing Acre'), from *The Crusade of Richard I, 1189–92*, selected by T. A. Archer, David Nutt, 1888

Bennett, Arnold ('The General Strike'), from *Journals*, Arnold Bennett, Newman Flower, Cassell, 1933

Bentley, Elizabeth ('Factory Conditions'), from *Report of Parliamentary Committee on the Bill to Regulate the Labour of Children in Mills and Factories*, 1832

Bentley, Thomas ('Machine Wreckers'), quoted in *Pandemonium 1660–1886: the Coming of the machine as seen by contemporary observers*, Mary-Lou Jennings and Charles Madge (eds), Papermac, 1995

Blakeney, Robert ('The Peninsular War: The Storming of Badajoz'), from *A Boy in the Peninsular War*, J. Sturgis (ed.), Murray, 1899

Bradford, William ('The Pilgrims' Land in New England'), from *History of the Plymouth Plantation*, William Bradford, 1899

Bride, Harold ('The *Titanic* Sinks'), from *New York Times*, 19 April 1912

Brittain, Vera ('Home Front: Death of a Brother'), from *Testament of Youth*, Vera Brittain, Virago, 1978. Copyright © Literary Executors of Vera Brittain 1970. Reprinted by permission of the Estate of Vera Brittain

Brontë, Charlotte ('A Visit to the Great Exhibition'), quoted in *The Brontes' Life and Letters*, Clement Shorter, Hodder & Stoughton, 1908

Brown, Cecil ('The Japanese Sink the *Repulse* and the *Prince of Wales*'), from *Suez to Singapore*, Cecil Brown, Random House, 1942

Bulstrode, Sir Richard ('Civil War'), from *Memoirs and Reflections upon the reign and government of King Charles I and King Charles II*, 1721

Burney, Fanny ('A Chance Meeting with Mad King George'), quoted in *English Diaries of the XVI, XVII and XVIII Centuries*, James Aitken (ed.), Pelican, 1945

Byrom, Elizabeth ('Bonnie Prince Charlie Invades Manchester'), quoted in *English Diaries of the XVI, XVII and XVIII Centuries*, James Aitken (ed.), Pelican, 1945

Byrom, James, ('D-Day: A British Paratrooper Lands in Normandy'), from *The Unfinished Man*, James Byrom, Chatto & Windus, 1957

Bystander ('The Burning of Archbishop Cranmer'), from *Memorials of Thomas Cranmer*, John Strype, 1848

Caesar, Julius ('Caesar Invades'; 'England: A Roman View'), from *The Conquest of Gaul*, trans. S. A. Handford, Penguin, 1951, revised Jane F. Gardner, 1982. Reprinted by permission of Penguin UK

Chadwick, Roy ('The Jarrow March'), from *Manchester Guardian*, 13 October 1936. Copyright © 1936 Guardian Newspapers Limited

Channon, Henry ('The Abdication'), from *Chips: Diaries of Sir Henry Channon*, Robert Rhodes James (ed.), Weidenfeld & Nicolson, 1967. Reprinted by permission of Weidenfeld & Nicolson

Chronicle of Lanercost ('The Battle of Bannockburn'), from *Chronicon de Lanercost, 1201–1346*, J. Stevenson (ed.), 1839

Churchill, John ('Blenheim: The Victor's View'), from *The Complete History of Spain*, John Churchill, 1707

Churchill, Winston ('Omdurman'), from *My Early Life*, Winston Churchill, Heinemann, 1930. Copyright © 1930 the Estate of Winston Churchill. Reprinted by permission of Curtis Brown Ltd

Churchill, Winston ('Armistice Celebrations'), from *The World Crisis*, Thornton Butterworth, 1927. Copyright © 1927 the Estate of Winston Churchill. Reprinted by permission of Curtis Brown Ltd

Churchill, Winston ('Churchill's War Speeches'), from the Parliamentary Debates, Fifth series, House of Commons, vols 361 and 362

Clark, Alan ('Thatcher Falls'), from *Diaries*, Alan Clark, Phoenix, 1994. Copyright © 1993 Alan Clark. Reprinted by permission of Weidenfeld & Nicolson

Clive, Robert ('Plassey'), from *Report to the Select Committee of the Court of Directors of the East India Company*, 26 July 1757

Cook, E. A. ('The Charge of the Light Brigade'), from *Letters*, E. A. Cook, 1855

Cook, John ('Climbing Boys'), quoted in *They Saw It Happen 1689–1897*, T. Charles-Edwards and B. Richardson (eds), Basil Blackwell, 1958

Crabbe, George ('The Gordon Riots'), quoted in *The London Anthology*, Hugh and Pauline Massingham, Spring Books, n.d.

Cromwell, Oliver ('Civil War', 'The Storming of Drogheda'), from *Cromwell's Letters and Speeches*, Thomas Carlyle (ed.), Chapman & Hall, 1845

Darwin, Charles ('Darwin in the Galapagos'), from *Journal of Researches into the Natural History and Geology of the Countries visited during the Voyage of HMS 'Beagle' round the world, under the command of Capt. FitzRoy*, Charles Darwin, Harper, 1846

Denbigh, Countess of ('Queen Victoria's Funeral Procession'), quoted in *The Feilding Album*, W. Elwes, Geoffrey Bles, 1950

De Saussure, C. ('Public Executions at Tyburn'), from *A Foreign View of England in the Reigns of George I and George II*, trans. Madame Van Muyden, Caliban, 1998

De Zarate, Francisco ('An Encounter with Drake at Sea'), from *New Light on Drake*, Z. Nuttall (ed.), Hakluyt Society, 1914

Elizabeth I ('The Armada: Elizabeth Addresses Her Troops'), quoted in *Readings in English History*, E. P. Cheyney (ed.), Ginn & Co., 1908

Engels, Friedrich ('Manchester Slums'), from *The Condition of the Working Class in England in 1844*, Friedrich Engels, Foreign Languages Publishing House, 1962

Epstein, Brian ('The Beatles in Performance'), from *Cellarful of Noise*, Brian Epstein, Souvenir, 1964

Evelyn, John ('Cromwell's Funeral'; 'Journal of the Plague Year'; 'The Great Frost Fair'; 'The Glorious Revolution'), from *The Diary of John Evelyn*, William Bray (ed.), J. M. Dent, 1907

Farrar-Hockley, Anthony ('The Korean War'), from *The Edge of the Sword*, Anthony Farrar-Hockley, Muller, 1954. Copyright © 1954 Anthony Farrar-Hockley. Reprinted by permission of Sutton Publishing Limited

Fawkes, Guy ('The Gunpowder Plot'), from *King's Book*, British Museum Press, 1940

Ferguson, W. H. ('Body-line Bowling'), from *Mr Cricket, Autobiography of W. H. Ferguson, as told to David R. Jack*, Nicholas Kaye, 1957

Flower, Desmond ('The Blitz'), from *The War 1939–45*, Desmond Flower and James Reeves (eds), Cassell, 1960

Freedland, Jonathan ('The Body of Diana, Princess of Wales, Is Flown Home'), from the *Guardian*, 1 September 1997. Copyright © The *Guardian* 1997. Reprinted by permission of Guardian Newspapers Limited

Froissart, Sir John ('The Hundred Years War: The Battle of Crécy'), from *Chronicles of England, France and Spain*, trans. Lord Berners, David Nutt, 1901–3

General Court of the Mayor of the City of London ('Some Public Nuisances'), quoted in *English Historical Documents 1327–1585*, A. R. Myers (ed.), Eyre & Spottiswoode, 1969

Gerard, John ('The Torturing of a Jesuit Priest in the Tower of London'), from *The Autobiography of an Elizabethan*, John Gerard, trans. Philip Caraman, Longmans, 1951

Gibson, Guy ('The Dambusters Destroy the Mohne Dam'), from *Enemy Coast Ahead*, Guy Gibson, Michael Joseph, 1946. Copyright © 1946 Guy Gibson. Reprinted by permission of the Estate of Guy Gibson

Giustinian, Sebastian ('A Portrait of Henry VIII'), quoted in *They Saw It Happen 1485–1688*, C. R. N. Routh (ed.), Basil Blackwell, 1956

Goldsmith, Oliver ('Bath under the Code of Beau Nash'), from *Life of Richard Nash, Esquire*, Oliver Goldsmith, W. Frederick, 1762

Greville, Charles ('The Coronation of Queen Victoria'; 'Chloroform in Surgery'; 'Chartist March'), from *The Greville Memoirs: A Journal of the Reign of Queen Victoria from 1837 to 1852*, Charles C. F. Greville (ed.), Longmans Green, 1895

Grim, Edward ('The Murder of Thomas-à-Becket'), from *St Thomas by Contemporary Biographers*, D. Nutt, n.d.

Harris, Rifleman ('The Peninsular War: Plundering a Dead French Soldier'), from *The Recollections of Rifleman Harris*, H. Curling (ed.), 1848

Harvey, William ('A Post-mortem'), from *The Circulation of Blood and Other Writings*, Kenneth J. Franklin (ed.), J. M. Dent, 1993

Hastings, Max ('Falklands War'; originally 'Max Hastings Leads the Way: The First Man into Port Stanley'), from *Evening Standard*, 15 June 1982. Copyright © 1982 Max Hastings and the *Evening Standard*. Reprinted by permission of Atlantic Syndication

Henry, Philip ('The Execution of Charles I'), quoted in *They Saw It Happen 1485–1688*, C. R. N. Routh (ed.), Basil Blackwell, 1956

Henry VIII ('Mine Own Sweetheart'), from *Intimate Letters of England's Kings*, Margaret Sanders (ed.), Museum Press, 1959

Henry of Huntingdon ('Cnut and the Waves'), quoted in *They Saw It Happen 55 BC–AD 1485*, W. O. Hassall (ed.), Basil Blackwell, 1957

Hentzner, Paul ('A Meeting with Queen Elizabeth'), quoted in *Life in Shakespeare's England*, John Dover Wilson (ed.), Cambridge University Press, 1911

Hillary, Edmund ('Everest Conquered'), from *High Adventure, Edmund Hillary*, Hodder & Stoughton, 1955. Copyright © 1955 Edmund Hillary

Hillary, Richard ('Battle of Britain: A Spitfire Pilot in Action'), from *The Last Enemy*, Macmillan, 1943. Copyright © 1942 Richard Hillary. Reprinted by permission of Macmillan

Holwell, J. Z. ('The Black Hole of Calcutta'), from *The Annual Register*, 1758

Hook, Henry ('Rorke's Drift, South Africa'), quoted in *Imperial Echoes*, Robert Giddings (ed.), Leo Cooper, 1996

Howard, Lord, et al. ('The Armada: The Commander's Report'), from *State*

Papers Relating to the Defeat of Spanish Armada, J. K. Laughton (ed.), Navy Records Society, 1894

Hughes, G. E. ('An Infantryman in Normandy'), from unpublished diary, Imperial War Museum

Hulse, Edward Hamilton Westrow '(Christmas in the Trenches'), quoted in *The Albatross Book of English Letters*, The First Earl of Birkenhead, Albatross Verlag, 1936

Jenkins, Peter ('The 1984–5 Miners' Strike'; originally 'A species threatened with extinction'), from the *Guardian*, 19 December 1984. Copyright © 1984 Guardian Newspaper Limited

Jenner, Edward ('Jenner Discovers Smallpox Vaccination'), from *On the origine of the Vaccine Inoculation*, D. N. Shury, 1801

Jesse, John H. ('Bad King George I'), from *Memoirs of the Court of England from the Revolution of 1688 to the Death of George the Second*, John H. Jesse and Francis A. Nicholls, n.d.

John et al. ('Magna Carta'), quoted in *Documents of Liberty*, Henry Marsh (ed.), David & Charles, 1971. Translation copyright © The British Library

Keating, Frank ('Wade Wins Wimbledon'), from the *Guardian*, 2 July 1977. Copyright © 1977 Guardian Newspapers Limited

Keith, Agnes Newton ('Tenko: An Englishwoman in a Japanese Prison Camp'), from *Three Came Home*, Agnes Newton Keith, Michael Joseph 1955

Kemble, Fanny ('First Excursion on the Liverpool–Manchester Railway'), from *Record of a Girlhood*, 1878

Kendall, H. G. ('The Arrest of Dr Crippen'), quoted in *Scrapbook 1900–1914*, Leslie Bailey (ed.), Frederick Muller, 1957

Kincaid, J. ('Waterloo: The Final Attack'), from *Adventures in the Rifle Brigade*, J. Kincaid, 1830

King, Lionel ('Doodlebugs'), from *People at War*, Michael Monahan (ed.), David & Charles, 1974. Copyright © 1974 Michael Moynihan. Reprinted by permission of David & Charles

Knighton, Henry ('The Black Death'), from *Chronicon Henrici Knighton*, J. R. Lumby (ed.), 1889–95

Knox, John ('The Death of General Wolfe on the Heights of Abraham'), from *Journal of John Knox*, Vol. II, Champlain Society, n.d.

Kray, Ronnie ('Ronnie Kray Murders George Cornell'), from *Our Story*, R. and R. Kray (with Fred Dineage), 1988. Copyright © 1988 Bejubob Ltd

Langland, William ('The Peasant's Life'), quoted in *The Portable Medieval Reader*, J. B. Ross and M. M. Mclaughlin (eds), Penguin, 1981

Lawrence, T. E. ('T. E. Lawrence Blows up a Train on the Hejaz Railway'), from *Seven Pillars of Wisdom*, T. E. Lawrence, Jonathan Cape, 1943. Copyright © 1926 T. E. Lawrence

London, John et al. ('The Dissolution of the Monasteries'), *Letters to Cromwell*, G. H. Cook (ed.), John Baker, 1965

Lydon, John et al. ('Never Mind the B******s: The Sex Pistols'), from *Rotten: No Irish, no blacks, no dogs*, John Lydon and Kent Zimmerman, Plexus, 2003. Reprinted by permission of the publisher

Lytton, Constance ('Force-feeding of a Suffragette'), from *Prisons and Prisoners*, Heinemann, 1914

Map, Walter ('The Virtues and Vices of Henry II'), quoted in *English Historical Documents 1042–1189*, D. C. Douglas and George W. Greenway, Eyre & Spottiswoode, 1953

Marchant, Hilde ('World War II: Children Evacuated'), from *Women and Children Last*, Hilde Marchant, Gollancz, 1941

Miller, David ('England Win the World Cup'), from *I Was There*, Collins, 1966. Copyright © 1966 The *Daily Telegraph* and *Sunday Telegraph*

More, Sir Thomas ('Richard III Murders the Princes in the Tower'), from *The History of King Richard III*, Thomas More, ed. R. S. Sylvester, Yale, 1963

Nasmyth, James ('The Black Country'), quoted in *Pandemonium 1660–1886: the coming of the machine as seen by contemporary observers*, Mary-Lou Jennings and Charles Madge (eds), Papermac, 1995

Neilly, J. E. ('The Siege of Mafeking'), from *Besieged with B–P*, J. E. Neilly, Pearson, 1900

Newton, Sir Isaac ('Isaac Newton Experiments on Light'), quoted in *The Ascent of Man*, J. Bronowski, BBC Books 1973

Nichol, John ('The Battle of the Nile'), from *Sailors Whom Nelson Led*, E. Fraser, Methuen, 1913

Nichol, John ('The Gulf War'), from *Tornado Down*, John Peters and John Nichol, Michael Joseph, 1992. Copyright © John Peters and John Nichol. Reprinted by permission of Penguin UK

Nightingale, Florence ('Florence Nightingale in the Crimea'), from *Florence Nightingale: Letters from the Crimea*, Sue M. Goldie, Mandolin, 1997

Orwell, George ('Down and Out: A Night in a Doss-house'), from *Down and Out in Paris and London*, George Orwell, Gollancz, 1933. Copyright © 1933 George Orwell. Reprinted by permission of A. M. Heath & Company

Panter-Downes, Mollie ('VE Day'; originally 'Letter from London'), from the *New Yorker*, 12 May 1945. Copyright © Mollie Panter-Downes. Reprinted by permission of the *New Yorker*

Paris, Matthew ('The Weather'), quoted in *English Historical Documents 1042–1189*, D. C. Douglas and George W. Greenway, Eyre & Spottiswoode, 1953

Pepys, Samuel ('The Restoration'; 'The Great Fire of London'), from *The Illustrated Pepys: Extracts from the Diary*, Robert Latham (ed.), Book Club Associates, 1978. Copyright © 1978 The Masters and Fellows and Scholars of Magdalene College, Cambridge, Mrs William Matthews and Mr Robert Latham

Piratin, Phil ('The Battle of Cable Street'), from *Our Flag Stays Red*, Phil Piratin, Lawrence & Wishart, 1948. Copyright © 1948 Lawrence & Wishart

Thompson, Leonard ('An Infantryman at Gallipoli'), quoted in *Akenfield*, Ronald Blythe, Allen Lane, 1969

Tristan, Flora ('Prostitutes and Peers'), from *The London Journal of Flora Tristan*, Jean Hawkes (trans.), Virago, 1982

Tynan, Kenneth ('Lady Chatterley's Trial'), from the *Observer*, 6 November 1960. Copyright © 1960 the *Observer*. Reprinted by permission of Guardian Newspapers Limited

Various ('Graffiti'), nos 2, 6, 7 from *The Romans in Britain: an anthology of inscriptions with translations and a running commentary*, Blackwell, 1932; nos 1, 3, 4, 5 from *The Archaeology of Roman Britain*, Methuen, 1930

Vergil, Polydore ('The Battle of Bosworth'), from *English History*, The Camden Society, 1844

Vergil, Polydore ('The Field of the Cloth of Gold'), from *Henry VIII*, E. Hall, T. C. and E. C. Jack, 1904

Victoria, Queen ('The Diamond Jubilee'), from *Letters of Queen Victoria*, George Earle Buckle (ed.), Murray, 1930–32

Vitalis, Orderic ('The Coronation of William the Conqueror'; 'The Harrying of the North'; 'The Loss of the *White Ship*'), from *The Ecclesiastical History of Orderic Vitalis*, trans. Majorie Chibnill, Oxford University Press, 1978

Von Uffenbach, Zacharias ('Cock-fighting'), from *London in 1710*, W. H. Quarrell and Margaret Mare (trans.), Faber and Faber, 1935

Walpole, Horace ('George II Interred'), from *Correspondence*, W. S. Lewis (ed.), Oxford University Press, 1937–83

Warkworth, John ('The Wars of the Roses'), from *Chronicles of the White Rose*, Bohn, 1843

Warwick, Sir Philip ('Cromwell in the House of Commons'), quoted in *They Saw It Happen 1485–1688*, C. R. N. Routh (ed.), Basil Blackwell, 1956

Weldon, Sir Anthony ('A Sketch of King James I'), quoted in *James I*, S. J. Houston, 1973

Wellesley, Arthur ('Wellington Meets Nelson'), quoted in *The Correspondence and Diaries: John Wilson Croker*, vol. II, Louis J. Jennings, Murray, 1884

Wesley, John ('John Wesley Preaches'), from *Journal*, John Wesley, Everyman's Library, J. M. Dent, 1906

Wheatley, Edmund ('Waterloo: Taken Prisoner'), from *The Wheatley Diary*, C. Hibbert (ed.), Longmans, 1964

Whitelock, Bulstrode ('Cromwell Purges the Long Parliament'), from *Memorials*, Sir Bulstrode Whitelock, 1682

Wilkinson, Jonny ('Rugby World Cup'), *My World*, Jonny Wilkinson, Headline, 2004. Copyright © 2004 Jonny Wilkinson Ltd.

William of Poitiers ('The Battle of Hastings'), from 'The Deeds of William, Duke of Normandy and King of the English', quoted in *English Historical Documents 1042–1189*, D. C. Douglas and G. W. Greenaway, Eyre & Spottiswoode, 1953

Wykes, Thomas ('Edward I Conquers Wales'), from *English History Illustrated from Original Sources*, Norman L. Frazer (ed.), A&C Black, 1907

Wynkfielde, R. K. ('The Execution of Mary, Queen of Scots'), from *Original Letters Illustrative of English History*, Henry Ellis (ed.), Harding, Triphook and Lepard, 1824–46

Index

WIN
A PLACE IN HISTORY

Were you part of or did you witness one of
the defining events in England in 2005?

Would you like to stand shoulder to shoulder with
Siegfried Sassoon, Winston Churchill and Jonny Wilkinson
and mark your place in England's history?

Tell us your story and help capture the nation's history.
The best account will be added to the paperback edition of
England: The Autobiography (to be published in 2006)
and published in *The Times*.

To enter this competition, send your account along
with the completed entry form below or a photocopy of the
entry form to the address below by 31st January 2006.
Your account should be no longer than 500 words and should be typed
(handwritten entries will be disqualified).

England Competition
Penguin General Marketing
80 Strand
London WC2R 0RL

In association with
THE TIMES
JOIN THE DEBATE

Name: ....

Address: ....

....

Email address: ....

Event recounted: ....

☐ Please tick the box if you'd like to receive exclusive news and further offers from Penguin. Your information will not be used for any other purpose, will be kept for only a reasonable time, and will not be passed on to any third parties.

✂

TERMS & CONDITIONS

1. This competition is open to all UK residents aged 18 and over. Employees of Penguin Books Limited and the News International Group are not eligible to enter. By entering this competition you will be deemed to have read and understood these terms and conditions and to be bound by them.

2. The address for entry is as stated in the entry details.

3. Closing date for receipt of entries is 31st January 2006.

4. No purchase necessary. Only one entry per person.

5. Entry to the competition is free and must be accompanied by a completed official entry form.

6. The piece must not be any longer than 500 words.

7. All entries shall be original, the authors' own work and should not have been previously published anywhere.

8. No responsibility can be accepted for incomplete, illegible, lost or damaged entries. Proof of sending is not proof of receipt. Entries via agents or third parties will be deemed invalid.

9. The winner will be chosen by a panel made up of judges from Penguin Books Limited and The Times. The winning entry will be the one which, in the opinion of the judges, most aptly captures the spirit of a defining event in England in 2005. It will be published in the paperback edition of England: The Autobiography (to be published in 2006). There is no cash alternative.

10. By entering, all entrants license their entry to Penguin Books Limited and Times Newspapers Limited ("TNL") on an exclusive royalty free perpetual worldwide basis to publish their entry in any and all forms of media, but the winner shall retain copyright in their entry. TNL reserves the right to publish any entries, but publication does not indicate the entrant has won. Entrants may be required to authenticate their entries.

11. The winner will be notified in writing by 31st March 2006. For the winner's details please send a stamped self-addressed envelope to the Promoter's address below, stating for which competition you would like details.

12. Entries will not be returned.

13. Entry into the competition does not constitute an agreement to publish the work.

14. The winner agrees to the use of his or her name and photograph for publicity purposes by Penguin Books Limited or TNL and the winner may be required to take part in publicity without additional payment or permission.

15. Events may occur that render the promotion itself or the awarding of the prize impossible due to reasons beyond the control of Penguin Books Limited. Penguin Books Limited may at its absolute discretion vary or amend the promotion and the winner agrees that no liability shall attach itself to Penguin Books Limited as a result.

16. The decision of the judging panel is final and binding for any situation, including any not covered in these terms and conditions. Correspondence will be entered into only at the absolute discretion of Penguin Books Limited. Competition rules published by Penguin Books Limited or TNL form a part of these terms and conditions.

17. Promoter: Penguin Books Limited, 80 Strand, London, WC2R 0RL.